PLACING THE GODS

PLACING THE GODS

Sanctuaries and Sacred Space in Ancient Greece

Edited by

SUSAN E. ALCOCK

AND

ROBIN OSBORNE

CLARENDON PRESS · OXFORD

*This book has been printed digitally and produced in a standard design
in order to ensure its continuing availability*

OXFORD
UNIVERSITY PRESS

Great Clarendon Street, Oxford OX2 6DP

Oxford University Press is a department of the University of Oxford.
It furthers the University's objective of excellence in research, scholarship,
and education by publishing worldwide in

Oxford New York

Athens Auckland Bangkok Bogotá Buenos Aires Cape Town
Chennai Dar es Salaam Delhi Florence Hong Kong Istanbul Karachi
Kolkata Kuala Lumpur Madrid Melbourne Mexico City Mumbai Nairobi
Paris São Paulo Shanghai Singapore Taipei Tokyo Toronto Warsaw

with associated companies in Berlin Ibadan

Oxford is a registered trade mark of Oxford University Press
in the UK and in certain other countries

Published in the United States
by Oxford University Press Inc., New York

ISBN 0-19-815060-1

CONTENTS

LIST OF ILLUSTRATIONS

LIST OF TABLES

ABBREVIATIONS

AA	*Archäologischer Anzeiger*
AAA	*Athens Annals of Archaeology*
AD	*Archaiologikon Deltion*
AE	*Archaiologike Ephemeris*
AION	*Annali dell'Istituto universitario orientale di Napoli, Dipartimento di studi del mondo classico e del Mediterraneo antico, Sezione di archeologia e storia antica*
AJA	*American Journal of Archaeology*
AJP	*American Journal of Philology*
AM	*Mitteilungen des Deutschen Archäologischen Instituts*
AR	*Archaeological Reports*
ARV²	J. D. Beazley, *Attic Red-Figure Vase Painters*, 2nd edn. (Oxford, 1963)
ASAtene	*Annuario della Scuola Archeologica di Atene e delle Missioni Italiane in Oriente*
BAR	British Archaeological Reports
BCH	*Bulletin de Correspondance hellénique*
BICS	*Bulletin of the Institute of Classical Studies of the University of London*
BSA	*Annual of the British School at Athens*
CAJ	*Cambridge Archaeological Journal*
CQ	*Classical Quarterly*
CSCA	*California Studies in Classical Antiquity*
EMC	*Échos du Monde Classique*
FrGrHist	*Fragmente der griechischen Historiker*, ed. F. Jacoby
GRBS	*Greek, Roman and Byzantine Studies*
HSCP	*Harvard Studies in Classical Philology*
HThR	*Harvard Theological Review*
IG	*Inscriptiones Graecae*
IstMitt	*Istanbuler Mitteilungen*
IPergamon	*Die Inschriften von Pergamon*, edd. E. Fabricius and C. Schuchart, 2 vols. (Berlin, 1890, 1895)
IPriene	*Inschriften von Priene*, ed. F. Hiller von Gaetringen (Berlin, 1906)
ISmyrna	*Die Inschriften von Smyrna*, ed. G. Petzl, 3 vols. (Bonn, 1982, 1988, 1990)
JFA	*Journal of Field Archaeology*
JHS	*Journal of Hellenic Studies*
JRA	*Journal of Roman Archaeology*
KrChron	*Kretika Chronika*
LSAM	*Lois sacrées d'Asie Mineure*, ed. F. Sokolowski (Paris, 1955)
LSCG	*Lois sacrées des cités grecques*, ed. F. Sokolowski (Paris, 1969)
LSS	*Lois sacrées des cités grecques, supplément*, ed. F. Sokolowski (Paris, 1962)
OJA	*Oxford Journal of Archaeology*
ÖJh	*Jahresheft des Österreichischen Archäologischen Instituts in Wien*
OpAth	*Opuscula Atheniensia*
PCPS	*Proceedings of the Cambridge Philological Society*
POxy	*The Oxyrhynchus Papyri* (London, 1898–)
PP	*La Parola del Passato*

Praktika	*Praktika tes en Athenais Archaiologikes Etaireias*
RA	*Revue Archéologique*
RE	*Paulys Real-Encyclopädie*
REA	*Revue des études anciennes*
REG	*Revue des études grecques*
RFIC	*Rivista di Filologia e Istruzione di Classica*
RPh	*Revue de Philologie*
SEG	*Supplementum Epigraphicum Graecum*
SIMA	Studies in Mediterranean Archaeology
SMEA	*Studi micenei ed egeo-anatolici*
SNG	*Sylloge Nummorum Graecorum*
ZPE	*Zeitschrift für Papyrologie und Epigraphik*

INTRODUCTION

THE publication of François de Polignac's *La Naissance de la cité grecque: Cultes, espace et société VIIIe–VIIe siècles* a decade ago which is now available, revised, in an English translation as *Cults, Territory, and the Origins of the Greek City-State* (Chicago, 1995), offered historians and archaeologists a radically new insight into the significance of where the gods were worshipped. De Polignac's insistence on the way in which the construction of a sacred landscape was central to the construction of the Greek polis not only gave a whole new way of understanding the formation of the Greek state, but also suggested that the relationship between religion and politics was in general more intimate and more involved than had often been assumed. For all that the placing of sanctuaries in the Greek landscape had attracted considerable attention from earlier scholars (one thinks, for instance, of Vincent Scully's *The Earth, the Temple, and the Gods*), de Polignac's work changed the focus of that attention and acted as a catalyst to further work.

The essays in this collection, which opens with de Polignac's own restatement of his position as he sees it ten years on, take up the challenge which *La Naissance de la cité grecque* made. They examine critically the relationship between sanctuaries and political units in the Greek world over the best part of two millennia, both extending de Polignac's sort of analysis back and forward in time, and also assessing the limits of that analysis. De Polignac stressed, and other scholars in different fields of archaeology have recently made similar points, that the sacred landscape was dynamic and not static. The contributors to this volume offer close analysis of how that dynamism worked within particular societies; they also look at factors influencing that dynamism which received less emphasis in de Polignac's work, as they bring out the different roles of different deities, the power of the weight of tradition, and the importance of the sacred landscape for mapping women's life, as well as the life of the male citizen. In stressing the complexity of the sacred landscape, the regional variations in the ways in which that landscape was constructed, and the ways in which the construction was always part of an ongoing history, we hope not only to show what *can* be achieved by paying detailed attention to the configuration of the sacred landscape but also to show what remains to be done.

The papers by Peatfield, Antonaccio, Osborne, Cole, and Alcock were first aired at the meeting of the Archaeological Institute of America in December 1991. We are grateful to all who participated in the discussion then and to John Cherry and Anthony Snodgrass for their help and encouragement with this volume.

Mediation, Competition, and Sovereignty: The Evolution of Rural Sanctuaries in Geometric Greece

FRANÇOIS DE POLIGNAC

Centre Louis Gernet, Paris

Any general theory which seeks to account for phenomena previously considered separately runs the risk of producing an interpretative model which is too rigid and which treats in an over-schematic way a reality which is rather more variable and nuanced than the explanations proposed for it. In the case of a theory based on archaeological data, there is a further danger of which one must be more or less aware: that of being proved false by a new discovery which brings into question facts until then held to be certain. Even in the best of circumstances it is not possible to escape from the necessity of adjusting the theory in the light of the development of archaeological knowledge and interpretation. Until now, perhaps simply by chance, the ideas advanced a decade ago in *La Naissance de la cité grecque*, about the early history of cults in the countryside and their role in the formation of cities during the Archaic period, have not been formally contradicted by the results of excavations carried out in the mean time. Nevertheless, the moment has come to return critically to some of the concepts which that work put into play, and to refine them in bringing more recent discoveries into the picture.[1]

According to the classic picture of the city, which still strongly influences *La Naissance*, the territory of a city is understood as the 'space of the citizens', a closed space under the control of a single sovereign body. Among the large number of cult places which are scattered over it, ranging from a simple altar, or sacred grove surrounded by a *peribolos*, to a monumental temple, some manifest particularly openly the authority whose exercise over this space each city determinedly reserved to itself. These great rural sanctuaries on the edge of the plain, and small sanctuaries in mountainous or coastal areas, constitute

---

[1] The analysis presented here represents a summation and completion of the changes which I have made to the text of *La Naissance de la cité grecque* (Paris, 1984) for the English edition, *Cults, Territory, and the Origins of the Greek City-State* (Chicago, 1995), and the new French edition (Paris, 1995).

what one might call sanctuaries of territorial sovereignty. The very term *extra-urban*, used to qualify these sites, shows clearly that they were still studied in relation to the central place of the city, and were sited with relation to the town, which gathers at its side the sanctuaries which protect its political institutions, often close to the agora where these institutions have their base, as well as the acropolis sanctuaries whose armed divinities (particularly Athena) keep a special watch over the integrity of the community and over its defenders (warrior aristocracies or an armed citizen body).

Because of the great political elaboration which is implied by the close link between each centre of sovereignty and the major rural sanctuary which depends on it, this notion of territory which suits the ideal type of the Classical city cannot be employed for Greece in the Geometric and early Archaic periods without caution. The limits are well illustrated by the case of the Argolid, which is certainly one of the best 'test cases' that the study of the ancient Greek world can offer, both because of the diverse historical situations which the region experienced and because of the relative richness of the documentation which it has left us.[2] In the Classical period, at least after 460 BC, when Argos regained regional hegemony, the Argive Heraion is incontestably one of the clearest examples of a great rural sanctuary where the sovereignty of a city, Argos, is made manifest, through the monumental buildings and the most solemn celebration of civic festivals accompanied by famous games.[3] The political situation is clear: Argos has forcibly subjugated Mycenae, Tiryns, and Nauplion, and rules over an undivided region. The axis, or at least symbolic axis (for the material traces remain uncertain), described by joining the sanctuary and the dominant city, the political centre of the region, traces a diagonal line across the plain which forms the heart of Argive territory, and the city on one side with its acropolis, and the Heraion on the other, like a beacon hung on the rising ground, flank and overlook the plain. But this schema cannot be applied just like that to the Geometric era, when the hierarchy of settlement sites was very different and during which their relations cannot be analysed in terms as abrupt as confrontation or submission, sovereignty or exclusion. Indeed, in the ninth century, Argos, for all that it was probably already a little more populous and its aristocracy a little more wealthy and more powerful than that of other small towns in the plain, was far from having gained the position of leadership which it would have in the Archaic period. The first traces of cult which can be detected at the Heraion perhaps go back to this period, but this rural, even rustic, cult place (no settlement of any importance seems to have been established there or in the vicinity at that time), which had no notable

---

[2] See my paper 'Cité et territoire: Un modèle argien', in *Argos et l'Argolide: Topographie et urbanisme*, Colloque de l'École française d'Athènes, 30 avril–2 mai 1990 (forthcoming).

[3] P. Amandry, 'Sur les concours argiens', in *Études argiennes*, BCH Suppl. 6 (Paris, 1980), 211–53.

building, cannot be considered to be exclusively or even principally Argive at that time. Its 'half-way house' position suggests, on the contrary, that it should be seen as a meeting point, a place where the communities which surrounded it gathered, and might even suggest a particular link with Mycenae, which is connected to the site of Prosymna by a Bronze Age paved road.[4]

Whatever the regional diversity in conditions of life and social organization, and whatever the ultimate destiny of these sanctuaries, most of the major rural cults can be considered, like the Heraion, to have originally been rallying and meeting points for the local populations. They were the locations of festivals which it is tempting to liken to fairs, those ritual gatherings which Louis Gernet has shown to have been occasions for exchanging hospitality and for sharing between the neighbouring communities which participated in them on a relatively equal footing, and which found in them an opportunity to settle trade deals, arrange alliances and marriages, and to compete in rustic games.[5] From this point of view there may have been scarcely any difference in origin between a future Panhellenic cult, such as that of Zeus at Olympia, whose small beginnings are to be found in the tenth century in a region perhaps dominated by pastoralism and where the settlement pattern was not yet stable, and other cults, like those at the Ida and Dikte caves in Crete, the Poseidonion at Isthmia, the Kabirion in Boiotia, the Amyklaion in Lakonia, and later, Pherai, Dodona, or the Argive Heraion. While all these cults are found more or less at the centre of a regional or local network of settlements, none of which can yet aspire to dominate or appropriate the sanctuary, Olympia in the ninth century plays the same role both on a larger scale, between several regions of the Peloponnese, and for a more restricted group, the offerings showing the aristocratic character of the cult.[6] The sanctuary at Isthmia also illustrates, from the second half of the eleventh century, the category of cults which are created close to communication routes (an isthmus, a pass, a col), and which constitute the only fixed point at which the scattered local population, in mountain areas only seasonally resident, can meet and exchange goods and eventually also welcome

[4] Most recent studies on the Heraion come together on this point: C. Morgan and T. Whitelaw, 'Pots and Politics: Ceramic Evidence for the Rise of the Argive State', *AJA* 95 (1991), 79–108; C. M. Antonaccio, 'Terraces, Tombs and the Early Argive Heraion', *Hesperia* 61 (1992), 85–105; Polignac (n. 2).

[5] L. Gernet, 'Frairies antiques', in *Anthropologie de la Grèce antique* (Paris, 1968), 21–61. The idea can be expressed in other terms by using the concept of the 'point of interaction' which is perfectly illustrated by the Heraion; cf. C. Renfrew, 'Peer-polity Interaction and Socio-political Change', in C. Renfrew and J. Cherry (edd.), *Peer Polity Interaction and Socio-political Change* (Cambridge, 1986), 1–18, and A. Snodgrass, 'Interaction by Design: The Greek City State', in the same volume, 47–58.

[6] Olympia: C. Morgan, *Athletes and Oracles: The Transformation of Olympia and Delphi in the eighth century B.C.* (Cambridge, 1990); H. Kyrieleis, 'Neue Ausgrabungen in Olympia', in W. Coulson and H. Kyrieleis (edd.), *Proceedings of an International Symposium on the Olympic Games* (Athens, 1992), 19–24. Dedications of figurines of cattle characterize the earliest period at the Kabirion as at Olympia, see B. Schmaltz, *Metallfiguren aus dem Kabirionheiligtum bei Theben* (Berlin, 1980).

offerings from passers-by. A variant of this type of sanctuary is represented by cults situated in more remote zones, *eschatia*, at the borders of two regions: research at the sanctuaries at Hyampolis in Phokis and Kombothekra in Elis suggests that these cults, most often cults of Artemis, also appeared at a very early date (eleventh or tenth centuries).[7]

A second form of mediation, which is useful for shedding light on the development of sanctuaries close to the sea, can be added to this first 'mainland' form. The increased amount of sailing in the Aegean from the tenth century on, and even more from around 800 when the Greeks recaptured the initiative in this domain, can be detected to some extent everywhere in the appearance or enrichment of cults on coasts, on capes, or at the mouths of rivers. The use of these sites itself reflects the important place which these cults held in processes of exchange. The coastal cults of Artemis in Attica, at Brauron and Mounykhia, which are associated either by their myths, particularly the figure of Iphigeneia, or by some of their rituals with the opening of the sailing season, seem to go back to a time when the contacts established between the Euboians of Lefkandi, and to a lesser extent Athens, and the Cypro-Levantine world show how important sailing was in the Euboian straits and around Attica.[8] As at Ephesos where, during the eighth and seventh centuries, the Artemision below the town, not far from the port, was regularly frequented by Phoenicians, the goddess of thresholds and passages between the unknown and the familiar could be patron of the sanctuary of a port-of-call, an intermediary in contacts and exchanges between foreigners and the coastal residents.[9] These circumstances have caused the foundation of some sanctuaries stretching along the routes of their maritime expansion in the Aegean to be attributed to the Phoenicians. Thus the sanctuaries of Herakles/Melquart, along the route leading to Thrace and to its mines by way of Thasos, and the sanctuary of Aphrodite/Astarte at Kythera on the route to the West, have often been considered Phoenician

[7] E. R. Gebhard and F. P. Hemans, 'Excavations at Isthmia, 1989', *Hesperia* 61 (1992), 1–23, and the paper by C. Morgan in this volume (esp. 109–28); R. C. S. Felsch *et al.*, 'Apollon und Artemis oder Artemis und Apollon?', *AA* (1981), 38–118, and 'Kalapodi: Bericht über die Grabungen im Heiligtum der Artemis Elaphebolos und des Apollon von Hyampolis', *AA* (1987), 1–99; U. Sinn, 'Das Heiligtum der Artemis Limnatis bei Kombothekra', *AM* 96 (1981), 25–71.

[8] At Mounykhia the earliest traces of activity on the site of the sanctuary seem to go back to the second half or end of the 10th cent.: L. Palaiokrassa, 'Neue Befunde aus dem Heiligtum des Artemis Munichia', *AM* 104 (1989), 1–40. As our knowledge currently stands the traces at Brauron would be a little later.

[9] Ephesos: A. Bammer, 'Spüren der Phöniker im Artemision von Ephesos', *Anatolian Studies* 35 (1985), 103–8; 'Neue weibliche Statuetten aus dem Artemision von Ephesos', *ÖJh* 56 (1985), 39–58; 'Gold und Elfenbein von einer Kultbasis in Ephesos', *ÖJh* 58 (1988), 1–23; 'Multikulturelle Aspekte der frühen Kunst im Artemision von Ephesos', *ÖJh* 61 (1991/2), 18–54. Artemis, Iphigeneia, and navigation: B. Sergent, 'Héortologie du mois Plowistos de Pylos', *Dialogues d'histoire ancienne* 16 (1990), 188–92. I have devoted more attention to the role of these 'contact' sanctuaries in my 'Influence extérieure ou évolution interne? L'Innovation cultuelle en Grèce géométrique et archaïque', in G. Kopcke and I. Tokumaru (edd.), *Greece between East and West 10th–8th centuries B.C.* (Mainz, 1992), 114–27.

foundations preserved by the Greeks and Hellenized once the Phoenician presence was a thing of the past.[10] Such hypotheses have not yet been confirmed by archaeology, but a probable Phoenician sanctuary has been found at the site of Kommos, on the south coast of Crete, which may have been a port-of-call for eastern sailors in the eighth century.[11] That case is but one particular example, part of a general system of mediation with foreigners, whoever they might be, of which a purely Greek sanctuary, such as that of Hera on Samos, may give a better idea. More than any other sanctuary, the Samian Heraion saw offerings from very diverse origins, but predominantly from the east, flood in during the eighth century.[12] It is important not to confuse the origin of objects and the origin of those who dedicated them to the divinity, but equally it is wrong to see this concentration of offerings as the result of purely Samian voyages and initiatives. Rather, the offerings dedicated at the Samian Heraion should be seen as at the end of a chain of exchanges whose forms, stages, and length are as variable as the agents involved: gifts from princes on the one hand and pillage on the other will have played a significant part, Phoenicians, Cypriots, Samians, and other Greeks travelling across the Aegean will all have been involved. In some ways Hera at Samos can be seen to reign over maritime space and Aegean relations in the same manner that Hera at Prosymna protects the Argive plain and the relations which unite its communities.

It is manifestly impossible to separate the opening up of these cults to outside elements and the general mediating role of rural sanctuaries from the role that they played in various rites of transition from one status to another. Cult as enacted at cult centres within settlements probably did not, until the eighth century, take the form of classical public cult before a temple, but consisted of sacrificial meals within a building in which the resident aristocracy, the *astoi* and their hosts for the occasion, gathered round their kings or princes, the *basileis*.[13] Such cult clearly expressed the local authority of the dominant groups

[10] D. Van Berchem, 'Sanctuaires d'Héraklès-Melquart', *Syria* 44 (1967), 76–108; J. Pouilloux, 'L'Héraclès thasien', *REA* 76 (1974), 305–16; G. Bunnens, *L'Expansion phénicienne en Méditerranée* (Brussels–Rome 1979), 282–4; *contra* C. Bonnet, *Melkart: Cultes et mythes de l'Héraclès tyrien en Méditerranée*, Studia Phoenicia 7 (Namur, 1988). Aphrodite on Kythera: Herodotos 1. 105.

[11] The latest research at the Herakleion on Thasos has added to our detailed knowledge of the Archaic cult but has not resolved the question of the 'Thasian Herakles': J. Des Courtils and A. Pariente, 'Problèmes topographiques et religieux à l'Héracléion de Thasos', in R. Etienne and M.-Th. Le Dinahet (edd.), *L'Espace sacrificiel dans les civilisations méditerranéennes de l'Antiquité* (Lyons–Paris 1991), 67–73. Kommos: J. W. Shaw, 'Phoenicians in Southern Crete', *AJA* 93 (1989), 165–83.

[12] I. Kilian-Ditlmeier, 'Fremde Weihungen im griechischen Heiligtümern von 8. bis zum Beginn des 7. Jahrhunderts', *Jahrbuch des Römisch-Germanischen Zentralmuseums* 32 (1985), 215–54, esp. 236–40; I. Ström, 'Evidence from the Sanctuaries', in Kopcke and Tokumaru (n. 9); F. de Polignac, 'Hera, le navire et la demeure', in J. de la Genière, *Cultes et sanctuaires d'Hera* (forthcoming).

[13] The architecture of these buildings seems to have directly inspired that of the first temples properly so called; cf. H. Drerup, 'Griechische Baukunst in geometrischer Zeit', in F. Matz and H. G. Buchholz (edd.), *Archaeologia Homerica*, ii, ch. O (Göttingen, 1969); A. J. Mazarakis-Ainian, 'Contribution à l'étude de l'architecture religieuse grecque des Ages obscurs', *L'Antiquité classique* 54 (1985), 5–48, and 'Early

who controlled access to the meal. But inversely, cults at a distance, a little way from the settlement or in the open countryside, were often consecrated to divinities who presided over the crossing of thresholds in life and in society, and over the various stages of integration of inside and outside, of wild and rule-bound—Artemis, Apollo, Hera, and indeed Poseidon.[14] To take charge of relations with neighbouring communities or with foreigners in transit was thus only a particular form of the general role of passage between two worlds.

The 'in-between' position of a cult either on the mainland or on the coast is a perfect illustration of the accommodation between the divinity's own particular character and the function of the sanctuary in the society, but it is not always sufficient to explain why it began at that point in the first place. This is another question which requires that some complex problems, such as that of what was inherited from the Bronze Age, are tackled. Developments in research now allow the much-debated problem of the nature of continuity and of discontinuity to be posed in terms which are not exclusive or antagonistic. There was a time when archaeologists tended to insist on the rupture which separated the Geometric sanctuaries from the Bronze Age remains on top of which they were mainly constructed, but new discoveries have tipped the balance of opinion, both by reducing considerably the chronological gap between the abandonment of Mycenaean sites and the appearances of the first traces of cult in the Dark Ages,[15] and by revealing the variety of forms of cultic continuity from one period to another.[16] This does not mean that one should return to the idea of universal and mechanical continuity and see a Bronze Age sanctuary under every Geometric sanctuary: on the contrary, the same recent

Greek Temples: Their Origin and Function', in R. Hägg, N. Marinatos, and G. Nordquist (edd.), *Early Greek Cult Practice* (Stockholm 1988), 105–19 has excessively systematized this view in gathering very different buildings under the term 'ruler's dwelling'. The Toumba building at Lefkandi may be an example of this type of building: M. P. Popham, P. G. Kalligas, and L. H. Sackett *Lefkandi*, ii: *The Protogeometric Building at Toumba* (London, 1990).

[14] Cf. *Cults, Territory* (n. 1), 32–88, and for the cities of Ionia: C. G. Simon, 'The Archaic Votive Offerings and Cults of Ionia' (Ph.D., diss. University of California, 1986).

[15] At Isthmia, for example, the first traces of renewed activity seem to date from the second half of the 11th century: Gebhard and Hemans (n. 7), 7–15. The interpretation of the earliest objects and therefore of the early history of a sanctuary is often uncertain: some objects from the Argive Heraion could date from the Protogeometric (see I. Ström, 'The Early Sanctuary of the Argive Heraion', *Acta Archaeologica* 59 (1988), 174–6) but have been deposited there only in the Geometric period (see Cl. Rolley, 'Argos, Corinthe, Athènes', in M. Piérart (ed.), *Polydipsion Argos: Argos de la fin des palais mycéniens à la constitution de l'Etat classique, BCH* Suppl. 22 (Paris, 1992), 39) or, indeed, have come from tombs. The same problem has been raised at Olympia and at Pherai in Thessaly for the 'Submycenaean' pins and fibulae: H. Philipp, *Bronzeschmuck aus Olympia*, Olympia Forschungen 13 (1981), 23; K. Kilian, *Fibeln in Thessalien von der mykenischen bis zu archaischen Zeit* (Munich, 1975), 168–70.

[16] The 'break' frequently found in the archaeological levels between the end of the Mycenaean period and the Geometric period does not exclude either the continuation of the cult in the same place or near by, in some way not detectable archaeologically, or the continued memory of the place as sacred. In this way it is possible to explain the way sanctuaries return to apparently deserted places. On this problem in general see Ch. Le Roy, 'Mémoire et tradition', in *Aux origines de l'héllénisme. La Crète et la Grèce: Hommages H. Van Effenterre* (Paris, 1984), 163–72, and Antonaccio (this volume) 86–90.

discoveries show that one must quit this game of balancing two opposed theses, and instead try to discover how different forms of continuity and of rupture combine in the history of cults. It remains very probable that some sanctuaries were founded on Bronze Age ruins during the Geometric period as a result of imagining a fictional continuity where there was no real continuity and by appropriating the past: even where the chronological gap at a site is very small the nature of the finds can imply that the use of places has altered.[17] In other cases, the refurbishment of a Geometric sanctuary on the site of a Bronze Age sanctuary may have been a completely conscious act, as in the sanctuary of Apollo Maleatas at Epidauros, and this implies that the sacred character of a place is remembered even if the place has not been used continuously over the centuries, especially when the divinity seems to have changed between the two periods.[18] Inversely, a sanctuary such as that of Apollo and Artemis Elaphebolos in the pass at Hyampolis in Phokis seems to have been regularly frequented from its foundation in Late Helladic IIIC, but this is the period of the transformation of the Mycenaean world after the end of the palaces, and the foundation of the cult is one of the many signs of the changes which affected social and religious life at that time: even in Mycenean times, 'continuity' is not a mechanical phenomenon.[19] The overall continuity of a sanctuary should not, therefore, be allowed to mask the developments which seem to indicate profound changes in the nature and significance of the cult. Throughout the Geometric and Archaic periods at Hyampolis it was the south temple, built above the Mycenaean cult place, and respecting some of its layout, which preserved the memory that this had been a sacred place since its foundation; but it was the north temple, built on virgin soil, which ended up being the most important in the sanctuary, and it was the north temple alone which was rebuilt after the Persian wars. The radical changes which occurred in cult practices there on several occasions, particularly in the choice of offerings, confirm that continuity, even where it can be established, though doubtless an important fact, is relative, and that one must get beyond the question of continuity if one is to understand the history of a cult and the evolution of its significance within society. To have determined that a sanctuary is, in one way

[17] Thus at Isthmia: Gebhard and Hemans (n. 7), 6–7 and 17–18; at Mounykhia: Palaiokrassa (n. 8) 11–12; and at Kommos: Shaw (n. 11). The possibility exists, in some cases, that the Iron Age sanctuary 'exteriorizes' the local cult which it overlays after a period of abandonment, and the memory of which has been perpetuated in one way or another among the population of the area.

[18] V. Lambrinoudakis, 'Remains of the Mycenaean Period in the Sanctuary of Apollo Maleatas', in R. Hägg and N. Marinatos (edd.), Sanctuaries and Cults in the Aegean Bronze Age (Stockholm, 1981), 59–65.

[19] R. C. S. Felsch, 'Mykenischer Kult im Heiligtum bei Kalapodi?', in Hägg and Marinatos (n. 18), 81–9. The marked break in cult practices between LH IIIB and IIIC is now well documented thanks to the excavations at Phylakopi: C. Renfrew, The Archaeology of Cult: The Sanctuary at Phylakopi (London, 1985). See also H. Gallet de Santerre, 'Les statuettes mycéniennes au type dit du "dieu Reshef" dans leur contexte égéen', BCH 111 (1987), 7–29.

or another, the heir of a Helladic sanctuary, or, alternatively, that it is a new foundation, does not mean that one does not also need to analyse why and how, in a particular historical context, the articulation of and relationship between the religious representations attached to the divinity, the forms which the cult takes, and the changes which affect the whole assemblage, give the sanctuary in question a central place in society.[20]

The hypothesis formulated above, about the nature of the festivals which periodically gathered the people round about at the rural sanctuaries, also permits us to construe the problem of continuity in a different way and distinguish what is really important. These gatherings, in the form of sacrificial banquets, did not in fact require either very strenuous formal organization or permanent management, and they do not necessarily imply continuous cult or any constant practice of dedication of figurines, pottery, or whatever. As a result they may sometimes have left only the slightest trace, or evidence which is difficult to date and liable to escape the attention of archaeologists, especially in early excavations.[21] The important question is not only one of knowing when evidence for cult first appears, but also of why, at some given moment, new cult practices, and particularly new offerings, make cult more visible not only to the eye of the archaeologist but also to ancient contemporaries; the simple phenomenon of quantitative accumulation cannot provide a sufficient explanation for this.[22] Thus, it follows from what has been said above that most probably the 'appearance' of a first generation of cults in the tenth century corresponds to a period of investigation and stabilization of contacts and exchanges following the instability and contraction of the earlier centuries. Such contacts might be established between neighbouring areas and regions (Olympia, Kombothekra, Tegea, Kabirion, Hyampolis, Hymettos, the Cretan caves, and cf. Amyklai) or with passing sailors (the Samian Heraion, Mounykhia, perhaps Brauron, the Polis cave on Ithaka, Kommos on Crete). But this is not sufficient to explain either the increasing number of sanctuaries thus rendered

[20] This is illustrated in a remarkable way by the work of P. Ellinger on the Hyampolis sanctuary, 'Hyampolis et le sanctuaire d'Artémis Elaphebolos dans l'histoire, la légende et l'espace de la Phocide', AA 42 (1987), 88–99, and Le Légende nationale phocidienne: Artémis, les situations extrêmes et les recits de guerre d'anéantissement, BCH Suppl. 27 (Paris, 1993).

[21] Such traces have now been found in the most recent excavations at Isthmia: Gebhard and Hemans (n. 7), 13–15. The importance of ritual meals in the organization of Archaic sanctuaries has been underlined by several recent studies: U. Kron, 'Kultmahle im Heraion von Samos archaischer Zeit', in Hägg, Marinatos, and Nordquist (n. 13), 135–48; R. A. Tomlinson, 'Two Notes on Possible Hestiatoria', BSA 75 (1980) 220–8; B. Bergquist, 'Sympotic Space: A Functional Aspect of Greek Dining-Rooms', and R. A. Tomlinson, 'The Chronology of the Perakhora Hestiatorion and its Significance', both in O. Murray (ed.), Sympotica (Oxford, 1990), 37–65 and 95–101. In the same volume, for the different possible forms of commensality, see P. Schmitt-Pantel, 'Sacrificial Meal and Symposion: Two Modes of Civic Institutions in the Archaic City?', and L. Bruit, 'The Meal at the Hyakinthia', at pp. 14–33 and 162–74.

[22] Analogous reflections are to be found in Morgan (n. 6), 59.

'visible' nor the sometimes spectacular development of certain of these cults in the ninth and again in the eighth century. Another transforming factor must be introduced, a factor of which the development of offerings allows a glimpse: the phenomenon of ritualized social competition, which can be seen in the flood of metal prestige offerings, particularly great bronze tripod cauldrons.

In talking of competition here I am not referring primarily or exclusively to the most well-known aspect, competition in games, those athletic and musical contests of funerary origin frequently associated with aristocratic funerals. That the very object which often constituted the victor's prize, the bronze tripod cauldron, appears in increasing numbers (mainly in Olympia (and Ithaka) in the ninth century, at Delphi from about 800, and afterwards, to a lesser degree, in places like Isthmia, the Argive Heraion, Amyklai, Athens, and Kalapodi), does not mean that the games were growing more common but rather that the sanctuaries were becoming the theatres for a more and more ostentatious rivalry in the expression of the power and authority which the tripod symbolized. One must nevertheless ask why this kind of ostentatious display is first of all exclusively (or almost exclusively taking Ithaka into account) focused on the sanctuary at Olympia, and has left no material traces in other cult places until the eighth century.[23] Remoteness in itself seems here to be a determining factor which distinguishes between two kinds of ritualized competition, one given material expression and 'visible' (in archaeological terms), the other not, corresponding to the different constraints which act on the princes in different contexts.[24] Because it is a selection criterion, distance confers a greater price, a greater prize, and a greater prestige on gathering at certain places: to take part in cults such as those at Olympia and Ithaka, situated on what was in the ninth century still the edge of the Greek world as well as the gateway to a semi-legendary West, was without a doubt a sign of belonging to a limited elite, particularly since the great myths of sovereignty attached to Pelops or the legends surrounding Odysseus could attract lively attention towards, respectively, the aristocracies of the Peloponnese or those more drawn by maritime adventures—even if those adventures developed more on the Aegean side of Greece, in, for

[23] The cult at the cave at Polis on Ithaka raises several problems: the number of tripods (13?), their considerable stylistic variety, and the uncertainty about their chronology and provenance make it difficult to interpret their role in the cult; the placing of some of them suggests that when in the 4th cent. the sanctuary was refurbished they may have been arranged to give it an image consistent with that of the cave of Odysseus in *Odyssey* 13. 13–14 and 363–71; see S. Benton, 'Excavations in Ithaca III', *BSA* 35 (1934/5), 51. That the cult after refurbishment was of Odysseus and the Nymphs, in conformity with the *Odyssey* (Benton, p. 54), does not mean that that was necessarily the cult in the 9th cent.: Odysseus the explorer king could be behind the cult without being in the religious sense the 'hero'. See my 'Offrandes, mémoire et compétition ritualisée', in P. Hellström (ed.), *Religion and Power in the Ancient Greek World* (forthcoming).

[24] For the notion of constraint see W. Burkert, 'Offerings in Perspective: Surrender, Distribution, Exchange', in T. Linders and G. Nordquist (edd.), *Gifts to the Gods* (Uppsala, 1987), 43–50.

example, Euboia from the beginning of the tenth century.[25] The symbolic capital of the tripod, which transferred into a public space the habit of making precious gifts which was characteristic of noble relations, was realized precociously in sanctuaries which were visited occasionally and selectively, because the conversion of the offering into a monumental material form, which was memorable and carried renown, gave the action a lasting permanence which preserved the glory of the dedicator among his peers.[26] Conversely, in sanctuaries which were near by and easy for the people around to attend, it was sacrifice which, by the sharing of food, the hospitality, and the commensality it occasioned, allowed the *basileis* regularly to bring into play and to strengthen the multiple networks of alliance, solidarity, and dependence which gave them authority over the inhabitants of the region; in this case the mediating role was performed by the goods that were shared and consumed, not by an object made to be taken out of the exchange network.

This distinction can be seen perpetuated under a different form in the eighth century, when the symbolic capital afforded by precious offerings became more generally dispersed. Sanctuaries at a distance from the major centres of power remained secure from seizure of direct control, and the competition for preeminence remained there symbolic, mediated by the memorial object.[27] Sanctuaries close by, by contrast, found themselves at the heart of complex processes of appropriation in which prestige offerings could play an important part, but where the decisive stage came when a city took in hand a major building programme (such as, and this is my point, only appeared later in sanctuaries that were outside the polis): the example of the Argive Heraion is again here the most enlightening.[28] It is indeed in the Heraion that bronzes, including

[25] Catling's connections between tripod moulds of around 900 discovered at Lefkandi and tripods from Olympia and Ithaka do not prove Euboian presence in sanctuaries in western Greece in the 9th cent., but show that it cannot be ruled out on stylistic grounds: see M. Popham, L. H. Sackett, and P. Themelis, *Lefkandi* i: *The Iron Age* (London, 1979), 93–7. Fibulae of Italian or Sicilian origin were able to get to Olympia already in the 9th cent. (H. Philipp, *Bronzeschmuck aus Olympia*, Olympia Forschungen 13 (1981), 13 no. 988) and the recent discovery near Rome (Osteria del'Osa) of an inscription in Greek characters on a pot dated to the late 9th or early 8th cent. shows how early were western contacts in which Euboians, given the role which they will later play in colonization, must have played a precocious part: A.-M. Bietti-Sestieri, *The Iron Age Community of Osteria del'Osa* (Cambridge, 1992), 185. Moreover, contrary to Rolley's suggestion, Olympia cannot be considered 'Argive' in the 9th cent. just because the bronzes there are Argive: the predominance of a style that was at the time without competitors does not necessarily signify political control: Rolley (n. 15), 49; see the remarks of F. Croissant in M. Piérart (ed.), (n. 15), 74–6.

[26] S. Langdon, 'Gift Exchange in the Geometric Sanctuaries', in Linders and Nordquist (n. 24), 107–13, discusses the transition from gift to offering, but her analysis depends on too rigid a notion of the gift—criticized by J. T. Hooker, 'Gifts in Homer', *BICS* 36 (1979), 79–90. I do not think that the idea of a 'reciprocal obligation' between giver and god will explain the appearance of precious offerings. These practices obviously do not exclude other 'levels' of cult.

[27] The cult at Delphi, which appears towards the end of the 9th cent., evidently finds itself in just this situation.

[28] This is a summary of my analysis in 'Cité et territoire' (n. 2). There are numerous analogies with

tripod cauldrons but, most of all, votive pins characterized by the same tendency to increase in size, pile up in the eighth century. In parallel with the increase of expensive dedications in the sanctuary, and more particularly in the second half of the century, burials in which the presence of arms, and particularly of complete sets of armour, appear to constitute a kind of claim to heroic status for the Argive aristocracy and more particularly its 'princes', as with other contemporary funerary customs in the Greek world.[29] Thus two rivalries find expression in the common sanctuary: one between the aristocracies of different small towns in the region, in which the Argives rapidly gain the upper hand, and the other extending the competition which the *basileis* at the head of the principal groups and power networks, and indeed other members of those groups, display in each community and particularly at Argos.[30] It is precisely because it is central and is shared that the rural cult becomes the principal place in which conflict is repeated and ritualized, and the only common place where the regional political pre-eminence acquired by one group or another can be displayed before the eyes of all. Whatever the form or extent of aristocratic participation in the early cult, it is clear that the medial sanctuary, and all that could be settled there on the occasion of the group festivals, became the site of an appropriation which was at first symbolic and then actual, as a power centre formed itself near by which reorganized regional relations for its own advantage and thus gave birth to a first form of state: at Prosymna the rearrangement of the sanctuary and of its cults at the end of the eighth century carries a clear imprint of Argos and establishes the fundamental town/sanctuary axis of the Archaic and Classical city, without other cities being excluded thereby from the cult.[31]

This fundamental mechanism gave birth to different situations according to the conditions in which it operated (Ill. 1.1). In some cases the nearby sanctuary which an emerging major political centre transformed into an expression of

the evolution of the sanctuary at Isthmia in the second half of the 8th cent., as analysed by C. Morgan in this volume.

[29] P. Courbin, *Tombes géométriques d'Argos*, i (Paris, 1974), 133–5 and 'Une tombe géométrique d'Argos', *BCH* 81 (1957), 322–86; R. Hägg, 'Burial Customs and Social Differentiations in Eighth-Century Argos', in R. Hägg (ed.), *The Greek Renaissance of the Eighth Century* (Stockholm, 1983), 27–31.

[30] These groups, of course, were not necessarily founded on a stable kin base, as 'clans', and their very instability may have been one of the causes of pressure and rivalry: see O. Murray, 'The Symposion as Social Organisation', in R. Hägg (n. 29), 195–9; the changes which took place in the 9th and 8th cents. (demographic growth, new opportunities brought by increased maritime activity, etc.) will have had an aggravating effect. B. Qviller, 'The Dynamics of Homeric Society', *Symbolae Osloenses* 56 (1981), 109–55, and J. Whitley, 'Social Diversity in Dark Age Greece', *BSA* 86 (1991), 341–65 have gone as far as comparison with Melanesian 'big men', but that must be considered the limiting case.

[31] Antonaccio (n. 4) proposes a lower date of 650–625 for the great terrace of the first temple, but despite the new elements that she brings, her demonstration does not finally solve this vexed question. For other datings of the terrace and temple see Ström (n. 15) 174–6, and M.-F. Billot, 'Terres cuites architecturales d'Argos et d'Epidaure', *Hesperia* 59 (1990), 95–104.

ILL. 1.1 Sanctuary and the creation of 'territories' in the eighth century

sovereign power was not a rural cult place, but the main sanctuary of a
subordinate community. The synoecism which led to the foundation of Sparta
and the unification of Lakonia in the eighth century, a double process in which
the small town of Amyklai, some kilometres to the south of Sparta, perhaps
took part, rather than to which Amyklai simply submitted, transformed the
local cult of Apollo Hyakinthos into the great territorial sanctuary of the city,
no doubt after a phase in which the cult served to link the two communities
and to be their meeting place. In Attica, the consolidation of social and cultural
unity and the mainland orientation of the city's politics during the sixth century
secured the integration of the cult at Eleusis after the model of the great
extra-urban sanctuaries, while the sanctuaries of Cape Sounion, the 'Cycladic'
extreme of the territory, had until that point been the principal manifestation
of Athenian sovereignty over the region.[32] In regions where no aristocracy

[32] See my 'Sanctuaires et société en Attique géométrique et archaïque', in A. Verbanck-Piérard and
D. Viviers (edd.), *Culture et cité: L'Avènement d'Athènes à l'époque archaïque* (Brussels, 1995), 75–101.

had succeeded in imposing its exclusive authority in the process of political
unification, and where relative equality prevailed between the cities or communities participating in the cult, rural sanctuaries often became the site and
protectors of practices and institutions of a federal kind in the Archaic and
Classical eras—Onchestos in Boiotia, the Phokikon and sanctuary of Artemis
Elaphebolos in Phokis, Thermon in Aetolia.[33]

This evolution obviously did not mean that cults were now closed to outside
elements, particularly not sanctuaries on coasts or at ports. In that case also a
variety of developments occurred in the eighth century. The Heraion at Samos,
established at a distance of some eight kilometres from the town, on remains
dating to the second millennium, or the Artemision at Ephesos, were, during
the Archaic period, incontestably the great sanctuaries at which each city
manifested its sovereignty by building mighty temples, by the organization of
the cult, and by ritual processions; they remained, however, closely associated
with the networks of exchange and circulation of the Aegean sea, and largely
open to foreign influences and foreign religious practices.[34] The Heraion at
Perachora, the sanctuary at Delphi, and perhaps that at Polis on Ithaka, well
illustrate the different degrees of dependence and mediation of cults whose
growth was largely bound up with that of a particular city, in this case of
Corinth. The sanctuary at Perachora, on the promontory facing Corinth,
reflects very closely the growth of Corinthian maritime activity in the eighth
century, but it also marks off the frontier of the territory of the city. Placed
outside direct Corinthian control, the other two sanctuaries escaped from any
exclusive sovereignty and established themselves as points of contact where
several influences could come face to face in juxtaposed dedications, even if
one particular influence may appear preponderant at a particular moment.[35]

Beginning from an initial situation that is analogous, or at least comparable,
the different blends of mediation and competition seem capable of explaining
the various developments at the majority of rural sanctuaries, giving birth to
sanctuaries expressive of the territorial sovereignty of a city, sanctuaries promoting regional federation, or sanctuaries suitable for interregional, even
Panhellenic, gatherings. It is, therefore, not surprising to find the same elements
in the world of the colonial foundations of the eighth and seventh centuries,
where Greeks were confronted by analogous problems of articulating the more
or less evident conflicts between different foundations, between different groups
within a single city, and between Greek and local populations. The peculiarity

[33] The links which unite the border sanctuary and the central sanctuary in Phokis have been lucidly
analysed by P. Ellinger, 'Hyampolis' (n. 20).

[34] Kilian-Dirlmeier (n. 12), 215–54; A. Bammer, 'Les Sanctuaires des VIIIe et VIIe siècles à l'Artémision d'Ephèse', RA (1991), 63–83.

[35] C. Morgan, 'Corinth, the Corinthian Gulf and Western Greece during the eighth century B.C.',
BSA 83 (1988), 313–38.

of the colonial world lies more in how speedily and systematically it develops what in the Aegean world is the outcome of an evolutionary process at work since the ninth century, and in its much neater identification of the city as both political unit (state) and social unit (community of inhabitants of a territory).[36] By contrast, in Archaic mainland Greece, the forms of organization remained more variable and often fluctuating, and it is scarcely possible to distinguish from the political point of view between a city and the decisions, actions, conflicts, and alliances of the leading members of its aristocracy.

This is why the non-urban sanctuaries of the colonial world display, combined in different ways according to local conditions, the same fundamental characteristics as those of the Aegean world, with the exception of the transformation into an interregional or Panhellenic sanctuary. Such a transformation could only occur at an 'intermediary' distance from the great political centres, a situation which the geopolitical configuration of the Greek West did not allow to materialize, and this role remained devolved upon the sanctuaries at Delphi and Olympia. Rather, the distribution of sanctuaries across the landscape there appears to be particularly neat, as, for example, at Croton (Ill. 1.2).[37] Situated like some enormous beacon on one of the most salient points of the coast of the Ionian Sea, the great Heraion on Cape Lacinium presents several analogies with that of Samos, in as far as it was simultaneously, by its position and the precious dedications, sometimes of non-Greek origin, that were made there, the main manifestation of the sovereignty of the city and the sanctuary which protected relations with the outside world. Much further from the town, some thirty kilometres away, the sanctuary of Apollo Aleos, founded in the coastal plain in the second half of the seventh century at the same time as a small Greek foundation, marked the northern frontier of the city and so also marked sovereignty, but in a context and a manner that were rather different. This part of the territory, beyond the River Neto, presents a landscape of more sharply broken relief than in the south and is home to a number of indigenous settlements of some importance which were established during the earliest Iron Age and continued to prosper there after the foundation of the city at the end of the eighth century.[38] The large number of non-Greek offerings found in the sanctuary, along with the plain and conservative temple architecture right up to the Hellenistic period, suggest that it was one of the main centres of regular public contact with the peoples of the hinterland who were in the sphere of

---

[36] The way in which the foundation of sanctuaries in colonial cities was systematically planned has been brought out by I. Malkin, *Religion and Colonization in Ancient Greece* (Leiden, 1987), 135–86.

[37] E. Lattanzi, 'Recenti scoperte nei santuari di Hera Lacinia a Crotone e di Apollo Aleo a Ciro Marina', in *Epeios et Philoctète en Italie*, Cahiers du Centre J. Bérard 16 (Naples, 1991), 67–73.

[38] Cl. Sabbione, 'L'insediamento delle Murge di Strongoli' in P. Poccetti (ed.), *Per un' identità culturale dei Brettii* (Naples, 1988), 195–200.

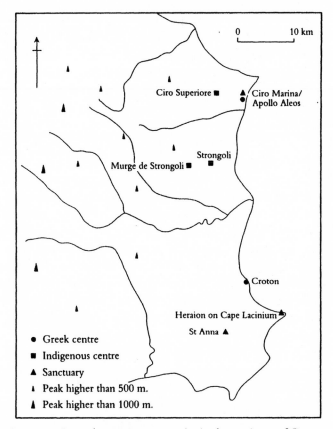

0   10 km

Ciro Superiore ■   ▲ Ciro Marina/
                         ● Apollo Aleos

Strongoli
Murge de Strongoli ■   ■

● Croton

Heraion on Cape Lacinium ▲
St Anna ▲

● Greek centre
■ Indigenous centre
▲ Sanctuary
▲ Peak higher than 500 m.
▲ Peak higher than 1000 m.

ILL. 1.2 Seventh-century sanctuaries in the territory of Croton

influence of the city but may not have been, strictly speaking, dependent politically.

Despite the variety of local conditions and the resulting adaptations, the articulation of a path between mediation and sovereignty, between border contacts and manifestations of authority, which is an essential feature of the genesis of extra-urban sanctuaries in the Greek world, retains a fundamental place in colonial cities. But it plays this role at the level of the city as a whole, rather than for certain eminent individuals or groups, and, as a result of this, the field of competition is moved from within the city, where the relatively egalitarian character of colonial societies in their early days gives it no place, towards the outside, towards the indigenous world. Non-urban Greek cult conveyed practices, images, cult forms—in short a cultural model which was as clearly identifiable as that of funerary rites. It offered indigenous elites a theatre in which they could all compete for prestige by adopting these cultural forms as distinctive signs of social superiority. Later, in the sixth century, the forms of

Greek cult, particularly the figurines characteristic of chthonic cults, were adopted within the indigenous communities, for their own cults. But this change is part of a series of social and cultural mutations which signal a new equilibrium at the heart of the indigenous societies and in their relations with Greek cities.[39]

The path from mediation to sovereignty which I have described explains how divinities of thresholds, of passage, of initiation—like Artemis—sometimes occupy a central place in great civic cults, and in the very idea of their own beginnings that cities or states create. Just as Pierre Ellinger has very truly said of the cult of Artemis at Hyampolis, which furnished the Phokian federal state with places and myths with which to think about its origins, the role of cults in Archaic societies invites us to replace our contemporary metaphor of the *birth* of the city, or of the state, by the rather more Greek metaphor of the *transition* towards a more finished, 'adult' stage of society and institutions, a metaphor which would be completely justified from the historic point of view.[40] In conjuring up change from one state to another, rather than a sudden rising out of darkness, this new model allows justice to be done to the research, such as that represented in this volume, which rightly tries to remove the study of society and cult in the Geometric and Archaic periods from the conceptual framework imposed through hindsight by the model of the Classical city. But it also insists, against a positivist conception of gradual and linear evolution, that historical societies can only be formed if crucial thresholds are crossed as the traditions and slow transformations of past centuries are brought together, remodelled, and transcended by large-scale changes, the skein of whose tangled interactions the historian must unravel.

Translated by Robin Osborne

---

[39] Sabbione (n. 38); D. Yntema, 'Oria', *Archivio Storico Pugliese* 39 (1986), 3–26.
[40] Ellinger, *Légende nationale* (n. 20) 296.

2

After the 'Big Bang'—What?
or
Minoan Symbols and Shrines
beyond Palatial Collapse

ALAN PEATFIELD

University College Dublin

An Historical Perspective

Beginning or ending, any Big Bang implies a fragmentation, a scattering of elements previously bound together in a structural form. This analogy is surely applicable to the end of the palatial system of Minoan Crete.[1] There we can see the breakup of political and economic structures; this breakup is equally apparent in the religious dimension, and this article examines it on two levels, a disintegration of shrine relationships, and a significant reformulation of one of the key symbolic belief elements of Minoan religion—the iconography of the Minoan Goddess.

This inevitably posits a contrast between Minoan religion in the Neopalatial period and in the Postpalatial period. In suggesting this contrast I am attempting to modify or progress from earlier analyses of Minoan religion which have tended to see their subject as a synchronic construct, created from sites and artefacts widely separated in time. Such a construct, labelled 'Minoan Religion', is inevitably artificial, and can offer only a partial perspective on the totality of religious belief and practice over two thousand years of Minoan cultural history. We have only to look back over two thousand years of Christianity to see how the faith of our own cultural heritage has been altered and redefined in relation to the events of history.

---

[1] For the purposes of this article I am assuming the end of the Minoan palatial system to be the conventional date of the final destruction of Knossos in Late Minoan IIIA2. But there is no intention here to contribute to the Destruction controversy; this article is entirely concerned with the religious dimension of Postpalatial Crete. Abbreviations: EM = Early Minoan, MM = Middle Minoan, LM = Late Minoan.

There are, of course, sufficient constant elements in Christianity for us to recognize that the faith of the first century AD is the same as that expressed in the established churches of today. Similarly, the Minoan artefacts allow us to recognize features constant in the development of Minoan religion—the focus on a female deity, the significance of symbols such as the double axe and the horns of consecration, meaningful animals such as bulls and birds, the emphasis on elements of the natural world. But the continued use of such features should not mislead us into believing that their meanings necessarily remained constant. Rappaport commented that only in its capacity to redefine its symbols does a society maintain its spiritual vitality.[2] The very continuity of Minoan religion does suggest the ability to redefine its symbols. The attempt to understand such redefinition is the duty of the historian of religion.

The historian of Minoan religion is inevitably constrained by the archaeological/artefactual nature of the material. Therefore this approach must start from the 'great events' of Minoan history, the transitions of the Pre-, Proto-, Neo-, and Postpalatial periods. Recent studies within the field of Minoan religion have started to take a more diachronic perspective. My own contribution to this has been the observations of changes in the peak sanctuary cult over the Proto- and Neopalatial periods.[3] That chronological focus, however, has been typical of recent studies; the cults, beliefs, and practices of the Pre-, Proto-, and Neopalatial periods have been emphasized, to the relative neglect of the Postpalatial period. Only Gesell has taken any consistent interest in Postpalatial Minoan religion.[4] This interest has been appropriately brought to fruition with the Kavousi excavations and the discovery of the Vronda shrine.[5]

Rural Sanctuaries in the Neopalatial Period

There is a pattern of evidence which suggests that during the Neopalatial period the expression and practice of religion became centralized on the palaces. This has been separately recognized by scholars looking at different aspects of Minoan culture. Gesell has observed that access to palace shrines becomes much more

[2] R. A. Rappaport, 'Ritual, Sanctity and Cybernetics', *American Anthropologist* 79 (1977), 53–76.

[3] A. A. D. Peatfield, 'The Topography of Minoan Peak Sanctuaries', *BSA* 78 (1983), 273–280; 'Palace and Peak: The Political and Religious Relationship between Palaces and Peak Sanctuaries', in R. Hägg and N. Marinatos (edd.), *The Function of the Minoan Palaces* (Stockholm, 1987), 89–93; 'Minoan Peak Sanctuaries: History and Society', *OpAth* 17 (1990), 117–31; 'Rural Ritual in Bronze Age Crete: The Peak Sanctuary at Atsipadhes', *CAJ* 2 (1992), 59–87.

[4] G. C. Gesell, 'The Minoan Snake-tube: A Survey and Catalogue', *AJA* 80 (1976), 247–59; *Town, Palace and House Cult in Minoan Crete*, SIMA 67 (Göteborg, 1985), esp. ch. V. See also now R. Mersereau, 'Cretan Cylindrical Models', *AJA* 97 (1993), 1–47, which appeared too late to be incorporated here but with which I broadly agree.

[5] G. C. Gesell, W. D. E. Coulson and L. P. Day, 'Excavations at Kavousi, Crete 1988', *Hesperia* 60 (1991), 145–77, esp. 161–3.

restricted in the Neopalatial period, in comparison to the Protopalatial period.[6] I have noted that the peak sanctuary cult, initially a peasant, popular cult, becomes palatially controlled in the Neopalatial period, centralized onto the peak sanctuaries of the various palatial centres.[7] Cameron went even further than this, by attributing the origin of figured fresco decoration at Knossos to that palace's appropriation of the cult of the Minoan Goddess in her capacity as 'Mistress of Animals and Peak Sanctuaries'.[8] Moody has contributed to this picture with her perception of religion as a prestige activity in palatial Crete, as important to elite domination as was control of material resources and prestige artefacts.[9]

Centralization of religion should not seem surprising in the Minoan context. It is a consistent social tool of elite hierarchical domination in many cultures. Modern scholars, in particular Cherry, have expanded the perspective of Minoan scholarship by applying this generalizing principle to Minoan society.[10] Wright has initiated a fruitful approach by offering a structuralist perspective of this religious centralization (see Ch. 3 below). He suggests a dyadic relationship (both complementary and oppositional) between palace cults and rural cults (correctly linking cave cults and what have been termed 'sacred enclosures' with peak sanctuaries as components of a broader earth/fertility cult).

I have already discussed aspects of peak sanctuaries elsewhere (see note 3), but in the context of the theme of this volume certain things may bear repetition. Crete is primarily a land of mountains. Its traditional economy is based on the Mediterranean staples of olive, vine, and pastoralism. These are the typical resources of a marginal landscape. Any culture that evolves in such a landscape is going to have an appropriate ritual response to it, and for the Minoans that response was the cult of the peak sanctuaries. A peak sanctuary is a sanctuary set on a mountain peak, but though this may seem an unnecessarily obvious definition, the twenty-five peak sanctuaries so far known on Crete all share features of topography and of finds so similar that we may identify a Minoan pan-Cretan peak sanctuary cult. The characteristic finds are terracotta figurines of three main types: human, animal, and separately modelled parts of the human anatomy, referred to as votive limbs. Most, though by no means all of these

---

[6] G. C. Gesell, 'The Minoan Palace and Public Cult', in Hägg and Marinatos (n. 3), 123–8.

[7] Peatfield, 'Palace and Peak' (n. 3); 'Minoan Peak Sanctuaries' (n. 3).

[8] M. Cameron, 'Theoretical Interrelationships among Theran, Cretan and Mainland Frescoes', in *Thera and the Aegean World*, i (London, 1978), 579–92.

[9] J. A. Moody, 'The Minoan Palace as a Prestige Artifact', in Hägg and Marinatos (n. 3), 235–41.

[10] J. F. Cherry, 'Generalisation and the Archaeology of the State', in D. Green, C. Haselgrove, and M. Spriggs (edd.), *Social Organisation and Settlement* (Oxford, 1978), 411–37; 'Evolution, Revolution and the Origins of Complex Society in Minoan Crete', in O. Krzyszkowska and L. Nixon (edd.), *Minoan Society: Proceedings of the Cambridge Colloquium 1981* (Bristol, 1983), 33–46; 'The Emergence of the State in the Prehistoric Aegean', *PCPS* 210, NS 30 (1984), 18–48; 'Polities and Palaces: Some Problems in Minoan State Formation', in C. Renfrew and J. F. Cherry (edd.), *Peer Polity Interaction and Socio-Political Change* (Cambridge, 1986), 19–45.

figurines seem to be Protopalatial in date. A significantly restricted group of nine (six certain, and three possible) peak sanctuaries also have more varied finds, e.g. bronzes (figurines, blades, double axes), stone vases and libation-tables, some with Linear A inscriptions, and very rarely seals and jewellery.[11] Many of these finds are Neopalatial in date.

Of these sites, only Jouktas, the peak sanctuary linked with the palace of Knossos, has anything approaching monumental architecture, with three huge terrace constructions, and a multi-roomed shrine building.[12] Only eight other sites (the same as those with Neopalatial finds, referred to above) have any trace of buildings, and these seem to have been rudimentary dry-stone structures, probably hypaethral (open to the sky). The smallest have single rooms, the largest have four or five rooms. Thus, most peak sanctuaries have no architecture. On these, however, the features of the natural rock seem to have served 'architecturally', e.g. as temenos boundaries or to demarcate special ritual areas.[13]

On the basis of the finds and the architecture (or lack of it) we can make some inferences as to the religious belief and practice associated with the peak sanctuaries. The finds are almost all votive offerings, very rarely are they cult symbols or equipment for use in ceremonies. As votives they seem to reflect the concerns of the worshippers, themselves (the human figurines), their health (the votive limbs), and their property and prosperity (the animal figurines). These personalized and agricultural, especially pastoral, concerns strongly suggest that, at its inception at least, the peak sanctuary cult was a genuinely popular, peasant one, based on the fertility of Nature. The few cult symbols, double axes and horns of consecration, do suggest that the divine focus of the peak sanctuary cult was the same as in the rest of Minoan religion, i.e. the Minoan Goddess.

In terms of practice, worship seems to have been primarily, perhaps exclusively, communal. Even on peak sanctuaries with buildings, the main focus of activity was an open space suitable for the gathering of groups of people. Ritual activity was not random, however; there is ample evidence for the demarcation of special ritual places, using natural rock features and/or pebble scatters. There is very clear evidence for this at Atsipadhes Korakias, where the lower of the peak's two natural terraces is an open flat space. Both its natural topography and the distribution of finds focus the Lower Terrace towards the Upper Terrace,

---

[11] Peatfield, 'Palace and Peak' (n. 3); 'Minoan Peak Sanctuaries' (n. 3), 127.

[12] A. Karetsou, 'The Peak Sanctuary of Mt. Juktas', in R. Hägg and N. Marinatos (edd.), *Sanctuaries and Cults of the Aegean Bronze Age* (Stockholm, 1981), 137–53; *Praktika* (1974), 228–39; (1975), 330–42; (1976), 408–18; (1977), 419–20; (1978), 232–58; (1979), 280–1; (1980), 337–63; (1981), 405–8; *Ergon* (1984), 111–15; (1985), 83–7.

[13] The available evidence of the peak sanctuaries is fully documented in my book, *Rural Religion in Prehistoric Crete* (forthcoming).

where an area covered with pebbles can be identified by its finds as a special liturgical zone.[14]

Before progressing to a discussion of spatial dimensions of peak sanctuary distribution, the sites should be placed in their chronological and historical context. The available evidence suggests that peak sanctuaries as a group and cult came into being sometime late in the Prepalatial period—probably EM III, and the very earliest sites possibly in EM II.[15] Almost certainly all twenty-five sites were in use by the Protopalatial period (MM IB–IIIA) (Ill. 2.1). Then, in the Neopalatial period (MM IIIB–LM IB) all but eight peak sanctuaries went out of use; these eight are the peak sanctuaries associated with palatial/urban settlements.[16] It is this restriction of the cult to the sanctuaries of elite political centres, that suggests its transformation from a diffuse peasant/popular cult to a centralized, elite-dominated cult.

From the preceding summary, the spatial significance of the peak sanctuaries can already be discerned. I have discussed the topographic characteristics of peak sanctuaries elsewhere.[17] In summary form these characteristics are as follows: 1) prominence and visibility of the peak from the area from which the worshippers came; 2) good view down onto that same area; 3) can 'see' and 'be seen' from other peak sanctuaries; 4) accessible; 5) proximity to areas of human habitation and exploitation.

The general point which underlies all these features is that peak sanctuaries are very much part of the 'human' landscape. Their geographical position is determined in relation to human factors, their interaction with the population who worshipped on them. This is not to deny the possibility that the Minoans regarded higher, more remote mountains as sacred; it is simply that they did not leave any material remains on them, i.e. did not build sanctuaries or leave offerings. Similarly, we should not assume that to the Minoans the peak sanctuary site was the only sacred part of a given mountain, the specific 'abode of the gods'; rather it may have been the most suitable location for a sanctuary from which those 'gods' could be worshipped.

This element of choice, to maximize the factors of human interaction, does make the Minoan peak sanctuaries an interesting variation of the general religious phenomenon of mountain worship. In most other cultures the sacred mountain is a remote, almost supernatural place; e.g. the mountain shrines of

---

[14] Peatfield, 'Rural Ritual' (n. 3), 68–69.

[15] Peatfield, 'Minoan Peak sanctuaries' (n. 3), 123–6; 'Rural Ritual' (n. 3) 71–2 and 86.

[16] These are: Gonies (serving the Sklavokampos villa and valley), Jouktas (serving Knossos, Archanes, and north central Crete), Kophinas (serving the Mesara plain and ?Phaistos), Petsophas (serving Palaikastro and its hinterland), Traostalos (serving the Epano Zakro sites and hinterland, and the Kato Zakro palace), Vrysinas (serving sites in the Rethymnon area), Zou Prinias (serving the Sitia coastal plain), and Pyrgos (serving the Tylissos villas).

[17] Peatfield, 'Topography' (n. 3); 'Minoan Peak Sanctuaries' (n. 3), 119–20.

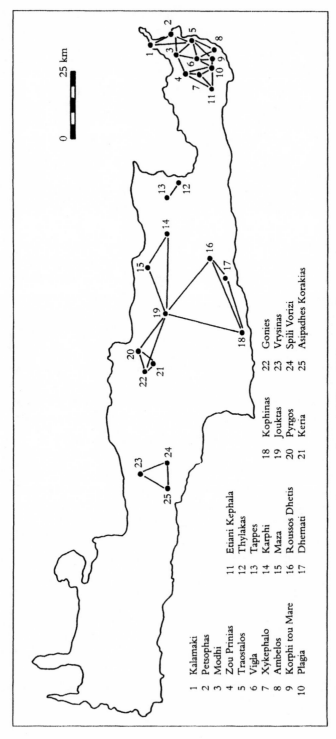

ILL. 2.1 Intervisibility of Minoan peak sanctuaries

1 Kalamaki	11 Etiani Kephala
2 Petsophas	12 Thylakas
3 Modhi	13 Tappes
4 Zou Prinias	14 Karphi
5 Traostalos	15 Maza
6 Vigla	16 Roussos Dhetis
7 Xykephalo	17 Dhemati
8 Ambelos	18 Kophinas
9 Korphi tou Mare	19 Jouktas
10 Plagia	20 Pyrgos
	21 Keria
	22 Gonies
	23 Vrysinas
	24 Spili Vorizi
	25 Asipadhes Korakias

Japan, the universe-mountain of Buddhist cosmology expressed in the domes of temples and embodied in certain Himalayan peaks, Mesoamerican holy mountains like Mt. Tlaloc. It is this contrast that I have had in mind when, in other articles, I have referred to peak sanctuaries as 'community shrines, not places of remote and arduous pilgrimage'.[18]

This does not invalidate, however, the symbolic 'otherness' of peak sanctuaries within the Minoan religious context; indeed it might almost emphasize it, for the very deliberateness of the choice of peak sanctuary location suggests that the Minoans were indeed cognizant, no doubt at various conscious and more subliminal levels, of the difference between the natural/rural world and the urban/palatial world. The recognition of the difference may have arisen through the impulse that first gave rise to the peak sanctuaries. Previously I have suggested that the absence of peak sanctuaries in the earliest Prepalatial periods (EM I–II) may have had some correlation with the comparative scarcity of settlements in the mountains during the same period, which may even have had the symbolic implications of a taboo; the impetus of economic expansion in the latest Prepalatial period (EM III–MM IA) certainly led to increased exploitation of the mountains, which may have required a placating of the spirits.[19] This suggestion received unexpected corroboration from the 1991 Ayios Vasilios Survey, when the upland area of the Kouroupas mountain (the location of the Atsipadhes Korakias peak sanctuary) proved almost entirely free of Minoan occupation; apart of course, from the peak sanctuary itself, Minoan material was found only in a small rock shelter. Seen in this way, one of the spatial elements of peak sanctuary distribution is that it is the symbolic and ritual expression of secular human exploitation of the mountain.

The wider spatial implications of peak sanctuaries are territorial. In the latest Prepalatial and Protopalatial phases any peak sanctuary is the spiritual focus of an expanded territory with multiple settlements—the spiritual focus, embodied in the landscape, for its community identity. On a regional level the intervisibility of peak sanctuaries provides an opportunity for the expression of ritual unity that may have transcended political boundaries (Ill. 2.1). This is most graphically represented by the intervisibility of Jouktas and Kophinas, the main peak sanctuaries of north central and south central Crete respectively, and, of course, the regions dominated by the great power blocs of the Minoan world, Knossos and Phaistos.

The Neopalatial centralization of the peak sanctuaries is expressive of political centralization. There is some correlation of the Neopalatial peak sanctuaries (noted above) with the palatial polities as suggested by Cherry.[20] This is again

---

[18] Peatfield, 'Minoan Peak Sanctuaries' (n. 3), 120.
[19] Ibid. 126.
[20] Cherry, 'Polities' (n. 10).

territorial, but it is with this centralization that the symbolic spatial dimension of peak sanctuary interaction with palatial urban cult is most profound. As has been already stated, however, this symbolic interaction is not exclusive to peak sanctuaries. It is a rural dimension which also includes caves and what Wright terms 'sanctuaries in a rural location'.

Caves are an intrinsic feature of the limestone geology of the Cretan mountains. Tyree has, however, persuasively argued that there were only around twelve caves sacred in Minoan times.[21] This radically reduces the number of Minoan sacred caves listed by Rutkowski and Faure.[22] But a consistent feature of these caves is that the finds which reveal their sacred usage are of high quality, e.g. fine pottery, bronze figurines and other objects, stone vessels (some with Linear A inscriptions), double axes in bronze, gold, and silver. They are, if only in a manufacturing sense, palatial objects.

In the present context 'sanctuaries in a rural location' should be defined as self-contained religious sites in a rural setting, i.e. not part of a larger, secular settlement site, such as a villa or farmhouse. They could be shrines associated with some numinous natural feature, a rock or stream or tree, or they are associated with agricultural land, perhaps for on-site rituals. Collectively these have been defined in the handbooks as 'sacred enclosures'.[23] As I have observed elsewhere, however, there are major problems with the identification of sites listed as sacred enclosures.[24] I conclude from first-hand examination that there are very few sites of the palatial period which may be confidently claimed as independent sacred enclosures; indeed, on the basis of currently available material, I would limit the certain ones to Anemospilia, Syme, and Piskokephalo.

One of the many ways in which the Syme sanctuary is remarkable is for the extremely high quality of its finds, and the elaboration of its architecture and layout, peaking in the Neopalatial period.[25] There are even suggestions, not simply of palatial involvement there, but specifically of Knossian involvement. The Anemospilia shrine is obviously within the Knossian sphere of influence, and judging by the personal objects among the finds, the people found therein, killed and buried by the earthquake which destroyed the shrine, were actual

---

[21] L. Tyree, *Cretan Sacred Caves* (Ann Arbor, University Microfilms, 1974).

[22] B. Rutkowski, *Cult Places of the Aegean* (London, 1986); P. Faure, *Fonctions des cavernes crétoises* (Paris, 1964); 'Chroniques des cavernes crétoises 1972–77', *BCH* 102 (1978), 629–40.

[23] Rutkowski (n. 22), 99–118.

[24] A. Brown and A. A. D. Peatfield, 'Stous Athropolithous: A Minoan Site near Epano Zakro, Sitias', *BSA* 82 (1987), 23–33, esp. 33 n. 32.

[25] A. Lebessi and P. Muhly, 'Aspects of Minoan Cult. Sacred Enclosures: The Evidence from the Syme Sanctuary (Crete)', *AA* (1990), 315–36. Lebessi and Muhly also address the issue of sacred enclosures with specific reference to Syme. I agree with their suggestion for closer definition of the term. I repeat, however, my basic point that the term has indeed been used as a catch-all for rural shrines that are associated with particular natural features, rocks, streams, trees, etc. (but not peak sanctuaries or cave sanctuaries), and which can be more closely defined through that association.

members of the palatial elite.[26] The Piskokephalo figurines, though clay, are also very fine, with elaborate forms of dress and hairstyle which can only be indicative of a local palatial or urban elite.[27]

In his discussion of sacred enclosures, Rutkowski acknowledged the difficulties of identifying the actual sites; he therefore focused his analysis on the iconography, i.e. religious scenes on seals, sealings, gold rings, frescos, stone vases, etc. which show rituals associated with natural features, most likely indicating a rural setting, actual as well as symbolic.[28] But recall what the objects are which present these scenes—they are objects of palatially controlled precious resources, made in palatial workshops, for wealthy elite palatial customers and reflecting their preoccupations.

Therefore, all the evidence—the sites themselves, the finds thereof, and the iconography which celebrates their importance—is consistent in revealing that Neopalatial elite interest was not just in the cult of the peak sanctuaries, but was extended to all the spiritual aspects of the natural world. At this point it is appropriate to draw a distinction between the peak sanctuary cult on the one hand and the caves and sacred enclosures on the other. As I have argued elsewhere, the basic material features of the peak sanctuary cult, finds and topography, fundamentally the same all over the island, suggest that it was a, perhaps the main, pan-Cretan Minoan cult.[29] The more individualized finds from the caves and sacred enclosures do not offer evidence of other pan-Cretan cults.[30] Rather they suggest that each was an individual sanctuary site, of, initially at least (viz. Syme), localized spiritual significance.

In political terms palatial interest in all these sites is very properly expressive of elite palatial centralizing control of rural popular cults, a concern with religious monopoly both on the pan-Cretan level and on the more parochial local level. Where Wright elaborates on his structuralist observation in spatial terms he does so on this territorial level, suggesting a balanced integration of palatial and rural sanctuaries, each having a place in actual and in hierarchical terms. We may, however, also observe a more symbolic spatial dimension to the binary relationship between palatial and rural: the hierarchical dominance of the 'inside', the urban/palatial elite cults, is expressed in the imagery of the 'outside', the rural popular cults.

We may conclude therefore, that by the Neopalatial period there had evolved

---

[26] J. A. and E. Sakellarakis, 'Drama of Death in a Minoan Temple' *National Geographic* (Feb. 1981), 205–22; *Archanes* (Athens, 1991), 137–56.

[27] N. Platon, 'To ieron Maza kai ta minoika iera koryphis', *KrChron* 5 (1951), 96–160, esp. 124–35.

[28] Rutkowski (n. 22), 99–118.

[29] Peatfield, 'Minoan Peak Sanctuaries' (n. 3); 'Rural Ritual' (n. 3), 61.

[30] Cf. Peatfield, 'Rural Ritual' (n. 3), 61. I note, however, that Warren in his reply to the same article expressed his disagreement with this interpretation of caves (p. 80). I shall present my full arguments for this interpretation at a later date.

a complex religious structure, which integrated both palatial and rural cults in terms of practical functions and of symbolic meaning. What then happened to this centralized religious structure after the destruction of Knossos and the end of the palatial system?

Postpalatial Religion

The primary evidence for Postpalatial religion is the phenomenon of the Goddess-with-Upraised-Arms, initially defined and catalogued by Alexiou.[31] It is the presence of these figures that allows the recognition of Postpalatial shrines. Goddesses-with-Upraised-Arms are relatively simply designed figures

ILL. 2.2 Goddesses-with-Upraised-Arms from Karphi

consisting of a cylindrical wheel-made skirt to which is attached a schematic torso. The name derives from the characteristically raised arms. The divinity of these figures is identified by the attributes which crown their heads: e.g. typical Minoan symbols such as horns-of-consecration, birds, discs, etc. (Ill. 2.2). Fortunately many of these figures have been found in shrines (mostly bench-sanctuaries) more or less *in situ* (Ill. 2.3): e.g. at Gazi (Ill. 2.4), Gournia, Kannia, Karphi, Kavousi Vronda, and Knossos (Shrine of the Double Axes). More problematic, but still demonstrably cultic, are other deposits at Knossos and at

[31] St Alexiou, 'He minoike thea meth' upsomenon cheiron', *KrChron* 12 (1958), 179–299.

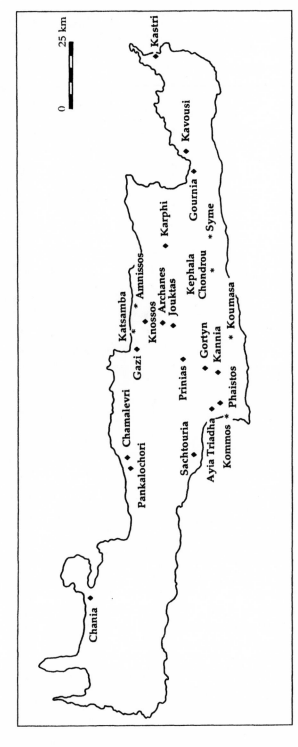

ILL. 2.3 Distribution of Late Minoan III Goddess-with–Upraised-Arms figurines (◆), and of snake-tubes in bench-sanctuaries (*)

ILL. 2.4 Goddess-with-
Upraised-Arms, with poppy-head
tiara from Gazi

Prinias. Fragments of Goddesses-with-Upraised-Arms have also been found
among the mixed finds in the large Postpalatial sanctuary at Ayia Triadha.
(Similarly, fragments of at least two Goddesses-with-Upraised-Arms are from
mixed deposits on the peak sanctuary of Jouktas.) Fragments have also been
reported from Chamalevri near Rethymnon. Two of the best preserved Goddesses-with-Upraised-Arms are chance finds from Sachtouria, on the south
coast of Rethymnon province, and from Pankalochori, near Rethymnon. Where
it is possible to date the context of all these finds more specifically than Late
Minoan III, they can be assigned to the LM IIIB and LM IIIC periods, which
is consistent with their stylistic characteristics.[32]

[32] For these sites I am giving only the relevant reference in Gesell, *Town* (n. 4); this is done purely for
convenience. For other references, interested readers should consult Gesell's entries. Gesell, *Town* (n. 4):
Gazi (no. 5, pp. 69–71); Gournia (no. 10, p. 72); Kannia (no. 21, pp. 77–9); Karphi (no. 22, p. 79);
Knossos, Shrine of the Double Axes (no. 37, pp. 90–2); Knossos (no. 68, p. 101); Prinias (no. 118, p. 132);

Frequently found with these Goddesses-with-Upraised-Arms have been the tubular offering vessels usually called 'snake-tubes'. Gesell has persuasively argued that where Goddesses-with-Upraised-Arms and snake-tubes have been found together, it is possible to observe the direct association of an individual snake-tube with an individual Goddess-with-Upraised-Arms, usually by virtue of identical clay fabric and/or painted decoration. Moreover this 'set' is often completed by the addition of a vase which seems to have been placed in the open mouth of the tube. Gesell's observation has been confirmed by the Kavousi finds.[33]

The Spatial Context of Postpalatial Shrines

This relationship between Goddesses-with-Upraised-Arms and snake-tubes opens up the possibility that sites which have snake-tubes in bench-sanctuaries, but do not have Goddesses-with-Upraised-Arms, may nevertheless represent the same cult. This would allow us to add several more sites: Katsamba, the port of Knossos, Kephala Chondrou, south of Mt. Dikte, Kommos, Amnissos, Koumasa, and Kato Syme.[34]

This is not an exhaustive list, but it reveals a minimum of eighteen separate sites which participated in the cult of the Goddess-with-Upraised-Arms, involving the greater portion of the island, at least as far east as Kavousi and at least as far west as the Rethymnon region. It is striking that many of the sites are relatively near one another: Ayia Triadha, Kommos, and Kannia; Gournia and Kavousi; Knossos, Jouktas, Gazi, Katsamba, and Amnissos. Despite this, however, there is little discernible hierarchical relationship between these near-neighbour sites in terms of size, richness, furnishings, and decoration. Certainly there is no evidence for selective luxury at especial shrines, such as is evident from Neopalatial sanctuaries. Another consistent feature revealed by the better preserved sites is that they are independent sanctuaries within settlements, i.e. they are public shrines. They are clearly a manifestation of *public* cult rather than simply private devotion.

Inevitably this is a simplification of the details, but what emerges is a broad picture of a single cult focused on a particular image of the Minoan Goddess, which was shared over most if not all of the island. It operated as a public, mostly

---

Ayia Triadha (no. 17, p. 76); Chamalevri (pp. 49–50); Sachtouria (p. 47); Pankalochori (p. 47). For Kavousi Vronda, Gesell *et al.* (n. 5), 161–3; for Jouktas, *Praktika* (1974), 235, pl. 175. On dating, Gesell, *Town* (n. 4), 47–50.

[33] Ibid. 50; Gesell *et al.* (n. 5), 162.

[34] Gesell, *Town* (n. 4): Katsamba (no. 30, p. 82); Kephala Chondrou (no. 31, p. 82); Kommos (no. 69, p. 102); Amnissos (p. 50); Koumasa (no. 70, p. 102). For Kato Syme, see no. 25.

settlement, cult. The material aspects of the cult (the buildings, equipment, idols themselves) reveal a moderate level of corporate prosperity.

This then is the basic material. What does it reveal of the social context of the Goddess-with-Upraised-Arms cult, especially in contrast to the earlier palatial periods?

The first point to highlight is that many of the sites are familiar more for their Palatial remains than their Postpalatial finds. These sites were clearly important for their role as greater or lesser regional centres in the political, economic, or indeed religious network of the centralized Neopalatial states, e.g. Knossos, Ayia Triadha—palaces; Gournia—town; Kommos, Katsamba, Amnissos—towns/ports; Kannia (perhaps also Gazi)—villa; Jouktas—central peak sanctuary.

Significantly, the two latest Goddess-with-Upraised-Arms sanctuaries, the LM IIIC sites of Karphi and Kavousi, are regional centres in the refuge site period.

These shrines are therefore strongly associated with secular sites; they are not independent sanctuaries, whose presence provides the *raison d'être* for any given site. In contrast there is very little evidence for other rural shrines in the Postpalatial period. If my reading of the evidence is correct, then already by the end of the Neopalatial period (if not earlier) Jouktas was the only peak sanctuary still in use.[35] Peak sanctuaries seem not to have been replaced by another form of sanctuary. Apart from the Syme sanctuary, the evidence of sacred enclosures in the Postpalatial period is apparently non-existent. These two sites, Jouktas and Syme, might seem to contradict the idea of no Postpalatial rural sanctuaries, but by the end of the Palatial period they had developed an individual pan-Cretan importance, independent of any association with a more general cult. Therefore their Postpalatial survival is expressed by incorporation into the main redefined cult of that era, i.e. that of the Goddesses-with-Upraised-Arms. Though they apparently have no material to link them directly with the Goddess-with-Upraised-Arms cult, the same is true of the two main sacred caves which survived in the Postpalatial period, Psychro and Ida. Significantly, too, Tyree suggests a diminution in the overall number of Postpalatial sacred caves, from eleven Neopalatial to nine Postpalatial, only eight of which are the same.[36]

This strongly indicates that the centralized Neopalatial structure of integrated palatial and rural cults had simply ceased to exist. Even without other evidence this argues that Wright's structuralist observation is correct, because in any structure, physical or symbolic, the removal of one component is going to affect the others; in this case the removal of the palaces (buildings and system) negated

---

[35] Peatfield, 'Minoan Peak Sanctuaries' (n. 3), 131.
[36] Tyree (n. 21), 98.

the importance of the rural sanctuary sites which had validated the palaces' importance. In Postpalatial society the physical spatial distinction between palatial and rural no longer had any significance, therefore the symbolic nature of the spatial distinction was also irrelevant and meaningless.

No structure simply evaporates, however; we need to understand what was left. Late Minoan IIIB Crete seems to have undergone a cultural 'Indian summer' after the destruction of the palace of Knossos. Perhaps the two are causally related. What is commonly perceived of the artefacts, however, especially the pottery, is that there was an increasing regionalism.[37] If this can be truly translated into social terms, then released from the centripetal energy flow of the centralized Minoan state, the towns and villas that had been the local provincial centres of the palatial political and economic network were perfectly placed to express independent control of their own small regions. The Goddess-with-Upraised-Arms sanctuaries, a public cult in public shrines, were the religious component of Postpalatial territorial definition.

A Symbolic Spatial Break-up

In the preamble to this paper I referred to the redefinition of symbols. It is clear that the Goddess-with-Upraised-Arms is the Postpalatial incarnation of that central symbol of Minoan religion—the Minoan Goddess. Moreover, the attributes of the Goddesses-with-Upraised-Arms include many of the symbols familiar from earlier manifestations of Minoan cult: bulls, birds, horns-of-consecration, double axes, snakes, solar or lunar discs, etc. In the Postpalatial use of these, however, there is a significant difference. Gesell has remarked that 'all the standard Minoan cult symbols—birds, bulls, snakes, agrimia, double-axes, horns-of-consecration—continued to appear; however, the majority of these are not independent objects, but are attached to other cult objects (goddesses, snake tubes, stands).'[38] Of the Gournia sanctuary in particular she says: 'it includes almost all the sacred symbols used in Neopalatial cult . . . with the distinction that all these have been reduced to attributes of the goddess and her cult equipment.'[39] This is surely a redefinition of fundamental importance. But what does it reveal?

Primarily it reveals that all these symbols are now specifically defined in relation to the Goddess. The Goddess-with-Upraised-Arms figures are crowned with various permutations of these symbols. The selective association of the symbols seems to be deliberately characterizing each particular Goddess-with-Upraised-Arms as an individual. For example, at Gazi the four preserved

[37] A. Kanta, *The Late Minoan III Period in Crete*, SIMA 58 (Göteborg, 1980).

[38] Gesell, *Town* (n. 4), 41.

[39] Ibid. 43.

Goddess-with-Upraised-Arms heads are quite distinctive, especially the largest figure with the incised poppy-head tiara (Ill. 2.4). Given the common medicinal use of opium in the Late Bronze Age, this figure surely represents the healing aspect of the Goddess, earlier celebrated by the votive limbs on the peak sanctuaries. This symbolic individualization of the Goddesses-with-Upraised-Arms harmonizes with the observation about the careful formation of 'sets', consisting of Goddess-with-Upraised-Arms figure, snake-tube, and offering vase. This is particularly clear at the better preserved sanctuaries, e.g. Gazi, Karphi, and Kannia.

Obviously the exact symbolic meaning of the permutations of attributes eludes us today, but the significant point is that the individualization of Goddess-with-Upraised-Arms figures was deliberate and, undoubtedly, meaningful to the Postpalatial Minoans. To be explicit, I am suggesting that a major feature of Postpalatial Minoan religion was a progression (probably no more than an intermediate stage) towards the developed polytheism familiar from later Greek religion, and that this was a feature new to Minoan religion.

The debate between Minoan monotheism and polytheism is not yet resolved. Nilsson and the scholars of his generation firmly believed in a multiplicity of Minoan goddesses,[40] but their synchronic approach to the material could not distinguish a progression through the cultural phases. By 'monotheism' I am not denying the probability that the Minoan Goddess had a consort; rather, I am suggesting that there is nothing in the iconography or cult places of the Pre-, Proto-, or Neopalatial periods to indicate that the Minoans of these phases characterized the aspects of the Minoan Goddess into separate deities. Branigan has already argued that the 'Minoan Household Goddess' and the 'Mistress of the Animals' are artificial definitions, and were in Minoan belief one and the same goddess. Warren too has argued for the basic unity of the Minoan Goddess.[41]

A possible analogy for the Palatial Minoan Goddess is the Virgin Mary as expressed in the imagery of the Roman Catholic and Orthodox Churches. The Virgin is worshipped under a variety of epithets, e.g. the Virgin of the Annunciation, Mary the Mother of Christ, Panayia Galaktrouphissa, Our Lady of the Sorrows, the Black Madonna. Each of these has a distinct and separate iconography, which for the outsider who sees only the material, would indicate separate goddesses, yet the insider, the believer recognizes these images as all of a single person.

---

[40] M. P. Nilsson, *The Minoan-Mycenaean Religion and its Survival in Greek Religion*[2] (Lund, 1950).

[41] K. Branigan, 'The Genesis of the Household Goddess' *SMEA* 8 (1969), 28–38; P. M. Warren, 'The Beginnings of Minoan Religion', in *Antichità Cretesi: Studi in onore di Doro Levi* (Catania, 1977), 137–47; *Minoan Religion as Ritual Action* (Göteborg, 1988). Also A. A. D. Peatfield, 'Water, Fertility and Purification in Minoan Religion', in C. E. Morris (ed.), *Klados: Essays in Honor of J. N. Coldstream*, *BICS* Suppl. 63 (London, 1995), 217–27.

Before the cynical reader suggests that this analogy may also be applicable to the Postpalatial Minoan Goddess, let me point out that the personalization of the Goddesses-with-Upraised-Arms is not of single figures, found in single shrines, but of *individuals within groups of figures*. Together, they need to be distinguished from each other. The association of offering vessels, too, suggests that the symbolic distinctions made by the permutations of attributes was accompanied by a practical ritual distinction, i.e. the distinctions were meaningful in terms of both belief and practice.

The factor which may account for this major difference between Palatial and Postpalatial religion is that crucial social change of the era—the presence of the Mycenaeans on Crete, and the Mycenaean cultural domination of the Aegean during Late Bronze III. Renfrew has argued for Mycenaean influence on Minoan religion in this period, which he termed a 'reflux' of the initial Minoan influence on the Mycenaeans.[42] Using the evidence of the Linear B tablets, Hooker has argued that there was a 'syncretism' of Minoan and Mycenaean features.[43] The limited scope of the tablets really only reveals names, names assumed to be divine from their receipt of offerings and their similarity to later Greek deities. Hooker argues that these names are essentially Mycenaean, but that the Knossos tablets show a syncretism by attributing Cretan epithets, e.g. Diktaian Zeus. If Hooker is correct, then the use of divine names suggests that Mycenaean religion was more overtly polytheistic than was Minoan. The individualization of the Goddess-with-Upraised-Arms figures would thus be the Minoan response to the 'reflux' of Mycenaean influence.

Conclusion

In this paper I have highlighted what seem to be the two most important aspects of Postpalatial Minoan religion: 1) the wide distribution of the Goddess-with-Upraised-Arms cult over Crete, and 2) the individualization of the Goddess-with-Upraised-Arms figures into separate personifications. The first can only be a response to the social and political fragmentation evident in the period, whereby the former local regional centres of the Neopalatial economic network evolved into independent political units. In other words, the Goddess-with-Upraised-Arms sanctuaries were a religious component to Postpalatial political and economic territorial definition. The second point is also a fragmentation, but of a more conceptual kind, a popular spiritual alienation against the centralizing religious impulses of the preceding political order.

Conventionally this material is defined as Postpalatial (after the Minoan

---

[42] C. Renfrew, 'Questions of Minoan and Mycenaean Cult', in Hägg and Marinatos (n. 12), 27–33.
[43] J. T. Hooker, 'Minoan Religion in the Late Palace Period', in Krzyszkowska and Nixon (n. 10), 137–42.

palaces), but many of the features which characterize post–Bronze Age (historic Greek) Crete are also apparent. In the fragmented regionalism of Postpalatial Minoan society lie the roots of the Archaic and Classical 'Crete of the hundred cities', an extreme example of the political divisions of ancient Greece. In the deliberately individualized Goddesses-with-Upraised-Arms are the first hints of the developed polytheism of ancient Greek religion. The end of something great provides its own impetus and continuity to the development of something more.

Viewed this way, it may well be that the analogy with which I began this paper is truly appropriate. The cosmic 'Big Bang' threw matter, in the form of galaxies and worlds, outwards to create the universe; in turn, the religious elements of Postpalatial Crete reveal a centrifugal scattering of religion and society from the 'Big Bang' of Palatial collapse, to provide the roots of later Greece.

3

The Spatial Configuration of Belief: The Archaeology of Mycenaean Religion

JAMES C. WRIGHT
Bryn Mawr College

Introduction[1]

The archaeological traces of Mycenaean religion demonstrate three broad types of religious sites. These are the megaron with its central hearth and throne, the shrine building, and open air settings. But there is no agreement among scholars as to how the available evidence fits into these categories. For example, Hägg has argued forcefully in favour of identifying a house shrine type, Lambrinoudakis has suggested that the remains at the Maleatas terrace at Epidauros are of a Minoan-type peak sanctuary, and Klaus Kilian has hypothesized that the remains from Ayios Ilias near Tiryns are part of a cult located in a small cavern.[2] These examples illustrate the need for clear-cut criteria that distinguish among the different types and that allow us to speak comprehensively about the nature of Mycenaean religious practice and belief.

Equally, estimates of the number and distribution of religious sites varies. Some scholars, such as van Leuven and Rutkowski,[3] using very loose criteria,

[1] Abbreviations: LH Late Helladic; LM Late Minoan; MH Middle Helladic; MM Middle Minoan. Acknowledgements: I wish to thank Susan Alcock, John Cherry, Andrew Cohen, Mary Dabney, Robin Hägg, Robin Osborne, and Ann Wright Parsons for commenting on earlier drafts of this article, suggesting references and lines of inquiry. They are, of course, in no way responsible for the views espoused here.

[2] R. Hägg, 'Official and Popular Cults in Mycenaean Greece', 'The House Sanctuary at Asine Revisited', and V. Lambrinoudakis, 'Remains of the Mycenaean Period in the Sanctuary of Apollo Maleatas', all in R. Hägg and N. Marinatos (edd.), *Sanctuaries and Cults in the Aegean Bronze Age* (Stockholm, 1981), 35–40, 91–4 and 59–65; Klaus Kilian, 'Patterns in Cult Activity in the Mycenaean Argolid: Haghia Triada (Klenies), the Profitis Elias Cave (Haghios Hadrianos) and the Citadel of Tiryns', in R. Hägg and G. C. Nordquist (edd.), *Celebrations of Death and Divinity in the Bronze Age Argolid* (Stockholm, 1990), 185–97.

[3] J. C. van Leuven, 'The Mainland Tradition of Sanctuaries in Prehistoric Greece', *World Archaeology* 10 (1978), 138–48; 'Problems and Methods of Prehellenic Naology', in Hägg and Marinatos (n. 2), 11–25; B. Rutkowski, *The Cult Places of the Aegean* (New Haven, Conn., 1986), 169–221.

include uncritically virtually all the suggested sites of Late Bronze Age date. Others, such as Hägg, Vermeule, and Hope Simpson and Dickinson are more cautious,[4] but neglect to state clearly the criteria for their selection. This state of affairs is not helped when one considers the history of religious sites, especially in relation to the formative stages of Mycenaean society. There is, as Mylonas has remarked,[5] virtually no evidence to go on for the Middle Bronze Age. Aside from the artefacts from Epidauros, there is almost nothing that can be safely identified for the early period of Mycenaean culture, though most scholars are content to utilize artefacts found in the many tombs of LH I and II. Plainly evident religious remains have only recently been discovered; these are the sanctuaries which came into being slightly after the formation of the Mycenaean palaces: LH IIIA:2 at the earliest.[6] As a result it is difficult to study the origins of Mycenaean religion and to see clearly how the sites of Mycenaean religion (not to mention the religion itself) changed over time.

The map (Ill. 3.1) illustrates the distribution of the three types mentioned above. It is easy to see that the best identified sites are located at the major palace centres and that there are relatively few obviously religious sites in the hinterlands surrounding them. This situation contrasts markedly with that mapped by Peatfield for Crete during its Palatial and Postpalatial periods where religious sites were widely dispersed over the landscape.[7] By taking a wider focus the situation is seen in greater relief: between MH and LH IIB there are only two securely and eight possibly identifiable sites, while after that date the numbers increase to fourteen and twenty-two respectively.[8] This contrast suggests that the formalization of religious activity in Mycenaean society was largely a phenomenon of the period of the palaces.

What other evidence is there that demonstrates that religious activity is closely linked to the palaces? What are the factors that caused this to happen? Why is there not more evidence of religious activity in earlier, Prepalatial times? These are questions to be pursued in this study. In doing so I hope to show

---

[4] R. Hägg, 'Mykenische Kultstätten im archäologischen Material', *OpAth* 8 (1968), 39–60; E. T. Vermeule, 'Götterkult', in F. Matz and H. G. Buchholz (edd.), *Archaeologia Homerica*, iii, ch. V (Göttingen, 1974), 32–8, 56; R. Hope Simpson and O. T. P. K. Dickinson, *A Gazetteer of Aegean Civilisation in the Bronze Age*, i: *The Mainland and the Islands*, SIMA 52 (Göteborg, 1979), 427, *passim*.

[5] G. E. Mylonas, *Mycenae and the Mycenaean Age* (Princeton, NJ, 1966), 137.

[6] E. French, 'Cult Places at Mycenae', in Hägg and Marinatos (n. 2), 41–8; C. Renfrew, 'The Sanctuary at Phylakopi', in Hägg and Marinatos (n. 2), 67–79; *The Archaeology of Cult: The Sanctuary at Phylakopi*, BSA Suppl. 18 (London, 1985), 80; W. Taylour, *Well Built Mycenae*, fasc. 1: *The Excavations* (Warminster, 1981), 8–9; K. Kilian, 'Zeugnisse mykenische Kultausübung in Tiryns', in Hägg and Marinatos (n. 2), 49–58.

[7] A. A. D. Peatfield, 'The Topography of Minoan Peak Sanctuaries', *BSA* 78 (1983), 273–80; 'Palace and Peak: The Political and Religious Relationship between Palaces and Peak Sanctuaries', in R. Hägg and N. Marinatos (edd.), *The Function of the Minoan Palaces* (Stockholm, 1987), 89–93.

[8] These numbers are derived from the lists compiled by Hägg (n. 4) and Hope Simpson and Dickinson (n. 4), and include sites discovered since their publication.

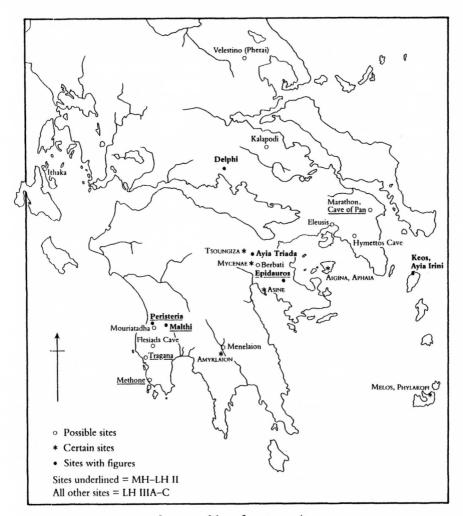

ILL. 3.1 Map of sanctuary sites

how the archaeological study of religion is an indispensable component for the reconstruction of ancient societies. Such an analysis, however, cannot succeed without a firmer foundation. There is a great need for an explicit archaeological statement that, like Renfrew's, establishes archaeological correlates of religious behavior and also articulates the structure of religion in its many levels and varieties.[9] Therefore a beginning must be made towards establishing the theoretical basis of an archaeological recognition of religion and in constructing a methodology for its reconstruction.

[9] Renfrew, *Archaeology* (n. 6), 11–26.

Issues in Theory and Method

The lack of a methodology for reconstructing religion in societies known only archaeologically has been acknowledged by several scholars.[10] Geoffrey Conrad and Arthur Demarest have offered compelling arguments for the centrality of religion as a primary agent in the evolution of the Aztec state, and much recent theory supports this perspective.[11] In particular the works of Bourdieu, Giddens, and Bell provide an integrated, comprehensive framework for incorporating the study of religion into an archaeological perspective.[12] What they offer is an argument for the centrality of religion in society. In particular, they show how the act of symbolizing, which is central to religion, pervades human action and the construction of social organization. In this regard their critiques overcome the limitations of structuralist analyses of symbols by urging their placement within a dynamic societal context. Their perspectives take account of the spatial and temporal dimensions of social action, dimensions that are central to archaeology. Thus implicit in Giddens's 'theory of action', and Bourdieu's notion of *habitus*, is a perspective that is vital for studying religion in relation to the evolution of society.[13]

These theoretical positions establish the fundamental relationship between belief and culture. They show how belief and values are closely interrelated in the construction of a society's cosmogony.[14] In addition they indicate directions for examining the cognitive geography of a society. Such a geography, though conceptual, becomes manifest in ritual practice. In this manner places are invested with sacred meaning and frequently (though not necessarily) referred back to the most intimately known place, the human body. Thus the *omphalos*, the arms and legs, the sensory organs, and the openings of the body, become metaphors for social and cosmic structures; and oppositions, such as day and night, earth and sky, can be framed in reference to gender. This process fleshes out cognitive space, which being non-linear and atemporal is now cloaked in a physical referent which can operate simultaneously at many levels, for example

[10] Notably in Aegean studies: S. G. Cole, 'Archaeology and Religion', in N. C. Wilkie and W. D. E. Coulson (edd.), *Contributions to Aegean Archaeology: Studies in Honor of William A. McDonald* (Minneapolis, 1985), 49–59; R. Laffineur, 'Archéologie et religion: problèmes et méthode', *Kernos* 1 (1988), 129–40. In the New World: G. Conrad and A. Demarest, *Religion and Empire* (New York, 1984), 209, and as a general issue, P. Garwood *et al.*, *Sacred and Profane* (Oxford, 1989), introd. pp. v–ix.

[11] Conrad and Demarest (n. 10), 215–26; C. Geertz, *The Interpretation of Culture* (New York, 1973), 119; C. Bell, *Ritual Theory, Ritual Practice* (New York, 1992), 82–5.

[12] P. Bourdieu, *Outline of a Theory of Practice* (New York, 1977); A. Giddens, *Central Problems in Social Theory* (Berkeley, 1979); *The Constitution of Society: Outline of a Theory of Structuration* (Berkeley, 1984); Bell (n. 11).

[13] Giddens, *Central* (n. 12), 45–8, *passim*; Bourdieu (n. 12), 97–8; Bell (n. 11) on practice, 69–93, on space and time, 124–30. Compare E. Zuesse, 'Meditation on Ritual', *Journal of the American Academy of Religion* 43 (1975), 519, and Conrad and Demarest (n. 10), 225.

[14] A. Wallace, *Religion: An Anthropological View* (New York, 1966), 71–5.

in common spaces such as dwellings and villages to less well-known regions like the world and the universe.[15] Thus it is theoretically possible to examine and to some extent derive meaning from the archaeological record of a society by studying the organization of dwelling, the spatial form of settlement and distributions in the landscape, especially if a long-term record can be documented.[16]

Scholars of settlement organization and architecture have explored these issues in the past and more recently incorporated the ideas of some of these social theorists in their writings.[17] In particular they have focused on differences in dwelling plan in relation to cultural habits and beliefs and attempted to relate differences in social organization to architectural complexity. In dwellings the division of space according to gender or cosmogonic orders is well illustrated in studies of contemporary architecture.[18]

In this chapter I will utilize these approaches to analyse the construction of space in Mycenaean society in order to show how such space reflects Mycenaean belief. In order to avoid a static and certainly incomplete analysis, I will consider the origins of this belief structure by examining first the spatial framework of Middle Helladic culture, as manifested on a regional basis at a number of sites on the mainland of Greece. I will then relate the central spatial components of this cultural tradition to the process of state formation as it evolves through

[15] Bourdieu (n. 12), 87–9, 114–30, *passim* in explaining his notion of *habitus*, discusses the importance of the body as a primary referent for conceptualizing space. He refers to this process as 'conceptual schemes immanent in practice' (p. 118). See the illuminating discussion by Bell (n. 11), 79–80, and the eloquent discussion of the spatial correlates of ritual by Zuesse (n. 13), 521–4.

[16] See n. 15 above and also: E. Guidoni, *Primitive Architecture* (New York, 1975) 8–31; P. Oliver, *Dwellings: The House across the World* (Austin, Tex., 1987), 153–79.

[17] Some early studies in this area are: C. E. Cunningham, 'Order in the Atoni House', and G. H. Gossen, 'Temporal and Spatial Equivalents in Chamba Ritual Symbolism', both in W. A. Lessa and E. Z. Vogt (edd.), *Reader in Comparative Religion: An Anthropological Approach* (New York, 1972), 116–35 and 135–49. A number of authors considered different aspects of this problem in P. J. Ucko, G. W. Dimbleby and R. Tringham (edd.), *Man, Settlement and Urbanism* (Cambridge, Mass., 1972), notably M. Douglas in a cautionary study, 'Symbolic Orders in the Use of Domestic Space' (513–52); see also R. Tringham, 'Territorial Demarcation of Prehistoric Settlement' (463–76); R. Martin, 'Concepts of Human Territoriality' (427–45); M. J. Rowlands, 'Defence: A Factor in the Territorial Demarcation of Settlements' (447–62); R. W. Schwerdtfeger, 'Urban Settlement Patterns in Northern Nigeria (Hausaland)' (547–56). Subsequent wide-ranging ethnographic surveys by Guidoni (n. 16) and Oliver (n. 16) provide many examples of contemporary settings among simple to complex societies for examining the variability in spatial expression of belief systems. S. Kent has explored theoretical issues with 'middle-range' studies in a variety of important studies: *Analyzing Activity Areas: An Ethnoarchaeological Study of the Use of Space*, (Albuquerque, N. Mex., 1984); 'A Cross-cultural Study of Segmentation, Architecture and the Use of Space' in S. Kent (ed.), *Domestic Architecture and the Use of Space* (New York, 1990), 127–52. L. Donley-Reid has made explicit the link between the above-discussed theoretical positions and the ethnographic record in 'A Structuring Structure: the Swahili House' in the same volume. See also E. Pavlides and J. Hesser, 'Sacred Space, Ritual and the Traditional Greek House' in J.-P. Bourdier and N. Alsayyad (edd.), *Dwellings, Settlements and Traditions: Cross-cultural Perspectives* (New York, 1989), 275–94.

[18] Guidoni (n. 16), 28–32, 284–88; Oliver (n. 16), 153–70.

contact with other Aegean cultures, notably Minoan, and show how a distinctive Mycenaean belief system emerges at the palace centres on the mainland.[19]

The Spatial Correlates of Religion in Mycenaean Greece

During the Early Mycenaean period there are virtually no cult installations. The map (Ill. 3.1) shows those sites identified as demonstrably and possibly associated with religious activity. The number is paltry and, in most instances, the sites are obscure. Subdivision of the sites by more specific periods (late MH, LH I, LH II) so fragments the record as to make it incomprehensible.

A survey of the history of scholarship of Mycenaean religion shows it to be largely intellectualist in approach, that is, speculative without placing the subject in the context of an explicit holistic cultural approach to reconstructing the evolving Mycenaean society.[20] Such an approach naturally focuses on the visible monuments and readily interpretable symbolic artefacts of a society. Consequently any interpretation is biased not only towards the cultural apices of a society but also towards a narrative that links such moments through time— much as if the method of archaeology were to be found in detective mysteries. Issues of collecting evidence to test theories of origins, evolution, process, and change are only considered piecemeal at best. Naturally, the scarcity of evidence for the Early Mycenaean period (MH III–LH II) encourages this kind of scholarship. Yet such a dearth of material should not be surprising in view of the fact that primitive religions are characteristically decentralized, personalized, and fluid.[21] Predictably they would have an underdeveloped symbolism that was neither standardized nor strongly under central control. Just as religion will be recognized in the monuments of a society, so should religion be reflected in the lack of centralizing forces in a society. In such instances we must seek our evidence of religion in different, less substantive manifestations. For example we might expect such ritual practice to focus on age distinctions, initiations, corporate membership, and community stability, and we must find our symbols in these concepts.

If religion, like mortuary custom, reflects to some degree the social organ-

---

[19] Since the focus of this study is religion, it is important to have a working definition in mind. For archaeological purposes that of Wallace (n. 14), 107, is useful: 'Religion is a set of rituals, rationalized by myth, which mobilizes supernatural powers for the purpose of achieving or preventing transformations of state in man and nature.' This definition is more inclusive and specific than that chosen by Renfrew, *Archaeology* (n. 6), 14, which permits only simplistic correlations between belief and archaeological evidence (cf. 18–20, 24–6).

[20] For references see: R. Hägg, 'Mycenaean Religion: The Helladic and the Minoan Components', in A. Morpurgo Davies and Y. Duhoux (edd.), *Linear B: A 1984 Survey*, Bibliothèque des cahiers de L'Institut de linguistique de Louvain 26 (Louvain-la-Neuve, 1985), 203–25; id. 'The Religion of the Mycenaeans', *II Congresso Internazionale di Micenologia* (Rome and Naples, in press).

[21] R. N. Bellah, 'Religious Evolution', in Lessa and Vogt (n. 17), 40–1; M. Bloch, 'Religion and Ritual', in A. Kuper and J. Kuper (edd.), *The Social Science Encyclopaedia* (Boston, 1985), 698–701.

ization of the society,[22] then it seems likely that in a primitive society in which relationship to the group, and especially the head of the group is important, the structure of these relationships will be manifested in symbolic action. As stated at the outset of this paper, likely places for this evidence to be preserved are in the organization of households and settlements, in the creation of central ceremonial spaces, and at cemeteries.[23] The sparse information about Middle Helladic settlement organization and the lack of ceremonial areas in settlements or at the burial sites of the Early Mycenaean period (as Mylonas has forcefully argued)[24] create difficulties in this venture. This paucity of evidence should not, however, lead to the conclusion that the religion of these people lacked organization, especially since much ritual expression will have left no physical trace, and in burial the rituals enacted will have been focused on the immediate corporate group to which the deceased belonged.[25] Instead information can be recovered by focusing our attention on detectable changes over time in the manifestation of ritual.

Middle Bronze Age

The dramatic upswing in marked or grouped burials at the end of the Middle Helladic period and the steady increase in the creation of monumental tombs in the immediately ensuing periods has long been recognized as a pivotal period of change in the Middle Bronze Age of Mainland Greece.[26] The events of that transformation permit us to reach backward and forwards to isolate continuities in Helladic culture and examine how they change. The process of recognizing continuities is, of course, essential to the identification of a 'Mycenaean' culture and its various characteristics, though it has been too often ignored in studies of Mycenaean institutions.[27]

In burial practices the focus of energy on a few important burials implies a radical change in the manner in which ancestors are venerated and, in the instance of the monumental tombs of the Early Mycenaean period, the way in which resources and people are managed. Similar developments are reflected

---

[22] E. Durkheim, *The Elementary Forms of Religious Life* (Glencoe, Ill., 1926). This was for Marx and Engels a central thesis: K. Marx and F. Engels, *The German Ideology* (New York, 1947), 20. But organized religion does not always support authority, Bloch (n. 21), 700; Wallace (n. 14), 87–8.

[23] H. Wright, 'Prestate Political Formation', in T. K. Earle (ed.), *On the Evolution of Complex Societies: Essays in Honor of Harry Hoijer, 1982* (Malibu, 1984), 43–4; I. Morris, 'The Archaeology of Ancestors: The Saxe/Goldstein Hypothesis Revisited', *CAJ* 1 (1991), 147–69.

[24] Mylonas (n. 5), 176–86; in fact most of the burials were not even marked: see O. T. P. K. Dickinson, 'Cist Graves and Chamber Tombs', *BSA* 78 (1983), 59–60.

[25] J. C. Wright, 'Death and Power at Mycenae', in R. Laffineur (ed.), *Thanatos: Les Coutumes funéraires en Égée à l'âge du bronze*, Aegaeum 1 (Liège, 1987), 174, 176.

[26] S. Iakovidis, 'Royal Shaft Graves outside Mycenae', *Temple University Aegean Symposium* 6 (1981), 17–28; Dickinson (n. 24), 60; C. B. Mee and W. G. Cavanagh, 'Mycenaean Tombs as Evidence for Social and Political Organization', *OJA* 3 (1984), 48–51.

[27] See for example, K. Kilian's important, but static study: 'The Emergence of the *Wanax* Ideology in the Mycenaean Palaces', *OJA* 7 (1988), 291–302.

in changes in the organization of settlements. As has often been pointed out, settlements begin to take on a more focused organization starting in the late Middle Bronze Age and continue increasingly to be oriented towards a centre of the settlement where the leader either resides or conducts business.[28] The fact that there are few known settlements of this period merely points up the fact that the process of centralizing power initially is highly variable, dependent upon regional factors that encourage it in one instance and delay or discourage it in another.[29] Thus particular examples must be cited to demonstrate the leading edge of the process, while recognizing that most settlements were not initially participating in any observable fashion in these changes.

At the only completely excavated site of the period, Malthi (Ill. 3.2), there is little direct artefactual evidence of religion, nor any obvious architectural focus of religious activity. The dispersed distribution of intramural burials throughout the settlement contrasts to the more focused organization of the settlement itself. Burials are neither grouped nor located in cemeteries outside

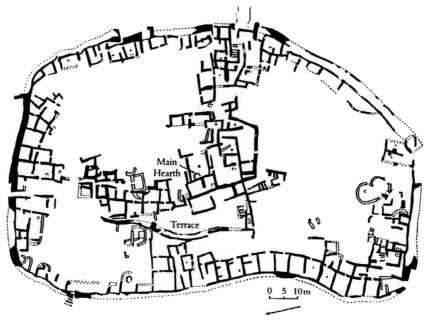

ILL. 3.2 Plan of Malthi

---

[28] Wright (n. 25); Kilian (n. 27).

[29] M. Dabney and J. C. Wright, 'Mortuary Customs, Palatial Society and State Formation in the Aegean Area: A Comparative Study', in Hägg and Nordquist (n. 2), 45–53; J. Lewthwaite, 'Why did Civilisation Not Emerge More Often? A Comparative Approach to the Development of Minoan Crete', in O. Krzyszkowska and L. Nixon (edd.), *Minoan Society* (Bristol, 1983), 171–83. Additionally, we are hampered by the extent to which early remains are covered over or irrevocably disturbed at the major palace sites.

the settlement. Instead they are distributed, perhaps in special areas within households and throughout the settlement.[30] This suggests, perhaps, that identity in death was strongly focused on the family rather than the community.[31] In contrast the layout of the settlement with a reserved area of large central rooms surrounded by clusters of regular rectangular small rooms built against the inside of the fortification suggests some segregation in architectural arrangement. This may reflect the inception of differentiation within the community.[32] It appears that Malthi has all the characteristics of a social group in transformation: it is sedentary, concerned with defence, becoming highly standardized in its organization of space, and reserving areas that may be used for centralized decision-making. These features are conditions for rudimentarily organized religion and should be traced to discern if there is any development in rituals to ancestors and signs of increasing centralization of authority, and especially, of any possible links between these two. Such a development is most apparent in the next phase of settlement when there occurs a dramatic shift in mortuary custom, such that two monumental tholos tombs were built into the hillside at the base of the hill on which the settlement is situated.[33]

Hägg considers the so-called Ceremonial Room at Malthi with its apsidal hearth as a probable focus of cult. Even though there is no hard artefactual evidence to demonstrate the hearth's importance in religion at this site during this time,[34] it is likely it was a major focus of rituals of the inhabitants, as will be shown below (pp. 57–60). Louis Deroy attempted to show how the hearth had a continuous history of religious importance from the arrival of the Indo-Europeans down to Roman times.[35] Although his arguments do not stand up to scrutiny, there is no question of the role the hearth played in historic times in both Greek and Roman culture as it does apparently in many societies,[36] and it is highly likely, as I shall later discuss, that it was central to the structure of Mycenaean religion during the Palace period. The appearance of the hearth as a central element in the architecture of the Early Mycenaean period is, therefore, highly suggestive of its position in the conceptual framework of these people.[37]

[30] N. Valmin, *The Swedish Messenia Expedition* (London, 1938), 233.

[31] A. Saxe, *Social Dimensions of Mortuary Practice* (Ann Arbor, University Microfilms, 1971), 65–71; Morris (n. 23), 147–69.

[32] Wright (n. 23), 44.

[33] Valmin (n. 30) 207–25; O. Pelon, *Tholoi, tumuli et cercles funéraires*, Bibliothèque des Écoles Françaises d'Athènes et de Rome 229 (Paris, 1976), 213–19, 402; O. T. P. K. Dickinson, *The Origins of Mycenaean Civilisation*, SIMA 49 (Göteborg, 1977), 93 and n. 45.

[34] Hägg (n. 4), 46, no. 11; Vermeule (n. 4) 37; see also J. C. van Leuven, 'The Sanctuaries of Malthi', *Scripta Mediterranea* 5 (1984), 1–26, for an optimistic interpretation of the meagre evidence from Malthi. I owe this reference to R. Hägg.

[35] L. Deroy, 'Le Culte du foyer dans la Grèce mycénienne', *Revue de l'histoire des religions* 137 (1950), 26–43.

[36] Guidoni (n. 16), 108; Oliver (n. 16), 158.

[37] Hägg, 'Religion' (n. 20).

The lack of associated artefactual evidence to demonstrate the special function of the hearth is predictable in a society that has yet no need for a highly controlled and centralized set of durable symbols. Yet it is important to consider these architectural remains as symbols themselves. Here, a structural analysis of the spatial order of the settlement is revealing (Ill. 3.2).[38]

A spatial hierarchy is announced in the planning of the settlement in a series of concentric rings. The first is the fortification wall. Within it peripheral structures, very uniform in plan, form an inner ring farthest from the centre of the settlement. On the higher central portion of the settlement is the inner terrace, rectilinear in shape and containing the largest structure of the settlement, a rambling association of rooms with a squarish one in the approximate centre. This room (Ill. 3.2) contains the apsidal hearth built against the centre of the rear wall.[39]

This centripetal spatial organization is not confirmed at other Middle Helladic or early Mycenaean sites. It would, in fact, be denied at Eutresis (Ill. 3.3),[40]

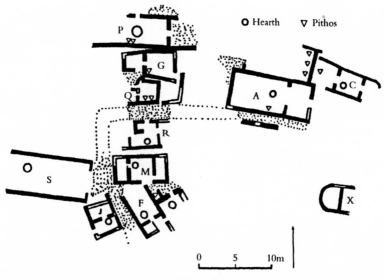

ILL. 3.3 Plan of Eutresis

---

[38] See above, n. 17, for the basis of this approach. I follow Bourdieu (n. 12), 87–95, 188, passim, Giddens, Central (n. 12) and Donley-Reid (n. 17), 115–16, in applying principles of post-structural analysis that do not seek binary opposites, but rather attempt to isolate the values or practices embedded in the symbolic ordering of space. The religio-philosophical underpinnings of this position are discussed in terms of the spatial correlates of ritual by Zuesse (n. 13) 521–4.

[39] Valmin (n. 30), 79–80, fig. 20. The hearth is 1.75 m. in diameter surrounded by a stone curb 0.15 m. high.

[40] K. Kilian, 'L'Architecture des résidences mycénienne: Origine et extension d'une structure du pouvoir politique pendant l'âge du Bronze récent', in E. Lévy (ed.), Le Système palatial en Orient, en Grèce et à Rome (Leiden, 1985), 203–17.

which merely confirms my insistence that we must examine individual cases and not seek uniformity over our self-imposed domain of study. The general notion of the enclosing circle, however, is a significant symbol, suggestive of inclusion and storage, and it is likely it reflects lineage ties extending beyond the nuclear family. Its wide application for most group and all monumental burials, whether in south-western Messenia, the Argolid, Attica, or Boiotia is a significant indicator of this concept in action. The circle is also represented in the apsidal end of many Middle Helladic buildings. The apsidal room at the back of the house suggests an innermost area of storage and often contains storage jars. Here too, the notion of inclusiveness is reinforced, but the plan of the houses is not circular, rather linear and axial.[41]

Middle and Late Helladic houses are organized along a linear axis with movement progressing from outer vestibule to inner rooms, one of which sometimes has a central hearth or even a column or two. In the example of House 98 and Room 45 at Middle Bronze Age Lerna V (Ill. 3.4) a simple combination of elements demonstrates an elaborate structure that constitutes probably a single homestead.[42] At one side is the main apsidal house. Attached is an enclosing wall forming a square compound with an additional small square storage room in the corner of the yard. In the one instance other than Malthi where a number of structures are grouped together, namely at Eutresis,[43] the striking fact is the independence each axially planned building takes (Ill. 3.3). A few rectilinear structures in the centre of the settlement are attached to each

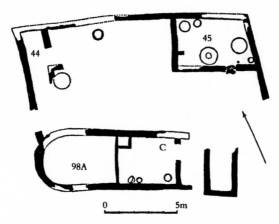

ILL. 3.4 Lerna, plan of House 98 and Room 45

[41] R. Hunter-Anderson, 'A Theoretical Approach to the Study of House Form', in L. Binford (ed.), *For Theory Building in Archaeology* (New York, 1977), 295–307.

[42] J. L. Caskey, 'Excavations at Lerna: 1956', *Hesperia* 26 (1957), 149–51; cf. G. Nordquist, *A Middle Helladic Village: Asine in the Argolid*, Boreas 16 (Uppsala, 1983), 88.

[43] H. Goldman, *Excavations at Eutresis* (Cambridge, Mass., 1931), 31–64; Kilian (n. 40).

other, but these are distinctly different from the main structures; they are
production areas with numerous hearths, ovens, and bins and are much less
formally organized than the larger buildings.

There seem to be some rules at work here, though the preserved sample
permits no quantitative measures. Circularity seems to represent small or highly
undifferentiated groups. These groups are stored, like undifferentiated grain, in
bulk containers. Axial arrangements are more focused and express heterogeneity
and differentiation.[44] These are spatial symbols of a society on the verge of
transformation from an undifferentiated to a highly differentiated order. They
do not spell out the content of the beliefs and value structure of the society but
indicate directions that can be pursued when more and diverse evidence is
available.

The transformation is most evident in changes in burial form. For example,
whereas in many areas burial in pithoi is common and these jars are frequently
placed within tumuli (e.g. Voïdokoilia, Papoulia, Argos, Aphidna), a change is
marked when rectangular stone-built cist burials are introduced. Thus at Marathon the core burial (grave 1) of tumulus 1 is an elaborate rectangular cist with

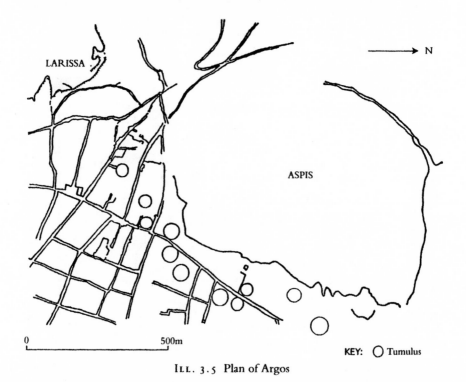

ILL. 3.5 Plan of Argos

<hr>

[44] Hunter-Anderson (n. 41), 304–12; Kent, 'Cross-cultural' (n. 17).

axial entrance, and later additions to the tumuli follow this lead.[45] At Argos, Asine, and Dendra cist tombs are prevalent forms whether placed in burial groups or within tumuli (Ill. 3.5).[46] At Mycenae the cist is normal but in Circle B it becomes a receptacle for important individuals and family groups whose lineages are accentuated by inclusion within the circle.[47] At Koukounara (Kaminia) in Messenia, emergent multiple tholoi first appear within a tumulus, and then, at Voïdokoilia the tholos assumes a more overtly individualistic focus with the construction of one tomb in the tumulus while still respecting the earlier burials.[48]

Discussion

These spatial habits can be understood as symbolizing bounded social groups recognizable in the layout and architecture of their settlements and their burials. Such social grouping is a natural result of a lineage system of descent. In her discussion of this system, Carol MacCormack points out that different marriage rules have different results regarding the origins of hierarchies, and, although the interest of her research on this question has to do with the origins of exchange,[49] clearly equal differences will be reflected in the spatial ordering of dwellings and settlements. Kent has proposed that changes towards complexity in social organization increase the segmentation of space and architecture, and this proposition, closely related to Hunder-Anderson's, is applicable in analysis of the remains of Middle Helladic and early Mycenaean Greece.[50]

On the surface these developments towards complexity in Mycenaean society seem to be largely social in nature, but they reflect an emerging conceptual framework of values and beliefs that later come to characterize Mycenaean religion. At the core of this conceptual development is the notion of centredness. Centredness is a general concept to describe the centripetal organization of Mycenaean society, an organizing principle common in many societies,

[45] Pithos burials: Pelon (n. 33); Dickinson (n. 24), 59. Marathon: S. Marinatos, 'Further News from Marathon', *AAA* 3 (1970), 162–3; 'Further Discoveries at Marathon', *AAA* 3 (1970), 351.

[46] Argos: E. Deïlaki, *Hoi tumboi tou Argous* (Athens, 1980). Asine: S. Dietz, *Asine* ii. 2: *The Middle Helladic Cemetery, The Middle Helladic and Early Mycenaean Deposits* (Stockholm, 1980); id. *The Argolid at the Transition to the Mycenaean Age* (Copenhagen, 1991), 145–7.

[47] Dickinson (n. 33), 40–1; G. Graziadio, 'The Chronology of the Graves of Circle B at Mycenae: A New Hypothesis', *AJA* 92 (1988), 343–72; 'The Process of Social Stratification at Mycenae in the Shaft Grave Period: A Comparative Examination of the Evidence', *AJA* 95 (1991), 403–40.

[48] Koukounara: G. S. Korres, 'Anaskaphe Pylou', *Praktika* (1975), 484–512; 'Anaskaphe ana ten Pulian', *Praktika* (1980), 125–9; 'Anaskaphe Voïdokilias Pylias', *Praktika* (1982), 230; *Ethnographisch-Archaeologische Zeitschrift* 28 (1987), 711–43; Dickinson (n. 24), 58.

[49] C. P. MacCormack, 'Exchange and Hierarchy', in A. Sheridan and G. Bailey (edd.), *Economic Archaeology*, BAR Int. Ser. 96 (Oxford, 1981), 161. See also: J. Friedman and M. J. Rowlands, 'Notes towards an Epigenetic Model of the Evolution of "Civilisation"', in J. Friedman and M. J. Rowlands (edd.), *The Evolution of Social Systems* (London, 1977), 201–76.

[50] Kent, 'Cross-cultural' (n. 17); Hunter-Anderson (n. 41), 295–307.

especially complex ones,[51] and it is validated in the case at hand because characteristic spatial components of it appear in the Middle Bronze Age, as just discussed, and carry over into the more fully developed Late Bronze Age. Centredness in Mycenaean society may be understood from three perspectives. First is the notion of inclusiveness within the circle which distinguishes the community as an undifferentiated yet highly distinct social entity. Second is the notion of the contents of the circle, which may be conceptualized as the multi-linear relations of kin groups. Third is the process of differentiation, which is lineage based and strongly affects burial, dwelling and settlement form. Naturally, as such a society constructs its cosmogony and belief system, social organization and religion will interact and be symbolized conceptually and, consequently, spatially, though the correlation between the two will not be precise.

Transitional Period

In Mycenaean society symbolic utilization of space becomes somewhat more evident during the period spanning LH I–LH IIB, which roughly would be considered the transitional stage from chiefdom to state.[52] The spread of the tholos across the mainland is one example of this process, for, aside from its monumental quasi-public character, the tholos establishes a distinct physical domain, usually around the outer perimeter of a settlement. As Cavanagh and Mee have pointed out, however, this relation is rarely explicit: the distribution of burials to settlements and of chamber tombs to tholoi and to roads, is neither regular nor in systematic alignment.[53] In architecture the evidence is less ubiquitous. The dearth of architectural remains of LH I–II date from both citadels and outlying sites precludes certainty about the level of planning and technical skills employed in central architecture. Evidence from elsewhere confirms only the tendency towards rectilinear and free-standing forms. Neither size nor organization appears to increase in any consistent manner. At the Menelaion, however, Mansion I shows (as did Malthi earlier) the advance guard of developments towards a monumental, standardized arrangement of complex forms. Although it may not be permitted to generalize a widespread contemporaneous phenomenon from a single example, the plan of Mansion I clearly exhibits the core principles of organization which subsequently governed

---

[51] P. Wheatley, *The Pivot of the Four Quarters* (Edinburgh, 1971), 257–67; D. H. Knipe, 'The Temple in Image and Reality', in M. V. Fox (ed.), *Temple in Society* (Winona Lake, Wis., 1988), 107–12; Guidoni (n. 16), 49, 59, 79, 92, 102–3, 130, 191, 252; Oliver (n. 16), 157.

[52] Wright (n. 25); Dabney and Wright (n. 29); Kilian (n. 40); Kilian (n. 27), 291–302.

[53] W. C. Cavanagh and C. B. Mee, 'The Location of Mycenaean Chamber Tombs in the Argolid', in Hägg and Marinatos (n. 2), 55–64; 'The Spatial Distribution of Mycenaean Tombs', *BSA* 85 (1990), 225–43.

palatial planning. At the centre is the central room of the megaron, fronted by a vestibule and flanked by corridors leading to secondary rooms. Here is the first strong architectural manifestation of the centripetal character of Mycenaean society, one which will become increasingly evident in the formal planning of the palaces and citadels during LH IIIA:1 and in subsequent periods.

Palatial Period

The developed spatial form of this ideology is well represented at Mycenae during its heyday (LH IIIB). Architectural icons form a series of concentric rings of symbols that increasingly focus on the centre of Mycenaean ritual and authority, which is the megaron with its monumental hearth and royal throne.

The most immediately visible encircling element in this iconic family is the Mycenaean fortification wall.[54] In its most elaborate form the magnitude of the fortification wall is clearly more concerned with making a statement of power than with practical defence.[55] Eight-metre thick walls or five-metre-long blocks, as are found at Tiryns, were hardly necessary to repel an attacker. A distinctive spatial characteristic of Mycenaean fortification is the elaboration of the gate by using special masonry forms; this creates accentuated nodes on the cognitive map of the onlooker.[56] At Mycenae (Ill. 3.6) this process achieves its most grandiose version in the plan and execution of the Lion Gate.[57] The plan with an exterior *dromos* focuses attention on the gate in the cross wall (Ill. 3.6). The material employed (massive rectangular blocks of conglomerate) stands out among the surrounding irregular, roughly faced limestone blocks that make up the wall (Ill. 3.7). The special slabs employed for the threshold, jambs and lintel of the gate provide focus to the entrance. The crowning limestone relief (Ill. 3.7) sends a triple message of natural power (the flanking lions) guarding the palace (represented by the column) and based on religion (the altars).[58] These icons are equally important as legitimating expressions of authority, much like the Lion of St Mark, because they are Minoan in origin and part of the

[54] The term 'iconic family' is borrowed from J. V. Knight, Jr., 'The Institutional Organization of Mississippian Religion', *American Antiquity* 51 (1986), 676.

[55] B. G. Trigger, 'Monumental Architecture: A Thermodynamic Explanation of Symbolic Behaviour', *World Archaeology* 22 (1990), 119–32.

[56] For a detailed examination of these phenomena at many sites, see J. C. Wright, 'Mycenaean Masonry and Elements of Construction' (Ph. D., diss., Bryn Mawr College, 1978), 168–70, 172, 179, 181, *passim*; see also S. Iakovides, *Late Helladic Citadels on the Mainland of Greece* (Leiden, 1983).

[57] Wright (n. 25), 182.

[58] P. Åström and B. Blomé, 'A Reconstruction of the Lion Relief at Mycenae', *OpAth* 5 (1964), 159–91; E. Protonatariou-Deïlaki, 'Peri tes pules ton Mykenon', *AE* (1965), 7–25; Mylonas (n. 5), 173–5; C. Kardara, 'He semasia tou anagluphou tes pules ton leonton', *AAA* 3 (1970), 238–46; M. Shaw, 'The Lion Gate Relief of Mycenae Reconsidered', in *Philia epe eis Georgion E. Mulonan*, i (Athens, 1986), 108–23.

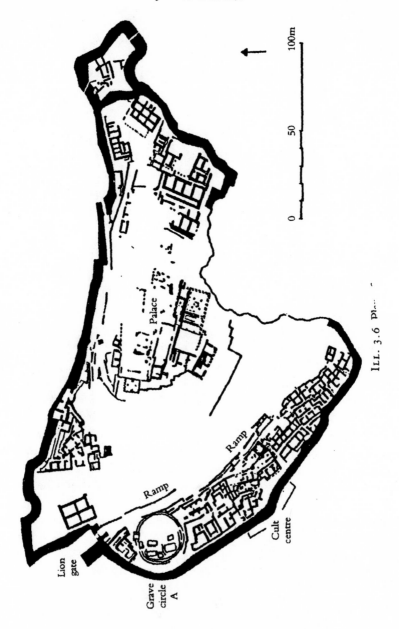

ILL. 3.6 Pl...

ILL. 3.7 The Lion Gate

iconography of power in Neopalatial Crete.[59] This use of Minoan symbols by Mycenaean rulers was part of the process of differentiation of their lineage groups from those of commoners. Mycenaean chiefs, who had access to the highest levels of the Minoan state, appropriated and adapted the symbols of Minoan religion and ruling authority as a means of removing themselves from the common beliefs and authority structure of Helladic custom, thus symbolically elevating themselves above the commoners.[60]

The passage through the gate is, naturally enough, the final destination of a system of state-operated roadways emanating from the palace. Placement of such symbols at the gate marks the transition into an area of special ritual significance. The monumental ramp that rises beyond the gate leads upwards to the crest of the citadel where another circle is perceived in the monumental terracing that supports the palace (Ill. 3.6).[61] Although the course of the road as it ascends is lost, the presence of two monumental entrances to the palace, the one through a formal propylon and the other up the Grand Staircase, reiterate the notion of passing through boundaries to the innermost seat of authority. The increasing repetition of special masonry forms and techniques, notably cut conglomerate stones used for column and anta bases, in these entrances emphasizes the architectural symbolism. From within these entrances the organization of corridors and courts provides another spatial surround before access to the megaron (Ill. 3.6). Here the architectural details are further enhanced by elaborate use of ashlar masonry, half-timbering, special flooring, and painted plaster. The plan at Tiryns (Ill. 3.8) is the most regular of all the palaces with a strict rectilinearity to its organization.

Analysis of the Megaron

The organization of the megaron produces one more shell around the core, (compare Ill. 3.8) for one must traverse first the porch (with its own special arrangement of cult furnishings),[62] then the vestibule before reaching the throne

[59] Vermeule (n. 4), 49–50; C. Boulotis, 'Villes et palais dans l'art égéen du IIe millénaire av. J.- C.', in Hägg and Nordquist (n. 2), 455–7; K. Krattenmaker, *Minoan Architectural Representation* (Ph.D., diss., Bryn Mawr College, 1991), 14–45, 92–7, 295–330; J. C. Wright, 'Empty Cups and Empty Jugs: The Social Role of Wine in Minoan and Mycenaean Society', in P. McGovern, S. Fleming, and S. Katz (edd.), *The Origins and History of Ancient Wine* (New York, in press). See the example at Athens in J. C. Wright, 'The Mycenaean Entrance System at the West End of the Akropolis of Athens', *Hesperia*, 63 (1994), 323–60.

[60] Friedman and Rowlands (n. 49); Wright, 'Empty' (n. 59).

[61] H. Lauter, 'Nouveaux aspects du palais de Mycènes au HR IIIB', in E. Lévy (ed.), *Le Système palatial en Orient, en Grèce et à Rome* (Leiden, 1987), 219–25, has suggested that some conglomerate blocks above the main ramp are part of another propylon in this area; the blocks, however, are no longer *in situ*.

[62] Between the southern column of the porch and the southern anta, I. Papadimitriou found what he interpreted as the remains of an altar, a carved offering table, and a compartmentalized basin set into the flooring slabs: 'Anaskaphai eis Mykenon', *Praktika* (1955), 230–2; see also H. Plommer, 'A Carved Block from the Megaron at Mycenae', *BSA* 60 (1965), 211, who thinks the block a column capital.

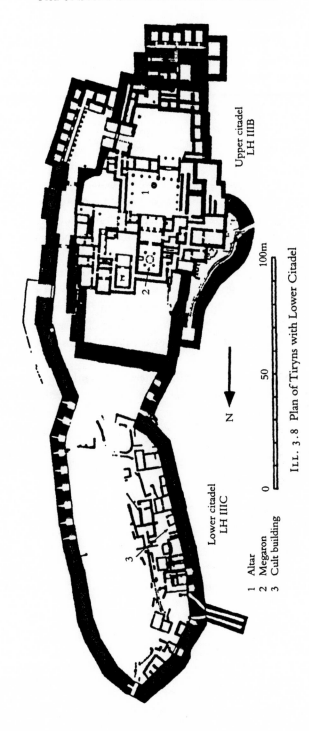

ILL. 3.8 Plan of Tiryns with Lower Citadel

room. This plan is a formalization of the linear, axial arrangement characteristic of Middle Bronze Age architecture, and it has as its goal the circular monumental hearth in the centre of the megaron which is itself surrounded by four monumental columns. The flanking throne against the centre of the wall on one's right is set on the cross axis of the hearth. It supports the human authority who administers the cults that are symbolized by the hearth.

From a structuralist viewpoint the organization of the megaron is of keen interest. For example, at Tiryns the axiality of the megaron is enhanced by its orientation to a circular stone-built altar in the great court (Ill. 3.8).[63] The megaron opens out to the court through its *distyle in antis* porch façade. From that point one is in liminal passage. The next room, a vestibule, is pierced by three doorways that retain the opening out into the more public court, but it also turns attention to the inner room, which is reached through a single doorway. Upon entering the room the plan and decoration focus and enframe the great central hearth. To the side, averted to the right, is the throne, which itself is centred on the hearth.[64] Thus, despite the presence of the seat of a powerful human in the room, the hearth is the centre of attention. The surrounding four columns support the opening in the ceiling that links the hearth with the heavens.

This overall organization is equally evident in the plans of other citadels, but thorough analysis of each case is not necessary here, though it is instructive to examine briefly the situation at Pylos. There, as recently argued by Lucinda R. McCallum, the vestibule and inner room of the megaron are linked by a programme of frescos. In the outer room a procession shows a bull being led inwards and in the inner room, at one's right, is a painted scene of sacrifice and ritual feasting.[65] Clearly this scene enhances the ritualistic nature of this room and provides a more detailed view than can be gained from the remains at the other palaces where these frescos were not preserved.

The Symbolism of the Megaron

Kilian has made the argument that the megaron arrangement of the palaces developed directly from the plan of Middle Helladic houses.[66] Although more complete studies of Early Mycenaean architecture caution against such an oversimplified notion of an architectural canon, there can be no question that

R. Hägg regards the basin as a place for libation: 'The Role of Libation in Mycenaean Ceremony', in Hägg and Nordquist (n. 2), 180, fig. 4.

[63] Hägg (n. 62), 181, 184.

[64] See now for Tiryns: K. Kilian, 'Die «Thronfolge» in Tiryns', *AM* 103 (1988), 1–9.

[65] L. R. McCallum, 'Frescoes from the Throne Room at Pylos: A New Interpretation', *AJA* 91 (1987), 296; R. Hägg, 'Pictorial Programmes in Minoan Palaces and Villas?' in P. Darcque and J.-C. Poursat (edd.), *L'Iconographie minoenne, BCH* Suppl. 11 (Paris, 1980), 216; Hägg, 'Religion' (n. 20). See also Wright (n. 59).

[66] Kilian (n. 40), 212–13; compare the discussion by G. Hiesel, *Späthelladische Hausarchitektur: Studien zur Architekturgeschichte des griechischen Festlandes in der späten Bronzezeit* (Mainz, 1990), 203–9.

the linear and axial principles of organization found in the palaces have a long history in Helladic architecture. What is missing in the Middle Helladic and Early Mycenaean period is evidence of the monumentalization of this architecture. Only the first 'mansion' at the Menelaion has a plan that suggests in its complexity the transition to the standard palatial plan, though there are several large rectangular buildings at other sites dating to LH II.[67] Clearly the peer polity interaction model is applicable when examining the creation of the homologous palace plans beginning in LH IIIA:1 with their focus on the monumental megaron.[68] Fundamental to the axial organization of the megaron is the central hearth, and nearly as important are the columns surrounding it.

The Hearth

As mentioned previously the hearth is commonly important in many Indo-European cultures and in Classical Greece. Jean-Pierre Vernant has argued that the goddess Hestia represents both the 'centre of the domestic sphere' and 'the navel which ties the hearth to the earth'. In Classical Greece the hearth fixed and oriented human space and was located at 'the centre of the cosmos'.[69] Its location at the centre of the physical sphere of Mycenaean society and its overtly symbolic nature in its monumentalized form in Mycenaean palaces supports a similar cognitive interpretation. Even the flame pattern painted on the stucco rim reinforces the notion of the sacred fire which it contained.[70] Paraphernalia found at Pylos around the hearth and the throne amplify its nature. Resting on a small tripod table next to the hearth were several miniature kylikes, which Hägg has cogently argued were used for libations. Next to the throne are the well-known interconnected plaster depressions that since Blegen's publication have been accepted as for receiving liquid libations.[71]

The orientation of the throne to the hearth suggests that the occupant of the throne, presumably the *wanax*, officiated in the rituals. He may have been the guardian of the hearth, and, in so far as the hearth represents the household, also the guardian of the family, protector of the household, and guarantor of its future. Vernant, explaining the role of the *hestia* in Greek thought, discusses at length the important roles symbolized by the hearth: patrilocality, fertility, the proper order of the household and the state, feasting, fraternity, and xenophilia.[72] Although there is neither epigraphic nor iconographic evidence to argue a

---

[67] Hiesel (n. 66), 204–7.

[68] C. Renfrew and J. F. Cherry (edd.), *Peer-Polity Interaction and Socio-Political Change* (Cambridge, 1986).

[69] J.-P. Vernant, *Myth and Thought Among the Greeks* (Boston, 1983), 128–31; Deroy (n. 35); compare Zuesse (n. 13), 521.

[70] C. W. Blegen and M. Rawson, *The Palace of Nestor at Pylos in Western Messenia*, i: *The Buildings and their Contents* (Princeton, NJ, 1966), 64.

[71] Hägg (n. 62), 183; Wright (n. 59).

[72] Vernant (n. 69), 133–42.

continuity between Mycenaean and Greek religion, the more complete picture of the symbolic content of the hearth provided in Vernant's analysis is useful for reconstructing the outlines of Mycenaean cosmology. Certainly, if one accepts the notion that Helladic culture was structured around the concept of lineage and that it evolved into a series of chiefdoms or paramount lineages, the idea of a powerful male ruling figure emerging in Mycenaean times is hardly far-fetched. Thus it is not improbable to suggest that the palace hearth symbolizes the centre of the state, and the *wanax* was in this sense its father and chief. Such an argument describes a cult institution of power and authority that reinforces the stability of the state,[73] but it also demonstrates the priority of religion in the organization of the seat of power. Again this distinction needs emphasis since it is common in anthropology to view religion and ideology only as tools of state power.[74]

The Columns

As Hiesel has observed, the columns surrounding the hearth are not merely decorative. We might suspect this from the frequency with which the column is imbued in many societies with fundamental symbolic meaning.[75] The column was an important icon in Minoan representation and becomes especially so in Mycenaean, appearing frequently flanked by animals and fantastic beasts and in association with altars.[76] In Mycenaean society, at one level the column represents the palace, which contains the hearth and the seat of the *wanax*, but it may well also represent something more substantive that relates different elements in Mycenaean cosmology.[77] Hence, in the two preserved locales where monumental entrance displays are preserved in the external fortifications, Athens and Mycenae, the column appears as a central element (Ill. 3.7). At Mycenae it is the central motive in the Lion Gate relief, which, as I have explained above, combines symbols of nature and the supernatural around the column. At Athens the column appears in the centre of the Cyclopean bastion before the west gate. We do not know if it stood alone or if other elements were placed in the niche that held it, but there are traces of burning and possible artefacts in the ledge below.[78] At Tiryns it is likely that a monumental relief may have been

---

[73] I use the term 'cult institution' in the sense of Wallace (n. 14), 75.

[74] Conrad and Demarest (n. 10), 203; M. Leone, 'Opinions about Recovering Mind', *American Antiquity* 47 (1982), 742–60; J. Haas, *The Evolution of the Prehistoric State* (New York, 1982) 174–80; compare Bell (n. 11), 83–5.

[75] Hiesel (n. 66), 225, 232; Guidoni (n. 16), 110, 152, 288; Oliver (n. 16), 162.

[76] M. P. Nilsson, *The Minoan-Mycenaean Religion and its Survival in Greek Religion* (Lund, 1950), 236–62; A. Evans, *The Mycenaean Tree and Pillar Cult and its Mediterranean Relations* (London, 1901), 58–65; Protonariou-Deïlaki (n. 58).

[77] Vermeule (n. 4), 49–50, 53.

[78] N. Balanos, 'He nea anastelosis tou naou tes Athenas Nikes (1935–39)', *AE* (1937), 776–807; Wright, 'Mycenaean Entrance' (n. 59).

placed above the Steintor and the remains of a monumental entrance-way atop the Larisa at Argos allow the possibility of another.[79] At Pylos, a fragment of wall-painting found in the inner propylon shows a variation where facing sphinxes repose *en gardant* above a monumental entrance with an ornate central post.[80] What is important to recognize here is that none of these primary symbols represents a human, a conclusion reinforced by the above observation that the throne is oriented to the hearth. Thus the column as a generic symbol may be strongly suggestive of the supernatural force that supports human authority.[81] The role of the column in the megaron, however, is fundamentally architectural. As such it supports an opening that allows smoke to vent from the building. But at the symbolic level it mediates between the human structure that contains the hearth and the heavens; it may be viewed as holding up the heavens or as connecting them with the hearth at the centre of the cosmos.

The Hearth as Cult Institution

Kilian has proposed a term for the phenomenon of emphasizing political authority in Mycenaean society; he calls it the *wanax* ideology.[82] In the light of the present study this term represents only half of the equation because it focuses only on the ruler and neglects the hearth and the associated rituals which the ruler performs; a preferable term might be the hearth-*wanax* ideology. In its most developed form the hearth-*wanax* ideology is a major cult institution of Mycenaean society. As we have seen, this ideology is composed of many all-embracing spatial elements, and as such, it probably is represented by contradictory and disparate symbols. For example, the increase of militaristic imagery in Mycenaean artefacts and art occurs in conjunction with the maintenance of the sylvan nature scenes of Minoan iconography.[83]

A significant architectural and spatial expression of this cult is in the re-organization and monumental display of the burials in Circle A at Mycenae, which, as I have argued elsewhere, is part of a highly organized iconic display of architecture focused on the palace at Mycenae but appealing to a very broad audience on the mainland of Greece, at least. By placing the Lion Gate before the refurbished grave circle the rulers at Mycenae emphasized the strength of ancestral authority (Ill. 3.6).[84]

The symbolism of the role of the *wanax* outlined here describes a centripetal

[79] K. Müller, *Tiryns*, iii: *Die Architektur der Burg und des Palastes* (Augsburg, 1930), 73; W. Vollgraff, 'Arx Argorum', *Mnemosyne* 56 (1928), 315–28; Åström and Blomé (n. 58), 180, figs. 3–5.

[80] M. L. Lang, *The Palace of Nestor at Pylos in Southwestern Messenia*, ii: *The Frescoes* (Princeton, NJ, 1968), fragment 1A2, 135–7; Shaw (n. 58), 123.

[81] The column is a dominant symbol, as in V. Turner, *The Forest of Symbols* (Ithaca, NY, 1967), 20–32; cf. Wallace (n. 14), 237–8.

[82] Kilian (n. 27).

[83] Compare P. Rehak, 'New Observations on the Mycenaean "Warrior Goddess" ', *AA* (1984), 542.

[84] Wright (n. 25), 181.

organization located in the megaron of the palace and focused on the hearth
where the ruler is responsible for the maintenance of the cult.[85] The history of
the development of this institution suggests an ever-increasing process of cent–
ring authority and power in the hands of an ecclesiastical primate ruler. Part of
this process, which distinguishes the Mycenaean system of belief from the
Minoan, is the appropriation of primary cult under the control of the ruler, a
process which continues throughout the Palatial period. This distinction,
however, is especially observable when comparing mortuary customs of the
Minoans and Mycenaeans. In Minoan society traditional community burials
are maintained at continuously inhabited Prepalatial settlements during Protopalatial and Neopalatial times. Individual burials only assert themselves during
the developed phase of the Neopalatial period.[86] In contrast in Mycenaean
culture ostentatious mortuary customs for individuals of high rank and status
precede palace formation and are characteristically located close by the locus of
power. The differences also are reflected in the lack of power-centred iconography in Minoan art and in the emphasis on rituals that show communal
participation, such as the 'Grandstand Fresco' or the 'Harvester Vase', or in
the architectural layout of the sanctuary at Simi Viannou.[87] In Mycenaean
iconography a contrasting emphasis on individual or restricted group activity is
more common, as in the frequent battle and hunt scenes in relief, on rings and
seals, and in wall-painting.[88] Places for communal worship are rare. Those that
are available, such as the great court at Tiryns, are in special, presumably
restricted, locations.

In terms of the process of the development of the citadels and the growth of
their territorial control, however, the centralized hearth-*wanax* cult may have
been too exclusive to effect the kind of integration necessary for a territorially
based state-level society. Local places of worship and assembly surely existed,
although not necessarily under the control of the palace. This problem, so far
discussed in Mycenaean studies in terms of official versus popular cults, may
also be viewed as a contrast between urban and rural cults. However viewed,
these dichotomies were not frozen in space and time, for the conditions of the
emergence and relations of these cults can only be viewed diachronically as part
of the process of the evolution of a complex society.[89] In the next part of this
paper the problem of this relationship will be examined.

[85] Wheatley (n. 51), 257–67.

[86] Dabney and Wright (n. 29), 46. Compare this situation to that described in Conrad and Demarest
(n. 10), 11–83, 218–20, for the Aztec state with its decentralized response to ideological custom.

[87] A. Lebessi and P. Muhly, 'Aspects of Minoan Cult. Sacred Enclosures: The Evidence from the
Syme Sanctuary (Crete)', *AA* (1990), 315–36.

[88] This is a much discussed issue; some recent research is N. Marinatos, 'Celebrations of Death and
the Symbolism of the Lion Hunt', and C. Morris, 'In Pursuit of the White-tusked Boar: Aspects of
Hunting in Mycenaean Civilization', both in Hägg and Nordquist (n. 2), 143–8 and 149–56.

[89] Conrad and Demarest (n. 10), 201–5; Wallace (n. 14), 86–8, 91–100; Bellah (n. 21), 42.

Citadel Cult Centres

We can begin by studying the other well-known focus of ritual activity at the citadels, the so-called Cult Centres. The process of centring also is manifest in the establishment of these cults within the citadels. The relationship of these areas to the palace has not been much examined and remains a major issue to consider.[90] The Cult Centres form an important part of our evidence for Mycenaean religion, in particular because they demonstrate the architectural form and artefactual content of Mycenaean shrines. The salient features of these installations are: 1. the late date of their establishment; 2. their construction in vernacular techniques using a vernacular plan; 3. their location within the citadel as far from the palace as possible and up against the circuit wall; 4. their use of large figures as cult statuary;[91] and 5. within the shrine buildings, the appearance of a bench as one focus of ritual activity. Finally, it should be stressed that the Cult Centres vary among themselves in degrees of complexity; some, such as those at Mycenae and Phylakopi, show evidence of a constellation of different cults probably located in different shrines.[92]

These distinguishing features differentiate the Citadel Cult Centres and their activities from those outlined above in the discussion of the megaron. They also suggest the centres were of lesser importance than the cults in the megaron of the palace. Their late establishment implies that they evolved out of circumstances that did not exist on a critical scale in the early years of the palaces. This is confirmed by the varying evidence for their establishment: LH IIIA:2 at Phylakopi, LH IIIB:1 at Mycenae, LH IIIB:2 at Tiryns, and the evidence that they continued to be used after the palaces were destroyed and abandoned.[93]

The notion of the Citadel Cult Centres as being less important than the cults in the palace is demonstrated by the lack of attention paid to their architectural adornment. Only rarely do any of the shrine buildings utilize the architectural techniques for monumental buildings, such as ashlar masonry, half-timbered wall construction and cut stone for column bases and antae. Only a few buildings preserve wall-paintings, and when they do at Mycenae—the most elaborate of the Cult Centres—the paintings are found at the entrance leading from, probably,

---

[90] See Cole (n. 10), 54. Some scholars now maintain that the megaron was not a centre of cult as I have argued, and that cult activity was focused in the shrines of the 'Cult Centres' within the citadels: see G. E. Mylonas, *The Cult Center at Mycenae* (Athens, 1972), 34–5, 40; Hägg, 'Official and Popular' (n. 2), 36; Renfrew, *Archaeology* (n. 6), 389, 401–2; but see Hägg, 'Religion' (n. 20).

[91] Renfrew, *Archaeology* (n. 6), 413–26.

[92] See French, 'Cult' (n. 6) and in Renfrew, *Archaeology* (n. 6); N. Marinatos, 'The Fresco from Room 31 at Mycenae: Problems of Method and Interpretation', in K. A. Wardle and E. A. French (edd.), *Problems in Greek Prehistory* (Bristol, 1988), 245–51; Mylonas (n. 90); I. Kritseli-Providi, *Toichographies tou threskeutikou kentrou ton Mykenon* (Athens, 1982).

[93] Renfrew, *Archaeology* (n. 6), 80 (Phylakopi); French, 'Cult' (n. 6) 42 (Mycenae); Kilian (n. 6), 53 (Tiryns).

the palace[94] decorating the altar area of the so-called House of the Frescos, and
located around and within the so-called South-west Building, a mudbrick
structure separated from the main cult area.[95] Most of the buildings have a
simple plan with a small floor area; the plan is often irregular and without a
strong orientation. The benches built within the shrines are constructed of
rubble and mud and sometimes contain deposits of the debris of worship.[96] The
third point in the list above, the location of the centres, suggests a secondary
nature. At Mycenae the Cult Centre is set alongside the circuit wall at its lowest
point—literally at the bottom of the citadel, tucked behind the display of Grave
Circle A and not obviously accessible, either from the area of the Grave Circle
or from the great ramp that leads up from the Lion Gate (Ill. 3.6). At Tiryns
the small one-room cult building is set against the wall of the Lower Citadel
and is hardly distinguishable among the architecture of this area (Ill. 3.8). At
Phylakopi, again, the cult is set along the inside of the fortification wall at some
distance from the location of the megaron. Only at Mycenae is there a suggestion
of a relationship between the Cult Centre and the palace. There, an elaborate
rampway with a monumentalized gate leads up from the Cult Centre to a cut
masonry-built stairway that ascends the citadel. Although the rest is lost, it is
not improbable that a 'sacred way', perhaps for processions, led from there up
to the Grand Staircase below the megaron.

After the architectural settings, the large human figures associated with the
Cult Centres seem to be their other most salient characteristic. Among the
figures, however, there is much variety—enough to indicate that they distinguish among different cults or rituals within sanctuaries. Thus the grotesques
and snakes from the 'House of the Idols' are unique to Mycenae and large male
figures are found only at Phylakopi. It is not merely the presence of these figures
which so impresses the viewer but also the aggregate of diverse finds: bovine
rhyta, all varieties of figurines, scarabs, beads, seals, objects in precious metals,
bronzes, ivories, etc. It is, however, the figures which stand out, and in
Mycenaean times they were clearly a major feature in Mycenaean religion,
since there is a strong relationship between them and the smaller figurines which
are distributed throughout the whole Eastern Mediterranean (see discussion
below).[97]

[94] Mylonas (n. 90), 19; Kritseli-Providi (n. 92), 19, 90–2, *passim*. Worth noticing is the construction
of the stairway leading down to the spacious landing to the ramp that descends to the Cult Centre. It is
built of cut poros ashlar blocks and is 2.5 m. wide. The entranceway itself is fitted with jambs of cut
conglomerate stone—the technique used in all the palace architecture.

[95] Marinatos (n. 92); Kritseli-Providi (n. 92), 16–18. Other frescos in the area come from the Ramp
House: A. J. B. Wace, 'Excavations at Mycenae', *BSA* 25 (1921–3), 79–80.

[96] Van Leuven (n. 3); G. Fernandez, 'Cult Places of the Bronze Age: The Identification Problem', in
Wardle and French (n. 92), 234; *AR* (1969–70), 12–13.

[97] E. French, 'Mycenaean Figures and Figurines, their Typology and Function', in Hägg and
Marinatos (n. 2), 172.

These features of the Citadel Cult Centres, especially the evidence for the variety of worship that took place within them, suggest they embraced the diversity of religious beliefs and customs in the territories of the palaces and thereby gave an official sanction to these beliefs by having a recognized centre within the citadel.

Locales of Cult Activity Outside the Palaces

As we know from the Linear B documents and from other studies the inception of a palatial society and the accompanying increase in the problem of administering a larger territory and population also resulted in a more complex religious life, in the growth of cult institutions and in the formalization of ritual practices and ritual places.[98] These developments are not restricted to the palace, however. Numerous sites of ritual activity are known at non-palatial centres, and it is important to try to understand what evidence they provide about Mycenaean religion prior to and independent of the palaces and how the religion changed after their formation. This task will be clearer after examining the evidence from these other sites.

An underlying assumption in current studies is that these 'non-palatial' cults represent 'popular' as opposed to 'official' religion. The following discussion will show, however, that this binary distinction sets up a false opposition between different aspects of an evolving Mycenaean religion. Rather than viewing these in opposition, it will prove more illuminating to understand them as different moments on a scale of increasing complexity.[99]

Citadel of Asine

The first instance to consider is that of 'House G' at Asine (Ill. 3.9). This structure has been recently republished by Hägg. The cult room contains an assemblage that includes a large head of a probable female figure,[100] female figurines, pottery (including a kylix and an up-ended vessel that seems to have served as a receptacle), and a stone hand-tool. All this material was found around a roughly built bench in a corner of the room.[101] The date of the complex is LH IIIC. The building does not easily fit categories for Mycenaean architecture, though with two centrally placed column bases it is not unlike

---

[98] See Bellah (n. 21), 42; Wallace (n. 14), 88–9.

[99] Hägg, however, has recently qualified this distinction by acknowledging intermediate scales of organization between these extremes.

[100] Hägg, 'House Sanctuary' (n. 2); E. French, 'The Development of Mycenaean Terracotta Figurines', BSA 66 (1971), 148.

[101] Hägg expresses concern about the evidence of the bench: 'House Sanctuary' (n. 2), 93. In 'The Role of Libation' he has identified the kylix as the standard vessel for ritual libations (n. 62). See also Wright (n. 59).

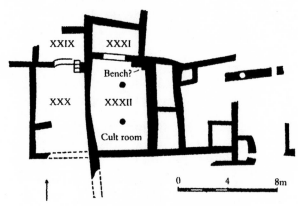

ILL. 3.9 Asine, plan of House G

contemporary buildings at Tiryns and Korakou, for example.[102] It is located at
the northern edge of the Lower Terrace of the citadel.

Hägg has urged the notion that this structure represents a 'house shrine', a
kind of intermediary between palace Cult Centre and rural shrine.[103] In the
same article he also classifies 'House G' as an example of popular cult, in
contrast to the official cults housed in the palatial Cult Centres. This is an
example of the problem with such formulations as 'popular' and 'official' and
'palace' and 'household'. They are also not formulations that make clear their
relationship to each other.

Meagre as they are, the contents of 'House G' (see Table 3.1) seem more in
accord with the paraphernalia at the Citadel Cult Centres than the material
from other sites; notable in this respect is the presence of the one large figure.
Although we have no reason to expect an elaborate building to house a shrine,
the architecture of House G is in fact rather formalized with its two rooms and
axially placed interior columns (Ill. 3.9). It also bears observing that House G
is located near the northern edge of the Lower Terrace of the citadel: in other
words in a position not unlike that of the shrines at the other sites. Furthermore,
Asine is apparently the central place in the immediately surrounding territory.
These observations seem to fulfil the criteria defined above (p. 61) for Citadel
Cult Centres. This shrine at Asine is perhaps best understood as another example
of a cult facility within a citadel that embraces the religious traditions of the
wider territory.

    [102] Asine: Hiesel (n. 66), 84–5. For Korakou (Houses L and M), Tiryns (Megaron W), Nichoria
(Unit IV4), see Hiesel (n. 66), 49, 63–9, 80, 107.
    [103] Hägg, 'Official and Popular' (n. 2), 39.

Amyklai

The site of Amyklai outside Sparta contrasts to House G at Asine. It is associated neither with a citadel nor a palace. In fact the architectural evidence is extremely scanty.[104] It does not seem likely that the sanctuary could be considered as part of a major settlement. Fragments of large figures are particularly intriguing: one shows a female with an elaborate coiffure, perhaps crowned with some kind of head-dress and another is a fragment of a hand grasping the stem of a chalice or goblet. There are also fragments representing a total of 28 bovine figures, 74 Psi-type female figurines, 32 animal, 2 horse, and 4 bird ones. In addition a group of bronze axes are thought to be contemporaneous dedications. The context of these remains is very late LH IIIB, or LH IIIC, and there are many indications of continuing use through much of the succeeding Dark Age.[105]

Despite the lack of architecture and the distance to a major settlement, the artefacts are similar to those of the Citadel Cult Centres. In fact the figure fragments fit into an important iconographic tradition of ceremonial drinking associated with the nobility and with divinities.[106] The absence of a palace complex to which to relate the sanctuary should not bias our interpretation of the remains at Amyklai, since in Lakonia there may have been a different resolution of the conditions that promoted the founding of the palaces: perhaps, for example, the ascendant groups in the region were content to share power among a group of strong communities, such as at Pellanes, the Menelaion, Vapheio-Palaiopyrgi, Geraki, and Ayios Stephanos.[107] In such an instance a site like Amyklai might have been the focus of regional ritual activity. None the less, the chronological evidence from this site suggests an absence of interest in it prior to the period of the palaces; in fact, as at many of the palace sites, the artefacts are Postpalatial and even Dark Age in date.

Epidauros

Excavations by Papadimitriou shortly after World War II discovered traces of Mycenaean activity beneath the Sanctuary of Apollo Maleatas at Epidauros.[108] During the last fifteen years Lambrinoudakis has clarified the nature of this site, uncovering traces of buildings within a terrace retaining wall on the

---

[104] K. Demakopoulou, 'To Mykenaiko iero sto Amyklaio kai i YE IIIC Periodos sti Lakonia' (Ph.D. diss., University of Athens, 1982).
[105] Demakopoulou (n. 104), 40, 43–78.
[106] Wright (n. 59); K. Kilian, 'Zur Darstellung eines Wagenrennens aus spätmykenischer Zeit', AM 95 (1990), 21–31.
[107] Hope Simpson and Dickinson (n. 4): Sites C 4, 12, 17, 56; pp. 109, 111–13, 123.
[108] I. Papadimitriou, Praktika (1944–8); (1950).

TABLE 3.1 *Cult locales and artefact assemblages**

Artefact type	Site									
	Phylakopi	Mycenae	Tiryns	Asine, House G	Amyklai	Tsoungiza	Epidauros, Apollo Maleatas	Delphi	Aphaia, Aigina	Agia Triada
Figure										
Female	×	×	×	×	×	×				
Male	×								×	
Grotesque		×					?			
Snake		×								
Rhyton										
Animal	×		×	×	×		×			×
Figurine										
Female	×	×	×	×	×	×	×	×	×	×
Animal	×	(×)	×		×	(×)	×	×	×	×
Horse			×		×		×		×	
Bird			×		×				(?)	
Driven ox	×									
Chariot	×		×			×	×		(?)	
Furniture	×							×	×	

Bronze
Human
Animal
Tool/weapon
Ivory/Ostrich/
Bone/Tortoise
Glass
Faience
Lead
Silver
Gold
Stone vase
Conch
Architecture
Building
Special technique
Altar
Hearth
Furnishing
Bench
Larnax
Fresco
'Baetyl'

* Because of the inconsistency of reporting among the sites it is not possible to provide accurate numbers in all cases, therefore only presence/absence is indicated. In addition, some sites are not reported yet in detail (e.g. Mycenae) which means more artefact types may have been recovered than are published.

slope of Mt. Kynortion.[109] Although some of the evidence from this area records the existence of a Mycenaean settlement, most documents the establishment of an Early Mycenaean ritual centre, which continued in use throughout the Mycenaean era.[110] The finds from this sanctuary are equally intriguing. Unlike the sites previously discussed, the Maleatas sanctuary lacks remains of large human figures, though a large bovine figure was found.[111] However, a normal mixture of figurine types is present: female, animal, horse, and furniture.[112] In addition a series of remarkable and in some instances unique artefacts (namely, a sheet-bronze animal face, bronze swords—and a stone pommel—and bronze miniature double axes) represent categories of objects scarcely known from the other sites.[113] An important fragment of a steatite relief vessel showing warriors in a boat fills out this unusual inventory.[114] Pottery from the site consists mostly of sherds; among other shapes Vapheio cups and kylikes are recognizable.

The remains have led the excavator and several other scholars to conclude that the site was a 'peak sanctuary' and to categorize it as an 'official cult'.[115] We are surely mistaken to apply both terms to the site. The former conclusion seems misleading, for it suggests a degree of borrowing of Minoan customs on the part of the Mycenaeans that is not demonstrated by the finds.[116] The latter ignores the fact that the site has so far presented us with none of the typical large figures of 'official cult' and seems clearly located in a setting well apart from any major citadel. Furthermore, on the basis of the evidence from the palace sites and others just discussed, an 'official cult' ought to have come into being with the founding of the palaces, not before. The very early date for the inception of this site surely is important evidence that some local places of ritual activity were coalescing during a period *prior* to state formation; thus providing prima facie evidence that the assemblage is independent of the palaces, which would seem to be the major characteristic of this sanctuary.

[109] Reports in *Praktika* (1974), 93–101; (1975), 162–75; (1977), 187–94; (1978), 111–21; (1979), 127–9; (1981), 158–60; (1983), 152–4; (1987), 52–8.

[110] Lambrinoudakis (n. 2).

[111] Except possibly a large grotesque: see Papadimitriou, *Praktika* (1950), 199, fig. 6. Bovine figure: Lambrinoudakis (n. 2), 63, fig. 8.

[112] *Praktika* (1983), 137.

[113] See, however, Delphi (below, p. 70).

[114] I. Papadimitriou, *Praktika* (1950), 200–2, fig. 10; B. Kaiser, *Untersuchungen zum minoischen Relief* (Bonn, 1976), 95, 133–4, 174.

[115] Lambrinoudakis (n. 2); Hägg, 'Official and Popular' (n. 2), 36.

[116] See A. A. D. Peatfield, 'Minoan Peak Sanctuaries: History and Society', *OpAth* 18 (1990), 120–2. Hägg has repeatedly argued against the interpretation of this site as a 'peak sanctuary': in 'Degrees and Character of the Minoan Influence on the Mainland', in R. Hägg and N. Marinatos (edd.), *The Minoan Thalassocracy: Myth or Reality* (Stockholm, 1987), 119–21; Hägg, 'Religion' (n. 20).

Tsoungiza

Recent excavation of a Mycenaean settlement on the hill of Tsoungiza at Nemea has disclosed evidence of what an 'official cult' in a rural setting might have looked like. In a large deposit of LH IIIA:2 pottery which contained numerous female and animal figurines was discovered the lower part of a figure (Ill. 3.10) like the 'Lady of Phylakopi'. In addition were found two rare figurines thought to represent someone making bread. Preliminary analysis of this large deposit suggests a selected series of shapes, primarily kylikes and bowls. The faunal remains, which are also still under analysis, may suggest selective disposal, possibly distinctive for feasting.[117]

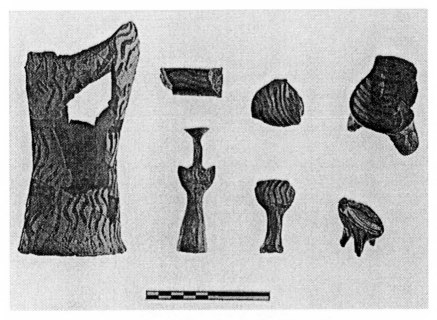

ILL. 3.10 Assemblage of votives from Tsoungiza

No architecture is associated with this deposit, though settlement architecture from earliest LH I down to the end of LH IIIB is well represented at the site. The deposit is located at the base of the crown of the hill which, it is thought, was the centre of the area of habitation. The deposit is clearly a dump, not unlike numerous others scattered over the site, and the remains almost certainly

[117] Preliminary notice in J. C. Wright et al., 'The Nemea Valley Archaeological Project: A Preliminary Report', Hesperia 59 (1990), 635–6. Prof. Patrick Thomas completed study of this deposit in the summer of 1992. Dr Paul Halstead has completed analysis of the faunal remains and informs me that he is fairly certain that the discard pattern is interpretable as relating to feasting.

originated from a structure, which is no longer preserved but which lay, perhaps, up the slope.

The presence of the figure provides an obvious linkage to the palaces, and the LH IIIA:1 date provides a *terminus post quem* for their invention which French had anticipated on the basis of her study of the remains from Phylakopi. This date corresponds with the best evidence for the initial construction of the palaces and the great fortifications around the citadels and it seems likely that their appearance is linked to these events.[118] The rural location of Tsoungiza probably falls within the territory of Mycenae, and the fortunes of the site throughout the Late Bronze Age seem closely tied to the rise and fall of that site.[119] Perhaps the settlement at Tsoungiza contained a rural shrine that was an extension of the cult located in the palace of Mycenae.

Aigina

Although inadequately published for the concerns of modern scholarship, the Mycenaean remains beneath the terrace of the historic period cult of Athena-Aphaia pose additional questions for the study of Mycenaean religion. First, the nature of the context—a fill beneath the terrace of the archaic temple—highlights the problem of evaluating to what extent the evidence represents the variety of material in use at the site. Second, the finds preserved focus the question of identifying a site of cult activity, for aside from numerous female figurines and others of horses, bulls, a bird (?), a charioteer, a throne, and a boat there are two fragments of probable large figures. One is a large arm and hand fragment, the other is the torso of a female figure.[120] As at Amyklai and Tsoungiza, the presence of these figures raises the question of the relation of this site to a central place.

Delphi

A recent restudy by S. Müller of early excavations at Delphi has published fragments of several bovine figures such as those known from Epidauros, the Amyklaion, and Phylakopi. In addition there is a fragment of a female figure. Unfortunately, the context of these finds is not known, but it seems fair to think that they were associated with the architectural remains in the sanctuary of Apollo.[121]

---

[118] French in Renfrew, *Archaeology* (n. 6), 215; Dabney and Wright (n. 29), 31.

[119] J. C. Wright, 'A Mycenaean Hamlet on Tsoungiza at Ancient Nemea', in R. Treuil and P. Darcque (edd.), *L'Habitat égéen préhistorique*, BCH Suppl. 19 (Paris, 1990), 347–54; J. L. Davis, 'If There's a Room at the Top, What's at the Bottom?', *BICS* 35 (1988), 164–5.

[120] H. Thiersch in A. Furtwängler, *Aegina: Das Heiligtum der Aphaia* (Munich, 1906), 370–5.

[121] S. Müller, 'Delphes et sa région à l'époque mycénienne', *BCH* 116 (1992), 478, fig. 16.1, 481. I thank R. Hägg for bringing this recent publication to my attention.

Discussion

Although the evidence of the establishment of shrines within the citadels and outside them in their territories may lead one to suspect a general phenomenon in the establishment of religion during the period of the establishment of the Mycenaean citadel-states, such a conclusion is only valid for heuristic purposes. The site of Epidauros stands out as an exception and a warning that the individual context of each case must be considered before any explanatory narrative can be constructed. This is equally true for consideration of the formalization of these sanctuaries, since only that at Tsoungiza has a clear date (LH IIIA:1) corresponding with the establishment of the palaces, and the others follow later: Phylakopi—LH IIIA:2; Mycenae—LH IIIB:1; Tiryns—LH IIIB:2; Amyklai—LH IIIB/C. Turning to another important category of evidence, Mycenaean figurines, the LH IIIA:1 date of the material from Tsoungiza lends support to French's assertion of 1971 that the earliest figurines dated to that period, but, as she has pointed out, the period of the formation of Mycenaean figurines must be assigned to LH II.[122] Taking this fact into account may further complicate the problem of identifying stages in the emergence of Mycenaean religion. In consideration of this problem it may be that the figurines are indicative of yet another level in the evolving scale of Mycenaean ritual activity. Thus a variety of possibly religious sites exist which are characterized solely, or almost so, by the presence of large numbers of figurines.

Ambiguous Examples

Places less clearly recognizable as centres of cult activity are well known.[123] Some, such as the site of Ayia Triada at Ayios Vasilios (Corinthia) or the remains at the Marmaria at Delphi, are characterized by having large quantities of figurines but little else that distinguishes them and nothing that ties them to the better known religious centres.[124] Both contain a heavy concentration of figurines of many varieties as well as other diverse material.[125]

[122] French (n. 100), 105–6.

[123] Deposits primarily consisting of figurines are known from a variety of sites that include Aigina (Aphrodite sanctuaries), Argos, Athens, Ayios Stephanos, Ayioi Theodoroi, Berbati, Dendra, Eleusis, Ialysos, Korakou, Lefkandi, Lerna, Nauplion, Prosymna, and Zygouries; in addition similar deposits were found at Mycenae and Tiryns in areas separate from the Cult Centres. This list is determined on the basis of French's chart (n. 100), 185–7, which is a summary of all the figurines found at a site, and does not represent their discrete contexts.

[124] Ayia Triada: the site was excavated eighty years ago by Frickenhaus and only recently well published by Kilian (n. 2), 185–90. It is near the village of Ayios Vasilios, not Klenies, as stated by Kilian. Delphi: R. Demangel, *Fouilles de Delphes: Le Sanctuaire d'Athèna Pronaia* (Paris, 1926), 5–26; Müller (n. 121), 481–6.

[125] Caves were also places of worship and have been well documented by Hägg (n. 4), 49–52 and Rutkowski (n. 3), 200–1, 210. When the function is in doubt, however, it is well to realize that caves can have been used for more than worship, as examination of any modern shepherd's fold will reveal, see P. Murray and C. Chang, 'An Ethnoarchaeological Study of a Contemporary Herder's Site', *JFA* 8 (1981), 372–81.

Åkerström has raised the question of household cults in his publication of two installations in rooms at Berbati.[126] To the informed sceptic the meagre remains of figurines, vessels, and small benches, could be seen as nothing more than a coincidental scatter of artefacts within a living area.[127] Yet it may be that the mere presence of such an assemblage within a building is indicative of the extent to which a uniform Mycenaean religion had been established during the period of the palace. Kilian has demonstrated at Tiryns that the distributional pattern of figurines favoured doors and hearths, which he interpreted as evidence of their use as protective devices.[128] Thus it remains highly possible that such meagre assemblages, when found in an architectural setting, may well be the remnants of Mycenaean belief manifested in the most accessible, humble and traditional forms of symbol and action.[129]

These examples sharpen the question of identifying a locus of ritual activity. Although French is justified in observing that the ubiquitous distribution of Mycenaean figurines in tombs, settlements, and sanctuaries all over the Eastern Mediterranean makes them unlikely indicators of cult activity, yet they are the most recognizable icon of Mycenaean society, one that was clearly accessible and utilized by many members of the society, perhaps as a ritual expression of belief.[130] Highly individualized religious activity, whether of an individual or a small community, may often leave nothing or only the barest of archaeological traces.[131]

Official or Popular Cults?

This review of sites clearly demonstrates the problem in applying dualistic categories to the interpretation of locales of Mycenaean ritual.[132] A more fruitful line of approach has been laid down by Anthony Wallace and been applied to

---

[126] Å. Åkerström, 'Cultic Installations in Mycenaean Rooms and Tombs', in Wardle and French (n. 92), 201–2.

[127] Thus French (n. 97), 173, has cautioned that 'the figurines take their function from their context and not vice versa', a position she had earlier stated (n. 100), 107–8.

[128] K. Kilian, 'Mycenaeans Up to Date', in Wardle and French (n. 92), 115–52; Hägg (n. 62), 178–84, has begun to define some of the common elements of a ritual assemblage, and certainly the conjunction of material at the cult locales at Mycenae, Tiryns, Phylakopi, the Amyklaion and elsewhere (see discussion and Table 3.1 below) demonstrate the wider range of material at major centres.

[129] Bourdieu's analysis of this problem is particularly helpful in understanding the nature of ritual as action, and the problems experienced by the external observer in explaining what is observed without losing in the process what is practised: (n. 12), 114–19, passim.

[130] Figurines are notoriously ambiguous in their interpretation. See P. J. Ucko, 'The Interpretation of Prehistoric Figurines', Journal of the Royal Anthropological Institute 92 (1962), 47–8; French (n. 100), 107–8; M. Voigt, Hajji Firuz Tepe, Iran: The Neolithic Settlement (Philadelphia, 1983), 186–95; L. E. Talalay, 'Rethinking the Function of Clay Figurine Legs from Neolithic Greece: An Argument by Analogy', AJA 91 (1987), 161–9.

[131] Wallace (n. 14), 85–6, 88–90, passim.

[132] Hägg, 'Official and Popular' (n. 2), 38–40; Renfrew, Archaeology (n. 6), 401–2.

archaeological settings by James V. Knight. Wallace organized religion according to levels of activity, from the smallest elements of ritual upwards through a variety of increasingly complex cult institutions.[133] Cult institutions are made up of rituals that fulfil social and religious needs according to the level of societal complexity. They also incorporate the diversity of ritual practices, such that contrasting notions like 'popular' and 'official' are not necessary categories for examining belief and action. Thus Wallace's division of cult institutions into four classes (Individualistic, Shamanic, Communal, and Ecclesiastical) reflects not only different levels of socio-political integration but also the belief systems of a society on a continuum. The model is inclusive so that the lower orders of institution may continue to be present and functioning even as the higher orders emerge and dwarf them by their greater visibility.

Knight recognized that this scheme for analysing religion had important applications to archaeology. His case-study of communal cult institutions among Mississippian mound builders shows how this method for reconstructing different cult institutions provides a way of discriminating among different rituals on the basis of their content, both in terms of consideration of location or date, and in terms of their level of integration into the socio-political matrix in which they flourished.[134] This approach requires the investigation of linkages (and their absence) among the artefacts associated with cult activity. Such assemblages Knight calls *sacra*—defined as 'the totality of representational art, artifact and icons that by inference appear to have been charged with conventional supernatural meaning, in the context of ritual activity or display'.[135]

The adoption of this approach to the study of Mycenaean religion permits a balanced treatment of cult places in the citadels and those outside them, facilitates appreciation of the variation evident in their location, architecture, and artefacts, and encourages interpretation according to the widest possible understanding of the socio-political level of the society of which they are a part. In addition this method respects regional variation such that the conditions evident at a primary centre, like Mycenae, will not have to be met elsewhere, such as at Amyklai. Finally this approach avoids the 'either-or' distinction forced by the categories of popular and official religion while also preserving the possibility of discovering important links between extra-palatial and palace-centred shrines on the basis of similar *sacra*.

Although it is beyond the scope of this study to examine each instance of purported cult places in Mycenaean Greece, some idea of the variation among

---

[133] Wallace (n. 14), 83; J. V. Knight, Jr., *Mississippian Religion* (Ann Arbor, University Microfilms, 1981), and (n. 54), 675–87.
[134] Compare Wallace (n. 14), 132, 256.
[135] Knight (n. 54), 687; cf. Turner (n. 81), 102.

the major ones may be gained from Table 3.1, where the complexity of artefact forms found at those discussed in this paper is displayed.[136]

Except for the Maleatas sanctuary, all of these sites were active only during the period of the palaces or after their destruction. Since many of these sites are situated outside the citadels, this relationship is important, for it conforms to our general understanding that the formalization of ritual practice and its codification and monumentalization are directly related to the scale of socio-political complexity. In spatial terms the establishment of such cult installations as that reconstructed at Tsoungiza appears to be evidence of the consolidation of territory by establishing external locations for conducting officially sanctioned rituals. These are secondary locations tied to the primary centres of the citadels. Several interesting questions are raised by taking this view.

First, is the cult established in such peripheral settings simultaneous with the establishment of the palaces, or in consequence of them? This question has been dealt with by Carla Antonaccio in a recent discussion (and in this volume, Ch. 4), and she has forcefully made the point, following the lead of de Polignac, that such activity usually is an *ex post facto* consolidation by the ruling power.[137] This is a fundamentally important observation since it relates closely to two problems that have centred in discussions of the role of religion in the formation of complex societies.[138] First, it indicates that the use of religion as a conscious instrument in the extension of power is not necessarily the case. Second, it suggests that religion is only used as a part of a process of rationalizing and justifying expansion after the fact. What is not demonstrated, however, is whether religion is the prime causal factor behind societal growth.[139]

Another important question arises when one considers the extremely late date of most of these installations, whether in the citadels or outside them. Since the true floruit of most of them follows upon the destructions at the palaces and citadels, after the loss of literacy and the administrative hierarchy, to what extent do they represent the state religion? This question has preoccupied Renfrew in various discussions, and in them he introduces the notion of popular cult. The core of his thinking on this subject seems to be that the ritual activity of these Cult Centres replaces the lost stability provided by the palatial society.[140]

---

[136] For a list, see Hägg (n. 4), and compare to maps in Renfrew, *Archaeology* (n. 6), 414–19.

[137] C. Antonaccio, 'Terraces, Tombs, and the Early Argive Heraion', *Hesperia* 61 (1992), 103–5; F. de Polignac, *La Naissance de la cité grecque: Cultes, espace et société VIIIe-VIIe siècles* (Paris, 1984).

[138] Conrad and Demarest (n. 10), 207, 215–16; see Bell (n. 11) 82–3.

[139] This is, of course, the thrust of the arguments of Conrad and Demarest (n. 10) regarding Aztec expansion. The theoretical aspects of the issue of intentionality and agency are clearly set forth by Giddens, *Constitution* (n. 12), 5–14, 244–62, 293–304, 319–27.

[140] C. Renfrew, 'Systems Collapse as Social Transformation: Catastrophe and Anastrophe in Early State Societies', in C. Renfrew and K. L. Cooke (edd.), *Transformations: Mathematical Approaches to Culture Change* (New York, 1979), 481–506; 'Questions of Minoan and Mycenaean Cult', in Hägg and Marinatos (n. 2), 28–31; *Archaeology* (n. 6), 396–8, 436–7. The problem with these discussions is that they are satisfied to list the symptoms of change without seeking also to offer an explanation of why.

In order to pursue this matter further, we must ask how this could be the case?

To answer this question we must reconsider the origins of 'official' religion—rituals controlled by the ruling powers. On the one hand is the hearth-*wanax* cult, which, as I have argued, represents the traditional value structure of Helladic society. As demonstrated here the maintenance of this cult by the ruler in the palace removed the commoners from direct participation. As the Helladic institution *par excellence*, however, the cult was celebrated at every household hearth by every head of household, and it is this redundancy that makes the cult so powerful when officially celebrated in the palace. On the other hand is the establishment of the Citadel Cult Centres, which, if they have a direct relation to cult locales outside the palaces, were probably much more open to public participation—a point underlined not only by their informal architecture but also by their removal from the palace. Temporally and, probably, functionally between these is the ubiquitous evidence of Mycenaean figurines. Although they may have origins in the Minoan practice of manufacturing figurines and have been influenced by such early examples as the statuettes at the sanctuary at Ayia Irini, Keos,[141] they only begin to become common with the founding of the palaces, and from the LH IIIA:2 period their popularity increases dramatically; they are found in large quantities at almost every kind of Mycenaean site. The formal similarity between the highly popular Psi figurines and many of the large figures suggests a strong relationship between them, one also recognized in the popularity in Crete of the 'Goddess-with-Upraised Arms'.[142] This relationship is important because it probably signifies the success of the effort by the ruling authorities to establish a viable ritual object for common use that was tied into the ideological structure controlled and administered by the palaces.[143] In so far as the figurine became a universal symbol of Mycenaean religion it meets Turner's definition of a dominant symbol—one, like a crescent or a cross, that embraces a host of religious associations.[144] Among other things the figurines may have symbolized the figures at Cult Centres and thereby provided a symbolic link to the seat of cult at the citadel centres. The fact that some are pierced to be suspended and others are decorated with necklaces adorned with pendants has been argued by Hägg and Kilian–Dirlmeier

---

[141] French (n. 100), 105; Renfrew, *Archaeology* (n. 6), 437; cf. the statuettes from Ayia Irini, Keos, which precede the Phi-type figurine: M. E. Caskey, *Keos*, ii. 1: *The Temple at Ayia Irini. The Statues* (Princeton, NJ, 1986).

[142] Peatfield, this volume (Ch. 2). See now: R. Mersereau, 'Cretan Cylindrical Models', *AJA* 97 (1993), 15; S. Alexiou, 'He minoike thea meth' upsomenon cheiron', *KrChron* 12 (1958), 179–299; cf. Caskey (n. 141).

[143] I treat this complicated phenomenon in 'From Chief to King in Mycenaean Greece', in P. Rehak (ed.), *The Role of the Ruler in the Prehistoric Aegean*, Aegaeum 11 (Liège and Austin, 1995), 63–80.

[144] Turner (n. 81), 20–32; see Wallace (n. 14), 237–8.

to imply their religious function.[145] In this sense they may not be any different from miniature and portable paraphernalia relating to saints sold at the site of their shrines and burial places. Believers purchase such items as a way of establishing a continuing immediate link with the object of veneration. Thus the popularity of these items over such a wide geography in Mycenaean times is illustrative of the success of palace-instituted ritual and cult locale. Once established and personalized, this religious object and its associations would take on a meaning independent of the palaces and hence would outlast them.

In conclusion there seem to be strong spatial and chronological similarities between territorially peripheral cult installations and the Cult Centres established in the citadels. Consequently, it is likely that the founding of these ritual areas represents an extension of cult from the palace centre outwards as an act of appropriation and incorporation of local and rurally based cults into the official palace-based religion. Presumably the palaces became interested in these external areas as they expanded or consolidated territory. This process of expansion may have occurred in several stages, from as early as LH I to as late as LH IIIB, depending upon the local conditions of state-formation. Whatever the case, it occurred in reference to existing autonomous local cults, the evidence of which is virtually impossible for us to recognize archaeologically.

As remarked, the sequence of the evolution of Mycenaean religion generally parallels that recognized by Conrad and Demarest in their analysis of Inca and Aztec expansion. Their evidence led them to argue for the importance of considering volition as a prime mover in societal evolution, such that societal institutions develop in irrational, often self-contradictory ways. This means that events are often only recognized, consolidated, and justified after the fact, instead of being planned.[146]

The traces for the evolution of Mycenaean religion, as Hägg has well established, are twofold: with origins on the one hand in the appropriation and adaptation of Minoan ritual and iconography,[147] and on the other in the consolidation of the indigenous practice of Helladic values. The amalgamation of these into a Mycenaean religion is seen as probably stochastic in process, corresponding to major stages in the evolution of Mycenaean society.

[145] Hägg, 'Official and Popular' (n. 2), 38; I. Kilian-Dirlmeier, 'Zum Halsschmuck mykenischer Idole', *Jahresbericht des Institutes für Vorgeschichte der Universität Frankfurt am Main* (1978–9), 29–43.

[146] Conrad and Demarest (n. 10), 207, 215–16. See Bell (n. 11), 82–3; the sequence that can be reconstructed on the basis of Conrad and Demarest's emphasis is as follows: Volition → Maladaptation → Contradiction → Crisis → Explosion → Collapse → Reformation. This sequence is anticipated in Wallace's notion of 'revitalization': (n. 14), 157–66; 'Revitalization Movements', *American Anthropologist* 58 (1956), 264–81. Compare Zuesse (n. 13), 522–9; Giddens, *Constitution* (n. 12), 5–14, 319–27.

[147] Wright (n. 59); Rehak (n. 83); Morris (n. 88); Marinatos (n. 88); Wolf-Dietrich Niemeier, 'Cult Scenes on Gold Rings from the Argolid', in Hägg and Nordquist (n. 2), 165–70.

Conclusion

Through the application of evolutionary and post-structural theories this chapter has examined the structure and functioning of Mycenaean religion from its origins in the Middle Bronze Age into the Palace period. I have argued for the pre-eminence of belief and custom as determining a social custom of lineage relations that evolves into a hierarchical descent-based political structure which historically had strong, if not permanent, control of the central rituals of the society. In so far as there existed a priesthood, it developed only in response to the managerial needs of an increasingly complex group of cults.[148] The complexity of the process of the evolution of Mycenaean religion is not readily apparent at any point in our study of this society. This analysis thus contradicts commonly held assumptions that the character of Mycenaean society was immediately formed upon contact with the Minoans during the Neopalatial period, for the view espoused here is neither static nor synchronic, and the position is maintained that only by studying a society in process can its institutions actually be examined and their various strands recognized and understood.

The earliest form of Mycenaean religion is probably manifested in individualistic and shamanistic cult institutions that are not easily detectable in archaeological remains. However, they may be inferred through spatial-structural analysis of the organization of dwellings, settlements, and mortuary facilities. Next occur communal cult institutions, which also are not easily reflected in the material record. They may be recognized in the establishment of the palaces, the erection of fortifications, and the first signs of cult areas segregated from the dwelling of the ruling lineage. As the consolidation of power at certain citadels continued, the needs of administering the cults gathered in through expansion of territory kept pace with demands on the decision-making system in political and economic terms. At this time, which marks the transition to statehood, the religion began to branch out like the roots and limbs of a tree, the former reaching back to and drawing from historic indigenous and external sources, the latter extending forward over new territory and through new leaves of expression. Thus the complexity apparent in the record of the Palatial and Postpalatial periods tends to overshadow the central sources of belief and custom and their accompanying institutional forms. This structure endures in many areas during the Postpalatial period. The continuing vitality of some of the institutions of Palatial society was achieved because the structure of Mycenaean society—its values and beliefs—were still nourished from ancient cultural roots. Finally, just as a tree that withers and dies may still regenerate itself with new

[148] Wallace (n. 14), 87–8; Bellah (n. 21), 42.

shoots from old roots, it seems likely, looking beyond the Bronze Age, that the beliefs and customs of the Helladic society continued to nourish new forms of ritual practice throughout the Dark Age.

4

Placing the Past: the Bronze Age in the Cultic Topography of Early Greece*

CARLA M. ANTONACCIO

Wesleyan University

The aim of this paper is to make a contribution towards understanding the development of one type of social landscape, the sacred landscapes of the protohistorical Greek Iron Age. This phase presents opportunities in some ways similar to those for Iron Age Europe; for example, in reconstructing the complex interplay of factors in a period strongly conditioned by the past and fundamental for the future. The Greek Iron Age requires different treatment from either the Bronze Age or the historical Archaic and Classical phases, however, as will become apparent.[1] From the beginning, the study of sanctuaries has always held a privileged position in classical archaeology. Focusing on the recovery and reconstruction of major monuments (a concern that persists to the present), votive offerings made at sanctuaries have been scrutinized to various ends, including identifying the cult, or the votaries. While new frameworks of enquiry and interpretation have been constructed, for example the class and gender of worshippers, most studies have remained within the confines of these traditional approaches, many of them grounded in some version of formal analysis.[2]

While studies of the Iron Age have hardly ignored the role of the Bronze Age in shaping it, most of the discussion has centred on whether or when later Greeks became aware of or acknowledged their predecessors, and on the

---

* Thanks to Sue Alcock and Robin Osborne for inviting me to contribute to this volume and the panel in which it originated, as well as for their editorial assistance, and to E. French, N. Klein, F. de Polignac, and I. Strøm for discussion and sharing unpublished work. Special thanks to Doug Charles for his insights.

[1] See D. Miles, 'Social Landscapes: Pattern and Purpose?', in M. Jones and G. Dimbleby (edd.), *The Environment of Man: the Iron Age to the Anglo-Saxon Period*, BAR Br. Ser. 87 (Oxford, 1981), 9–18.

[2] To choose just two studies, cf. B. Bergquist, *The Archaic Greek Temenos* (Lund, 1967), and F. van Straten, 'Votives and Votaries in Greek Sanctuaries', in A. Schachter (ed.), *Le Sanctuaire grec*, Entretiens de la Fondation Hardt sur l'antiquité classique 37 (Geneva, 1992), 247–86.

continuity of cult from prehistory through a 'Dark Age'.[3] Although this last is an important issue, it has mostly been framed to argue an essential conservatism in Greek religion. By extension, the essential identity of the Greeks across the 'Dark Ages' can be inferred, though the reality and effects of the Dorian invasion are far from settled issues (see further below).[4]

The contributions of François de Polignac represent a new strategy. De Polignac examined the interplay of cult and its locations in space with social developments in the eighth and seventh centuries BC in several regions of Greece, identifying how sanctuaries were placed so as to articulate the territory of emerging poleis.[5] This paper builds on de Polignac's insights about the significance of location for sanctuaries in Iron Age and early Archaic Greece, elaborating discussion of the role of Bronze Age features in the topography, and argues that an important factor in the construction of a bounded (and a sacred) landscape is the presence of Bronze Age remains.[6] While the Iron Age is clearly a critical period, its developments are less a sudden emergence into the light (a 'Greek Renaissance') than the culmination of a continuous and intensifying development.[7]

An important aspect of the Bronze Age and its effects on the Iron Age which has seen extensive discussion is the treatment of Mycenaean tombs in the Iron Age, in hero or tomb cult.[8] In this paper, I will attempt instead to consider how Bronze Age sanctuaries, tombs, and habitation sites structured the landscape in certain parts of Greece. Recent emphasis on material culture as symbolic of ethnicity in the Iron Age offers a particularly promising way to explore how sanctuaries might have expressed corporate identity and shaped cult in the

---

[3] See the following note, and A. Schachter, 'Policy, Cult, and the Placing of Greek Sanctuaries', in Schachter (n. 2), 2–57. Schachter's parameters are very close to mine: the end of the Dark Age and early Archaic periods, limited to the mainland and the Aegean. However, his project considers 'the relationship of a sanctuary to the people who used it and to the deity worshipped at it' (p. 2). His purposes and mine therefore diverge, as will be apparent.

[4] On this question see the work of B. Dietrich, *The Origins of Greek Religion* (Berlin, 1974), and *Tradition in Greek Religion* (Berlin, 1986); S. Hiller, 'Possible Historical Reasons for the Rediscovery of the Mycenaean Past in the Age of Homer', and C. Rolley, 'Les grands Sanctuaires panhelléniques', both in R. Hägg (ed.), *The Greek Renaissance of the Eighth Century BC: Tradition and Innovation* (Stockholm, 1983), 9–14 and 109–114; C. LeRoy, 'Mémoire et tradition: Réflexions sur la continuité', in *Aux origines de l'Héllenisme: la Crète et la Grèce: Hommage à H. van Effenterre* (Paris, 1984), 163–73; W. Burkert, *Greek Religion* (Cambridge, Mass., 1985), 43–53, and Schachter (n. 3), 2–4.

[5] *La Naissance de la cité grecque* (Paris, 1984), now rev. and trans. as *Cults, Territory, and the Origins of the Greek City-State* (Chicago, 1995). See also his paper in this volume (Ch. 1); I am grateful to him for sharing the unpublished paper, 'Cité et territoire au géométrique récent; un modèle argien?', delivered at the French School at Athens in 1990. The papers in Schachter (n. 2), are also apropos (more below).

[6] I have profited from D. Lowenthal, *The Past Is a Foreign Country* (Cambridge, 1985), in thinking about the relationship of past to present.

[7] On the concept of a Greek Renaissance, see R. Hägg in *The Greek Renaissance* (n. 4), 208–10, and S. Hiller (n. 4); in the same volume, J. N. Coldstream pointed out (p. 49) that P. N. Ure (in 1922) and A. R. Burn (in 1936) had both used the concept of a Renaissance for early Greece; *contra* Coldstream, Burn was not the first to use the term 'Greek Renaissance', cf. P. N. Ure, *The Greek Renaissance* (London, 1921).

[8] See below, pp. 90–2.

aftermath of the Bronze Age.[9] I begin with a brief survey of archaeological approaches, placing current work and my own approach in perspective.

Approaching Frontiers and Boundaries

There is an archaeology of frontiers and boundaries, and it tends to be strongly processual, though various methods have been brought to bear.[10] Outside classical archaeology, the study of frontiers and boundaries generally concentrates on the peripheries of entire societies, cultures, and empires, and what takes place there within the structure, as well as the interactions between it and any neighbours. These approaches identify frontier and boundary not only with topography, but with culture: 'In archaeology [the] boundary problem involves the definitions of types and patterns: artifact types and settlement patterns, for example, rest upon theoretical and empirical considerations concerning behavior, material culture, and their expression in the archaeological record.'[11]

De Polignac's is the only study of its kind for ancient Greece. Though concerned with centres and peripheries, frontiers and boundaries, it has less in common with the studies of these concepts already mentioned than with structuralism. In structuralism, the language of culture is formed around opposites: nature and culture, male and female, centre and periphery, city and country.[12] Structuralists working on Archaic and Classical Greek culture have explored the structures of youth and age, public and domestic, freeborn and slave, citizen and alien, Greek and barbarian. Though highly effective in identifying underlying patterns which articulate social relations, structuralism polarizes its subject into paired extremes, without any middle ground. It has been text-driven; archaeological evidence is inconsistently utilized, and written sources from all periods are used to build up a composite which cannot reflect any single moment. Gaps between ideal, text-based constructs and ancient lived experience are not acknowledged. Recent critiques of archaeology, while by no means widely adopted in practice, have strongly questioned structuralism, and a few archaeologists have attempted to articulate post-structural archae-

---

[9] I expand here upon my paper 'Territory, Competition, Community, and the Early Argive Heraion' in the colloquium 'Sanctuaries in Outer Space', organized by S. E. Alcock and R. Osborne at the Annual Meeting, Archaeological Institute of America, Chicago, December 1991. This paper has appeared as 'Terraces, Tombs, and the Early Argive Heraion', *Hesperia* 61 (1992), 85–105. The present paper has benefited from discussion in Chicago, as well as from work by I. Strøm and F. de Polignac which came into my hands after the earlier article went to press.

[10] On processual archaeology, see I. Hodder, *Reading the Past*, 2nd edn. (Cambridge, 1991).

[11] S. Green and S. Perlman, 'Frontiers, Boundaries, and Open Social Systems', in S. Green and S. Perlman (edd.), *The Archaeology of Frontiers and Boundaries* (New York, 1985), 4. Cf. S. De Atley and F. Findlow (edd.), *Exploring the Limits: Frontiers and Boundaries in Prehistory*, BAR Int. Ser. 223 (Oxford, 1984).

[12] C. Tilley, 'Lévi-Strauss: Structuralism and Beyond', in *Reading Material Culture* (Oxford, 1990), 5–6.

ologies.[13] Others have recognized the slippage between the archaeological record and ideal structures, not to mention the conflicts arising between textual and archaeological accounts.[14] In this paper, a contextual approach will be used, encompassing many factors in the formation of the cultic landscape, not only location in space but local traditions including the Bronze Age past. I will not be concerned so much with interactions or conflicts between states or regions as with interactions between communities within a region. This will require first a definition of what a territory or region is.

Both ethnographic cases and complex societies in the past often provide more data for analysis than we have for Iron Age Greece, in the form of information on settlement patterns, subsistence, and environment. Through survey, our understanding for some areas of Greece is better than only a decade ago, but the important survey in the Argolid has only just been published, the survey in Boiotia awaits full publication, and other surveys are still in progress.[15] It is still difficult to do the kind of fine-grained analysis which analyses the relationship of settlement and territory diachronically.[16] A major result is that political boundaries and cultural boundaries, subsistence zones, and cultic territories are often assumed to be coextensive.[17] Such conclusions may not be warranted; consider the role of political territory in historical Greek warfare. As Robert Connor has observed, the basic aim in war was not the wholesale acquisition or annexation of territory.

Apart from the anomalous seizure of Messenia by the Spartans, territorial acquisition ... appears primarily in the change of sovereignty over marginal border lands. Each state retains control over its main agricultural land ... The ideology of ancient Greek land warfare, the representation of war as a matter of honour, affects its conduct and results. Underlying the violence and destruction of war is a logic based not on the use of war as a means to certain ends but on its effectiveness as a way of self and civic representation.[18]

Yet, even in this particular construction of warfare and its purposes, borders were crucial symbolically, as well as tactically and politically. Hoplite battles were frequently fought at the edge of agricultural plains, which were also often

---

[13] Cf. the papers in I. Bapty and T. Yates, *Archaeology after Structuralism* (London, 1990).

[14] Osborne (this volume); see also the papers in B. Little (ed.), *Text-Aided Archaeology* (Boca Raton, 1992).

[15] M. H. Jameson, C. N. Runnels, and Tj. H. van Andel, *A Greek Countryside: The Southern Argolid from Prehistory to the Present Day* (Stanford and Cambridge, 1994); J. Bintliff and A. Snodgrass, 'Mediterranean Survey and the City', *Antiquity* 62 (1988), 57–71.

[16] Cf. P. Rubertone and P. Thorbahn, 'Urban Hinterlands as Frontiers of Colonization', in Green and Perlman (n. 11), 231–49, for 18th- and 19th-century Rhode Island, using both archaeological and documentary evidence.

[17] Cf. P. Cartledge, *Sparta and Lakonia: A Regional History 1300–362 BC* (London, 1979), 3–12, on the concepts of region and territory for Lakonia; the observations are extendable to any part of Greece.

[18] R. Connor, 'Early Greek Land Warfare as Symbolic Expression', *Past & Present* 119 (1988), 3–29 at 16–17.

at the very boundary of the invaded state, and it was the border areas that were likely to change hands, if anything.[19] As recognized by de Polignac, extra-urban sanctuaries are also often located in these areas, and the common symbolic language of warfare and cult may be noted here. A crucial point for de Polignac is that the rise of major sanctuaries was inextricably linked with the rise of the polis, the very birth of the Greek city. It is essential, therefore, to examine the formation of boundaries in the Iron Age, the period which saw the emergence of the polis, and strategies for their definition and maintenance. If sanctuaries are truly linked with communal self-definition and symbolize sovereignty, then both a dia-chronic perspective, and methodologies for distinguishing cultural and political boundaries in the archaeological record, must accompany further enquiry.

Before proceeding, a brief review of de Polignac's essential points follows. His study combined archaeological information with myth, history, and the literary record, and covered mainland Greece, the Aegean islands, and Greek colonies in North Africa, Asia Minor, and the West. He challenged previous constructions of early Greek history and the growth of the polis. For the mainland, de Polignac questioned whether the Athenian pattern as commonly construed was appropriate for all Greek communities. In the Athenian model, the imposition of civic cult atop the Bronze Age palatial site on the Acropolis symbolized the devolution of power from monarchy to polis. In this process, although the powers of the old monarchy were dispersed, symbolically they were located with the deity which presided over the new order. The organization of space formed an important correlative, a concentric arrangement of territory around the urban core with the acropolis at the centre, its temple embodying political unity.[20] De Polignac, however, challenged this account, calling attention to recent re-examinations of the institutions of *basileia*, *genos*, and tribe which have undermined the presumed transfer of power from Bronze Age ruler to Iron Age king and ultimately to the institutions of the polis, with the concomitant transformation of early Greek society. He also pointed out that Athens had come to stand for the Greek polis generally, whereas it is in fact a unique case; other city-states had very different patterns of cult during their emergence.

De Polignac went on to describe how sanctuaries articulate the territory of nascent poleis, the appearance of a sanctuary signifying a new attitude towards space, the formation of a frontier between sacred and profane.[21] The con-

---

[19] Connor (n. 18), 12. These observations should be compared with C. Sourvinou-Inwood, 'What is Polis Religion?', in O. Murray and S. Price (edd.), *The Greek City from Homer to Alexander* (Oxford, 1990), 295–322. See also G. Daverio Rocchi, *Frontiera e confini nella Grecia antica* (Rome, 1988), 25–40; M. Sartre, 'Aspects économiques et aspects religieux de la frontière dans les cités grecques', *Ktema* 4 (1979), 213–24.

[20] De Polignac, *La Naissance* (n. 5), 16; cf. 85–6; for some revisions see De Polignac, *Cults, Territory*, and Ch. 1.

[21] De Polignac, *La Naissance* 30.

struction of a temple embodied the sacred in the countryside. The new importance of agricultural territory, according to de Polignac, was a function of increasing population and pressure on subsistence strategies. The delimitation of
agricultural space with the landmark of a sanctuary divided it from the uncivilized,
wild world of nature and from the arable land of other communities.[22]

De Polignac assigned this 'monocentric' pattern to Athens alone, and
developed a 'bipolar' model for other communities. The two poles were formed
of city and territory, and their political and social unity symbolized by the
procession from urban centre to rural margin enacted regularly in honour of
the deity situated at the border. This unity fundamentally depended on military
control, made possible by hoplite armour and organization, and was underlined
by the participation of hoplite warriors in the processions.[23]

The details of myth, ritual, and ceremony which de Polignac outlined for
these sanctuaries conflate sources which range widely in time, and need not be
considered here.[24] For this study, the most important point to emerge from de
Polignac's work is that sanctuaries mark the centre and especially the boundaries
of a polis, 'stress points in the social and political territory of states'.[25] Much
work in anthropology has concerned the construction of boundaries between
groups using material culture.[26] It will be important to consider how these
stresses are expressed in what is found at the sanctuaries, in addition to their
location, and how (or whether) different groups expressed difference or identity.
A growing literature on Greek categories of difference expands on familiar (and
essentially structuralist) distinctions between barbarian and Hellene, citizen and
metic, slave and free, male and female.[27] One approach is to examine stylistic
and typological variations in votive offerings with a view to discerning the
identities of the votaries, locating women, foreigners, or slaves, the marginal
groups within a community in the Archaic and Classical periods.[28] The question

---

[22] De Polignac, *La Naissance* n. 5, 44–7. Not all extra-urban sanctuaries served this function; some
were involved in rituals of transition, and here 'l'indétermination culturelle d'un espace contigu à deux
cités a pu permettre à certains sanctuaires de demeurer à cheval sur une frontière politique' (p. 47).
Similarly, Albert Schachter identifies a list of actions in establishing a polis, including the delimitation
of territory and the defence of both the city and the territory, and the unification of the population.
Among the strategies employed, he mentioned 'the establishment or confirmation of common sanctuaries at critical places, namely, in the town, where the town joins the country, in the countryside, at
the edges of the territory': Schachter (n. 3), 11.

[23] De Polignac, *La Naissance* (n. 5), 48–50, 54–6, and esp. 85–92. Cf. I. Morris, *Burial and Society*
(Cambridge, 1987), 195–201, who argues against the reality of the 'hoplite revolution'.

[24] See Schachter (n. 3), 36–56 on the roles of specific gods in choice of site.

[25] C. Morgan, 'Ethnicity and Early Greek States: Historical and Material Perspectives', *PCPS* 37
(1991), 144. *Ethne* are different, as Morgan outlines.

[26] See e.g. the papers in De Atley and Findlow (n. 11).

[27] See e.g. Daverio Rocchi (n. 19), 11–12 and n. 3 on Greeks and non-Greeks.

[28] See especially C. Simon, 'The Archaic Votive Offerings and Cults of Ionia' (Ph.D. diss., Berkeley,
1986); I. Strøm, 'The Early Sanctuary of the Argive Heraion and its External Relations', *Acta Archaeologica*
59 (1988), 173–208, and de Polignac, this volume (Ch. 1), touch on these issues (see further below).

of boundaries between Greeks and various 'Others', particularly non-Greeks, however, will not be addressed here; rather, the emphasis will be on the ways in which Greeks marked off divisions between and within their own communities. This amounts to the study of ethnicity, defined as 'the way in which social groups consciously choose to assert their identity and to define and constitute themselves in relation to others in any given set of circumstances'. Morgan employs ceramic styles in the Iron Age to identify correlates of group identity. As she notes:

ethnic behaviour affects only those categories of artefact selected to carry social or political meaning under particular circumstances, rather than the totality of a society's material culture. So in identifying patterns of behaviour underlying the regional 'cultures' evident across Early Iron Age Greece, one should look to distinguish between those aspects which reflect state organisation and elements of the social structure tamed to it, those which result from underlying social organisation with no implication of institutionalisation and those which are manipulated to express ethnicity within this wider framework.[29]

Variations discernible in Iron Age pottery styles, then, articulate regional, and intra-regional, distinctions and affiliations. While some Iron Age artefact styles basically coincide with later political territorial boundaries, however, it is not sufficient to assume total conformity between style, region, and people, invariable through time.[30]

Using these concepts to identify different groups, it can be suggested that in communities which developed into poleis, especially Athens, Corinth, Sparta, and Argos, early Iron Age conflict over land was expressed in a variety of strategies: within communities, burial customs and tomb cult for some (see below, pp. 90–2); between communities, hero cult and the foundation of sanctuaries. At the end of the period, Isthmia provides an example of a former 'roadside shrine' which became a pre-eminent Corinthian sanctuary in the early seventh century (see Morgan, this volume). In *ethne* the identity of this form of state did not depend on strong regional boundaries,[31] but beginning in the eighth century, sanctuaries arose or expanded in both *ethne* and poleis, with equal attention and expense on the part of both. Still, some early cult places

[29] Morgan (n. 25), 134, and C. Morgan and T. Whitelaw, 'Pots and Politics: Ceramic Evidence for the Rise of the Argive State', *AJA* 95 (1991), 79–108.

[30] Ian Hodder notes: '. . . many, if not most, stable material culture and social boundaries cannot be equated with coherent and stable groupings of people . . . Differences between cultural units are maintained in relation to organizational differences and sets of social interests, and the human populations may be transient, especially when looked at over the long term', in 'Boundaries as Strategies: An Ethnoarchaeological Study', in Green and Perlman (n. 11), 141–59 at 142–3. Compare the closing remarks of Morgan (n. 25), 148–9: '. . . ethnicity . . . may thus help to account for the appearance and disappearance in the material record of local subgroups within various regions and for differences in their organisation and development'.

[31] Morgan (n. 25), 142. See also Schachter (n. 3), 8–11.

located in *ethnos* and polis territory cannot be readily interpreted as articulating this particular conflict, and we must guard against searching for a single covering explanation; sanctuaries such as Olympia, the Polis cave on Ithaka, and Mt. Hymettos in Attica all have individual histories, though we may trace their origins or efflorescence to the same period.[32]

The Iron Age landscape had been intensively inhabited by the ancestors of its first millenium inhabitants. Greek communities of this phase encountered natural features such as rivers, mountains, and plains, and neighbouring inhabitants, but also remains of past inhabitants. It remains to be seen what impact the traces of the Bronze Age past had in constructing the landscape and articulating boundaries.

Bronze Age Traces in the Iron Age Landscape

Three types of Bronze Age site will be considered: sanctuaries, cemeteries, and settlements. These play different roles, of different duration, in different times and regions in the development of Iron Age cultic landscapes. After outlining the types and distributions of Bronze Age sites, and at the risk of further trampling already well-trodden ground, discussion will concentrate on the Argolid, Lakonia, and Attica. These choices are based on the availability of information on both sanctuaries and material culture in these regions. The amount of data for the Argolid makes it possible to discuss the Bronze and Iron Ages in some detail; the same is true to a lesser degree for Attica, which also seems to present a very different situation for comparison; Sparta's singular social structure and history ought to provide clear comparisons to the other two regions.

Sanctuaries

Though the issue is critical to considering Bronze Age cult sites, no more than a brief statement on continuity of religion into the Iron Age is possible here. The Linear B evidence so far shows that some deities were lost after the palatial destructions, though many were to re-emerge into the Archaic period.[33] As mentioned, much research has focused on the issue of continuity at Iron Age

---

[32] Morgan (n. 25) 144: 'A shared need to come to terms with "the other", human or divine, offered a ready frame of reference and mutual awareness, and thence in time a basis for institutionalised panhellenic communications.' See also C. Morgan, *Athletes and Oracles: The Transformation of Olympia and Delphi in the 8th c. BC* (Cambridge, 1990), for Olympia and Delphi, both in regions with *ethne*.

[33] See J. Chadwick, *The Mycenaean World* (Cambridge, 1976), 84–101, for a convenient summary of Mycenaean religion and the textual evidence, and S. Hiller, 'Mykenische Heiligtümer: Das Zeugnis der Linear B-Texte', in R. Hägg and N. Marinatos (edd.), *Sanctuaries and Cults in the Aegean Bronze Age* (Stockholm, 1981), 95–125. See also B. C. Dietrich, 'Tradition in Greek Religion', in Hägg (n. 4), 85–9, arguing as elsewhere strongly for continuity.

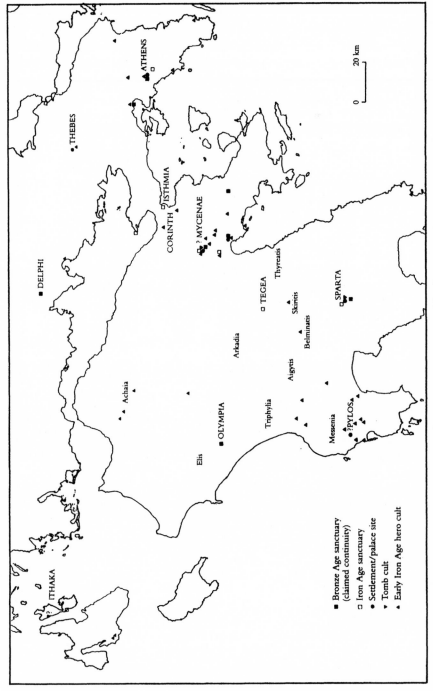

ILL. 4.1 Sites mentioned in the text

and Archaic sanctuaries for which cult is also claimed during the Bronze Age. The sites in this category fall into two groups: Bronze Age sanctuaries where cult is supposed to be continuous into the Iron Age; and sanctuaries founded on former palace sites, which supposedly continue (or revive) a palace-centred cult.

Few sites of the first group actually offer strong evidence for ritual activity during the Bronze Age. Bronze Age sherds or other remains certainly occur on many, but cultic continuity cannot be proved by projecting Iron Age cult back into the Bronze Age with this kind of evidence.[34] It is possible that some sites were never forgotten after the destruction of the palaces, though an early Iron Age hiatus is not easily eliminated. At Amyklai in Lakonia, for example, adjustments in Lakonian pottery chronology have narrowed the gap to only fifty or so years, little enough to be filled by oral memory. Besides Amyklai, sites usually mentioned include Eleusis, the sanctuary of Apollo Maleatas near Epidauros, the Bronze Age sanctuary at Ayia Irini on Keos, Olympia, and the Artemision on Delos.[35] Cultic continuity in each case has been challenged, however, and cannot be definitely proved at this point. The second group includes the megaron on the acropolis of Tiryns, supposedly reconstructed to house a cult of Hera which continued a palace-based religion, besides the cult of Athena on the Athenian Acropolis, which also takes up a palace cult. The same scenario is proposed for Athena at Mycenae.[36] The assumption that citadel

---

[34] See above, pp. 79–81 and nn. 3–4, and de Polignac, *La Naissance* (n. 5), 37, as well as Morgan (this volume, Ch. 5) on the lack of solid evidence for Bronze Age cult at Isthmia.

[35] On Mycenae, see E. French, 'Cult Places at Mycenae', in Hägg and Marinatos (n. 33), 41–8; G. Mylonas, 'The Cult Centre of Mycenae', *Proceedings of the British Academy* 67 (1981), 307–20. For Amyklai, see Cartledge (n. 17), 80–96 with references; and esp. K. Demakopoulou, 'To mukenaiko iero sto Amyklaio kai i YE III periodos sti Lakonia' (Ph.D. diss., University of Athens, 1982), and W. D. E. Coulson, 'The Dark Age Pottery of Sparta', *BSA* 80 (1985), 29–84. Ayia Irini: M. Caskey, 'Ayia Irini, Kea: The Terracotta Statues and the Cult in the Temple', in Hägg and Marinatos (n. 33), 127–35; M. Caskey, *Keos*, ii: *The Temple at Ayia Irini, Part I: The Statues* (Princeton, NJ, 1986), esp. 39–41. Eleusis: J. Travlos, 'I Athena kai i Eleusina ston 8° kai 7° p.Ch. aiona', *ASAtene* 45 (1983), 323–8 and cf. P. Darque, 'Les Vestiges mycéniens découverts sous le Télestérion d'Eleusis', *BCH* 105 (1981), 593–605. Apollo Maleatas: V. Lambrinoudakis, 'Remains of the Mycenaean Period in the Sanctuary of Apollon Maleatas', in Hägg and Marinatos (n. 33), 59–65 (see also Felsch on Kalapodi in the same volume). Olympia: A. Mallwitz, 'Cult and Competition Locations at Olympia', in W. Raschke (ed.), *The Archaeology of the Olympics: The Olympics and Other Festivals in Antiquity* (Madison, Wis., 1988), 79–109; Morgan, *Athletes* (n. 32), and the papers in W. Coulson and H. Kyrieleis (edd.), *Proceedings of an International Symposium of the Olympic Games* (Athens, 1992). Delos: H. Gallet de Santerre, *Délos primitive et archaïque* (Paris, 1958); 'Notes Déliennes 1. De Délos mycénienne à Délos archaïque: L'Artémision', *BCH* 99 (1975), 247–62; C. Rolley, 'Bronzes géométriques et orientaux à Délos', in *Études Déliennes*, *BCH* Suppl. I (Paris, 1973), 523; 'Les Trépieds à cuve clouée', in *Fouilles de Delphes* 5.3 (Paris, 1977), 139–40.

[36] Athenian Acropolis: out of a vast bibliography, C. Kardara, 'O pukinos domos tou Erechtheos', *AE* (1960), 165–84; against Bronze Age cult on the Mycenaean bastion, see I. Mark, *The Sanctuary of Athena Nike in Athens*, Hesperia Suppl. 26 (Princeton, 1993), 3–5; the archaeological evidence for any Bronze Age palace has been totally obliterated by later building. Tiryns: A. Foley, *The Argolid 800–600 BC: An Archaeological Survey*, SIMA 80 (Göteborg, 1988), 145–7 with references; see also Morgan and Whitelaw (n. 29), 87–8 and C. M. Antonaccio, *An Archaeology of Ancestors: Tomb Cult and Hero Cult in Early Greece* (Lanham, Md., 1995), ch. 3.

sanctuaries carried on palace-centred Mycenaean cult is ultimately based on the presumed divinity of the Mycenaean king, grounded in two Homeric passages (*Iliad* 6. 546–51, *Odyssey* 7. 80–1). One describes how Athena raised Erechtheus and installed him on the Acropolis, where the young men of Athens supplicate him with bulls; in the other, Athena leaves Scheria and comes to Athens (via Marathon), entering the well-built house of Erechtheus on the Acropolis. The notion follows that Dark Age *basileis* were kings who assumed authority from the Mycenaean *wanax*, and then passed it to the polis. Citadel sanctuaries, serving the tutelary deity of the polis, would then be the last link in an unbroken chain. The natures of Mycenaean and Iron Age kingship have not gone unchallenged, however, and the archaeology does not support the accompanying cult scenario, so the meaning of citadel sanctuaries should be reconsidered.[37]

When we can locate Mycenaean religion elsewhere, it seems to have been localized either in open-air sanctuaries, or in shrines identifiable by specific items, like wheelmade terracottas.[38] Some of the few certain Bronze Age shrines on the mainland, like the Cult Centre at Mycenae, certainly do not demonstrate continuity of cult to the Iron Age; the temple on the acropolis of Mycenae was situated over the megaron of the palace, not the shrine itself. De Polignac noted that many sanctuaries, especially non-urban ones, were constructed on the ruins of the Bronze Age. He did not subscribe to unbroken continuity with Bronze Age cults, however, but explained such cases as a rediscovery which became a 'quête d'une sacralisation légitimante'. The presence of Bronze Age remains, especially at non-urban sanctuaries, either fortuitously rediscovered or simply still visible, was often of minimal impressiveness, in contrast to ruins to which legends attached (Mycenae, for example).[39] But aside from the question of continuity, de Polignac does not further consider what types of Mycenaean sites become which sort of sanctuaries.

De Polignac convincingly argues that Athens, with Athena Poliouchos installed on the Acropolis, is exceptional, but though there may be continuous occupation here, continuity with a Bronze Age palace cult is not the same thing. At any rate, Athenian claims to autochthony complicate evaluating this case, and Athens cannot be used as a model for other, 'bipolar' poleis. The choice of a Bronze Age palace site for a cult in the Iron Age might be due to both topography (urban centre and geographically prominent) and co-opting

[37] On Mycenaean kingship, see Burkert (n. 4), 49–50, with references. On Iron Age 'kingship', cf. R. Drews, *Basileus: The Evidence for Geometric Kingship* (New Haven, Conn., 1983); B. Qviller, 'The Dynamics of the Homeric Society', *Symbolae Osloenses* 67 (1985), 109–55. See also de Polignac, *La Naissance* (n. 5), 85–92.

[38] Cf. the Cult Centre at Mycenae and Amyklai (above, n. 35); see Wright, this volume (Ch. 3).

[39] De Polignac, *La Naissance* (n. 5), 38–9 and n. 42.

of Bronze Age remains. These cases cannot be considered further without first discussing Bronze Age tombs and habitation sites.

Tombs

The treatment of Mycenaean tombs in the Iron Age (and after) has engendered several competing interpretations. Though my views on tomb and hero cult are set out in detail elsewhere,[40] a brief summary follows. I separate hero cult from tomb cult on the basis of a few observations: 1) Archaic hero cults which can be identified with confidence are never located at Mycenaean tombs; 2) tomb cults which are located at Bronze Age tombs are uniformly anonymous; 3) tomb cults are occasional rituals, often one-time visits, not true cults marked by festivals, monumentalization, and duration; 4) the reuse of these tombs for burial seems to exclude hero cult for Mycenaean tombs; 5) tomb cult does not evolve into hero cult: tomb cult continues, with varying intensity and frequency, into the Classical period and beyond; 6) the literary descriptions of hero cult, which claim that a hero's tomb and bones are essential, describe the cult of relics which characterized the Archaic and Classical periods, rather than the Iron Age, and these relics did not have to originate in Mycenaean tombs.[41]

While ritual activity at Mycenaean tombs in the eighth century BC has been considered hero cult, an interpretation of votive deposits at Bronze Age tombs as a form of ancestor cult has emerged, and the term tomb cult is often applied, a usage made here as well.[42] The reuse of Mycenaean tombs in the Iron Age for burials, however, has gone relatively unnoticed. This reuse is a recurring, though intermittent, feature of the archaeological record for Greece throughout antiquity to the Christian era. Funerary reuse is not the only reuse, either. Both tholos and chamber tombs were transformed into kilns, mills, reservoirs, and shelter for people and animals.[43] The varieties of reuse must condition any assessment of the meanings of reuse in post-Bronze Age periods.

Iron Age reuse of tombs and adoption of earlier monuments includes those as early as the Middle Helladic period. Variable uses are evident even in prehistory: at Mycenae, Grave Circle A was carefully preserved and incorporated

---

[40] I have covered much of this ground in 'The Archaeology of Ancestors', in C. Dougherty and L. Kurke (edd.), *Cultural Poetics of Archaic Greece* (Cambridge, 1993), 46–70.

[41] Ibid. See also my article, 'Contesting the Past: Tomb Cult, Hero Cult, and Epic in Early Greece', *AJA* 98 (1994), 389–410.

[42] Hero cult: J. Coldstream, 'Hero-cults in the Age of Homer', *JHS* 96 (1976), 8–17 is a basic study. Ancestor cult: for comprehensive treatment, see Antonaccio (n. 36). See also A. Snodgrass, 'Les Origines du culte des héros dans la Grèce antique', in G. Gnoli and J.-P. Vernant (edd.), *La Mort, les morts dans les sociétés anciennes* (Cambridge, 1982), 107–19; 'The Archaeology of the Hero', *AION* 10 (1988), 19–26, and V. Lambrinoudakis, 'Veneration of Ancestors in Geometric Naxos', in R. Hägg, N. Marinatos and G. C. Nordquist (edd.), *Early Greek Cult Practice* (Stockholm, 1988), 235–46.

[43] Coldstream (n. 42); A. Snodgrass, *The Dark Age of Greece* (Edinburgh, 1971), 191–4, and Morris (n. 23), 182–3, all remarked the reuse of Bronze Age tombs without drawing any particular conclusions. See Antonaccio (n. 36) and (n. 40).

into the Late Helladic defensive circuit, while Grave Circle B was left outside the walls. The Tomb of Aegisthus encroached upon the second Grave Circle, which rather than indicating disregard or disrespect for the early monument, perhaps forms a deliberate gesture which co-opted an older monument into the mound of the tholos. Late Helladic votive deposits were made around the curb wall of the mound, as well as further burials.[44] There is a continuum of such practice from the Bronze Age to the Iron, though not continuity at any one monument or grave or site. Post-Bronze Age funerary reuse may be linked with the votive deposits (tomb cult). This is clearly different from hero cult and better related to tomb cult, especially in the early Iron Age in the Argolid and Messenia.[45]

The practice of tomb cult was contested in the later Iron Age, no longer restricted to local élites; true hero cult perhaps first developed in the singular polis of Sparta, while tomb cult continued into the seventh and sixth centuries in the Ionian islands, the Argolid, and Attica.[46] Three early hero cults are always mentioned: Menelaus and Helen at Therapne (Lakonia), Agamemnon near the citadel at Mycenae, and Odysseus in the Polis cave on Ithaka. While the Iron Age origins of the last two as hero cults have been questioned, it remains true that none of these are located at Mycenaean tombs. Menelaus and Helen's shrine is built at the premier Bronze Age palace site in Lakonia; the shrine identified with Agamemnon at Mycenae is located near a Bronze Age bridge opposite the Treasury of Atreus, nearly a kilometre from the citadel, and can only be confidently assigned to Agamemnon in the fourth century. The cave on Ithaka was probably a Bronze Age shrine, and identified with Odysseus in the Hellenistic period only. Prior to that, cults of Athena, Hera, and the Nymphs are attested.[47]

Monumental tombs in other prehistoric cultures (for example, megaliths in Europe, and native American burial mounds in North America) may have served as territorial markers, as expanding population put pressure on resources in the form of arable land or subsistence territory. Their significance changed through time, as subsistence strategies, environment, and population fluctuate, and the landscape becomes marked with these cultural traces. In Iron Age Greece, monumental chamber and tholos tombs from the Bronze Age may

[44] Discussed in Antonaccio (n. 36), ch. 2 and (n. 40). See on this E. Protonotariou-Deïlaki, 'The Tumuli of Mycenae and Dendra', in R. Hägg and G. Nordquist, *Celebrations of Death and Divinity in the Bronze Age Argolid* (Stockholm, 1990), 85–106, and 'Burial Customs and Funerary Rites in the Prehistoric Argolid', pp. 69–83 in the same volume. Cf. E. French, 'Cult Places, and "Dynamis" in the Archaeological Record at Mycenae', in M. Mackenzie and C. Roueché (edd.), *Images of Authority*, PCPS Suppl. 16 (1989), 122–30.
[45] For specifics, cf. above, n. 41.
[46] Detailed in Antonaccio (n. 36) and (n. 40).
[47] See Antonaccio (n. 36), ch. 4 and (n. 40); Morgan and Whitelaw (n. 29), 89–90, for Agamemnon, and recently W. D. E. Coulson, 'The "Protogeometric" from Polis Reconsidered', BSA 86 (1991), 43–64.

have symbolized access to resources without actual continuity in their use; their reuse stakes claims to the ancestors.[48] Hero cults, located at non-mortuary sites, were creations of the polis, each according to specific circumstances, manipulating local history perhaps in competition with, or as an extension of, the ancestor cults at Mycenaean tombs.

Palace and Settlement Sites

After the end of the Bronze Age three possibilities for Bronze Age palace and settlement sites (apart from permanent abandonment) emerged: some were reinhabited in the Iron Age or later; some became burial areas; others were transformed into sanctuaries. There is no formula which will fit all circumstances, and local variations again come into play.

The number of sites to consider is limited: Athens, Tiryns, Mycenae, Therapne (Lakonia), and Pylos. Several of these were touched on earlier in discussing the issue of cultural and religious continuity.[49] At Athens, the Acropolis became the sanctuary of Athena Polias, but we have no information on any Bronze Age cult on the site. At Tiryns, the megaron itself was once thought to have been reconstructed as a shrine in the Geometric period, and was assigned to Hera on the evidence of a votive deposit found nearby. The megaron reconstruction has been redated to LH IIIC, though Schwandner has recently discussed other evidence for monumental architecture on the site. Hera is not the only candidate for a sanctuary, either: cults of Athena, Herakles, and Zeus in the late seventh or early sixth century are epigraphically attested.[50] Meanwhile, Mycenae's acropolis sees construction of a temple in the seventh century, assigned to Athena on the basis of an inscribed bronze plaque, but perhaps belonging to Hera.[51] At Pylos, on the other hand, which was not a fortified citadel, no sanctuary ever arose; there is some evidence for a post-destruction habitation in the early Iron Age, but its extent and purposes are not clear as yet.[52]

Thus former habitation and palace sites were often transformed in the Iron

---

[48] See e.g. R. Chapman, 'Archaeological Theory and Communal Burial in Prehistoric Europe', in I. Hodder, G. Isaac, and N. Hammond (edd.), *Pattern of the Past* (Cambridge, 1981); 'The Emergence of Formal Disposal Areas and the "Problem" of Megalithic Tombs in Prehistoric Europe' in R. Chapman, I. Kinnes, and K. Randsborg (edd.), *The Archaeology of Death* (Cambridge, 1981), 71–81. I am grateful to D. Charles for his discussion of the North American Midwest with me.

[49] Above, pp. 79–81, 86–92.

[50] See above, n. 36. On the epigraphic evidence, M. Jameson and I. Papachristodoulou, 'Die archaischen Inschriften von Tiryns', *Akten VI. Int. Kongresses gr. u. lat. Epigraphik* (Munich, 1973), 421–5; N. Verdelis *et al.*, 'Archaikai epigraphai ek Tirynthos', *AE* (1975), 150–205. See E. L. Schwandner, 'Archaische Spolien aus Tiryns: Ausgrabungen in Tiryns 1982/83', *AA* (1988), 269–84.

[51] N. Klein, 'A New Study of the Archaic and Hellenistic Temples at Mycenae', *AJA* 97 (1993), 336–7 (abstract). Other cults at the citadel include Perseus; Enyalios is discussed below.

[52] See W. Coulson, *The Dark Age Pottery of Messenia*, SIMA 43 (Stockholm, 1986); M. Popham, 'Pylos: Reflections on the Date of its Destruction and on its Iron Age Reoccupation', *OJA* 10 (1991), 315–24; C. Griebel and M. Nelson, 'Post-Mycenaean Occupation at the Palace of Nestor', *AJA* 97 (1993), 331 (abstract).

Age into sanctuaries, probably unrelated to any prior cult activity, but symbolic of a unified community. For Sparta, a hero shrine was constructed at Therapne where the major Bronze Age site was located, a monumental symbol of authority utilizing transformed ancestors. In a few cases, former habitation sites become locations for burials, a further link to ancestors.[53] Former habitation sites, therefore, were put to different uses in different areas: there is no Panhellenic template. The key to their use is their location in space, and their local history.

Argos and its Boundaries

Argos is critical to all studies of the Bronze Age and Iron Age because it furnishes the greatest amount of information. The Argive plain, though small, is clearly defined by sea and mountains.[54] In de Polignac's bipolar model, the Argive Heraion forms one pole, and the settlement (and its sanctuaries) is the other. At Argos, there are two peaks, the Aspis and the Larissa, rather than a single acropolis; the Aspis may have been the citadel in the Bronze Age. Each peak was the location of sanctuaries in the Classical period: the ravine called the Deiras, where tomb cult was extensively practised in the Bronze Age cemetery, was in the historical period the location of a sanctuary of Apollo Pythaios and one of Athena Oxyderkes. The Larissa had another sanctuary of Athena Polias and one of Zeus Larissaios, and one of Hera Akraia on the slope; it also produced a seventh-century dedication to Enyalios. Geometric and Archaic sherds and an Archaic votive deposit of the seventh–sixth century were recovered on the Deiras; Foley notes that there is no preserved architecture from earlier than the sixth century, but extends cult activity to the Iron Age on the basis of the other finds. Eighth- and seventh-century votives from the Larissa cannot be readily connected with any of the cults of the Classical period.[55] But ritual activity does seem demonstrable on the heights of Argos in the late Iron Age, complementing that at the Heraion.

De Polignac, focusing on Argos and her neighbours and rivals, has also suggested a special role for non-urban sanctuaries in the earlier Iron Age. These second-order sanctuaries, according to de Polignac, were critical in two ways. First, they served as common ground on which the élites of various communities met to compete. Second, they served as arenas for competition within local élites. In this model, during the ninth century, these sanctuaries need not have

---

[53] As at Naxos: Lambrinoudakis (n. 42), and the Athenian Acropolis, and Asine (see below).

[54] See Morgan and Whitelaw (n. 29), 80–2 with references.

[55] See R. Hope Simpson and O. T. P. K. Dickinson, *A Gazetteer of Aegean Civilisation in the Bronze Age*, i: *The Mainland and Islands*, SIMA 52 (Göteborg, 1979), 43–5 (site A8); Foley (n. 36), 139–40; Schachter (n. 3), 12–13; Morgan and Whitelaw (n. 29), 84. The cults are described by Pausanias 2. 24. 1–2. Cf. the 7th-century sanctuary of Enyalios near Mycenae (below).

been monopolized by any single community, but by the eighth century the control of a sanctuary like the Argive Heraion or the Amyklaion by Argos or Sparta respectively would be a powerful claim to territorial control. De Polignac touches briefly on the issue of the location of Bronze Age remains at these sites, but only as an adjunct factor to their position in the *chora*.[56]

I suggest that in the case of Argos and the Heraion, the concentration of chamber tombs at Prosymna perhaps attracted the sanctuary, after tomb cult played itself out in significance. The location of this sanctuary, on the margins of the Argive plain, is peculiarly well suited to articulate Argive claims to this territory, as well as provocative in relationship to Mycenae and Tiryns. The presence of the chamber tombs, though, must not have been coincidental in the choice of this site. In fact, tomb cult including reuse of the Prosymna cemetery cannot be confidently ascribed to a particular community: Mycenae and Argos may have both been involved.[57] Certainly, the Mycenaeans and Argives were both practising tomb cult in the chamber and tholos tombs located close to their own citadels, and the tombs of Prosymna located between them would be a suitable venue for symbolic conflict.[58] Furthermore, a 'Secondary Shrine', located near the tholos at the western limit of the Prosymna chamber tomb cemetery, was founded in the Late Geometric period. It lies near the old Bronze Age route from Prosymna to Mycenae, and was interpreted by Carl Blegen as an outlying altar of the main shrine of the Heraion. I have argued that it may in fact predate the construction of the monumental Old Temple Terrace, and its placement out in the direction of Mycenae might be a ritual gesture defending the Prosymna tombs, which do not clearly belong to any contemporary settlement, against Mycenaean claims.[59]

This argument, however, is largely made from location; it does not consider types of finds and their origins, nor what they might tell us of the actors in ritual activity. Morgan has suggested that Argive ceramic style in particular undergoes 'politicization' during the course of the Iron Age, and (consciously or not) expresses 'increased communication, interaction, and presumably competitive emulation between sites', among communities on the plain.[60] By contrast, Argive metalwork was from an early date much more widely distributed, and influenced by outside contacts, than pottery. Left unexplored,

---

[56] See de Polignac, this volume (Ch. 1), on the presence of tombs at Prosymna and the issue of continuity. The 9th century is little attested at the Heraion: I cannot agree with Strøm (n. 28) on the early Iron Age at the Heraion.

[57] De Polignac, in his discussion of the Heraion delivered at the French School in Athens in 1990 (n. 5 above), claims this activity for members of the Argive élite, but I do not see that the evidence makes this conclusion necessary.

[58] Submycenaean burials in this area could either be evidence for local habitation, or for the transport of corpses from elsewhere for burial. De Polignac interprets all tomb activity as cult.

[59] See further below and Antonaccio (n. 9), 103–4.

[60] Morgan and Whitelaw (n. 29), 101; similar arguments for Achaia in Morgan (n. 25), *passim*.

however, is the issue of local context. Unfortunately, at the Argive Heraion it is difficult to be specific about the local place of origin for pottery insufficiently studied, now often lost, and described according to decorative scheme only as 'Geometric', 'Argive', and '(Proto)corinthian'. The overwhelming majority of pottery from the Heraion is Argive, with small numbers of imports from Corinth and possibly Lakonia.[61] Foley observes that two specifically votive terracotta types, pomegranates and cakes, are found only at the Heraion, Tiryns, and Argos.[62] While she claims that variations in the colour of fabric among the Argive material can be accounted for 'if one takes into account the fact that worshippers may have brought these vases from all over the Argolid', Morgan and Whitelaw have argued that Foley generally 'underestimates the degree of site-specific variation in fabric' in Argive production.[63] If we accept that both ceramic style and ritual action make statements about identity, we must then consider what it means to find a seventh-century child burial in a Corinthian-style Subgeometric krater in a chamber tomb at Mycenae. Another conundrum is a kotyle at the Secondary Shrine on the road between Mycenae and the Argive Heraion, inscribed in what is identified as Kleonian script.[64] It is as clearly unsatisfactory to assume simply that individuals from Corinth or Kleonai were responsible for these circumstances, as it is unnecessary to assume that foreign objects require foreign visitors at sanctuaries. Attempts to match votive types with types of cult have also been unsatisfactory, and we may not be able to expect that general patterns in artefact use and meaning will always apply everywhere.

The placement of the Old Temple Terrace and Old Temple in conjunction with the Prosymna cemetery may be directly competitive with the citadel cults at Mycenae, Tiryns, and Asine, but would form an extension of Argive power into the plain, since Argos had its own acropolis as well. Such a strategy did not involve Argive fabrication of a Mycenaean ruin in the eighth century, however, as is commonly held; the Old Temple and Terrace probably date to the first half of the seventh century, and the structural and display functions of the Terrace, rather than deliberate archaism, determine its form.[65] But its construction by the Argive state, coming after the destruction of Asine, is a massive

---

[61] Cf. the discussion of Isthmia and Perachora by Morgan in this volume (Ch. 5).

[62] Foley (n. 36), 65.

[63] Ibid.; Morgan and Whitelaw (n. 29), 92 n. 60. On this subject see also Strøm (n. 28).

[64] L. Jeffery, *The Local Scripts of Archaic Greece* (Oxford, 1990), 149, 150 no. 11, and pl. 25. Jeffery had initially (and tentatively) attributed this to Kleonai, but commented that it might also be Tirynthian; she excluded an Argive origin because of the form of epsilon used. Even the discovery of the Tiryns inscriptions (here n. 50), which show that the Tirynthian script is in fact very close to the Argive, still allows for a Kleonian origin.

[65] See J. Wright, 'The Old Temple Terrace at the Argive Heraeum and the Early Cult of Hera in the Argolid', *JHS* 102 (1982), 186–201; Antonaccio (n. 36) and (n. 9); Strøm (n. 28); J. Hall, 'How Argive was the "Argive" Heraion? The Political and Cultic Geography of the Argive Plain 900–400 BC', *AJA* 99 (1995), 577–613.

Argive demonstration of power, and settled the argument over ritual control of Prosymna. The Mycenaeans in the seventh century ritually defended their north-western border with a sanctuary of Enyalios, and posted other markers in their citadel cult (or cults), including the sanctuary at the Chaos, and continuing tomb cult at the chamber tombs and tholoi.[66] As de Polignac has observed, the Argives also staked their claims at the Deiras chamber tombs and with cults on the Larissa and Aspis. Perhaps the same transformation, from tomb cult to sanctuary, can be followed there as at the Heraion.

Finally, at Asine, destroyed by Argos in the late eighth century, tomb cult again can be attested, with reuse or deposit as early as Protogeometric. This activity took place in the tombs on Barbouna, the mount opposite the ancient acropolis. Interestingly, it was this eminence, not the prehistoric acropolis, which was the ultimate site for a cult of Apollo Pythaios, and Protogeometric tombs were located in the lower city of the prehistoric settlement. Apparently, activity continued at this sanctuary even after the Argive destruction.[67] The limited autonomy of this community as well as Mycenae and Tiryns into the Archaic and early Classical period may explain continued cult at these sites, even after the foundation of the Heraion, as a form of local resistance.

Though the cult trajectory of Argos has become a major exemplum since de Polignac, this is probably no more appropriate than to regard Athens as a typical polis. The use of Bronze Age remains varies regionally, and while élite communication and mutual awareness, as well as competition, would account for the Panhellenic distribution of these behaviours, they need not all mean the same thing.[68] As in so much else, we must allow for the operation of local tradition and variation. This seems acutely important in Lakonia, and Athens is a different story again.

Sparta: Another Model

The heartland of Lakedaimon was topographically bounded by the two for-midable ranges of Taygetos on the west and Parnon on the east, sectioned by the Eurotas river, and limited absolutely by the Aegean Sea to the south and east. The additional territory under control of the Spartans was liable to

---

[66] Morgan and Whitelaw (n. 29), 106, state: 'The key to Mycenae in regional terms must lie in its location near the principal passes into the Corinthia, and when domination of the territory of the plain became a really pressing issue, probably during the latter part of the eighth century, one might expect Argos to show a greater interest in this area. Signs of local independence at Mycenae, including distinctive Subgeometric pottery, linger relatively late and accord well with the trend of potentially threatening divergence from Argos.'

[67] Foley (n. 36), 142–3 with references; Schachter (n. 3), 13 (but destruction of Asine is end of the 8th, not end of the 7th century). Discussion: Morgan and Whitelaw (n. 29), 83 and Antonaccio (n. 36), Chs. 2 and 4.

[68] See Antonaccio (n. 9) and (n. 40).

fluctuation. Schachter claims the 'main limitary sanctuaries' of Karyai and Limnai were those dedicated to Artemis, delimiting the northern and western borders with Arkadia and Messenia. Unfortunately, we again have no archaeological evidence to draw upon for the antiquity or form of these shrines.[69]

The known early sanctuaries of Sparta construct a different sort of cultic landscape from that of Argos (or Athens), and Bronze Age traces play a perhaps unique role.[70] Sparta's social structure was unique among Greek communities; it was also anomalous for a polis that the settlement was dispersed and unwalled. Five villages made up the 'city': Pitana, Limnai, Mesoa, and Kynosoura grouped around the acropolis; Amyklai, the fifth, was apparently added, at some early but controversial date.[71] Sparta's central sanctuary, located on the Spartan acropolis, belonged to Athena; a major sanctuary crucially important to Spartan transition rituals, that of Artemis Orthia, was located in the marshes on the west bank of the Eurotas river. South of this core, the outlier Amyklai harboured the sanctuary of Apollo Hyakinthos, which presents one of the strongest cases for continuity with the Bronze Age (though not incontrovertible; see above). Alexandra or Kassandra together with Agamemnon also had a cult near this sanctuary; it had its start in the eighth century and continued until at least the Hellenistic period.[72] An early cult was also located at Therapne, site of the Menelaion, built on the ruins of the major Bronze Age site in Lakonia, dominating the plain. The Dioskouroi were also associated with this location, but there is nothing in the way of archaeological evidence to confirm this.[73]

These locations circumscribe the core of Sparta *per se*. Lakedaimon, however, was a much bigger, and variable, area, one which changed over time as the Spartans annexed Messenia, the borderlands of Arkadia and Argos (Thyreatis, Aigytis, Skiritis, Belminatis, and Triphylia), and made attempts on Arkadia itself.[74] Furthermore, two very different social-political (and perhaps ethnic)

---

[69] Schachter (n. 3), 35.

[70] A different view of Lakonian cultic landscape: C. Calame, 'Spartan Genealogies: The Mythological Representation of a Spatial Organisation', in J. Bremmer (ed.), *Interpretations of Greek Mythology* (Totowa, NJ, 1986), 153–86.

[71] See Cartledge (n. 17), 107–8 for the villages of Sparta.

[72] See above. I am not convinced by identifications of several *heroa* in Lakonia: one, within the confines of Sparta herself near the Eurotas and ascribed to Astrabakos; the others are at Angelona and Chrysapha. See Antonaccio (n. 36), Ch. 3, and (n. 40). On Agamemnon/Alexandra, see also the work of G. Salapata, 'Lakonian Plaques and their Relation to the Stone Reliefs', *Akten des XIII. internazionalen Kongress für klassische Archäologie* (Mainz, 1990), 525; 'Pausanias 3.19.6: The Sanctuary of Alexandra at Amyklai', *AJA* 95 (1991), 331 (abstract).

[73] Alkman fr. 7; cf. S. Wide, *Lakonische Kulte* (Leipzig, 1893), 309–25; Salapata (n. 72). On the Lakonian 'hero reliefs', which appear to be related to the Dioskouroi and the Spartan double kingship, see D. Hibler, 'Three Reliefs from Sparta', and J. M. Sanders, 'The Early Lakonian Dioskouroi Reliefs', both in J. M. Sanders (ed.), ΦΙΛΟΛΑΚΩΝ: *Lakonian Studies in Honour of Hector Catling* (Athens, 1992), 115–22 and 205–10.

[74] Cartledge (n. 17), fig. 1 and ch. 7; J. Christien Tregaro, 'De Sparte à la côte orientale du Péloponnèse', in M. Piérart (ed.), *Polydipsion Argos*, BCH Suppl. 22 (Paris, 1992), 157–70.

statuses marked this system: the helots and the *perioikoi*. This is not the place to embark on a necessarily complex discussion of the origins of these two groups; it is enough, and uncontroversial, to note their clearly differentiated status and distribution. The *perioikoi* inhabited both Lakonia and Messenia after the conquest, with the exception of the five villages mentioned which were the preserve of the Spartans; they were free but not of equal status with the Spartans. The helots, however, were essentially slaves, scattered on the land owned by the Spartan citizens, enjoying certain limited rights to property, marriage, and asylum. Many aspects of Sparta's material culture and cult were also peculiar, and Lakonia would appear to be a likely test case for the expression of difference through material culture.[75] The lack of archaeological information for this enormous region is proverbial, and immediately imposes limits on analysis. Still, little evidence in literature, and less in archaeology, attests to specifically helot cults or their participation in cults already mentioned. Even the *perioikoi*, with their own sanctuaries and festivals, apparently adopted the same divinities and practices as their Spartiate masters, and also participated in some Spartan rituals. Furthermore, similar forms of votives, reliefs, and other artefacts are distributed throughout Lakonia.[76]

I have noted elsewhere that among features unique to Sparta were the early cults of epic figures, Helen and Menelaus, and a relative paucity of tomb cult, though this last point should not be pushed too far given the state of our evidence. The few instances of tomb cult, however, are suggestive: at Pellana and Analipsis, on the border with Arkadia, and at Epidauros Limera, in what would be (presumably) perioikic country. These are areas of stress from early in Lakonian history. On the other hand, Messenia featured intense tomb cult until the end of the eighth century, and then again in the late Classical period. This periodicity corresponds to Sparta's conquest of the area and then to Messenian independence. Interestingly, some of the most important examples of Lakonian Iron Age pottery come from these tombs, again raising the question of how style and material culture express identity.[77]

Schachter claims that 'Where other poleis tried to bind the different elements of their populations together, the Spartans were concerned to keep them apart. The sanctuaries we know about are mostly those of the ruling class and represent

---

[75] See Cartledge (n. 17), 94–100, 160–95; R. Osborne, *Classical Landscape with Figures* (London, 1987), 121–3. On Sparta's material culture: C. Rolley, 'Le Problème de l'art laconien', *Ktema* 2 (1977), 125–40.

[76] R. Parker, 'Spartan Religion', in A. Powell, (ed.), *Classical Sparta: Techniques Behind her Success*, Oklahoma Series in Classical Culture 1 (Norman, Okla., 1988), 142–72: cf. n. 15: 'Spartans often used and may in some cases have controlled sanctuaries in perioecic territory: the details of ownership, rights of access and administrative responsibility are wholly unknown.'

[77] Antonaccio (n. 36), ch. 2; cf. W. D. E. Coulson, 'Geometric Pottery from Volimidia', *AJA* 92 (1988), 53–74.

its overriding concern with military and political supremacy.'[78] This statement is made categorically and ahistorically, however. It is essential to consider when Lakonian sanctuaries were established, when the state invested in each location and what evidence there is for the interaction of different groups at these locations. This is precisely the sort of evidence lacking for Lakonia. Unification of the scattered core villages was enacted with the cults of Athena Chalkioikos, Artemis Orthia, and the Amyklaian cults, which linked the fifth village in the network. The Menelaion represents a strategy of élite legitimation and self-definition, which is also expressed by its position dominating the territory. I have also suggested that the Spartan construction of the Menelaion parallels and competes with Argive monumentalization of the Heraion.[79] The choice of a site with habitation remains from the Bronze Age is common to both sites. The complex of cults at Amyklai is focused on an important Bronze Age site.[80] The liminal sanctuaries of Karyai and Limnai mentioned by Schachter, and disputed with Arkadia and Messenia, apparently belong to a later phase of state and boundary definition.

Athens and Introspection

Athens has one of the largest territories of any polis (though Sparta wins the prize), and this fact alone conditions any consideration of cultic landscape. Its chief natural boundary was the sea; the mountains surrounding the Attic plain were no obstacle to the inclusion of the *mesogeia* in the political unification of Athens by the Archaic period. The central Athenian settlement was always focused on the Acropolis, and some have proposed that the countryside was resettled from this centre during the Iron Age.[81] Divisions among the population in the territory were expressed in terms very different from those on the Argive plain or Lakonia. Athenian use and reuse of the past differs, too. The Acropolis was discussed earlier; the Bronze Age citadel, and a dominant topographical feature of the landscape, makes apt de Polignac's designation of it as the central pole for the state. Only Eleusis was as important a sanctuary in Attica; its early history, and relation to Athens itself, is fiercely debated. Much later than the late Iron Age, the Peisistratids unified Attica, cultically and politically.[82]

---

[78] Schachter (n. 3), 34.

[79] Interestingly, Lakonian Iron Age pottery is known at the Heraion: see Cartledge (n. 17), 83, 99 (Protogeometric, doubtful), 135. On the Menelaion, see now R. A. Tomlinson, 'The Menelaion and Spartan Architecture', and R. W. V. Catling, 'A Votive Deposit of Seventh-Century Pottery from the Menelaion', both in Sanders (n. 73), 247–55 and 57–75 respectively.

[80] See Antonaccio (n. 9).

[81] See Osborne (n. 75), 128–30; A. Snodgrass, 'The Rural Landscape and its Political Significance', *Opus* 6/7 (1987/89), 53–70, at 60–2; J. Whitley, 'Early States and Hero Cults: A Re-appraisal', *JHS* 108 (1988), 173–82, for Attic tomb cult as local resistance to this internal colonization.

[82] Two items from a vast bibliography: H. A. Shapiro, *Art and Cult under the Tyrants in Athens* (Mainz, 1989) and R. Garland, *Introducing New Gods: The Politics of Athenian Religion* (Ithaca, NY, 1992).

Athenian material culture presents the most complete, continuous, and best understood sequence in antiquity. As distinct from the patterning observed by Morgan for the Argive plain and Achaia, Attic pottery is widely distributed and does not locally vary to the degree observed in the Argolid and Achaia. One exception occurs in the seventh century, with a split between early Orientalizing forms and Subgeometric. James Whitley has suggested that the contexts differ in which these contemporaneous forms are found: the elaborate, innovative, and eastern-influenced styles from high status graves in the Kerameikos and the Attic countryside; the Subgeometric from ritual contexts like the sanctuary on Mt. Hymettos. Whitley suggests that Protoattic 'is best understood as an exclusive, elite style, with a restricted range of uses ... whereby the aristocratic elite helped to define itself through a restricted access to the Orientalizing iconography and heroic or mythological subject matter'.[83] If the split in style can be so understood, it is the first time that such a pattern has been observed for Athenian material culture. It remains to be seen if this sort of pattern can be observed earlier.

The cultic strategies of tomb cult and hero cult, particularly the latter, can be traced in Attica. Athens is famous for the multiplicity of her heroes and heroines, named, epic, and totally obscure. Yet there is little early evidence for hero cult; it seems to emerge clearly only in the Archaic period. Nock pointed out long ago that Athenian hero cult (as seen in epigraphical evidence) did not require a tomb, at least not in the historical period, and early hero cult may be archaeologically invisible in Attica.[84] Tomb cult, however, has an interesting distribution. The major concentrations (so far as known) are at the West Cemetery at Eleusis, in the Agora, and at Thorikos. There is none at the major Late Helladic chamber tomb cemetery at Perati; other, less extensive instances occur in chamber tombs at Aliki (Glyphada) and near the north slope of the Acropolis. These correspond to the dispersed pattern of Iron Age settlement; their distribution, with few on the borders, may also reflect the inward-looking character proposed for Athenian society at this time.[85] The majority of this activity occurs at the core settlement (Agora, north slope), the shore (Aliki), the country (Menidhi), and the Megarian border (Eleusis), and prefigures the divisions which feature prominently in Athenian history and politics of the

---

[83] See Morgan and Whitelaw (n. 29), 93, about assumptions for similar social function of ceramics in different areas; cf. J. Whitley, 'Protoattic Pottery: A Contextual Approach', in I. Morris, *Classical Greece: Ancient Histories and Modern Archaeologies* (Cambridge, 1994), 51–70.

[84] Definitive on this, using literary evidence: E. Kearns, *The Heroes of Attica*, BICS Suppl. 57 (London, 1989); see A. D. Nock, 'The Cult of Heroes', HThR 37 (1944), 141–74. The earliest reference to heroes is in Drako (as quoted by Porphyry, *De Abstin.* 4. 2), but without any details of the rituals observed.

[85] See J. Whitley, *Style and Society in Dark Age Greece: The Changing Face of a Pre-Literate Society 1100–700 BC* (Cambridge, 1991); 'Social Diversity in Dark Age Greece', BSA 86 (1991), 341–65.

Archaic and Classical periods.[86] It should be kept in mind, however, that this summary thins out the extremely complex interaction with the past which occurs in the Agora as changing use of this area encountered tombs ranging in date from the Bronze Age to the Archaic period, and the manipulation (and creation) of the past on the Acropolis and in Athenian cult.

Conclusions: Pushing the Limits

Cultic landscapes form the original focal point for the papers in this volume. The idea of a sacred landscape, conditioned by methods developed for other cultures, China, for example, or India, represent a perspective different from that usually encountered in Greek sanctuary studies.[87]

Sacred landscapes emerge as both culturally constructed and historically sensitive, immensely variable through time and space ... Far from being immune to developments in other aspects of human life, they can reflect a very wide cultural and political milieu. Yet they also provide more than a simple mirror of change by their active participation in the conditions of social reproduction.[88]

A sacred landscape constructed according to a mythological script seems not to be an appropriate model with which to generalize about Greece: so much about Greek sacred places was not just mutable, but contingent on the variabilities of Greek poleis, their politics, and local traditions. Although Keos, Athens, Sparta, and Argos were all city-states of Old Greece, they differed greatly among themselves: for example, in the size of their territory, patterns of cult, and political institutions. The concept of a scripted sacred landscape may in fact best suit colonial foundations, where ideal civic and sacred space was deliberately laid out in a relatively constricted timeframe, in a context where no Bronze Age traces were encountered, but an indigenous presence instead. It would therefore be inaccurate to consider the colonial landscape a blank slate— natural features and indigenous cults certainly played a role, as did myths, the construction of which construed colonization as a Greek 'return'. Colonies must be seen as special cases, which do not mirror conditions in the mother city, but, if anything, lead the way in organizing space, and therefore of cult.[89]

---

[86] See Antonaccio (n. 36), ch. 3, and (n. 40). Tomb cults at Menidhi and Thorikos both have a long duration, in marked contrast to the usual one or two incidents. It remains the case that neither of these cults is ever named or monumentalized. If ancestor, rather than hero cult, this durability may be an Attic variation on the pattern, or an example of an anonymous hero *per se* which the written record for Athens records later.

[87] I am grateful to my colleague P. Wagoner for sharing his work on Vijayanagara with me.

[88] S. Alcock, *Graecia Capta: The Landscapes of Roman Greece* (Cambridge, 1993), 172–214 at 172.

[89] Cf. de Polignac, *La Naissance* (n. 5), ch. 3. For colonial sites, see esp. I. Malkin, *Religion and Colonization in Ancient Greece* (Leiden, 1987), esp. 135–86 and on Etruscan and Greek Italy, I. Edlund, *The Gods and the Place: Location and Function of Sanctuaries in the Countryside of Etruria and Magna Graecia (700–400 BC)* (Stockholm, 1987), and, recently, B. Bergquist, 'The Archaic Temenos in Western Greece: A Survey and Two Inquiries', in Schachter (n. 2), 109–52.

Greek 'sacred landscape' is constructed differently in different times and places, and depends very strongly on local knowledge.[90] For the Classical period, Christiane Sourvinou-Inwood claims that the framework for Greek religion depended on the polis, each city developing a separate system, a claim she extends even to Panhellenic sanctuaries. The differences between poleis arose from their pasts, and were locally expressed in hero cults.[91] An emphasis on identity and ethnicity is a vital part of this local knowledge. I would argue, however, that such formulations are important and useful, but not adequate without a consideration of context and the relations of production. Ceramic style can perhaps be shown to reflect political affiliation, but it is unknown what the categories of material culture, like metal objects, which have a wide circulation outside the home territory, signify. The implications in the assumption that craftsmen travel from Argos to Olympia, or that some Argive painters could work in different communities on the Argive plain, are potentially very important.[92] If only pottery is selected to carry ethnic (intra-group) information for home consumption, while regional style has broader implications and audiences, it would be important to know who is producing these categories of culture and controlling their distribution. What does seem clear is that the venues for display and interaction provided by shared ritual sites like Olympia dictate the use of different categories of material culture. These issues are beyond the scope of this paper, but deserve further research.

It is important to keep in mind, as Alcock remarks in considering Roman Greece (Chapter 11, below), that the reuse of monuments is not frugality. Rather, the rededication (or other manipulation) of monuments taps the past for use in the present. Recycled monuments over time acquire multiple meanings in addition to their original one (which is transformed through myth and local history).[93] In the Greek Iron Age and Archaic period, original messages may be erased when literacy is lost and a massive interruption of population and transformation of culture and society takes place. Yet the significance of durable monuments, whether originally cult places, habitation sites, or tombs, remains;

[90] From C. Geertz, 'Local Knowledge: Fact and Law in Comparative Perspective', in *Local Knowledge: Further Essays in Interpretive Anthropology* (New York, 1983), 167–234. Cf. the comments of Morgan (n. 25) 140; Sourvinou-Inwood (n. 19), 295–322.

[91] Sourvinou-Inwood (n. 19), 295–6, 300–1, citing Thucydides 4. 97. 2–3; 4. 98. 2. The author divorces secular and divine, observing that since sanctuaries could move from the control of one community to that of another, they were thought of as part of the human, and not the divine, world. A polis which controlled a territory also had its sanctuaries, and would retain the rites customary before a change in control: since the gods did not change, and religion was part of a wider system, it was natural that possession of land would include its sanctuaries. See the continuation of this study in 'Further Aspects of Polis Religion', *AION* 10 (1988), 259–74.

[92] Morgan and Whitelaw (n. 29), 92–3; Morgan this volume (Ch. 5) for the presence of Corinthian metalwork in Olympia, but little at the Isthmus.

[93] Alcock (n. 88), 196–8.

though their meaning was mutable and manipulable, their power was still felt.[94] It is significant that so many of the Bronze Age monuments so adopted were tombs. These are well-suited to the creation of ancestors, and of a sense of the depth of time, and this seems to intensify as the Iron Age progresses, along with the struggle between different groups for legitimacy and power.

Bronze Age sites, in different ways, served as anchors in a system of moorings which strengthened or unified a territory, confronting the claims of another state or integrating several communities (as at Prosymna in the Argolid). These anchors, fastening on to a site of past significance, used the past to lay claim to present power. The cables of these anchors could consist of natural features (streams, mountains), or artefacts (cemeteries, walls, roads, and newly created sanctuaries like that of Enyalios at Mycenae). Territories were not formed simply by the natural limits of arable land, nor boundaries by the mountains, rivers, and sea which divide Greek poleis and *ethne* from each other, but were actively structured by the Bronze Age traces in the landscape.[95] Tombs might provide reinforcement, if located at the margins (like Prosymna), or a venue for local display, if near a settlement (Mycenae, Argos, and Attica for instance). It is significant that bona fide hero cults rarely arise at a Mycenaean tomb; rather, one named hero receives cult at a Bronze Age habitation site (Menelaion), though by the sixth century others are 'discovered' and 'transported' to a significant place in a polis. True hero cult is a function of the seventh century, more than the eighth, if separated from tomb cult and predicated on the coalescence of authority and identity which the polis represents.

Cult is located not only to structure physical territory, but to articulate borders at points of contact between different groups. Sanctuary histories feature multigroup competition preceding the monopolization of control by a single community. In the end, they act to dissipate tension, by structuring competition. The proliferation of hero cult, while Panhellenic in scope, is a particularly local phenomenon, intended for home consumption more than the cults in Olympian sanctuaries, but still loaded with significance for outsiders and at times responding to similar, local claims. The struggle over relics in the Archaic and Classical periods embodies this mutual awareness and the importance of such figures for relations between communities.

The peak of tomb cult and the rise of hero cult coincide with the decline of burial as a symbolic arena for display. The expressive and symbolic power of burial was directed into tomb cult, and then into hero cult, over the course of the Iron Age, perhaps by different groups within communities. Hero cult,

---

[94] On long term manipulation of funerary monuments, see J. C. Barrett, 'The Living, the Dead and the Ancestors: Neolithic and Early Bronze Age Mortuary Practices', in J. C. Barrett and I. A. Kinnes (edd.), *The Archaeology of Context in the Neolithic and Bronze Age: Recent Trends* (Sheffield, 1988), 30–41.

[95] On both natural and man-made delineations, see Daverio Rocchi (n. 19), 49–68.

however, as often observed, represents a transformation of the power of the past, not as a devolution of control from some Dark Age kingship to a nobility, but as part of the emergence of certain groups within a community, and certain communities, at the end of the Iron Age. This is the formation of the polis, though even *ethne* felt the need for self-definition and turned to cult to articulate it. But this is another matter.

5

The Evolution of a Sacral 'Landscape': Isthmia, Perachora, and the Early Corinthian State

CATHERINE MORGAN

Royal Holloway, University of London

In *La Naissance de la cité grecque*, François de Polignac described the creation of networks of sanctuaries and shrines as a direct and conscious response to the immediate social and political needs of newly emerging poleis. He thus saw it as an essentially eighth- and seventh-century phenomenon. Whilst recognizing the importance of city-centre shrines as focal points for the expression of community identity, de Polignac laid particular stress on the emergence of sanctuaries situated in marginal or border locations, and especially on their role in cementing relations between town and country and in focusing and defining the inherently ambiguous relationship between the community and its human or divine 'neighbours'. Since these sanctuaries embodied all the relations essential to the polis (linking town and country, human and divine, citizen and non-citizen), for de Polignac their creation represented the 'acte constitutif' of the polis itself.[1]

It is most appropriate that a volume dedicated to the wider exploration of de Polignac's central thesis should include a study of the early development of cult in the Corinthia (Ill.5.1). Not only does this region contain rich 'rural' eighth-century sanctuaries and seventh-century 'urban' and 'rural' temples (which offer the earliest evidence for the Doric order on the Greek mainland), but it has also produced evidence for cult activity dating back to the very start of the Protogeometric period (*c.*1050 BC). Central to this study is a review of this earliest evidence, and in particular, reappraisal of the nature of Mycenaean and Early Iron Age activity at the sanctuary of Poseidon on the Isthmus of Corinth. This is largely based on a new study of material excavated by Oscar Broneer for the University of Chicago during a series of campaigns conducted between 1952 and 1967.[2] Broneer published a small amount of early material

---

[1] F. de Polignac, *La Naissance de la cité grecque* (Paris, 1984), NB ch. 2.

[2] Perachora: H. Payne, *Perachora* i (Oxford, 1940), 27–30; H. Drerup, 'Griechische Baukunst in geometrischer Zeit', in F. Matz and H. G. Buchholz (edd.), *Archaeologia Homerica* ii ch. O (Göttingen, 1969), 28; K. Fagerström, *Greek Iron Age Architecture* (Göteborg, 1988), 38–40. Corinth: H. Robinson,

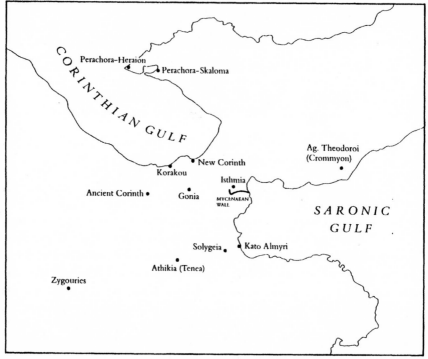

ILL. 5.1 Principal sanctuary and settlement sites in the Late Bronze Age and Early
Iron Age Corinthia

(especially pottery) in his preliminary reports, but the full extent of his discoveries has only recently been revealed. Thanks in no small measure to his policy of retaining a large proportion of all his finds, some 83 kilos of very fragmentary sherds have now been identified from the Protogeometric and Geometric periods alone, along with a variety of metal items and terracottas, a range of evidence which promises rare insights into the nature of cult activity in the Corinthia during the Early Iron Age.[3]

Clearly such material is of interest in its own right, but it also raises issues of

'Temple Hill, Corinth', in U. Jantzen (ed.), *Neue Forschungen in Griechischen Heiligtümern* (Tübingen, 1976), 240–50; 'Excavations at Corinth: Temple Hill 1968–1972', *Hesperia* 45 (1976), 203–39. Isthmia: O. Broneer, *Isthmia*, i: *The Temple of Poseidon* (Princeton, NJ, 1971); *Isthmia*, ii: *Topography and Architecture* (Princeton, NJ, 1973); 'The Isthmian Sanctuary of Poseidon', in Jantzen, *Neue Forschungen*, 39–62; E. Gebhard and F. Hemans, 'University of Chicago Excavations at Isthmia, 1989: I', *Hesperia* 62 (1992), 1–77.

[3] e.g. O. Broneer, 'Excavations at Isthmia: Third Campaign, 1955–1956', *Hesperia* 27 (1958), pls. 12c, 13a. The Mycenaean and Early Iron Age finds are to be published by the present author in a volume in the *Isthmia* series (Princeton, NJ, ASCS forthcoming; henceforth, Morgan, *Isthmia*). I am grateful to Prof. David Mitten and Dr Alastar Jackson for permission to refer to their catalogues of terracottas and arms and armour respectively (to be published as *Isthmia* volumes; both authors have also contributed chapters to Morgan, *Isthmia*).

interpretation which both complement and challenge the framework established by de Polignac in 1984 and considerably developed and revised in his stimulating introduction to this volume. Before moving to examine the material evidence in greater detail, it is therefore worth pausing to consider some of these issues and their implications for the wider application of de Polignac's ideas. De Polignac's analysis was structured from a Classical perspective; his starting point was the cult organization of the Classical polis and his forays into earlier, specifically eighth-century, evidence were conducted with the express aim of understanding the origins of that organization. Although he addresses this bias explicitly in the English edition of his book, these limitations have not been wholly overcome. There is nothing inevitable in the patterns of development of future poleis or *ethne*, and although it would be unwise to underrate the extent of change on a general level, a superficial approach will only obscure its nature and variability. Perhaps more seriously, the Classical polis is such an elusive, transitory and variable phenomenon that it is tempting to regard it as less of a model than a mirage. Not only is de Polignac's analysis focused on the polis, but much of the evidence which he adduces comes specifically from colonies. Although colonies are in some ways paradigm poleis, they are also exceptional as creations forged and maintained in the face of strong and continuing external pressure, and their complexities and traditions therefore differ from those of the old mainland cities (compare, for example, the cult history of Corinth and its colonies, Kerkyra and Syracuse).[4] It might be argued that the polis in its various guises was the most developed and influential form of political organization in the Classical Greek world, yet it was not the only one, and it would be a serious omission to ignore the *ethnos*, especially when examining sanctuary development. It is not simply that much of the richest evidence for pre-eighth-century cult comes from regions which did not develop into poleis (indeed, it is hard to make any meaningful distinction between these two groups of state-forms until the eighth century at the earliest), but from the eighth century onwards, it is very hard to distinguish between sanctuaries in poleis and *ethne*, since their physical form, the nature of offerings made, and

---

[4] De Polignac, *Cults, Territory and the Origins of the Greek City-State* (Chicago, 1995), xii–xiv, 1–9; O. Murray, 'Cities of Reason', in O. Murray and S. Price (edd.), *The Greek City* (Oxford, 1990), 1–25. For a somewhat extreme view of the variability of poleis: E. Ruschenbusch, *Untersuchungen zu Staat und Politik in Griechenland vom 7–4 Jh v. Chr.* (Bamberg, 1978); H.-J. Gehrke, *Jenseits von Athen und Sparta: Das dritte Griechenland und seine Staatenwelt* (Munich, 1986). Equally, the argument that the polis is an essentially modern concept, as presented by W. Gawantka, *Die sogennante Polis: Enstehung, Geschichte und Kritik der modernen althistorischen Grundbegriffe der griechische Staat, die griechische Staatsidee, die Polis* (Stuttgart, 1985), whilst interesting appears overstated. The point is shown clearly in the elaborate ritual structures with which colonies surrounded themselves: I. Malkin, *Religion and Colonisation in Ancient Greece* (Leiden, 1987); I. Edlund, *The Gods and the Place* (Stockholm, 1987), chs. I and IV. I. Malkin, 'Review of de Polignac, *Naissance*', *JHS* 107 (1987), 227–8 makes many of the same criticisms; as he notes, de Polignac's suggestion that colonies were formed gradually is contrary to the mass of literary and historical evidence for emphasis on the act of foundation.

the cults instituted are to all intents and purposes identical. The role of ritual as a means of regulating relations with human and divine 'others' was hardly exclusive to the polis.[5]

As a direct consequence of this focus on the Classical polis, de Polignac's discussion was predicated on a model of pre-polis Greek religion which stressed the contrast between eighth-century developments and the relative scarcity of formalized cult places in earlier periods; his analysis thus betrayed preconceived, if hardly unique, notions about the nature of Early Iron Age cult. Only recently has he allowed issues such as the pattern of incorporation or rejection of pre-existing religious organizations or the existence of indigenous traditions which may influence later developments to become central in his discussion. Rather than pursue individual cases, he assumed that pre-polis institutions were absorbed and emasculated within the new state structure and that this process was cemented by the establishment of a cult for the new state.[6] The resulting model was essentially static; although de Polignac did not deny that change and development occurred within the cult systems of individual regions, he did not allow this to become a central issue. Within many Archaic and Classical poleis, there is considerable evidence for a near-continuous process of rewriting and reshaping of ritual structures which spans many centuries, even though this is often difficult to trace in detail (Athens is a case in point, as Robin Osborne's discussion in this volume shows). Yet even in the case of Athens, it is questionable whether this reshaping ever constituted the total shift which would be required if earlier institutions were to be completely absorbed or emasculated; and if this cannot be traced in Attica, it is even more questionable in a smaller and politically more conservative state like Corinth.[7] If nothing else, the fact that the polis *sensu stricto* occupied a relatively short period of the political life of even the most renowned Classical states should make clear the importance of considering the longer term evol-

[5] C. Morgan, 'Ethnicity and Early Greek States: Historical and Material Perspectives', *PCPS* 37 (1991), 131–63, religion 144–5; ead. *Athletes and Oracles* (Cambridge, 1990), 7–16. I. Morris, 'The Early Polis as City and State', in J. Rich and A. Wallace-Hadrill (edd.), *City and Country in the Ancient World* (London, 1991), 25–57. J. Whitley, *Style and Society in Dark Age Greece* (Cambridge, 1992), ch. 6.

[6] De Polignac (n. 1), 15–31. For a contrary view of the importance of the eighth century, e.g.: C. Sourvinou-Inwood, 'Early Sanctuaries, the Eighth Century and Ritual Space: Fragments of a Discourse', in N. Marinatos and R. Hägg (edd.), *Greek Sanctuaries: New Approaches* (London, 1993) 1–17; C. Sourvinou-Inwood, '*Reading*' Greek Death to the End of the Classical Period* (Oxford, 1994), ch. 2. R. Hägg, N. Marinatos and G. C. Nordquist (edd.), *Early Greek Cult Practice* (Stockholm–Athens, 1988) for a recent conspectus of Early Iron Age (EIA) evidence.

[7] R. Osborne, *Demos: The Discovery of Classical Attika* (Cambridge, 1985). For discussion of myth/cult continuities and innovations accompanying political developments: R. Parker, 'Myths of Early Athens', in J. Bremmer (ed.), *Interpretations of Greek Mythology* (London, 1987) 187–214; E. Kearns, *The Heroes of Attica, BICS* Suppl. 57 (London, 1989); H. Parke, *Festivals of the Athenians* (London, 1977), 183–91. Corinth: J. Salmon, *Wealthy Corinth* (Oxford, 1984), 205–9, 231–9.

ution of cult systems.[8] De Polignac has surely been correct to stress the desir-
ability of investigating the variety of interests expressed at different cult places
within the territory of a particular community, but it is also vital to recognize
that such a system is not a one-time construct but develops through accretion
and builds on tradition.

All of these issues are directly relevant to the case of Corinth and its
sanctuaries. The region was discussed briefly by de Polignac, who mentioned
the case of eighth-century Perachora and noted Isthmia as an example of a
border sanctuary with eighth-century evidence for cult and a major temple
built early in the seventh century. Since he wrote, however, new evidence of a
much earlier shrine at Isthmia has emerged to challenge this picture.[9] The fact
that the cult place at Isthmia can now be seen to have played a collective role
through many centuries, from c.1050 until the sack of Corinth by Mummius
in 146 BC (subsequently being revived during the first century AD), raises directly
the question of its evolving meaning in relation to the nature of the collectivity.
Although this study will focus on just one phase of transition within this long
history (from the eleventh to the seventh century), the issues raised are more
generally applicable.

The Origins of the Isthmian Shrine

Reappraisal of Broneer's results, complemented by a further campaign of excavation in 1989, has now enabled us to form a clear picture of the early history
of the Isthmian sanctuary. The origins of religious activity can be fairly securely
placed at the very beginning of the Protogeometric period (in the mid-eleventh
century BC).[10] Not only does this make Isthmia one of the earliest post-
Mycenaean shrines in the Greek world, comparable to sites like Olympia,
Kalapodi, and Kommos, but it is also worth reiterating that it is one of the very
few early religious sites to have been discovered in an area which was later to
develop into a polis, and which sustained its major communal role through the

---

[8] W. G. Runciman, 'Doomed to Extinction: The Polis as an Evolutionary Dead-end', in Murray
and Price (n. 4), 347–67.

[9] De Polignac (n. 1), 33, 46, 61 (Isthmia); 29, 33–4, 46, 51, 60–1 (Perachora). De Polignac (n. 4),
51–2, takes account of this earlier evidence but continues to emphasize 8th c. change.

[10] The case is presented in Ch. II. 2 of Morgan, *Isthmia* (n. 3). P. Mountjoy and V. Hankey, 'LH IIIC
Late *versus* Submycenaean: The Kerameikos Pompeion Cemetery Reviewed', *Jahrbuch des Deutschen
Archäologischen Instituts* 103 (1988), 26, 33–7 propose to redate the start of Attic and by implication
Argive PG to c.1020/1000, but since nothing in the Isthmia evidence allows us to test this hypothesis, a
relative date remains most reliable.

life of that polis and beyond.[11] The site has produced no evidence of any building
earlier than the first monumental temple (for which the 1989 excavations gave
a *terminus post quem* of 690–650).[12] Evidence for cult activity in earlier times
consists of a concentration of redeposited ash in the south-east temenos which
was packed with animal bone (mostly heavily burnt) and also unburnt pottery.
The pottery forms a continuous sequence from the Earliest Protogeometric to
the Early Protocorinthian period and beyond, and mostly consists of the open
shapes usually associated with drinking and dining. The ash also contained
figurines and jewellery dating from the Late Protogeometric period onwards,
and, from the late eighth century, tripods, artefacts which rarely occur outside
cult contexts. This combination of ash, bone, pottery, and votives clearly points
to cult activity, and since the ash mixture is homogeneous and cannot be divided
chronologically, it must be concluded that the sanctuary was established at the
beginning of the Protogeometric period.[13]

   Prior to this, there is evidence for Mycenaean activity at Isthmia which spans
the period from LH I to LH IIIC Late. Yet the material record from this long
period is very different, and there is no reason to assume that the sanctuary had
Mycenaean origins. Mycenaean evidence consists of a series of small scatters of
pottery with no spatial focus, plus a few small Psi and Phi figurines (which are
not in themselves diagnostic of function); no structures or graves have yet been
discovered.[14] There is nothing here to suggest that Isthmia was anything more
than a small settlement, especially as this pattern of evidence is typical of most
of the eastern Corinthia. In the vicinity of Isthmia (Ill. 5.2), similar sites have
been found in the area of the West Cemetery, the Sacred Glen, and on the
Rachi, and further afield pottery scatters have been identified all around the
Perachora peninsula and on promontories along the coast of the Saronic Gulf.
A small number of tombs dating to the earlier phases of the Mycenaean period

---

[11] Kalapodi: R. Felsch *et al.*, 'Apollon und Artemis oder Artemis und Apollon? Bericht von der Grabungen im neu entdeckten Heiligtum bei Kalapodi, 1973–1977', in R. Hägg and N. Marinatos (edd.),
Sanctuaries and Cults in the Aegean Bronze Age (Stockholm, 1981), 81–9; R. Felsch *et al.*, 'Bericht über die
Grabungen im Heiligtum der Artemis Elaphebolos und des Apollon von Hyampolis 1978–1982', *AA*
(1987), 3–26. Kommos: J. Shaw, 'Excavations at Kommos (Crete) during 1981', *Hesperia* 51 (1982), 164–
95; J. W. Shaw, 'Phoenicians in Southern Crete', *AJA* 93 (1989), 165–83 (temple B). Olympia: Morgan,
Athletes (n. 5), ch. 3; H. Kyrieleis, 'Neue Ausgrabungen in Olympia', *Antike Welt* 21 (1990), 177–88; 'Neue
Ausgrabungen in Olympia', in W. Coulson and H. Kyrieleis (edd.), *Proceedings of an International Symposium
on the Olympic Games* (Athens, 1992), 19–24. A. Mallwitz, 'Cult and Competition Locations at Olympia'
in W. Raschke (ed.), *The Archaeology of the Olympics* (Madison, Wis., 1988), 79–109.
[12] Gebhard and Hemans (n. 2), 39, pl. 13.
[13] C. Morgan and E. Gebhard, in Gebhard and Hemans (n. 2), 9–22. C. Morgan, 'Archaeological
Evidence for Dark Age Cult at Isthmia', *AJA* 92 (1988), 268. Full discussion will appear in Morgan,
Isthmia (see n. 3).
[14] C. Morgan in Gebhard and Hemans (n. 2), 6–9, pl. 8a; Morgan *Isthmia* (n. 3), chs. I. 2 (pottery
cats. 1–180), I. 5 (figurines), I. 6 (context). Function of Mycenaean figurines: E. French, 'The Development of Mycenaean Terracotta Figurines', *BSA* 66 (1976), 101–87; ead. 'Mycenaean Figures and
Figurines: Their Typology and Function', in R. Hägg and N. Marinatos (edd.), *Sanctuaries and Cults of
the Aegean Bronze Age* (Stockholm–Athens, 1981), 173–7.

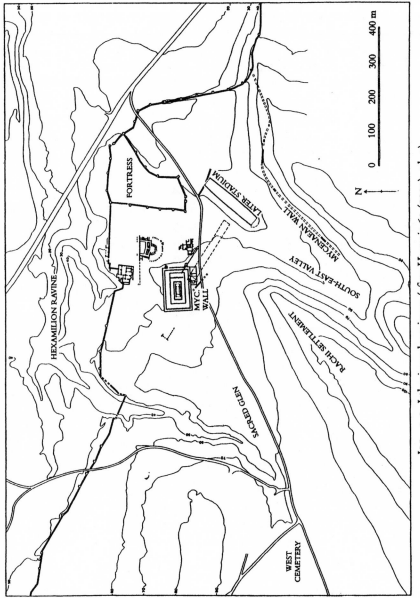

ILL. 5.2 Isthmia and environs (after *Hesperia* 62 (1992), pl. 3)

near Galataki, but from LH IIIA onwards there are also substantial chamber tomb cemeteries at Kato Almyri on the Saronic Gulf, Perachora-Skaloma, and at Yiriza near Gonia. It is very likely (on analogy with evidence from other regions, such as Lakonia) that much early evidence is missing, but it is also possible that at least from LH IIIA onwards, a sizeable proportion of the local population lived in scattered settlements but buried their dead in shared cemeteries (especially as the Kato Almyri cemetery included multiple burials which may perhaps be interpreted as family tombs).[15] Like Isthmia, those sites which have been excavated (cemeteries included) continue no later than LH IIIC. The sole exception is Corinth itself, which has produced evidence of continuous activity into the Early Iron Age in the area of the later sanctuary of Demeter and Kore.[16]

In short, there is nothing to distinguish Mycenaean Isthmia in its local context, and had all activity ceased at the end of LH IIIC the question of a Mycenaean sanctuary would surely never have arisen. On this basis, we should have no hesitation in placing the introduction of cult at the beginning of the Protogeometric period and no earlier. Whatever later developments in myth-history may have been intended to imply, sanctuaries are not by definition primeval and there is no logical reason to question an Early Iron Age origin where this is indicated by the material remains. Unfortunately, there is no evidence with which to identify the deity worshipped at Isthmia, although Poseidon may be a safe assumption, not least since there is nothing to suggest a change in cult. The name Poseidon, apparently referring to a divinity, was already well established (appearing in the LH IIIB Linear B record at both Pylos and Knossos), and it is worth noting the presence of a high percentage of bulls

[15] West Cemetery: *AD* 26 (1971), B 1, 105, pl. 79d (I thank Prof. Tim Gregory for permission to study this material). Mycenaean Corinthia: H. N. Fowler and R. N. Stillwell, *Corinth, i: Introduction, Topography, Architecture* (Cambridge, Mass., 1932), 107–14; C. W. Blegen, 'Corinth in Prehistoric Times', *AJA* 24 (1920), 1–13; J. Wiseman, *The Land of the Ancient Corinthians* (Göteborg, 1979) *passim*; K. Gebauer, 'Forschungen in der Argolis: Korinthia' *AA* (1939), cols. 268–87; Morgan, *Isthmia* (n. 3), app. 3. I thank the Blegen archivist of the American School of Classical Studies in Athens, Dr Carol Zerner, for permission to consult Blegen's accounts of his informal survey work in the Corinthia. Payne (n. 2). 20; T. J. Dunbabin, *Perachora ii: Pottery, Ivories, Scarabs, and Other Objects from the Votive Deposit of Hera Limenia* (Oxford, 1962) 531–2. Kato Almyri (19 chamber tombs forming part of LH IIIA–IIIC cemetery on site of Rachi-Bechri): *AR* 35 (1988/9), 24; *AD* 35 (1980 [1988]), B 102–5. Solygeia/Galataki (LHI–IIIA): N. Verdelis, 'A Sanctuary at Solygeia', *Archaeology* 15 (1962), 185–8. New Corinth graves: Wiseman (n. 15, above), 72–3, figs. 97–100 (erroneously captioned); Corinth NB 272, 70. Old Corinth graves: Corinth NB 207, 153; NB 241, 187 (Pitsa area). Perachora-Skaloma: *AD* 35 (1980 [1988]) B 109–10 for the first phase of a continuing excavation. On tomb distribution and the range of arguments for the social meaning of chamber tomb burial: C. B. Mee and W. Cavanagh, 'The Spatial Distribution of Mycenaean Tombs', *BSA* 85 (1990), 225–43.

[16] J. B. Rutter, 'The Last Myceneans at Corinth', *Hesperia* 48 (1979), 348–92. N. Bookidis and J. E. Fisher, 'Sanctuary of Demeter and Kore on Acrocorinth. Preliminary report V: 1971–73', *Hesperia* 43 (1974), 286–9. I am grateful to Dr Christopher Pfaff for discussion of the EIA pottery in advance of publication.

among the early terracotta figurines at Isthmia (see below pp. 119–20).[17] It is, however, important to stress that nothing can be proved, especially as there is no unequivocal evidence for Poseidon at Isthmia until the sixth century and the appearance of inscriptions and Penteskouphia-style plaques and figurines which stress his maritime attributes (a particularly appropriate association in a city by then renowned for its colonization and trading activity, and where only a fraction of state territory lay more than 10 kilometres from the sea).[18]

Early Activity at Isthmia

Such an early date for the sanctuary naturally raises many questions. It seems most unlikely that its institution had anything to do with a change in population in the Corinthia. Not only is there no positive archaeological evidence for this, but the continuous sequence of activity at Corinth speaks more of peaceful transformation than externally forced change. The reasons for instituting a cult place must therefore lie within contemporary society, and here the nature of activity at the sanctuary itself offers the best evidence.[19] The material record indicates that drinking and dining were the principal activities; completely burnt as well as unburnt bone suggest not only a sacrifice but its natural accompaniment, a shared meal of some kind.[20] By contrast, early votives are relatively few in number and bear no comparison with the rich sequence of bronzes from Olympia.[21] At Isthmia emphasis seems to have been placed on communal dining rather than on the display of wealth, and no investment was made in building, in contrast to sites like Kalapodi or Kommos. Here it is worth stressing the very great variety of evidence which has emerged in recent years from a growing number of Early Iron Age sanctuaries. It is now abundantly clear that there is no such thing as a normal course of sanctuary development and that Early Iron Age religion is not susceptible to interpretation through any single model. In view of the variability of evidence from early cult places, the lack of a cult building at Isthmia need not surprise us; many shrines existed in more or less open form into the Archaic period, and built shrines coexisted

[17] J. T. Hooker, 'Cult Personnel in the Linear B Texts from Pylos', in M. Beard and J. North (edd.), *Pagan Priests* (London, 1990) 157–74. M. Ventris and J. Chadwick (edd.), *Documents in Mycenaean Greek*[2] (Cambridge, 1973), 126, 276, 279–80, 286–8, 308–9, 311–12, 458–65, 478–80, 484.

[18] Penteskouphia plaques: H. Geagan, 'Mythological Themes in the Plaques from Penteskouphia', *AA* (1970), 31–48, for iconography; Broneer (n. 3) 35–6 no. 25, pl. 11b. The Isthmia plaques are to be published by Wendy Thomas. Poseidon: O. Broneer, 'Excavations at Isthmia: Fourth Campaign, 1957–1958', *Hesperia* 28 (1959), pls. 67e, 68e–h, 73c, 328 fig. 5, 333 fig. 9, 338. Geography: A. Philippson, *Die griechische Landschaft*, iii. 1 (Frankfurt, 1959), ch.V; Salmon (n. 7), 1–7, 19–37.

[19] Cf. U. Sinn, 'Der Kult der Aphaia auf Aegina', in Hägg *et al.* (n. 6), 148–59 for a similar approach.

[20] On the range of evidence for sanctuary dining in later times: M. S. Goldstein, *The Nature of the Ritual Meal in Greek Sanctuaries, 600–300 BC* (Ph.D., diss., Berkeley; Ann Arbor, University Microfilms, 1978).

[21] Olympia: Morgan, *Athletes* (n. 5), ch. 3.

with open sites for centuries. It is, though, a clear sign of the nature of early investment.[22]

The Isthmia pottery assemblage is dominated by open vessels, and specifically by two forms, Late Protogeometric high-footed cups and their successors, Geometric teacups, which together form over half of the Early Iron Age fineware assemblage by weight (Ill. 5.3). When the very small range of earlier

ILL. 5.3 Principal Early Iron Age cup forms

Protogeometric skyphoi and later eighth-century kotylai is also taken into account, the functional assemblage appears to be concentrated around an exceptionally restricted sequence of forms, implying a strong tradition of what was appropriate to the occasion.[23] Throughout, however, these standard cup forms were accompanied by more elaborate skyphoi and a growing range of painted kraters and oinochoai which become ever more plentiful and elaborate through time. This may be taken to indicate increasing differential investment in the celebration, although there is no spatial evidence for this until the eighth century (below, pp. 125–7). Furthermore, the consistently clean breaks on sherds found in the east temenos imply that vessels were quickly swept away and perhaps deliberately broken after the meal (although the area was so disturbed by later

[22] Kommos and Kalapodi, above, n. 11. Diversity of evidence: A. Mazarakis Ainian, 'Early Greek Temples: Their Origin and Function', in Hägg et al. (n. 6), 105–9; 'Contribution à l'étude de l'architecture religieuse grecque des Ages Obscurs', L'Antiquité classique 54 (1985), 5–48. For a general review of EIA architecture and the relation of temples to domestic structures: Fagerström (n. 2); cf. J. J. Coulton, Ancient Greek Architects at Work (New York, 1977), 30–50, on the origins of Doric architecture.

[23] V. R. Desborough, Protogeometric Pottery (Oxford, 1952), 101–2; J. N. Coldstream, Greek Geometric Pottery (London, 1968), 10, pl. 1n. The teacup is rare in the Corinthia, both in graves and settlement-related deposits: e.g. C. Pfaff, 'A Geometric Well at Corinth: Well 1981–6', Hesperia 57 (1988), 58; C. K. Williams II, 'Corinth and the Cult of Aphrodite', in M. del Chiaro (ed.), Corinthiaca (Columbia, 1986), 13, fig. 11, J. Unpublished fragments from the Rachi, Isthmia, probably relate to settlement (I thank Prof. Virginia Anderson-Stojanović, for permission to discuss material from this site).

activity that it is now impossible to support this argument with distribution or join patterns). Since the pottery is not burnt, there can be no suggestion that it was deliberately thrown into the fire; instead it seems that vessels used for the feast were left on site, perhaps in an act of sacralization.[24] It seems likely that some form of altar existed, probably close to the ash concentration, but nothing survives (not least because the planing of the bedrock for the Archaic temple would have destroyed anything located on the west side of the ash).[25]

Who participated in this celebration and who, if anyone, was excluded is of course a vital but unanswerable question. We might expect adult males to have been involved, although there is also evidence to suggest that women used the site too (below, pp. 118, 121). Who would *need* to meet is a parallel problem. It is probably safe to assume, albeit tentatively, that the Early Iron Age population of the Corinthia was highly dispersed and is now largely archaeologically invisible or unresearched (and it is important to stress that large areas of the city of Corinth and its cemeteries remain to be dug). This is not a licence to speculate, but simply a recognition that the scale of activity at Isthmia does not accord with the lack of early settlements and graves. Apart from Corinth itself, only a very few widely scattered sites (mainly graves) have produced Early Iron Age evidence, and these span only one or two phases at most.[26] Were we to rely on preserved remains alone, the pre-eighth-century population of the Corinthia would at times appear so low as to be barely viable, and there must surely have been a change in the nature of material representation at the end of the Bronze Age which is not yet fully understood.[27] If the population was indeed dispersed, it is tempting to think of the Isthmia celebration as a meeting of scattered households.

Indirect evidence for a regional framework of community identity exists in the form of a shared pottery style and burial practices.[28] Beyond that, there is very little evidence for social structure, although this is hardly a problem peculiar

[24] Cf Olympia: W. Gauer, *Olympische Forschungen*, viii: *Die Tongefäße aus dem Brunnen untern Stadion-Nordwall und im Südost-Gebiet* (Berlin, 1975). Samian Heraion: U. Kron, 'Archaisches Kultgeschirr aus dem Heraion von Samos', in H. A. G. Brijder (ed.), *Ancient Greek and Related Pottery* (Amsterdam, 1984), 292–7. Contrast Apollo Maleatas: V. K. Lambrinoudakis, 'Remains of the Mycenaean Period in the Sanctuary of Apollo Maleatas', in Hägg and Marinatos (n. 14), 59–65.

[25] Gebhard and Hemans (n. 2), 3–4.

[26] e.g.: S. Charitonides, 'More Geometric from the Corinthia', *AJA* 61 (1957), 169–71; 'A Geometric Grave at Clenia near Corinth', *AJA* 59 (1955), 125–8; P. Lawrence, 'Five Grave Groups from the Corinthia', *Hesperia* 33 (1964), 91–3. C. Blegen, *Zygouries* (Cambridge, Mass., 1928), 67–9, figs. 171–2. Ay. Theodoroi: *AD* 17 (1961/2), B 52–3, pls. 55–6; *AD* 24 (1969), B 103. Rachi: above, n. 22.

[27] Comparable changes in the archaeological record are evident in later times when there is no suggestion of population change; e.g. R. Osborne, 'A Crisis in Archaeological History? The Seventh Century in Attica', *BSA* 84 (1989), 297–322.

[28] Pottery: Coldstream (n. 23), ch. 3; 'The Meaning of the Regional Styles in the Eighth Century BC', in R. Hägg (ed.), *The Greek Renaissance of the Eighth Century BC* (Stockholm, 1983), 17–25. Burial practices: Salmon (n. 8), 43–4; K. Dickey, *Corinthian Burial Customs, c.1100–550 BC* (Ph.D., diss., Bryn Mawr College; Ann Arbor, University Microfilms, 1992).

to the Early Iron Age at Corinth, where the scarcity of inscriptions of any kind from the period before 146 BC is notorious. Later evidence gives only passing hints of varying reliability. The proverbial 'πάντα οκτώ' certainly reflects a strong tradition of eight divisions of some sort, and this is also represented in the recurrence of multiples of eight in the post-Kypselid constitution (eight chief magistrates or *probouloi* and an eighty strong *boule*, for example). A notice in the *Souda* ascribed these divisions to Aletes, the first Dorian king of Corinth, and implied that they were interrupted during the period of Bacchiad rule. If we were to accept this statement at face value and follow Diodoros' implicit placing of the start of Bacchiad rule ninety years before Kypselos, this would put the interruption of an early tribal constitution somewhere around the mid-eighth century. This would, however, be most unwise. Attractive as the suggestion may seem at first sight, especially given the pattern of development of activity at Isthmia (below, pp. 124–8), the sources are late and questionable, and they rest on versions of Corinthian genealogy and Dorian myth-history which are unlikely to belong earlier than the eighth century (below, pp. 121–2) and which stress the disruptive aspects of Bacchiad rule and the Kypselid tyranny.[29]

Independent evidence for the post-tyrannical tribal system has been reconstructed, chiefly by Dow and Stroud, from four Classical inscriptions. These give abbreviations for four tribes (*ΣΙ, ΛΕ, ΣΥ, ΚΥ*, of which the full name only of the last, Kynophaloi, is known) and they also indicate that each tribe had at least three subdivisions, designated *Ε, F*, and *Π*. Whether more tribal names or subdivisions remain to be discovered is a matter of conjecture, nor is it clear on what basis subdivisions were made and tribes constituted. Since such subdivisions seem too simple and readily confusable to represent demes, Stroud proposed a trittyes organization similar to that instituted in Athens by Kleisthenes, and in order to guarantee Athenian-style full regional representation, he suggested that the trittyes may have been drawn from the city itself and the areas north and south of the Isthmus. Stroud advanced this suggestion with suitable caution, but if he is correct, such a division would again stress the Isthmus as a central point in Corinthian geography, a convenient dividing line for that element of the population resident outside the city. If we assume that the existence of an urban population was a largely Archaic or at least post-ninth-century phenomenon (a point to which I shall return), the issue of the antiquity of the trans-Isthmian divide becomes as important as it is problematic. Does this hypothetical later system represent a return to, or a development from, pre-tyrannical organization, or did it result from a more radical political reorganization? It might be argued that the lack of epigraphical references to tribal affiliations implies that the system was so simple or so well known that there was rarely any need to make formal reference to it. In other words, it may have rested on what were already well-established divisions. On the other hand, it is equally likely that at least by post-tyrannical times, individual identity was not expressed primarily in this way (and here it is notable that there are no inscribed stelai from the North Cemetery, and only nine from Corinth itself prior to 146 BC). It should also be stressed that the extent of excavation in the Corinthia and the quantity of inscriptions on vases show that this is not a result of bias of investigation or limited literacy. The infrequent occurrence of stone inscriptions is reinforced by the context and likely purpose of the preserved examples, some or all of which *may* have military and/or bureaucratic overtones (they include a clearly identified casualty list, and those found within the city may be boundary markers for the defence of the city walls, or more probably mark tribal assembly areas within the city of Corinth).[30] In short, a variety of later sources provide continuing evidence for the existence of a strong regional identity, but although there is limited evidence for internal divisions in which the Isthmus may have played a role, the antiquity of such a system and the divisions embodied in it are matters of speculation.

It is therefore clear that even though a strong perception of regional identity surely existed during the Early Iron Age, we can speak only in the most general terms of the nature of the social divisions within the Corinthia in pre-tyrannical times. A ceremonial meeting of the kind which seems to have been held at Early Iron Age Isthmia would certainly have served to cement this regional identity, but the precise basis on which it was constituted remains unknown.

In assessing the extent of the territory served by Isthmia, it is worth stressing that about one third of the basic high-footed cups and teacups are made in Attic or (to take a more cautious view) in a red, probably trans-Isthmian fabric. The limited evidence available from the eastern Corinthia and the Megarid during the Early Iron Age suggests that similar-looking fabrics were in use across the Isthmus, at, for example, Ayioi Theodoroi, and there is thus no need to assume that Athenians took an interest in such a distant sanctuary at this early date, even though this cannot be ruled out. The constituency of the sanctuary almost certainly extended across the Isthmus, but the precise location of its boundary is at present impossible to determine on the basis of pottery alone. From the

---

[30] R. S. Stroud, 'Tribal Boundary Markers from Corinth', *CSCA* 1 (1968), 233–42 (based on Corinth inscriptions I 2562, 2624, 2184, 734). S. Dow, 'Corinthiaca', *HSCP* 53 (1942), 113–19. G. R. Stanton, 'The Territorial Tribes of Korinth and Phleious', *Classical Antiquity* 5 (1986), 139–53. C. Roebuck, 'Some Aspects of Urbanisation in Corinth', *Hesperia* 41 (1972), 114–16. Salmon (n. 8), app. 1. The earliest example of an ethnic on a tombstone is *SEG* 23. 219 (Ἀγαθῶν Κρωμνίτης) late 4th/early 3rd century. Inscriptions and dipinti on vases: D. Amyx, *Corinthian Vase-Painting of the Archaic Period* (Berkeley, 1988), 547–615.

Late Protogeometric period onwards, more elaborate Attic vessels are also found. These may have been brought by Athenians, but they could as well have come via Corinth, especially as the rate of imports at the two sites corresponds quite closely. This would certainly be the simplest explanation for a small group of the most unusual imports which includes, for example, fragments of a Late Geometric prothesis scene on a large closed vessel and a horse pyxis from the Middle Geometric II Filla workshop. Since these vessels are rarely exported and in Attica are exclusive to graves, it may be easier to accept that it would take a non-Athenian to use them for such an alien purpose.[31] The plainer cups are a separate problem though, as it is difficult to envisage Corinthians bothering to import simple vessels identical to their own products, and here we have clear evidence that the sanctuary had a wide constituency on both sides of the Isthmus. The idea of a community of cult centred on the Isthmus accords well with the pattern of local Mycenaean settlement, but it is unfortunate that so little evidence survives for Early Iron Age activity of any kind in this area, a point to which we will return (below, pp. 121–2). It is sufficient here to stress that Isthmia's location was of continuing significance; not only is it within reach of the Corinthian and Saronic Gulfs, it is also beside what must have been the main road from Athens to Corinth and within reach of the road south to Kenchreai and Epidauros, a crossroads indeed.[32]

Further evidence for the interests represented at the early shrine comes from figurine types and jewellery. Ten items of jewellery have been discovered dating from the Protogeometric period to the eighth century. These are mainly very simple types, mostly of bronze and, with the exception of one Attico-Boiotian fibula, probably all local. They look like normal personal possessions, with none of the usually large or fragile ceremonial items found at sanctuaries elsewhere, Perachora included.[33] At a number of later sanctuaries a close link has been proposed between jewellery dedications and women, with the suggestion that women dedicated this kind of personal possession to mark occasions of particular personal significance such as childbirth or marriage.[34] If this is true here also, it is interesting to consider whether such dedication formed part of the dining

---

[31] LG prothesis scene, IP (Isthmia Pottery) 867: Morgan *Isthmia* (n. 3), ch. I. 2 cat. 370. MG II horse pyxis from the Filla workshop, IP 7931: Morgan (n. 3), ch. I. 2 cat. 265; Gebhard and Hemans (n. 2), no. 20 p. 22, pl. 10c. B. Bohen, *Kerameikos*, xiii: *Die Geometrischen Pyxiden* (Berlin, 1988), 57–60 (Filla workshop).

[32] Salmon (n. 8), 16, fig. 4. Roads: *BCH* 113 (1989), Chronique, 598 and fig. 25.

[33] Isthmia: I. Raubitschek, *Isthmia*, vii: *Metal Objects, 1982–1987, 1989* (in press, Princeton, NJ, ASCS), hereafter *Isthmia*, vii: cat. 177a (IM (Isthmia Miscellaneous) 2221), 177b (IM 1338), 178 (IM 2174), 197 (IM 5037), 198 (IM 2387), 199 (IM 2165), 224 (IM 3140), 226 (IM 2263), 225 (IM 2314), 248 (IM 446). Ceremonial jewellery: Payne (n. 2), 73–4; J. N. Coldstream, *Geometric Greece* (London, 1977), 41–2, 123–6.

[34] C. G. Simon, *The Archaic Votive Offerings and Cults of Ionia* (Ph.D., diss., Berkeley; Ann Arbor, University Microfilms, 1986), 170–82, 198–205, and n. 186. M. B. Hollinshead, 'Against Iphigenia's Adyton in Three Mainland Temples', *AJA* 89 (1985), 425–6, 432–5. L. Kahil, 'L'Artémis de Brauron: Rites et mystère', *Antike Kunst* 20 (1977), 86–98. For examples of women's dedications: I. Kilian, 'Weihungen zu Eileithyia und Artemis Orthia', *ZPE* 31 (1978), 219–22; *Palatine Anthology* 6. 274.

celebration, or whether it was a distinct activity, in which case the sanctuary must have operated on a number of levels from the very beginning. Here also, it is interesting to compare evidence from Olympia, where jewellery dedications appear in quantity only from the eighth century onwards, at approximately the same time that evidence for settlement on a large scale reappears for the first time since the end of the Bronze Age.[35]

Terracotta figurines are also found from the early tenth century onwards; the earliest securely datable example is an unusually elaborate leg from a hollow-bodied wheelmade bull, akin to Attic and Lakonian figures and indeed to the Lefkandi centaur.[36] The vast majority of the Isthmia figurines are terracotta (thirty-one pieces as opposed to only three eighth-century bronzes, two of which are probably attachments from a single tripod, a remarkable scarcity in a region later renowned for its metalworking). This is a striking point of contrast with Olympia where terracotta and bronze continued side by side throughout the Early Iron Age, even if they did not carry the same value. At Isthmia there can be no suggestion that terracotta was the poor man's bronze. The assemblage includes Attic imports, mostly of the eighth century, but the majority of finds are Corinthian and at present unique; with the exception of one probable eighth-century figurine from Perachora, Isthmia is the first Corinthian site to have produced Early Iron Age terracottas. In view of the strength of the local pottery industry it is hardly surprising to find that terracottas were produced locally at this early date, since the two crafts usually go hand in hand, but it is interesting to find this confirmed.[37]

The most popular subject in the figurine assemblage is the bull. Here Isthmia contrasts with the majority of other sites which have produced early figurines, including Olympia, the Samian Heraion, and Artemis Orthia, where horses and oxen dominate. Most of the seventeen examples are crude, handmade, and undecorated, and are therefore difficult to date; the discovery of three examples in the fabric of East Terrace 1 (see below) indicates that they were being offered by the mid-eighth century at the latest, but they could, in theory, continue still later, into the seventh century and beyond, although it is notable that with one exception from the area of the sanctuary of Aphrodite on Acrocorinth (which has no datable context), no comparable examples have been found in any of the many deposits of Archaic Corinthian figurines (including those from Perachora and the

[35] Olympia: Morgan, *Athletes* (n. 5), 34–5, 49–56.

[36] Isthmia leg, IM 1078: Morgan, *Isthmia* (n. 3), ch. I. 5. cat. 32; R. V. Nicholls, 'Greek Votive Statuettes and Religious Continuity', in B. F. Harris (ed.), *Auckland Classical Essays: Presented to E. M. Blaiklock* (Auckland–Oxford, 1970), 9–14; K. Kübler, *Kerameikos* iv: *Neufunde aus der Nekropole des 12. bis 10. Jahrhunderts* (Berlin, 1939), 20, 40, no. 641, pl. 26; V. R. Desborough, R. V. Nicholls, and M. Popham, 'A Euboian Centaur', *BSA* 65 (1970), 21–30.

[37] W. D. Heilmeyer, *Olympische Forschungen* xii: *Frühe olympische Bronzefiguren* (Berlin, 1979). Payne (n. 2), 66. Archaic Corinthian industry: A. Stillwell, *Corinth*, xv. 2: *The Potters' Quarter, the Terracottas* (Princeton, NJ, 1952).

Potters' Quarter at Corinth). On the analogy of the Olympia sequence these figurines could go back as far as Protogeometric, but it is perhaps safer to stick to a vague 'Early Iron Age' date. There are several possible explanations for the popularity of bulls; a connection with Poseidon is one,[38] another is that they served as symbols of economic wealth (although it is unfortunate that we lack comparative evidence to compare such ideological statements with the realities of the contemporary local economy). It seems unlikely that bull figurines were dedicated to represent sacrificial animals, not least because bulls are poorly represented in the early bone deposits (they could have served as symbols only in the limited sense of removing the need to sacrifice a real animal). This is also the case at Kommos, one of the very few other Early Iron Age sanctuaries to have produced bull figurines in quantity; indeed in no case yet discovered does the bone and figurine evidence truly tally.[39] If economic symbolism does underlie the Isthmia figurine dedications, it is more likely to have operated on a general level; it is, for example, tempting to use the popularity of terracotta bulls and the stress put on the consumption of food and drink to argue, however tentatively, for an agricultural and/or pastoral celebration, 'first fruits' perhaps.[40]

A further subject represented among the pre-eighth-century terracottas suggests quite different interests. A pair of very realistic Attic model boots and a further close Corinthian copy are almost identical to examples found in graves in Athens and Eleusis.[41] Scholars who have studied the Attic boots have tended to assume from their context that their significance was primarily funerary, and that they perhaps symbolized the journey to Hades, yet clearly this creates difficulties at a Corinthian sanctuary. The Isthmia dedications may have been just curiosities (although in this case the Corinthian copy would be unexpected), or alternatively the idea of a journey may have been retained (especially at a

---

[38] W. D. Heilmeyer, *Olympische Forschungen* vii: *Frühe olympische Tonfiguren* (Berlin, 1972); Kyrieleis, *Antike Welt* (n. 11), 127–8, figs. 13–14. D. Ohly, 'Frühe Tonfiguren aus dem Heraion von Samos I', *AM* 65 (1940), 57–102. R. M. Dawkins (ed.), *The Sanctuary of Artemis Orthia at Sparta, JHS* Suppl. 5 (London, 1929), 157–8. *RE* s.v. Poseidon, section 19, cols. 484–5. A single animal body from the area of the sanctuary of Aphrodite on Acrocorinth forms the closest parallel yet discovered for the Isthmia bulls, but is finer and better finished, closer still to Archaic figurines from the Potters' Quarter: Williams (n. 23), 13, fig. 1D, 18 n. 26, 19.

[39] Isthmia bones, unpublished report by David Reese. Kommos: J. Shaw, 'Excavations at Kommos (Crete) during 1977', *Hesperia* 47 (1978), 142–5; 'Excavations at Kommos (Crete) during 1978', *Hesperia* 48 (1979), 163 n. 43; 'Excavations at Kommos (Crete) during 1979', *Hesperia* 49 (1980), 229–37, 245–8, pl. 65b; 'Excavations at Kommos (Crete) during 1982–3', *Hesperia* 53 (1984), 279–84, and Shaw (n. 11). I am grateful to Peter Callaghan and Joseph and Maria Shaw for discussion of EIA evidence from Kommos. A. M. Snodgrass, *An Archaeology of Greece* (Berkeley, 1987), 205–7, attempts to relate the pattern of figurine dedication at Olympia to a predominantly pastoral economy, but his argument is weakened by the scarcity of contemporary settlement evidence.

[40] E. Simon, *Festivals of Attica* (Madison, Wis., 1983), 105–8 for the argument that most Attic festivals originated as agricultural celebrations; cf. R. Osborne, *Classical Landscape with Figures* (London, 1987), ch. 8.

[41] Isthmia boots, IM 1102, 1128, 3508*bis*: Morgan *Isthmia* (n. 3), ch. I. 5. R. S. Young, 'An Early Geometric Grave in the Athenian Agora', *Hesperia* 18 (1949), pls. 70, 71; *AD* 19 (1964), B 54–5, pl. 49.

roadside shrine). A further possibility, since the Attic finds all appear to come from the graves of subadult women, would be a specifically female association; and here we may suggest marriage boots, the *nymphides* worn for the journey to a bride's new household (since there would be a nice irony in including *nymphides* in the graves of girls who never lived to marry). The two interpretations are not far removed, as there is a close conceptual link between the journeys involved in death and marriage, but the latter would certainly fit more readily at Isthmia, perhaps indicating that the boots were another form of women's dedication.[42]

Other offerings are less immediately helpful in defining the nature of sanctuary activity. Non-dining vessels, including pyxides and kalathoi, could have held perishable offerings, but there are no miniatures and no obviously votive vessels earlier than the eighth century.[43] Diverse and stylistically significant as the pottery assemblage is, it gives few clues to the full range of functions it may have fulfilled.

In summary, evidence for pre-eighth-century sanctuary activity indicates a need (and the organization) to bring together people from a wide area. It points to the existence of some sort of community of cult which did not behave competitively, at least with its durable material wealth, and which allowed women to participate in some way (at least to celebrate specifically female interests). Here it is worth pausing to consider two issues concerning the sanctuary's place in the contemporary Corinthia. The first is that although by the standards of, for example, Olympia, comparatively little durable wealth appears to have been invested in offerings, this compares favourably with the contents of contemporary graves. Throughout the Early Iron Age, such graves as have been discovered are not conspicuously rich (although it is important to emphasize that there are almost certainly cemeteries remaining to be dug), and the sanctuary may have been the main place of display.[44] One might assume that the wealthy graves of the Corinthian élite remain to be found, or that the Bacchiads preferred to be buried on their country estates rather than in the major cemeteries. Yet it is very surprising that not one wealthy grave has yet

---

[42] e.g. Young (n. 41), 282–3; S. Immerwahr, *Early Burials from the Agora Cemeteries* (Princeton, NJ, 1973), with figs. 1, 37; E. Vermeule, 'Myth and Tradition from Mycenae to Homer', in D. Buitron-Oliver (ed.), *New Perspectives in Early Greek Art* (Hanover–London, 1991), 107–8. Nymphides: R. F. Sutton, *The Interaction Between Men and Women Portrayed on Attic Red Figure Pottery* (Ph.D., diss., University of North Carolina; Ann Arbor, University Microfilms, 1981), part II, section I. Death/Marriage: I. Jenkins, 'Is There Life After Marriage? A Study of the Abduction Motif in Vase Paintings of the Athenian Wedding Ceremony', *BICS* 30 (1983), 137–45; M. Alexiou, *The Ritual Lament in Greek Tradition* (Cambridge, 1974); L. M. Danforth, *The Death Rituals of Rural Greece* (Princeton, NJ, 1982), ch. 4.

[43] MG II pierced kalathos, IP 7475: Morgan, *Isthmia* (n. 3), ch. I. 2 cat. 273.

[44] Dickey (n. 28). C. Blegen, H. Palmer, and R. Young, *Corinth*, xiii: *The North Cemetery* (Cambridge, Mass., 1964), 13–20. A. N. Stillwell, *Corinth*, xv. 1: *The Potters' Quarter* (Princeton, NJ, 1948), 6–15; A. N. Stillwell and J. L. Benson, *Corinth*, xv. 3: *The Potters' Quarter, the Pottery* (Princeton, NJ, 1984), 13–34.

been found in such an intensively cultivated region, and it would seem more relevant to speculate about the impact on mortuary display of rule by a closed élite.

A second issue arising from consideration of the early sanctuary concerns changes in settlement, and the process by which Corinth emerged as the *asty* of the Corinthian polis. Although it would be unwise to draw firm conclusions in the light of current archaeological exploration of the region, as yet Corinth is the only site to have produced a continuous material sequence from Mycenaean into historical times. Yet the pace and nature of its emergence as a central place are by no means clear. The archaeological record remains the only reliable source of contemporary evidence in view of eighth-century manipulation of the myth-historical tradition (below, pp. 135–8), and here we may document shifting and expanding nuclei of settlement (revealed by graves and wells) within a relatively small area. Yet the degree of real integration and the site's regional significance remain open to question (a problem common to all the mainland 'urban' centres of the Early Iron Age). Indeed, the urban structure of Corinth may have remained very loose as late as the sixth century, with only gradual filling in of the areas between house clusters and relatively late development of any monumental buildings other than temples.[45] As noted, the site of Isthmia is central in relation to the Late Bronze Age settlement pattern in all but the far west of the Corinthia (the area of Zygouries which in many ways remained closer to Nemea and Mycenae), but this contrasts markedly with the Corinth-centred pattern of the Archaic period. The rise of Corinth as the central place of the post-Bronze Age state must have taken time, and it is important to stress that there was nothing inevitable about the site's eventual status. Following Roebuck, it is possible to argue for a date as late as the eighth century for the emergence of Corinth as a political centre, if one wishes to align physical changes to the political developments of Bacchiad rule, but the connection cannot be pressed, and an earlier and more gradual emergence seems equally likely. Whichever case one prefers, it is significant that on present evidence, Isthmia seems to have been the only sanctuary in the Corinthia until the establishment of a shrine to the first temple of Hera at Perachora during the first half of the eighth century, with no real rivals at Corinth until the construction of the first temple on Temple Hill in the first decades of the seventh century. There is no secure earlier evidence for cult at Corinth itself (Ill. 5.4); the few sherds found on Temple Hill and Acrocorinth could as well

---

[45] Salmon (n. 8), 38–54, argues for a LPG shift in settlement corresponding with the refoundation of the Dorian city, but this can no longer be sustained by the archaeological evidence. Cf. A. Mazarakis-Ainian, 'Geometric Eretria', *Antike Kunst* 30 (1987), 3–24; C. K. Williams II, 'The Early Urbanisation of Corinth', *ASAtene* 60 (1982), 9–19; P. Aupert, 'Argos aux VIIIe–VIIe siècles: Bourgade ou métropole?', *ASAtene* 60 (1982), 21–31. C. K. Williams II, 'Pre-Roman Cults in the Area of the Forum of Ancient Corinth' (Ph.D., diss., Pennsylvania, 1978), ch. 1. Roebuck (n. 30).

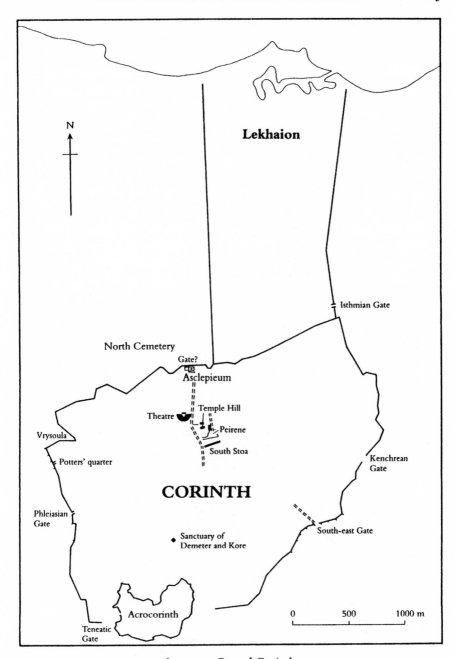

ILL. 5.4 Central Corinth

and the nature of early activity at the Sacred Spring is by no means clear. The spring does seem to have been regarded as special from an early date, even though it is less copious than, for example, Peirene; during Middle Geometric II large round pits were sunk into the natural rock of the valley, and with the construction of the south retaining wall during the Late Geometric period the spring area was demarcated and protected. In view of its later development as a shrine, it is tempting to infer cult use from the beginning, but this is unprovable; and in any case, the later cult with its funerary overtones contrasts markedly with the Olympian worship conducted at Isthmia and Perachora.[46] The evidence from Early Iron Age Isthmia is unparalleled, and the development of the twin sites of Isthmia and Corinth thus reflects a bipolarity which was a natural consequence of the growth of Corinth as a regional centre, and strengthened as the Early Iron Age progressed. It is, however, interesting to note that in this case it is the sanctuary which developed first, before the settlement, the reverse of the model of bipolarity proposed by de Polignac.

Eighth-Century Isthmia

This pattern of activity at Isthmia continued essentially unchanged in nature until the second half of the eighth century. A short-lived increase in the level of activity occurred during the Late Protogeometric and Early Geometric periods. If, in seeking to interpret these fluctuations, we work from the assumption that the greatest investment in ritual or ideological activity tends to occur at times of major change or insecurity, and relate this to developments at Corinth (Ill. 5.4), it becomes clear that this peak coincides with an expansion of settlement into the upper Lekhaion road valley, as well as, for example, the earliest evidence for Corinthian external contact, with Medeon in Phokis.[47] Middle Geometric II saw a more lasting escalation in activity with a marked increase in the quantities of pottery deposited (especially vessels such as conical oinochoai not associated with dining). This coincides with the start of a series of major urban changes at Corinth (although as noted, these do not include the development of a cult place). To this period belongs the establishment of

[46] Roebuck (n. 30). Temple Hill: I am grateful to Dr Julie Bentz for information on the Geometric pottery from this area in advance of her publication. Although the planing of the rock for the construction of the temple may well have removed EIA evidence, it is notable that very little early material of any description has been found anywhere in the immediate vicinity. Aphrodite: Williams (n. 23), 13 fig. 1. Sacred Spring: Williams, Pre-Roman Cults (n. 45), 93; C. K. Williams II and J. E. Fisher, 'Corinth 1970: Forum Area', Hesperia 40 (1971), 3. A. Steiner, 'Pottery and Cult in Corinth: Oil and Water at the Sacred Spring', Hesperia 62 (1992), 385–408.

[47] Williams, Pre-Roman Cults (n. 45), ch. 1. C. Vatin, Médéon de Phocide (Paris, 1969); Morgan, Athletes (n. 5), 248–50. A similar case for a link between cult investment in the broadest sense and political stability may be made in Ionia; e.g. C. Morgan, 'Divination and Society at Delphi and Didyma', Hermathena 147 (1989), 17–42.

settlement in the Potters' Quarter and the opening of the North Cemetery, the latter significant not only as the first use of this area for burials since the Middle Helladic period, but also as the first move away from a long-established pattern of burying the dead near settlements and towards isolating them in separate burial areas (a shift completed in Early Protocorinthian, with the latest adult burial in the forum area dating to the transition between Late Geometric and Early Protocorinthian). A new shrine to Hera was established at Perachora, contacts with Italy were also renewed, and from this period, Corinthian trade developed in many directions.[48] Expansion at Isthmia may therefore be seen as part of a general pattern of change at Corinth, where developments through the second half of the century include the construction of retaining walls either to protect graves or as the first sign of design for habitation; such a wall redirects the stream in the area below Peirene and other examples include a wall further south-west in an area of Late Geometric wells and residences, and the Sacred Spring terrace which supports a Protocorinthian house. New cemetery areas are also opened; the first grave in the Lekhaion cemetery belongs early in the seventh century (c.680).[49]

The second half of the eighth century was also marked by real changes in the material expression of religious belief not only at Isthmia, but also at Perachora, and from the very end of the century at a new small shrine at Solygeia (below, pp. 136–8). Almost inevitably, an increase in the number of sanctuaries demanded closer definition of the particular role of each. It is, though, notable that on present evidence, cult developments were still concentrated outside the settlement of Corinth; here the first temple was established only at the very end of this phase of development (probably during the first quarter of the seventh century, see below, pp. 138–9).

At Isthmia the most striking development is the construction of East Terrace 1 in the mid-eighth century, the first of a series of formal surfaces which served to accommodate dining and other gatherings, with a refuse area provided close by (Ill. 5.5). On this surface were found a burnt plank and a series of randomly spaced post-holes; their profile, spacing, and angles suggest that these holes accommodated removable poles wedged in, rather than any fixed structure. A

---

[48] North Cemetery and Potters' Quarter, n. 43 above. Latest forum burial: S. Weinberg, *Corinth*, vii. 1: *Geometric and Orientalising Pottery* (Harvard, 1943), 34–5 (sarcophagus within the foundation of Temple F). Trade: C. Dehl, *Die korinthische Keramik des 8. und Frühen 7. Jhr. v. Chr. in Italien. Untersuchungen zu Ihrer Chronologie und Ausbrietung*, AM Beiheft 11 (Berlin, 1984); C. Morgan, 'Corinth, the Corinthian Gulf and Western Greece during the Eighth Century BC', BSA 83 (1988), 313–38; Salmon (n. 8), 139–47.

[49] Williams, *Pre-Roman Cults* (n. 45), ch. 1, 93. Williams and Fisher (n. 46), 3–5. C. K. Williams II and J. E. Fisher, 'Corinth 1971: The Forum Area', *Hesperia* 41 (1972), 144. Lechaion (grave B20): C. W. J. and M. Eliot, 'The Lechaion Cemetery near Corinth', *Hesperia* 37 (1968), 346–50 (the authors note that no other graves of this period were found, but also report that 15 of the 46 graves excavated were empty and 13 held sherds only).

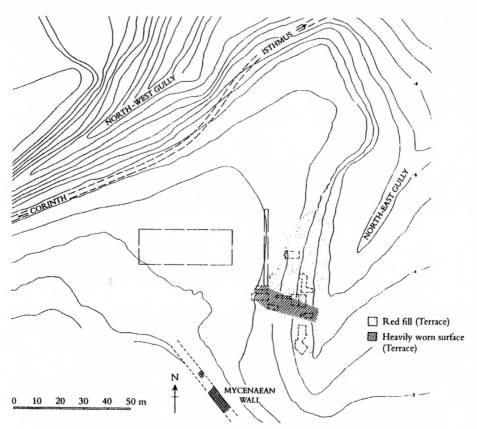

ILL. 5.5 Isthmia East Terrace 1, late eighth century (after *Hesperia* 62 (1992), fig. 1)

stand for offerings is one possible explanation (perhaps similar to those posited at Tegea), or they may have held tent poles of the kind common in many later shrines, including the Samian Heraion and the Sacred Spring at Corinth. Tents could shelter votives or visitors with varying degrees of elaboration; in later times provision could be very large (the proto-Pompeion in the Kerameikos of Athens is a case in point), but evidence from the section of East Terrace 1 so far excavated suggests that the structures erected on it were relatively small. The development of the terrace certainly implies a need to cater for growing numbers of people, and also raises the possibility of social differentiation, both in terms of access to shelter and in the overall use of space (especially as the distribution of the finest pottery is far from even). How this related to the earlier conduct of the dining celebration, and whether the expansion in activity strained existing organization to the point of collapse or whether it could be accommodated via the introduction of changes and refinements must unfortunately remain matters of conjecture.[50]

New kinds of dedication also appear at Isthmia at this time, including artefacts which are rare elsewhere in the Corinthia. Tripods are a case in point; the eight examples so far discovered are few in comparison with Olympia, but they form a large group by the standards of the Corinthia.[51] It is notable that even though the Corinthian school of bronzeworking is well established by the Late Geometric period (shown principally in the tripods and especially horse figurines which circulated widely, particularly in western Greece), within the Corinthia tripods are found in quantity only at Isthmia and even here there are no free-standing horses. The early deposits from the sanctuary of Hera (Akraia) at Perachora include only one possible iron leg and one clay lebes (perhaps dedicated as a poor man's bronze, although the votives from this time onwards are otherwise very rich), and they are no more plentiful in the otherwise oustandingly rich Hera Limenia deposit. They are next found in the Archaic destruction debris of the first temple on Temple Hill at Corinth.[52] Of particular interest among the Isthmia tripods is a leg which has a twin (made from the same patrix) dedicated at Olympia. Since it seems likely that both pieces were Corinthian and the Olympia leg was probably brought to the site by a Corinthian who had acquired it from a local workshop, this parallel suggests that at least by this time, Isthmia was regarded as the appropriate local context for such a rich dedication, a Corinthian parallel for distant Olympia.[53]

Arms and armour constitute a similar case. From the late eighth or early seventh century, Isthmia has produced fragmentary military dedications (a *Kegelhelm*, an Illyrian helmet, and a spearhead), again offerings which are unparalleled at Perachora.[54] In the wider Greek context it is not surprising to find that such rich personal possessions were offered at a sanctuary during this period, since this is precisely the time when a transfer of personal wealth and especially arms and armour, from the personal context of the grave to the

[50] East Terrace 1: Gebhard and Hemans (n. 2), 12–15. Samos: E. Buschor and H. Schlief, 'Heraion von Samos: Der Altarplaz der Frühzeit', *AM* 58 (1933), 146–73. U. Kron, 'Kultmahle im Heraion von Samos archaischer Zeit', in Hägg *et al.* (n. 6), 144. Kerameikos: W. Hoepfner, *Kerameikos* x: *Das Pompeion und seine Nachfolgebauten* (Berlin, 1976), 16–23, 127. Sacred Spring: C. K. Williams II, 'Excavation at Corinth, 1968', *Hesperia* 38 (1969), 43–6; id. 'Corinth 1969: Forum Area', *Hesperia* 39 (1970), 21–5.

[51] Isthmia tripods, bowls, and attachments: *Isthmia*, vii, cat. 60 (IM 5080), 61 (IM 2308), 295 (IM 2826), 301 A–G (IM 1656, 5024, 5068, 5121a and b, 5815), 302 (IM 234), 303 (IM 1795a and b) (legs); 296 (IM 2224), 297 (IM 1335) (attachments). M. Maass, *Olympische Forschungen*, x: *Die geometrischen Dreifüße von Olympia* (Berlin, 1978).

[52] Corinthian bronzeworking. J.-L. Zimmermann, *Les Chevaux de bronze dans l'art géométrique grec* (Mainz, 1989), 176–83. Hera Akraia: Payne (n. 2), 55, pls. 14:6, 124:1 (clay lebes), 75 (possible iron leg), 126–30, pl. 38 (griffin protome from Hera Limenia deposit). Temple Hill: Robinson, 'Excavations' (n. 2), pl. 56.

[53] Maass (n. 51), no. 110a, B4350, pl. 30; Isthmia IM 2826: (*Isthmia*, vii, cat. 295). Cf. Argive pair at the Argive Heraion and Delphi: M. Maass, 'Die geometrischen Dreifüße von Olympia', *Antike Kunst* 24 (1981), 12.

[54] A. Jackson, 'Three Possible Dedications of Arms and Armour at Isthmia', in Morgan (n. 3).

communal sanctuary is becoming very noticeable.[55] In the Corinthia, however, it is interesting to find that Isthmia was the sanctuary chosen as the appropriate place for such display. This may be a result of its prominent roadside location, more widely visible to passing traffic than even Corinth itself, since such dedications were surely intended for show. Perachora may therefore have seemed too remote. Yet it may also have been a matter of tradition; the aristocratic wealth implied by tripods, and the wealth and willingness to fight for the community symbolized by arms and armour, were probably most appropriately displayed at the traditional community shrine which had played a long standing role in regional affairs. Here also we may compare Olympia as the only Greek shrine to have received arms and armour dedications in any quantity, and then only from the late eighth century onwards.[56] So during the latter part of the eighth century, we first find rich aristocratic dedications appearing at Isthmia alongside smaller personal dedications and the debris of dining.[57]

Lesser changes are evident in the nature of the pottery used and the figurine types dedicated. During the third quarter of the eighth century we find a breakdown in the dominant sequence of simple cup forms which lasts until kotylai grow in popularity during the Early Protocorinthian period. In the interim, a much wider range of Corinthian open vessels, including early kotylai, skyphoi, kyathoi, and mugs, was used for the dining celebration. The significance of this departure should not be overrated, but it is interesting to note any break in a pattern so long established, especially where it is a temporary one which coincides with other changes in material behaviour.[58] During the eighth century the range of figurine dedications also widens with the addition of, for example, Attic and Corinthian wheeled horses and a mule. In Athens the fact that such models have been found in graves, wells, and sanctuaries makes it hard to identify their function, although it seems likely that at least some were children's toys. Model cart wheels are also very appropriate at a roadside shrine, and are reminiscent of the rich collection of Archaic cart models found in the Potters' Quarter at Corinth. The range of figurines and the interests they represent is considerable, and the Isthmia finds are at present unique in the Early Iron Age Corinthia.[59]

[55] A. M. Snodgrass, *Archaic Greece* (London, 1980), 52–4.

[56] A. Jackson, 'Arms and Armour in the Panhellenic Sanctuary of Poseidon at Isthmia', in Coulson and Kyrieleis (n. 11), 141–4; id. 'Hoplites and the Gods: The Dedication of Captured Arms and Armour', in V. Davis Hanson (ed.), *Hoplites: The Classical Greek Battle Experience* (London, 1991), 228–49. Snodgrass (n. 55), 99–107 (p. 105 for Olympia statistics).

[57] Cf. H. Kyrieleis, 'Offerings of the Common Man in the Heraion at Samos', in Hägg *et al.* (n. 6), 215–21.

[58] Morgan, *Isthmia* (n. 3), ch. II. 3.

[59] Morgan, *Isthmia* (n. 3), ch. I. 5. Nicholls (n. 36), 1–37; I am grateful to Dr Nicholls for discussion of unpublished finds from the Athenian Agora. G. Raepsaet, 'Charettes en terre cuite de l'époque Archaïque à Corinthe', *L'Antiquité classique* 57 (1988), 56–88.

Perachora

Parallel to the changes evident at Isthmia, the second half of the eighth century also saw a great expansion in cult activity at the sanctuary of Hera at Perachora (Ill. 5.6). Cult activity there seems to have begun in the Middle Geometric II phase, perhaps as early as the first and certainly by the second quarter of the eighth century. If we follow Payne in assuming that the 'first temple' is indeed an Early Iron Age building and with the earliest pottery (and in the absence of stratigraphical support this must be recognized as an assumption), then it must have been constructed by 750 at the latest. It should, however, be stressed that there is no independent dating evidence for the structure. Very little of the material which Payne illustrates in his publication of the early (Hera Akraia) deposit has to go far back into Middle Geometric II; most appears to date from around the middle of the century, with a considerable increase in the number, range, and wealth of finds during the last decade or so. It therefore seems that the period of expansion at Isthmia is mirrored at Perachora.[60] Dining activity at Perachora is indicated by burnt debris and a high concentration of drinking vessels in the ceramic assemblage (albeit much more varied in form, with few teacups), as well as fragments of amphora and cooking vessels. As at Isthmia, the early assemblage contains few large vessels, and forms such as plates and kalathoi only became popular during Early Protocorinthian. Perachora's remoteness may indicate that the celebration was a more exclusive affair than that at Isthmia, a point reinforced if the so-called second temple of Hera (Limenia) in the upper valley is a seventh-century dining-room which could have held only a few people. Unfortunately, though, the nature of the early dining celebration and the participants involved remain a mystery.[61]

Eighth-century cult activity at Perachora therefore bears a certain resemblance to that at Isthmia, yet almost from the very beginning there is a marked difference in the wealth of offerings. Although there is no evidence of tripod, armour, or figurine dedications at Perachora, the site has produced much more gold, purpose-made votives including thin sheet gold and votive jewellery, and also imports such as scarabs and faience.[62] Unfortunately, it is difficult to equate the pattern of dedication with the broader development of the sanctuary and its cults. The architectural sequence at Perachora is by no means clear, and the nature of votive deposition is also a matter of debate. Rather than arguing for

---

[60] Temple (n. 2). Early pottery: Payne (n. 2), e.g. pl. 12:1, 4, pl. 14:1, pl. 15:3. Overview: R. Tomlinson, 'Pechora', in A. Schachter (ed.), Le Sanctuaire grec, Fondation Hardt Entretiens, 37 (Geneva, 1992), 321–46.

[61] Payne (n. 2), 53–66. J. Salmon, 'The Heraeum at Perachora and the Early History of Corinth and Megara', BSA 67 (1972), 159–204. R. A. Tomlinson, 'The Upper Terraces at Perachora', BSA 72 (1977), 197–202.

[62] Payne (n. 2), 69–77.

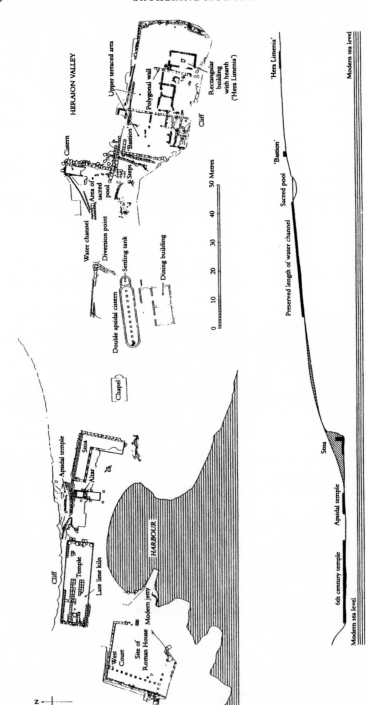

ILL. 5.6 The Sanctuary of Hera at Perachora (by kind permission of R. A. Tomlinson)

two separate cults or cult places, with a spatial distinction between the cults of Hera Akraia and Hera Limenia, I prefer to regard the whole valley as one complex, with the upper terraces holding overspill dedications and the focus of cult activity (meeting areas and cult buildings) remaining by the harbour. It is clear from Payne's reference to the upper chronological limit of the 'Geometric' (Akraia) deposit in the lower valley as the 'époque des aryballes pansus' (i.e. Early Protocorinthian, a phase characterized by what we now know as the globular aryballos) that the upper (Limenia) and lower (Akraia) deposits overlap chronologically. Furthermore, as Payne notes, the lower deposit was cut away in the course of fourth-century construction by the harbour and we can only guess at what may have been lost. It would therefore be unwise to place too much stress on the spatial separation and apparently different chronological emphasis of the two preserved deposits to argue for separate areas of cult activity. Yet whatever the precise distribution of votives, it is true to say that from the last quarter of the eighth century, Perachora increased greatly in wealth, and by the seventh century it had become the richest shrine for miles around, richer by far than contemporary Delphi. By this time, Perachora was receiving a wealth of small portable items and imports unparalleled at Isthmia.[63]

Why such a rich shrine was maintained in such an isolated position, and what role it played in Corinthian society are both questions to which there is no straightforward answer. The site is rugged and has a poor water supply, and at least into the early Archaic period there is no evidence for neighbouring settlement (or indeed for much settlement on the Perachora peninsula as a whole, although historically, this was always oriented more towards the centre and the north rather than the mountainous south). Excavation, however, has largely been confined to the public buildings of the Heraion valley and the headland has not been fully investigated; so whilst it is clear that settlement was established on the promontory and the central Peiraion by the sixth century, it is impossible to be certain that we have the earliest material from either area, and we cannot therefore exclude the possibility of a sanctuary established to serve a settled area. Nevertheless, the shrine's close relationship with Corinth is clear; as Payne emphasized, only Corinth could have created the Heraion as we know it. As is often pointed out, the name 'Peiraion' implies a Corinth-centred viewpoint, and strategically, the promontory is so close to Corinth that control by any other region would pose a threat not only to Corinthian trading links to the north and west but also to the territorial integrity of the state itself.[64]

---

[63] U. Sinn, 'Das Heraion von Perachora: Eine Sakrale Schutzzone in der korinthischen Peraia', AM 105 (1990), 61–6; contra Salmon (n. 61). Payne (n. 2), 31 (see chs. V and VI. 2 for bronzes and terracottas from the Hera Limenia deposit). Dunbabin (n. 15).

[64] Penteskouphia plaque inscribed Περαιόθεν ἵκομες, IG iv 329; A. Furtwängler, Beschreibung der Vasensammlung im Antiquarium, i (Berlin, 1895), 91 no. 838. Thucydides 4. 42 refers to Κορίνθιοι ἔξω Ἰσθμοῦ. Payne (n. 2), ch. 1 for summary of peninsula and its archaeological remains (Payne notes (p. 15),

Furthermore, if Payne's reconstruction is correct, the early monumental development of the sanctuary implies that it had more than a purely local significance; the construction of what would be the earliest temple in the Corinthia was followed by what is now interpreted as an early dining-room and a sixth-century predecessor of the later hestiatorion (the plan and function of which is unclear, although in addition to dining, housing administration or protecting visitors and/or votives are also possibilities).[65] It is tempting to assume that Perachora's position on the Corinthian Gulf made it a natural repository for western colonial wealth, but it is notable that an increasing majority of imports were of eastern manufacture (the earliest instance of such orientalia in the Corinthia). It is therefore possible to make a case for dedication at Perachora as a more random reflection of Corinthian trading interests at this period, even if we cannot be specific about the representation of individual routes or connections.[66] The harbour was surely too small, shallow, and unprepossessing to be an attraction in its own right (most ships would probably have had to anchor in the bay outside), and it is interesting that Corinth's long-standing trading arrangements with settlements near the coast of Phokis (with Medeon from the Late Proto-geometric period and Delphi from c.800) do not seem to be reflected in early activity on the peninsula, probably indicating that Corinthian shipping ran directly for harbour closer to home. It is, though, worth noting that Perachora's location in a notoriously difficult area of the Gulf, with irregular and fierce cross-winds and currents, may have made it attractive as an occasional shelter.[67]

As noted, some indication of the interests represented at Perachora is provided by the debris of dining and personal dedications which include valuable imports unparalleled at Isthmia. Two further categories of votive deserve mention: terracotta koulouria are characteristic of Hera cult but architectural models are harder to interpret. Perhaps the most distinctive type of votive yet discovered at Perachora, they have not so far been found elsewhere in the Corinthia; they should therefore offer insight into the local role of the cult, yet they remain very hard to interpret. They appear to represent real buildings (especially as the most complete example compares well with the ground-plan of the so-called first temple of Hera), although in view of the continuing popularity of the form

referring to the Archaic town on the Heraion, that it is 'a safe guess that this town goes back to the Geometric period'). Wiseman (n. 15), 32–37. An unpublished EG/MG I oinochoe from the area of the Perachora-Skaloma cemetery probably comes from a grave in view of its state of preservation, but no further EIA evidence has been noted.

[65] R. A. Tomlinson, 'Perachora: The Remains Outside the Two Sanctuaries', BSA 64 (1969), 170.

[66] I. Kilian-Dirlmeier, 'Fremde Weihungen in griechischen Heiligtümern vom 8. bis zum Beginn des 7. Jahrhunderts v. Chr.', Jahrbuch des Römisch-germanischen Zentralmuseums Mainz 32 (1985), 225–30; 'Ἀφιερώματα μὴ Κορινθιακῆς προλεύσεως στὰ Ἡραῖα τῆς Περαχώρας (τέλος 8ου–ἀρχὴ 7ου αἰ. Π Χ)', Peloponnesiaka 16 (1985/86), 369–75.

[67] D. J. Blackman, 'The Harbour at Perachora', BSA 61 (1966), 192–4. Morgan, Athletes (n. 5), 106–26. Payne (n. 2), 24.

period, when temple architecture had been completely transformed, it seems more reasonable to interpret them as private houses than as temples (although here it must be admitted that the architectural relationship between early temples and large houses is ill-understood). The four surviving Perachora models probably began quite early in the eighth century (in view of the form of the decorative meander which on pottery appears closer to Middle Geometric I than to Late Geometric); they are thus amongst the earliest such finds known, and are second in number only to the thirty five examples from the Samian Heraion which span the eighth to the sixth centuries (and it may be significant that these also come from a Hera sanctuary). Elsewhere, occasional terracotta and poros models of a variety of types have been found widely scattered in Late Geometric and Archaic contexts, including the Argive Heraion, the Athenian Acropolis, Khaniale Tekke, Aetos on Ithaka, Larisa on the Hermos, Sardis, Sellada on Thera, Skillous in Elis, the sanctuary of Artemis Orthia at Sparta, Lemnos (probably representing a fountain house), and Ano Mazaraki. Although these models are found in a variety of contexts, including later seventh- and sixth-century burials, the only Geometric example known outside a sanctuary is that from Khaniale Tekke on Crete, a region notorious during the Early Iron Age for its idiosyncratic material behaviour. Elsewhere, the models from the two Hera shrines on Samos and at Perachora are likely to be contemporary, and these are followed, probably in the early seventh century, by finds from a further Hera shrine, the Argive Heraion, as well as the sanctuary of Apollo at Aetos and a rural shrine perhaps dedicated to Artemis at Ano Mazaraki in Achaia (although here the models are clearly granaries rather than houses). The possibility of an early (if short-lived) link between building dedications and Hera cannot therefore be discounted, and in view of Hera's associations with matrimony, women, and the oikos, the link would seem appropriate. It may, however, be argued that remote Perachora was a strange place for Corinthians to place a sanctuary of Hera linked to the oikos, and this has led Kåre Fagerström to suggest that the dedications were made by colonists concerned for the prosperity of their future homes, echoing the proposed western connection discussed earlier. Such a specific connection poses chronological problems though, and it is surely more likely that Corinthians would have chosen to celebrate their personal wealth, as well as the strength of their households within the rapidly expanding city, at such a marginal shrine. Perachora, which lacked the long communal tradition of Isthmia, may have seemed a freer and more open place at which to make such personal statements.[68]

[68] T. G. Schattner, *Griechische Hausmodelle*, AM Beiheft 15 (Berlin, 1990): Schnattner wants the Perachora models to begin in the 9th century, although he accepts the general preference for a later date. Lemnos: H. Payne, 'Archaeology in Greece, 1929–30', *JHS* 50 (1930), 245–7. Ano Mazaraki: M. Petropoulos, 'Τρίτη ανασκαφική περίοδος στο Άνω Μαζαράκι (Ρακίτα) Αχαίας', in Πρακτικά

Two further suggestions concerning the role of Perachora must be regarded as more speculative, at least when considering the origins of the sanctuary. Strabo (380) refers to an oracle of Hera Akraia at the Heraion as existing in former times, with the clear implication that it was defunct in his day. Since this is the only reference to such an oracle, we can have no real idea of whether Strabo was correct, and if so, how the oracle worked or when it was established and to what end. We also have no clue as to its location; Dunbabin suggested that a deposit of bronze phialai in the so-called sacred pool may have been linked with divination, but this seems less likely than Tomlinson's hypothesis that the pool provided the water supply for the adjacent dining-room and that the phialai were discarded banqueting equipment. It is tempting to speculate about the role of an oracle during the eighth century, and it is easy to see how some provision for divine sanction of decision making might be advantageous during a period of major political and physical change in the community, but the evidence is too scanty to move beyond speculation.[69]

An alternative explanation for the location and role of the sanctuary has been proposed by Ulrich Sinn, who stresses Perachora's isolation from Corinth in arguing that the site served as a place of refuge and asylum within the Corinthia for many centuries.[70] His case rests on one of the very few literary references to Perachora: Xenophon (*Hellenika* 4.5) remarks that the inhabitants of the Perachora took refuge in the sanctuary as the Spartan army under Agesilaos advanced during the war between Corinth and Sparta in 390. While it is true to say that Greek sanctuaries were generally used as places of refuge, it is less clear that this should be identified as a specific role for Perachora within the Corinthia. Xenophon is a relatively late and isolated source; if he refers to a regular local practice (and the evidence here does not permit any conclusion) it is still doubtful whether this was a factor in the sanctuary's foundation or whether it was a role acquired over time. Much depends on Perachora's relations with Corinth, and here it is interesting to consider the possibility of an early cult of Hera in the city centre. The myth of Medea and her children, and specifically the tradition that the children were buried in the temenos of Hera

Γʹ *Διεθνούς Συνέδριου Πελοποννησιακών Σπουδών*, ii (Athens, 1987/8), fig. 9. Samian Heraion (35 models, 8th to mid-6th century + ?); Argive Heraion (1, 1st quarter 7th century); Athens acropolis (1, Archaic; 1, 6th century); Khaniale Tekke (Geometric reuse of tholos grave); Aetos (1, late 8th/early 7th century); Larisa on Hermos (1); Sardis (2, 6th century); Sellada (1, 6th century); Skillous (3, 6th century); Sparta (Artemis Orthia, 1, 6th century); Ano Mazaraki (3, EPC, late 8th century, probably granaries); Lemnos (2, *c.*700 BC, ?Greek?). Hera: Fagerström (n. 2), 155–7.

[69] Salmon (n. 61), 165–8. T. Dunbabin, 'The Oracle of Hera Akraia at Perachora', *BSA* 46 (1951), 61–71. R. Tomlinson, 'Water Supplies and Ritual at the Heraion, Perachora', in Hägg *et al.* (n. 6), 167–71; 'The Chronology of the Perachora *Hestiatorion* and its Significance', in O. Murray (ed.), *Sympotica* (Oxford, 1990), 95–101. Morgan, *Athletes* (n. 5), ch. 5 on the political role of oracles in early states; Morgan (n. 47).

[70] Sinn (n. 63), 53–116; 'La funzione dell'Heraion di Perachora nella «peraia» corinzia', in F. Prontera (ed.), *Geografia storica della Grecia antica* (Bari, 1992), 209–32.

Akraia where they received hero honours, is most fully explored by Euripides (*Medea* 1378–83) and mentioned by Pausanias (2. 3. 6, 11), but it may also have been known to Eumelos as early as the late eighth century. Arguments for the identification of the sanctuary of Hera Akraia with that at Perachora have been thoroughly reviewed by Payne and more recently Williams, both of whom dismiss the idea and instead suggest that the shrine should be located in the city centre of Corinth, where an annual festival was held until the sack of the city in 146 BC. Pausanias refers to the 'mnema' of the children (usually, if not strictly accurately, translated as 'tomb') by the Odeion along with a statue of Terror, and although the archaeology is inconclusive, there is no reason to doubt that this was the site of a Greek cult. Eumelos' reference may date the myth to the end of the eighth century, but the date of the cult, and its relationship to that at Perachora, remain unknown.[71]

In conclusion, although it is perhaps easier to define the interests which were not represented at Perachora rather than those which were (not least, thanks to comparison with Isthmia), it seems likely that the foundation of the sanctuary reflected a complex of interests, including celebrations of the household, trade, and control of land essential to Corinth. These were all interests which would not have fitted readily into the existing pattern of activity at Isthmia, in view of its position and historical traditions, nor indeed in any new city-centre sanctuary had one been established. There is thus a strong case to be made for the utility of a new, truly marginal shrine.

Corinthian Cult and Myth

Mention of Eumelos raises the wider issue of the impact upon cult of the rewriting of Corinthian mythology which seems to have begun during the second half of the eighth century.[72] So little of Eumelos' work survives that we can only speculate on the basis of passing reports and references in later authors, Aristotle and Pausanias included. Negative argument is therefore impossible, but positive hints of the issues covered allow some insight into contemporary Corinthian concerns, since the act of enshrining an issue in myth implies that it was of some significance to the community. We may therefore consider how such issues relate to existing cults and how they are reflected and enhanced by

---

[71] E. Will, *Korinthiaka* (Paris, 1955), 81–129. Williams, *Pre-Roman Cults* (n. 45), 46–9; Payne (n. 2), 19–20; G. Roux, *Pausanias en Corinthie* (Paris, 1958), 120–2; *contra* de Polignac (n. 1), 51 (who also cites Herodotos' (5. 92) account of Periander's dealing with the women of Corinth, even though Herodotos does not give the location of the relevant temple of Hera). See postscript to this paper.

[72] Eumelos' date is based on his composition of a prosodion for the Messenians, referring to Zeus of Ithome, before the First Messenian War: C. M. Bowra, 'Two Lines of Eumelus', CQ 13 (1963), 145–53; G. L. Huxley, *Greek Epic Poetry* (London, 1969), 62. For general reviews of Eumelos: Huxley, pp. 22–4, 60–79; M. H. Jameson, 'Labda, Lambda, Labdakos', in del Chiaro (n. 23), 6–8.

later cult developments. Most prominent are details of Corinthian royal genealogy and the Dorian pedigree of the city, and Eumelos also takes a somewhat
optimistic view of Corinth's relations with neighbouring states (putting Ephyre
or Corinth at the head of the dynasty of Lakedaimon, for example, and creating
a similarly propagandist genealogy for Arkadia).[73] The Isthmus features as the
burial place of Neleus father of Nestor, although the context of the story is
lost. Perhaps of greater interest is an anonymous hexameter verse recording the
dispute between Poseidon and the Sun over the land of Corinth, for which a
possible source is Eumelos' *Korinthiaka*. A further fragment ascribed to Eumelos
or Arkitios by Athenaios (22c) may record the episode immediately preceding
this, the victory celebrations of Zeus after the Titans had been shut up in
Tartaros.[74]

Contemporary with, or immediately following Eumelos' reshaping of Corinthian myth comes the establishment of a shrine on the ridge of Solygeia
(modern Galataki, Ill.5.7), an isolated site but of particular significance in the

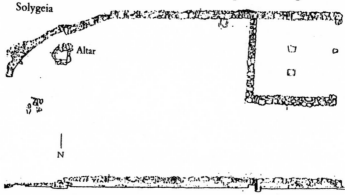

ILL. 5.7 The Shrine at Solygeia (after *Archaeology* 15 (1962), 186)

newly enshrined Corinthian myth-history.[75] The shrine is close to the site of
six Mycenaean chamber tombs, but although the collapsed *dromos* of one tomb
was used to hold a votive deposit, there is nothing to suggest that the presence
of earlier remains influenced the choice of location (and certainly no evidence
for continuity of activity). The earliest votives date from the Early Protocorinthian period, and the site has produced over one thousand vases, including

[73] Lakedaimon: reported by scholiast to Apollonius Rhodios 1. 146–9a; C. Wendel, *Scholia in
Apollonium Rhodium vetera* (Berlin, 1935), 19–20; Apollodoros, *Lib.* 3. 11. 1. Arkadia: *FrGrHist* 451 F 2c;
Apollodoros, *Lib* 3. 9. 1. Huxley (n. 72), 74–5, 77. P. de Fidio, 'Un modello di "mythistorie" Asopia ed
Efirea nei «Korinthiaka» di Eumelo', in Prontera (n. 70), 233–63.
[74] Neleus' tomb reported by Pausanias 2. 2. 2. Arbitration: cited Pharorinos in Corinthian Oration,
Dio Chrysostom 37. 11–12; J. de Arnim (ed.), *Dionis Prusaensis quem vocant Chrysostomum quae extant
omnia* (Berlin, 1893–6), ii. 19. Scholiast on Apollonius Rhodios, *Argonautika*, 1. 1165c; Wendel (n. 73),
106.
[75] Verdelis (n. 15), 184–92; *Praktika* (1958), 135–45.

many miniatures, and over fifty figurines (mainly seated goddesses and poppies, plus koulouria and offering trays, probably indicating a cult of Demeter).[76] The building was restored by its excavator, Nicholas Verdelis, as an apsidal temple built of mud brick on a stone footing, oriented east to west, and with a west entrance and an internal hearth-altar; according to Verdelis, such an archaizing, megaron-like structure, reflected the presence of a hypothetical Middle Helladic predecessor.[77] The remains are, however, very fragmentary, and Verdelis' reconstruction is hypothetical in many respects. In particular, the foundation seems too insubstantial for the kind of superstructure he proposes, and may well be more suitable for a simple peribolos. The building may therefore have begun life as an enclosure of some sort with an altar, and may only have been elaborated during the sixth century, when we have evidence (in the form of Corinthian tiles) for a roof. Whatever the case, the site appears to have been abandoned at the end of the sixth century.[78]

Nicholas Verdelis was surely correct to identify Solygeia as the site of the battle between Dorian invaders and the native Aeolian inhabitants of Corinth recorded by Thucydides (4. 42. 2), an episode of the greatest importance in the history of Dorian Corinth. Whether or not Eumelos also knew the story is unclear, although it fits well with his interest in local genealogy and myth-history.[79] That this story is a creation of the eighth century (or later) and not earlier is shown not only by the discrepancy with the early archaeological record (which indicates continuity of occupation at Corinth), but also by the way in which the story of the first Dorian king Aletes' refoundation of Corinth is linked to the oracle of Zeus at Dodona (the only foundation legend associated with this oracle). Such a connection would be anachronistic in earlier times both in terms of the development of the sanctuary at Dodona, and in relation to the pattern of Corinthian connections in north-west Greece.[80] If the Solygeia shrine did celebrate the refounding of Corinth, it emphasizes discontinuity and

[76] Verdelis (n. 15), 192, identified the deity as Hera on the basis of the koulouria and offering trays, although the presence of poppies and the close similarity of the votives overall to those from the sanctuary of Demeter and Kore on the lower slopes of Acrocorinth has encouraged more recent commentators to identify the shrine with Demeter. R. Stroud, 'The Sanctuary of Demeter and Kore on Acrocorinth. Preliminary Report I: 1961–1962', *Hesperia* 34 (1965), pl. 11; Williams, *Pre-Roman Cults* (n. 45), 190–1; (n. 23), 18 n. 28.

[77] Verdelis (n. 15), 188–92.

[78] A. Mazarakis-Ainian, 'From Rulers' Dwellings to Temples: A Study of the Origins of Greek Religious Architecture in the Protogeometric and Geometric Periods' (Ph.D. diss., University of London, 1987), 748–54, also believes that there may have been no roofed building during the first phase, and that the addition of such a building alongside the retaining/peribolos wall may have been a feature of the second phase. M. O. Knox, 'Megarons and Megara', *CQ* 23 (1973), 16, takes a similar view.

[79] Verdelis (n. 15), 184. T. Dunbabin, 'The Early History of Corinth', *JHS* 68 (1948), 67. R. Stroud, 'Thucydides and the Battle of Solygeia', *CSCA* 4 (1971), 227–47.

[80] H. Parke, *Oracles of Zeus* (Oxford, 1967), 129; Schol. Pindar, *Nemean* 7. 155a, A. B. Drachmann (ed.), *Scholia Vetera in Pindari Carmina* (Leipzig, 1927), iii. 137. G. Huxley, 'The Malian Boat (Aristotle F544)', *Philologus* 119 (1975), 140–2. Morgan (n. 48).

renewal of the kind which is celebrated by Eumelos rather than the continuity and tradition represented at Isthmia. It is the earliest archaeologically demonstrable embodiment of this new tone of myth, and although it would be unwise to infer cause and effect, the coincidence of the two developments is striking. Similar echoes are also evident in later cults, such as those of at least two of the four daughters of Timandros (Chryse, Eurytione, Hellotis, and Kotyto) who were burned to death whilst taking refuge in the temple of Athena when the Dorians took Corinth; Hellotis was celebrated in the festival of the Hellotia and the cult of Kotyto may be associated with the Sacred Spring at Corinth.[81]

The First Temple at Corinth

The final piece in this jigsaw is the first temple on Temple Hill at Corinth itself, the first undoubted shrine in the city centre. The building, a proto-Doric stone structure with a painted tiled roof and painted stucco, marks a wholly different level of investment from what had gone before. Its date, c.680 or soon afterwards (established on the basis of Early Protocorinthian pottery in the construction fill), puts it roughly contemporary with, or slightly later than, Solygeia. Unfortunately, its destruction in the sixth century and the subsequent remodelling of the area means that very few votives can be securely associated with it, although tripods do seem to have been offered (and so we may tentatively suggest that the temple had begun to attract some of the interests hitherto represented at Isthmia).[82] The deity involved is also unclear. Apollo is commonly assumed (largely on the basis of Pausanias' reference (2. 3. 6) to an Apollo temple close to the road to Sikyon), and this would certainly fit the myth of the apportionment of the Corinthia mentioned above, yet the evidence is slight, and the probable double aisle of the temple may indicate that more than one deity was involved. Alternatively, it has been suggested, by Dengate among others, that before 146 BC the temple belonged to Athena and was rededicated to Apollo only after the foundation of the Roman colony.[83] A balance between cults of Athena in Corinth and Poseidon at the Isthmus is certainly attractive, not least because of the common association of the two deities on the Penteskouphia

[81] Hellotia: Pindar, *Olympian* 13. 56; *Etym. Mag.* s.v. 'Hellotis'; O. Broneer, 'Hero Cults in the Corinthian Agora', *Hesperia* 11 (1942), 140–61; S. Herbert, 'The Torch-race at Corinth', in del Chiaro (n. 23), 29–35; Williams, *Pre-Roman Cults* (n. 45), 44–5, 135–6. Heschyius s.v. Κοτυτώ; *Souda* s.v. Κότυς; Steiner (n. 46), 385–408, highlights the funerary nature of the votives at the Sacred Spring and evaluates the evidence for a cult of Kotyto here.

[82] Corinth temple (n. 2).

[83] Fowler and Stilwell (n. 15), 115–16, 130–3. C. Dengate, *The Sanctuaries of Apollo in the Peloponnese* (Ph.D., diss., University of Chicago; Ann Arbor, University Microfilms, 1988), 15–17. Roman remodelling of temple: C. K. Williams II, 'The Refounding of Corinth: Some Roman Religious Attitudes', in S. Macready and F. H. Thompson (edd.), *Roman Architecture in the Greek World* (London, 1987), 31–2; *BCH* 103 (1979), Chronique, 550–3, fig. 65.

plaques (and also for the way this invokes one of the most commonly depicted Corinthian myths, the story of Bellerophon), but there is no clear evidence to support either case.[84]

The location of the temple is also significant in relation to the urban development of Corinth. It lies in the upper Lekhaion road valley, one of the principal residential areas of the Archaic and Classical city which was only settled to any real extent from the early seventh century onwards (coinciding with the further elaboration of the principal local water source, the Sacred Spring, with the addition of a stone floor, water channels and flanking walls). It is easy to exaggerate the extent of this change; the real development of the upper Lekhaion road valley belongs in the sixth century and later, and is accompanied by the appearance of numerous small cult places. Nevertheless, the temple is the first major public building of any kind erected in Corinth, and the choice of a location in what was to become a rich residential area must have been a matter of some significance. The relationship of the temple to the Greek Agora is also a matter of considerable debate. Although it lies beside the Roman Agora, there is no clear evidence to show that the same area served as an agora in both the Greek and Roman periods, and indeed, Charles Williams prefers to locate the Greek Agora on the north side of Temple Hill, closer to the Roman theatre. Whatever the truth, it should be stressed that the temple is the first securely identifiable cult place in the city centre which receives anything like the material investment accorded to earlier rural shrines, a clear reflection of the changing role of the city centre in the social geography of the Corinthia.[85]

Continuity and Change in Corinthian Religion

It is clear that the eighth century was a period of considerable development and reorganization at Corinth, with rapid changes in the cult organization and myth-history of the community accompanying developments in urban structure and probably a population increase. Without seeking to identify any immediate cause of ritual change, it is worth stressing the variety and severity of contemporary upheavals. The colonization of Kerkyra in 734 and Syracuse in 733, for example, may imply land hunger as well as political disaffection (indeed, one of the reforms attributed to the early lawgiver Pheidon was the redivision of land to ensure that the number of plots corresponded with the number of citizens). Equally, even allowing for the traditional hostility shown by ancient commentators towards the Bacchiads, Kypselos' *coup d'état* which ended their 'arbitrary' rule does hint at stresses in government at least during the latter part

---

[84] *Antike Denkmäler*, i, pls. 7–8; ii, pls. 23–4, 39–40. Will (n. 71), 145–68.
[85] Sacred Spring: n. 46. Agora: Williams, *Pre-Roman Cults* (n. 45), 38 (see ch. 8 for summary of later, 7th/6th century, developments); Williams (n. 50), 32–9.

of the eighth century. These are problems which must have affected the entire Corinthia and which could not readily have been addressed via new institutions in the city centre alone. According to Strabo (830), many of the colonists who joined the expedition to Syracuse came from Tenea, and this may be taken to imply that such pressures affected different parts of the Corinthia in different ways.[86] It is therefore not surprising to find that a shrine like Isthmia, which had long played a pan-regional role, was adapted to suit new circumstances; it would perhaps have been more surprising if it had stayed the same. Yet here I differ from François de Polignac in suggesting that the many and various changes described in this chapter are unlikely to have been mere reflections of the needs of the new urban élite of the emergent polis. Instead, I suggest that we are dealing with a community-wide re-evaluation of existing practices, changes required and instituted as much by the rural as the urban population, and that this process extended to the provision of new shrines to deal with interests which could not readily be accommodated within the existing cult framework.

In this climate of change, Isthmia's importance could easily have diminished. That it did not is shown most strikingly by the construction in the mid-seventh century of the second monumental stone temple in the Corinthia, an even grander building than that at Corinth with a colonnade and exterior wall-paintings, and also by the establishment in 582/0 of the Isthmian games, *the* Panhellenic festival under Corinthian patronage.[87] I suggest that two principal factors governed Isthmia's continuing role. The first is its location; as has been emphasized, the sanctuary lies close to a main road that must have taken an increasing weight of traffic from the eighth century onwards. De Polignac has described Isthmia as a marginal sanctuary, and whilst it is not actually on the Corinthian border (and always remained in Corinthian control), it lies on a very dramatic narrowing of the Isthmus, a real 'doorway' as Pindar describes it (*Olympian* 13. 4–5), with Acrocorinth visible immediately behind, a location which is both accessible and highly symbolic of Corinthian territorial control. De Polignac in Chapter 1 of this volume makes a case for marginal (as opposed to true border) sanctuaries as prime sites for the enactment of aristocratic rivalries, and as he points out, the case of Isthmia fits this model very well. The second factor, of equal weight, is Isthmia's long-standing role as a community meeting place, a tradition more powerful than any individual myth.

Isthmia therefore represented a tradition of ritual behaviour which had to be incorporated or manipulated within the expanded order. How the sanctuary's

---

[86] Pheidon: Aristotle *Politics* 1265[b] 12–16. Government: Nikolaos Damaskenos, *FrGrHist* 90 F 57; Salmon (n. 8), 186–95. J. Boardman, *The Greeks Overseas*[1] (London, 1980), 172–4, 225–9. For a different interpretation of the role of Tenea, see I. Malkin, 'Apollo Archegetes and Sicily', *ASNP.* ser.3, 16 (1986), 61–74.

[87] Broneer, *Isthmia* i (n. 2); Gebhard and Hemans (n. 2), 25–40. E. R. Gebhard, 'The Early Stadium at Isthmia and the Founding of the Isthmian Games', in Kyrieleis and Coulson (n. 11), 73–9.

role evolved through many centuries of activity is a subject which demands a much longer discussion than is possible here. It is, though, clear that the distinction between cults established at Isthmia and Corinth remained strict, and we have no evidence for any policy of using specific cults to relate the city to the countryside. Poseidon belonged at the Isthmus, and we have only limited and later evidence for his worship in the city centre (even allowing for the difficulty of locating cults in the archaeological record as well as identifying known cult places in Corinth). Pindar (*Olympian* 13. 69) refers to a cult of Poseidon Damaios which may be linked to the myth of Bellerophon, a particularly popular story in Corinthian art and literature. A circular poros altar dedicated to Poseidon has been discovered in the upper Lekhaion road valley, and Oscar Broneer has also associated an isolated dedication to Zeuxippos with a Poseidon cult. Yet this is scant evidence, and we have no reason to believe that it represents the same cult as that at Isthmia, especially as the horse imagery implied by the name Zeuxippos and the link between Poseidon Damaios and Bellerophon does not form part of Poseidon's image at Isthmia. Transfers of cults tend to be explicit, as for example the institution of Artemis Brauronia on the Athenian Acropolis, and this is simply not the case here.[88]

In this paper, I have focused on Early Iron Age developments and the transformation of Corinthian cult during the eighth and early seventh centuries, but as I have stressed, there is no reason to suppose that the pace of change in any way diminished in later times. New shrines of Demeter and Kore were instituted in the late seventh or early sixth century on the slopes of Acrocorinth and probably on the Rachi at Isthmia also, and in the city of Corinth, the development of public and private cult is intimately linked to changes in the urban fabric. From this time onwards, we may also observe a variety of eastern influences on the nature and form of Corinthian cults, notably that of Aphrodite. At Isthmia, the construction of the Archaic temple during the seventh century was accompanied by that of a monumental altar over 100 feet long, the first of such dimensions. The purpose of this altar remains unclear; it may have been intended for mass display, for Syracuse-style mass slaughter, or perhaps (as Elizabeth Gebhard has suggested) to enable different social groups each to maintain their own place of sacrifice, although if the latter, it is unclear whether this reflects continuity of an earlier social order or a newly established practice based more or less on what had gone on before.[89] It is tempting to try to read

---

[88] Broneer (n. 81), 136–9. J. H. Kent, *Corinth*, viii, 3: *The Inscriptions* (Princeton, NJ, 1966), 5 no. 14. Williams, *Pre-Roman Cults* (n. 45), 24–5 on Poseidon. Cf. Pindar, *Olympian* 13. 69.

[89] Demeter: V. R. Anderson-Stojanović, 'Cult and Industry of Isthmia: A Shrine on the Rachi', *AJA* 92 (1988), 268–96. R. Stroud, 'The Sanctuary of Demeter and Kore on Acrocorinth. Preliminary Report I: 1961–1962', *Hesperia* 34 (1965), 1–24; id. 'The Sanctuary of Demeter and Kore on Acrocorinth. Preliminary Report II: 1964–1965', *Hesperia* 37 (1968), 299–330; N. Bookidis, 'The Sanctuary of Demeter and Kore on Acrocorinth. Preliminary Report III: 1968' *Hesperia* 38 (1969), 297–310; N.

early seventh-century developments back into the eighth century, but in view of the pace and nature of social change in Corinth at this time, this would surely be a mistake.

In short, interpreting the complex of evidence available from a region like Corinth is largely a matter of considering the place of innovation in the context of an essentially accretional tradition. François de Polignac is surely correct to stress that the choice of sanctuary location is a meaningful political statement, but it should not be considered in isolation or on a simplistic level; developments in cult, perhaps more than in any other area of human action, are reflexive, both representing and shaping communal perceptions, and these perceptions have their own traditions which may not easily respond to sudden changes in political circumstances.[90] For this reason, if for no other, it is surely impossible to understand later developments without full consideration of Early Iron Age evidence; in the old mainland cities at least, we can hardly expect to find ritual systems created anew in the eighth century without the accommodation or transformation of existing patterns of activity. That this viewpoint may have early echoes in the Corinthian myth tradition is, I think, suggested by the story of the arbitration over Corinth and the apportionment of Acrocorinth to the Sun and Isthmia to Poseidon, perhaps a mythological accommodation of the growing divide between the old meeting place at Isthmia and the new political centre of Corinth.

Postscript: The case for identifying the Hera Akraia of the *Medea* with Perakhora has recently been restated by B. Menadier, 'The Sanctuary of Hera Akraia and its Religious Connections with Corinth', in R. Hägg (ed.), *Peloponnesian Sanctuaries and Cults* (Stockholm, forthcoming). See also, F. M. Dunn, 'Euripides and the Rites of Hera Akraia', *GRBS* 35 (1994), 103–15, and 'Pausanias and the Tomb of Medea's Children', *Mnemosyne*, 48 (1995), 348–51.

Bookidis and J. E. Fisher, 'The Sanctuary of Demeter and Kore on Acrocorinth. Preliminary Report IV: 1969–1970', *Hesperia* 41 (1972), 283–331; 'The Sanctuary of Demeter and Kore on Acrocorinth. Preliminary Report V: 1971–1973', *Hesperia* 43 (1974), 267–307. E. Pemberton, *Corinth* xviii. 1: *The Sanctuary of Demeter and Kore. The Greek Pottery* (Princeton, NJ, 1989). Potters' Quarter: C. K. Williams II, 'The City of Corinth and its Domestic Religion', *Hesperia* 50 (1981), 408–21. Aphrodite: Williams (n. 23). Long altar: Gebhard and Hemans (n. 2), 41–2; Broneer, *Isthmia* i (n. 2), 98–100. E. Gebhard, 'Evidence for Corinthian Control of the Isthmian Sanctuary', *AJA* 96 (1992), 355, citing Pylian sacrifice in *Odyssey* 3. 5–224. For a general overview see E. Gebhard, 'The Evolution of a pan-Hellenic Sanctuary: From Archaeology towards History at Isthmia,' in Marinatos and Hägg (n. 6) 154–77.

[90] S. Shennan, 'Cultural Transmission and Cultural Change', in R. Torrence and S. van der Leeuw (edd.), *What's New? A Closer Look at the Process of Innovation* (London, 1989), 330–46.

6

Archaeology, the Salaminioi, and the Politics of Sacred Space in Archaic Attica

ROBIN OSBORNE

Oxford University

Historians and archaeologists have generally pursued rather different lines of enquiry in their work on Archaic Athens. Archaeologists have tended to concentrate on artefacts, occasionally raiding Greek texts for possibly relevant snippets. Historians have immersed themselves in texts and raided the work of archaeologists for certain items of archaeological interpretation (such as population growth). Few archaeologists show much awareness for the problematic status of the texts which they plunder, and few historians show any awareness of the nature of the archaeology whose interpretations they come to depend upon.

There are some grounds for claiming that archaeologists have been less remiss than historians in this: given the poverty of the texts, even for sixth-century Athens, historians might reasonably be held to have little to offer. But certainly there can be no real justification for the way in which historians have proceeded: there can be no historical questions to which the nature and distribution of human settlement and activity in Attica are irrelevant. Ignoring the archaeological data, historians simply dream up a picture of what Athens and Attica were like in the seventh and sixth centuries, and they make their judgements of what is and what is not likely to have been the case on the basis of how well it conforms to that dream. The archaeological data do not, of course, form a ready-made picture that is simple to interpret. But to ignore the material evidence entirely should no longer be considered a viable option.

In this paper I want to argue that both history and archaeology have more to contribute to our understanding of cult development in Archaic Attica than has previously been realized. I will suggest that the commonly held and often repeated views about the development of cult activity in sixth-century Athens are plausible only against the background of an imaginary Athens, and that both the archaeological data which are now available for the period and the historical information on cult activity in the classical city point to a society that was rather differently organized and in which cult played a rather different part.

Cult and Politics in Classical Athens

Regular Greek cult practice was this-worldly. There were Mystery cults which concerned themselves with what happened to human beings when they died, but although such cults receive considerable attention in the surviving literature, the vast bulk of the very considerable amount of religious activity in classical Athens was devoted to cults whose sphere of activity was this world rather than any other. This fact is of profound importance for our understanding of the relationship between cult and politics. Cults which are other-worldly inevitably concentrate on the fate of the individual soul, and, although the behaviour which they may require of the individual who would ensure a good lot in the other world may have social and political consequences, it is not this world as such that they seek to change. But the this-worldly cults of the classical world were precisely directed at changing this world, and in seeking to change this world, in attempting to impose some beneficial pattern on happenings outside human control, they inevitably sought to change this world for all who dwelt in it, or in a particular little bit of it, and not just for the individual. And so cult practice always and necessarily involved a community, and the relationship that the individual had with the gods was a community concern.

But if cult activity was of communal concern so also was political activity. Although a this-worldly cult might be credal, the religious cults of the Greek city were not, as A. D. Nock classically demonstrated.[1] What mattered was the performance of cult acts, not the state of mind of the actor. In as far as individuals were recognized as especially 'religious' it was for what they did, not for what they thought. An impious individual might bring disastrous effects upon the community by his or her impiety, but so also an individual who was perceived to be harming other people within or outside the community might bring disastrous effects on the community. That in the one case there would be no possibility of solving the problem by rational argument and in the other there could be expected to be some such possibility did not mean that the community had no interest in the former case. And although the means of political and the means of religious communication were different there was no necessary separation of personnel between those members of the community who looked after that community's relations with the gods and those members of the community who looked after the community's relations with other men.

---

[1] A. D. Nock, *Conversion: The Old and the New in Religion from Alexander the Great to Augustine of Hippo* (Oxford, 1933).

The great overlap between those who dealt with the gods and those who dealt with politics is very easy to demonstrate from Classical Athens. The Assembly began with an act of sacrifice and regularly made decisions about religious matters—establishing priesthoods, regulating the use of sanctuaries, and determining the rules of behaviour at and nature of religious festivals.[2] As its agents in all this it appointed not a separate body of religious specialists but members of the Council of 500, which in any case both prepared and executed its business.[3] The members of the Council and other magistrates were routinely involved in sacrificial and other cult activities, as is clear from the following passage of Antiphon:

These men, knowing all the laws, saw that I was a member of the Council and entered the Council chamber, and in that Council chamber there is a shrine of Zeus Boulaios and Athena Boulaia, and as the Councillors enter they offer prayers, and I was one of those who also did these things, and I went into all the other sanctuaries with the Council and made sacrifices and prayers on behalf of this city and in addition to that I was a prytaneis for all but two days of the first prytany and acted as *hieropoios* and sacrificed on behalf of democracy and put matters to the vote and spoke opinions about matters of the greatest moment and it was clear to everyone that I was an important citizen.[4]

Nor was this identity of 'political' and religious personnel something that occurred only at the level of the city: it is equally to be observed in the divisions of the people, in demes, phratries, etc. So, the deme of Eleusis was as likely to regard itself as the body which would appropriately praise the official who looked after the temple of Demeter and Kore and the Mysteries as was the city as a whole, and just as the city decided what sacrifices should be made when and to what god by the city as a whole, so the divisions of the demos decided upon their own religious calendar, and might make their own sacrifices, either locally or in Athens, on the occasion when the city had a central celebration in honour of a particular deity.[5]

The political implications of all this are important and should be clear. Changes in the definition of a community and the development of new communities inevitably had implications for cult practice, and might have

---

[2] Priesthoods: *IG* i³ 35, 36 (424/3) Priestess of Athena Nike; use of sanctuaries: *IG* i³ 84 (sanctuary of Kodros, Neleus, and Basile); behaviour at festivals: *SEG* 30. 61 with Demosthenes 21. 175–7.

[3] See e.g. *IG* i³ 82 (421/0 BC) the appointment of members of the Council as *hieropoioi* for the festival of the Hephaistia.

[4] Antiphon 6. 45. For the religious role of the archons see [Aristotle], *Constitution of the Athenians* 56–8.

[5] *IG* ii² 1192 (321/0 BC) for Eleusis and the *epimeletes* Xenokles; Lysias 30 and F. Sokolowski, *Lois sacrées des cités grecques* (Paris, 1962), no.10, for the central calendar (of which the latest discussion is P. J. Rhodes, 'The Athenian Code of Laws, 410–399 BC', *JHS* 111 (1991), 87–100); *SEG* 21. 541, 542, 23. 80, 26. 136 for calendars of single demes; *IG* ii² 1358 for calendar of the Marathonian Tetrapolis; D. Whitehead, *The Demes of Attica 508/7–ca.250BC: A Political and Social Study* (Princeton, NJ, 1986), 185–208, and R. Parker, 'Festivals of the Attic Demes', *Acta Universitatis Upsaliensis Boreas* 15 (1987), 137–47, for recent discussions.

implications for cult personnel. Performing religious actions for a community was a source of pride. Theophrastos' man of petty ambition (*Mikrophilotimia*) 'wants to be in on the chores of the prytaneis, so that he can announce the sacred rites to the people, and having got himself kitted out in a splendid cloak and put on a crown goes public and says "Athenians, we prytaneis have sacrificed the Galaxia to the Mother of the Gods and the sacrifices were good and you receive the blessings." And when he has made this announcement he goes away home to his wife exceedingly happy' (Theophrastos, *Characters* 21. 11). The community reflects this in the bestowal of honours on cult officials.[6] But the body with the power is the sovereign body within the community, and it makes no effective distinction between secular and sacred decisions. In as far as there are people recognized as cult experts in Classical Athens they are at most so recognized *informally*, and enjoy special status only in as far as they can persuade the sovereign body, the Assembly, to grant that to them.[7]

It follows from this that in investigating cult activity in Archaic Attica the crucial question is the question of the definition of communities. To what extent are the cult acts, for which there is archaeological evidence, a reflection of a single community and to what extent are they a reflection of a number of communities? In as far as they reflect a number of communities, are these communities conscious of belonging to a single larger community (in the way that Athenian demes of the Classical period recognize centrally appointed cult officials and mark with acts of their own centrally organized cult acts), or are they consciously independent of any larger community? Any answer to these questions, and any understanding of cult in Archaic Attica, has to look at the wider question of community and not simply at the narrower question of cult activity, for only against a picture of the community and its organization can cult activity be understood.

---

[6] An excellent example of this is *IG* ii² 1749 (341/0BC): 'The prytaneis of Aigeis under the archon Nikomakhos made this dedication having been crowned by the Council and the People for their excellence and justice [list of names of prytaneis by deme follows]. Tharrias of Erkhia said: the tribesmen have decided, since Poseidippos of Hestiaia, the Treasurer of the tribe, has been a good and just treasurer for the tribesmen and has caused all the sacrifices that should be sacrificed to be sacrificed for the prytaneis, to praise him for his justice towards the prytaneis and crown him with an olive crown. Aristophanes of Ikaria said: the tribesmen have decided, since they looked after bringing the People together well and justly and the giving out of tokens and made a donation to the tribesmen, to praise for their excellence and justice towards the tribesmen and crown each with a crown of olive for their excellence and justice towards the tribe: Diodoros son of Philokles of Gargettos, Timokritos son of Timokratos of Ikaria, Tharrias son of Tharriades of Erkhia. Tharrias of Erkhia said: Praise the *hieropoioi* who were *hieropoioi* for the Mysteries at Eleusis and crown each of them with a crown of olive for their excellence and justice towards the tribesmen: Poseidippos of Hestiaia, Timokritos of Ikaria, Aristophanes of Ikaria, Khairias of Plotheia, Kallistratos of Teithras, Python of Kydantidai, Eubios of Ankyle, Theomnestos of Phegeia, Theophilos of Myrrhinoutta, Melieus of Ionidai. The People. The Council. Diodoros of Gargettos said: praise Aristophanes son of Eukleidos of Ikaria for his justice towards the tribe Aigeis and crown him with a crown of olive.'

[7] So Lampon in *IG* i³ 78. Note that the *hieropoioi* whose advice, together with that of the priest of Dionysos, is taken by Council and People in *IG* ii² 410 (*c*.330 BC) were elected from the Council.

Cult and Politics in Archaic Athens: The Current Orthodoxy

The orthodox view about the development of cult in Archaic Athens is well represented by two recent works, ironically both by archaeologists: Catherine Morgan's *Athletes and Oracles*, and Alan Shapiro's *Art and Cult under the Tyrants at Athens*.[8] Morgan provides a succinct summary:

the appearance of temples and formal festivals, with their implications of state investment, provide unequivocal evidence for the emergence of ordering of social and political territory on a regional basis. Many of these developments date from Peisistratid times and were perhaps conscious attempts to solve a major problem for the emergent Athenian state, that of defining an exceptionally large territory and relating it to the civic centre. In view of the scale of the problem, it is not surprising that the mythological and cult mechanisms employed are sophisticated and relatively late in their final development.

The role of the Peisistratids in centralising cults has long been recognised, but the way in which centre and boundaries are balanced deserves greater attention. Peisistratos, for example, is credited with the institution of the cult of Artemis Brauronia on the Acropolis, and this was balanced by the contemporary development of a major festival at his home town, Brauron. The institution of the Little Bears at Brauron also involved the movement of young daughters of leading Athenian families from their homes, for a period of residence and service at the sanctuary. The development of the Great Mysteries at Eleusis and their incorporation into Athenian state religion also date to this period. In this case, connections between the border town, Eleusis, and Athens were complex and functioned in several ways. There were physical links, with a procession from Athens to Eleusis forming an integral part of the cult celebration, a link between the Mysteries located in Eleusis and the lesser Mysteries close to Athens (and also the presence of the Eleusinion in Athens itself), and a mythological connection, with Herakles playing a parallel role in the foundation of both celebrations. (pp. 12–14)

Advocates of the orthodoxy will admit that the specific evidence linking any cult to Peisistratos is slim.[9] Shapiro, for example, admits that 'Of all the cults later known in Athens, the establishment of only two is explicitly attributed to Peisistratos or his family by written sources, in one case not necessarily reliable ones: the peribolos of the Twelve Gods in the Agora ... and the sanctuary of Pythian Apollo' (p. 13). Shapiro minimizes the significance of this by claiming that 'The only Athenian cults for which we have fairly secure evidence earlier than the sixth century are ... those of the city goddess Athena and Zeus' (p. 12), a statement only credible if archaeological evidence, such as that from Hymettos, is reckoned to be insecure.[10] He then proposes that Peisistratid interference with cults can be assumed because 'the Tyrants would have had good reason to

---

[8] Catherine Morgan, *Athletes and Oracles: The Transformation of Olympia and Delphi in the Eighth Century BC* (Cambridge, 1990); H. A. Shapiro, *Art and Cult under the Tyrants at Athens* (Mainz, 1989).

[9] Compare also R. Garland, *Introducing New Gods* (London, 1991), 39: 'Yet the evidence for all this remains tantalisingly inconclusive.'

[10] M. K. Langdon, *A Sanctuary of Zeus on Mount Hymettos, Hesperia* Suppl. 16 (Princeton, NJ, 1976).

establish other cults and sanctuaries' and because 'Parallels with sixth century tyrants elsewhere in Greece show that manipulation of cult was one of the principal political tools at a tyrant's disposal' (p. 13). This leads him to a position where he can both acknowledge that the evidence for Peisistratos having had influence in or control over several regional cults in Attica is 'circumstantial and indecisive' and also suggest that 'it would if true accord well with our picture of a tyrant who relied heavily on cults both to consolidate his own power and to give a strong identity to the polis' (p. 15). This is clearly a very unsatisfactory way of arguing, and if we can find any sort of evidence that will bring a way out of this sort of circularity it will clearly be welcome. My claim here is that the archaeological evidence does offer just such an exit.

Religious Activity in Archaic Attica: The Archaeological Picture

Archaeological finds enable us not only to observe the distribution of cult activity across the landscape but to date that activity and to compare it with contemporary patterns of habitation and other activities.[11]

Prior to Late Geometric, archaeological evidence indicative of cult activity in Attica is known from Athens, Brauron, Eleusis, Peiraieus (Artemis Mounykhia), Phyle (a single vessel), and Hymettos. During the Late Geometric evidence also appears from Akharnai (the Menidhi tholos), Kiapha Thiti, Marathon, and Tourkovouni, although there is no further trace of activity at Phyle (Ill. 6.1). In the seventh century, down to 630 BC, evidence for cult activity disappears from Marathon but appears additionally at Merenda, Prophitis Elias, perhaps Rhamnous, Sounion, Thorikos, Vari (Lathouresa), and Varkiza (Ill. 6.2). This list has no chance of being at all complete, but the pattern of cult activity expanding steadily into more and more of the Attic countryside which it offers cannot for that reason be ignored.

This pattern of steady expansion contrasts with the archaeological record for settlement as attested by habitation sites and by burials. Here there is a very distinct rise in the number of known burial and settlement sites in the later part of the eighth century, but only a small number of those sites have also yielded clear evidence of seventh-century presence and there are relatively few new seventh-century burial and habitation sites. Indeed it seems that on some sites, at Lathouresa perhaps and Thorikos, the ceramic evidence points to cult activities being the only activities sustained during part at least of the seventh century.

---

[11] Compare F. de Polignac, 'Sanctuaires et société en Attique géométrique et archaïque: réflexion sur les critères d'analyse' in A. Verbanck-Piérard and D. Viviers (edd.), *Culture et cité: L'Avènement d'Athènes à l'époque archaïque* (Brussels, 1995), 75–101. De Polignac's analysis is a good deal more detailed and nuanced than that traditionally offered. I am very grateful to the author for allowing me to see a copy of this paper in advance of publication.

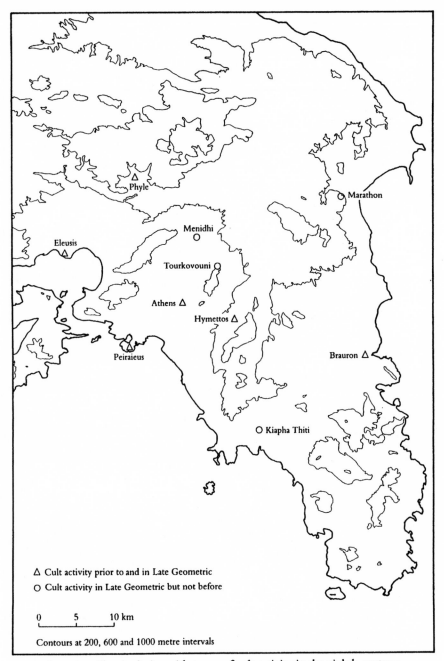

ILL. 6.1 Sites in Attica with traces of cult activity in the eighth century

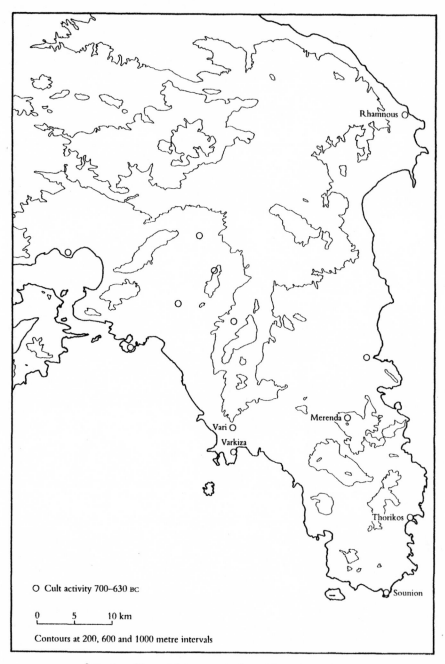

ILL. 6.2 Sites with traces of cult activity, c.700–630 BC

It is not my intention here further to discuss the problems of the seventh-century evidence.[12] What I wish to draw attention to is (a) the continued spread of cult activity in the face of declining evidence for other forms of activity; (b) the persistence with which energy and material goods continue to be devoted to cult activity on sites far from the centre.

What we are to make of patterns of cult activity in the sixth century must depend on what we have made of the patterns of activity in the seventh century and before. Do Brauron and Eleusis, the two sites round which the traditional interpretation of Peisistratos' activity revolves, constitute, as the orthodoxy presupposes, somehow rival centres of religious power in the eighth and seventh centuries? And if they do, is the same true of all the other places of cult activity outside Athens established before the activity of Peisistratos? If it is not true of those other places, what is it that makes Brauron and Eleusis different and in what ways does that difference manifest itself in the archaeological record?

Both Brauron and Eleusis were sites of Mycenaean activity, but at Brauron certainly and at Eleusis not improbably, there was a break in human activity before it was re-established at Brauron in the ninth century and at Eleusis in the tenth. At Brauron the details of activity in the Geometric and Protoattic periods are ill known but the presence of cult activity is not in question, and a vase attributed by Beazley to the Burgon Group and dated to c.560 which shows dancing to an *aulos* may be hard evidence that the ritual involving young girls was already established by that date.[13] The temple there seems to date to the end of the sixth or beginning of the fifth century, and it is in the late sixth century that krateriskoi, vases of a shape which derives from a Protogeometric prototype and which are particularly associated with the worship of Artemis, first appear on the site, though most of them apparently date to the early fifth century.[14] The krateriskoi, although a peculiarly Artemisian shape, are not at all unique to Brauron (they are found at the sanctuary of Artemis Mounykhia in the Peiraieus, at Eleusis, and in Athens). All the vases published from Brauron are very much Attic mainstream, and indeed are remarkable for their quality: many of them can be associated with particular painters and workshops in Athens. For the antiquity of the festival of the Brauronia we have no literary

---

[12] See R. G. Osborne, 'A Crisis in Archaeological History? The Seventh Century in Attica', *BSA* 84 (1989), 297–322 where references to the sources of archaeological information exploited here will be found. To the list there add: Kiapha Thiti: H. Lauter, *Der Kultplatz auf dem Turkovuni 302,1, AM* Beiheft 12 (1984), 129; *Lathuresa: Beiträge zur Architektur und Siedlungsgeschichte in spätgeometrischer Zeit* (Mainz, 1985), 3; Peiraieus: L. Palaiokrassa, 'Neue Befunde aus dem Heiligtum der Artemis Munichia', *AM* 104 (1989), 1–40; Rhamnous: *Ergon* (1982), 34–6; Varkiza: H. Lauter and H. Lauter-Bufe, 'Ein attisches Höhenheiligtum bei Varkiza', in R. Hanauer (ed.), *Festschrift Werner Böser* (Karlsruhe, 1986) 285–309.
[13] See *Ergon* (1961), 28; *Praktika* (1949), 79; L. G. Kahil, 'Quelques vases du sanctuaire d'Artémis à Brauron,' in L. G. Kahil (ed.), *Neue Ausgrabungen in Griechenland, Antike Kunst* Beiheft 1 (1963), 5–29, no. 3 pl. 1.4.
[14] L. G. Kahil, 'Autour de l'Artémis attique', *Antike Kunst* 8 (1965), 20–32 at 20.

evidence at all, and support for the assumption that Peisistratos had a hand in promoting the Brauron cult comes from the tradition that his family hailed from the neighbourhood and from Photios' statement that he 'equipped the sanctuary' (which may itself be an elaboration of the tradition of his links with the area).[15]

At Eleusis, burial practices in the later Dark Age differ in some observable ways from those at Athens but none of the differences could not adequately be accounted for by a certain time-lag between centre and periphery. In terms of pottery, the assemblage at Eleusis does include vessels of Corinthian origin (e.g. North-West Cemetery grave G 11 has a Corinthian MG krater (no. 133) and oinochoe (no. 136) but also Attic pyxides (nos. 134–5)) but it remains predominantly Attic and not significantly distinct in any way from the assemblages from e.g. the Kerameikos.[16] Several painters and workshops whose wares can be distinguished are represented in both Eleusis and Kerameikos cemeteries (as well as elsewhere in Attica).[17] There is no sign that the community at Eleusis is using material culture in any way to mark out its distinction from the community at Athens, and it is reasonable to assume that relations between the two communities were as close as those between Athens and the rest of Attica, throughout the Geometric period, whatever we take to be the political implications of that.[18]

Nor is it reasonable to suppose that things were any different in the seventh century. Eleusis offers a rich sequence of fragments of Early and Middle Protoattic vessels, almost all of which are closely paralleled elsewhere in Attica. Indeed the Analatos painter is well represented at Eleusis and by a plaque from Sounion (one of the earliest finds from Sounion) as well as in Athens itself. With the exception of rich Middle Protoattic black and white style finds on Aigina, which may indeed have been manufactured there, Protoattic pottery is notoriously limited to Attica in its distribution. Again this cultural uniformity, indeed cultural exclusiveness, would seem to have political implications.

Against this background of cultural homogeneity scholars have long attempted to paint a picture of hostility and separation between Athens and Eleusis. The evidence for this (legends of *sunoikismos* by Theseus of twelve

---

[15] Photios, *Lexicon* (ed. Theodorides) s.v. Brauronia: καὶ ἦν τὸ ἱερὸν πρὸς τῷ Ἐρασίνῳ ποταμῷ κατασκευασθὲν ὑπὸ Πεισιστράτου. See also R. G. Osborne, *Demos: The Discovery of Classical Attika* (Cambridge, 1985), 156–7.

[16] Corinthian is in fact better represented at Thorikos: see M. Devillers, *An Archaic and Classical Votive Deposit from a Mycenaean Chamber Tomb at Thorikos*, Miscellanea Graeca, fasc. 8 (Ghent, 1988).

[17] J. N. Coldstream, *Greek Geometric Pottery* (London, 1968), 32, 55, 64.

[18] For sophisticated arguments about the connection between cultural and political homogeneity see C. Morgan and T. Whitelaw, 'Pots and Politics: Ceramic Evidence for the Rise of the Argive State', *AJA* 95 (1991), 79–108. Compare also C. Rolley, 'Argos, Corinthe, Athènes: Identité culturelle et modes de développement (ixe–viiie siècles),' in M. Piérart (ed.), *Polydipsion Argos: Argos de la fin des palais mycéniens à la constitution de l'état classique*, BCH Suppl. 22 (Paris, 1992), 37–49 at 46.

independent communities, of which Eleusis was one, Herodotos' anecdote about Solon's story of Tellos who dies when the Athenians were fighting at Eleusis against their neighbours (1. 30), and the supposedly partisan *Homeric Hymn to Demeter*) is extremely weak.[19] When Shapiro says (p. 67) 'The exact period of Eleusis' incorporation into Attica, together with Athens' takeover of control of the sanctuary, is also not to be found in our sources. A plausible reconstruction of events, however, would place this takeover in or just before the time of Solon', his plausibility is baseless, and is in part a result of his never questioning that there has to be a moment of incorporation and take-over at all. I suggest that the archaeological evidence rather supports the idea that Eleusis was part of Attica from whenever Attica first began to be an entity, and that questions of take-over of control of the sanctuary should also be viewed critically.

De Polignac in *La Naissance de la cité grecque* devotes some attention to what he calls 'l'exception athénienne'.[20] Moved by the way in which, in the parallel stories of Kleomenes' military intervention at Athens and at Argos, there is no Athenian equivalent of the Argive Heraion—a religious site whose capture constitutes a symbolic victory over the city as a whole—de Polignac suggests that while Argos was 'bipolar', Athens was 'concentric' with a major procession (the Panathenaia) which marched into rather than out of the town centre (pp. 87–8).[21] De Polignac traces Athens' exceptional formation back to her exceptional continuity from the Bronze Age, a continuity that enabled the myth of autochthony and which resulted in her possessing 'la seule acropole où une divinité effectivement poliade se substitue vraiment aux derniers vestiges d'une royauté déliquescente' (p. 90).

De Polignac is too quick to dismiss the possibility of shrines outside Athens serving symbolically for Athens as a whole: the mythical rape of Athenian women from Brauron (Herodotos 6. 138) and the story of the attempted rape from Halimous (Plutarch, *Solon* 8), both sites with classical processions linking them to the town, surely rotate around precisely this possibility. But he must be correct in supposing that the significance of cult activity at Eleusis for Athens is different from the significance of cult activity at the Argive Heraion for Argos. Central to the difference is the fact that Eleusis is a settlement at least as soon as it is a cult centre. The Argive Heraion was an isolated foundation, the Telesterion at Eleusis was in the midst of a community.

As de Polignac points out, while the worshipping community of the Argive

[19] See K. Clinton, 'The Author of the Homeric Hymn to Demeter', *OpAth* 16 (1986), 43–9, and R. Parker, 'The *Hymn to Demeter* and the *Homeric Hymns*', *Greece and Rome* 38 (1991), 1–17.

[20] F. de Polignac, *La Naissance de la cité grecque* (Paris, 1984).

[21] For some reservations about bipolarity see C. Calame, *Thésée et l'imaginaire athénien: Légende et culte en Grèce antique* (Lausanne, 1990), Ch. 5.

Heraion is the whole city, the worshipping community at Eleusis comes to be comprised of all initiates regardless of their place of origin or affiliation within Greece. But the fact that the interested public for cult activities at Eleusis is potentially very much wider than the local community or even the city should not be allowed to obscure the particular connection of the cult with both local and wider community. As the cult gains fame so it brings wealth and prestige to the community, raising the profile of individuals within the community and of the community within the wider community of the city.

Culturally Eleusis is Athenian from as far back into the Dark Age as we can go. I have suggested that there is no reason to believe that Eleusis was not also politically Athenian from as early a date as it makes sense to talk of a political unit (and dating the rise of the polis is no part of my task here). The wider cult clientele that the Mysteries attracted did not jeopardize the cultural identity, and there is no case for believing that it jeopardized the political identity. Rather, Eleusis offered to Athenians a cult centre which was within their territory and recognized as such but which attracted, rather than repelled as the Argive Heraion did, outside participants, thus actually signalling the unusual power and facilities of Athens without compromising the integrity of the community whose exclusively Athenian cultic activities could be maintained quite distinctly elsewhere.

The Place of the Salaminioi

What we make of the maintenance and establishment of other cult places in Attica is very largely dependent on who worships at them. That in the Classical period many of the sanctuaries in the countryside were claimed by the Athenians as a whole is clear both from what we know of cult practices, and from associated myths (like those involving Brauron and Halimous to which reference has been made above). But these stories are of unknown antiquity, a fact which has been instrumental in enabling the theory of 'sixth-century take-over' to get off the ground.

There are archaeological arguments that are relevant here (including those involving hero cults[22]), but I want here to try one that is independent of detailed analysis of the archaeology. This concerns the *genos* of the Salaminioi. Our knowledge of the Salaminioi derives almost entirely from inscriptions, and for our purposes here there is just one inscription that is important. This is a record, dated to the archon year of Kharikleides (363/2 BC), of the results of the arbitration of a dispute between two branches of the *genos*, the Salaminians of

---

[22] On the (peculiar) pattern of hero cult in Attica see A. J. M. Whitley, 'Early States and Hero Cult: A Re-appraisal,' *JHS* 108 (1988), 176–8.

the Seven Tribes and the Salaminians from Sounion (*SEG* 21. 527). The opening lines read: Θεοί | Ἐπὶ Χαρικλεῖδ v ἄρχοντος Ἀθηναίοις· ἐπὶ τοῖσ[δ]|ε διήλλαξαν οἱ διαιτηταὶ Σαλαμίνιος τὸς ἐκ τῶ|v Ἑπταφυλῶν καὶ Σαλαμινίος τοὺς ἀπὸ Σονίο. The settlement of the dispute involved going through all the property and obligations of the *genos* and deciding which groups had responsibility for what. We thus learn about the priesthoods belonging to the *genos*, and about the land owned by the *genos*. This reveals the geographical spread of the obligations of the *genos*, a spread which has implications for the nature of the geography of sacred space in archaic Attica.

A list will make clear what is involved. The *genos* looks after the priesthood of Athena Skiras, of Herakles at Sounion at a location called Porthmos, of Eurysakes, and of Aglauros, Pandrosos, and Kourotrophos. It owns land at the Herakleion at Porthmos, at Koile. The members of the Salaminioi of the Seven Tribes who take the oath come from the demes of Boutadai, Agryle, Akharnai, and Epikephisia.

We know that the sanctuary of Athena Skiras was at Phaleron (Pausanias 1. 1. 4, 1. 36. 4) and that the Eurysakeion was in Athens where it served as the repository for decrees of the tribe Aiantis. The location of Epikephisia is uncertain but it is likely to be close to the town of Athens, and thus the demes to which the members of the Salaminioi of the Seven Tribes belong are all relatively close to the town of Athens. It therefore looks as if the *genos* of the Salaminioi had two foci—Sounion and the town of Athens. The important question in assessing the significance of this is the question of the date from which this had been true.

A *terminus ante quem* for the Salaminioi being thus disposed is provided by the title 'of the Seven Tribes'. This title must post-date the Kleisthenic reforms of *c.*507, since previously Athens had had but four tribes. But the title presupposes the dispersion of the Salaminioi across parts of Attica sufficiently disparate to belong to seven of the ten Kleisthenic tribes, and that dispersion must have been pre-Kleisthenic, since once an Athenian of the time of Kleisthenes was registered in a deme and tribe all his descendants, barring their adoption into other families, remained members of that deme and tribe whether they kept their old residence or whether they moved. The question thus becomes, how long before 507 had the Salaminioi been established at both Athens and Sounion?

Broadly speaking previous scholars have held one of three positions. Ferguson, who first published the inscription and whose general view has gained most support, argued as follows: 'The Salaminioi as an organisation so named cannot antedate the opening of the struggle between Athens and Megara for Salamis.' 'It was only on the annexation of Eleusis that the possession of Salamis became a sort of geographical necessity for Athens.' 'In fact the struggle did not open till the end of the seventh century BC at the earliest.' 'The Salaminioi came into being to promote and justify the claims of Athens to possession, on the basis of rightful ownership, of Salamis.'[23] Ferguson thus favours a date c.600 BC.

Nilsson reacting immediately to the publication of the decree, took a different view.[24] He argued that the Salaminioi are people from Salamis resettled by the Athenians after Salamis had been granted to Athens by the arbitration of Kleomenes and others (attested in Plutarch, Solon 10) which he dates to c.509 BC. He imagined the Athenians handing over to the Salaminioi old Attic cults and organizing them as a genos. This was all in the interest of winning the favour of the people of Salamis.

Guarducci moved in the opposite direction.[25] Arguing that on the basis of names similarly formed from place-names the Salaminioi ought to be made up of Athenians who owned land on Salamis, she suggests that these were Athenians who went to Salamis not later than 700 BC when Athens annexed Eleusis and who were then thrown out by the Megarians in the course of the seventh century, prior to Solon's further action to recover the island.

The issues here are complex. The Salaminioi do not fit into the pattern of a normal genos.[26] They have a name which refers to a place rather than to an apical ancestor, they look after more than one cult, and they are geographically dispersed. How did this group come to be responsible for a goddess who presides over a festival, the Oskhophoria, which is evidently of considerable antiquity (on the basis of such features as the 'fivefold cup' drunk by the winner of the race, and of the complexity of the mythical nexus into which it is tied)? Nilsson's solution is to go as late as possible and make the Salaminioi a very artificial construct. Guarducci's is to push the date back far enough for no detailed questions to be asked. Ferguson adopted a middle path between the two solutions, going for as early a date as he thought possible given the historical background which he assumed.

Of all these scholars the only one to attempt to bring archaeological evidence into play was Guarducci, who noted that John Young had suggested that there might be a connection between some seventh-century plaques from Sounion showing Herakles and the Herakleion at Porthmos. Given the fragility of evidence of that sort it might be as well to start at the other end. The archaeology of Salamis is very unsatisfactory, but that is not to say that nothing is or can be known.

Salamis enjoys its greatest burst of archaeological limelight in the Sub-

[23] W. S. Ferguson, 'The Salaminioi of Heptaphylai and Sounion,' Hesperia 7 (1938), 1–74, quotations from p. 42. Calame (n. 21), 422 adopts a similar position (cf. also 445–6).

[24] M. P. Nilsson, 'The New Inscription of the Salaminioi,' AJP 59 (1938), 385–93.

[25] M. Guarducci, 'L'Origine e le vicende del γένος attico dei Salaminii', Rivista di filologia e di istruzione classica NS 26 (1948), 223–43.

[26] See also, on this, F. Bourriot, Recherches sur la nature du genos (Lille, 1976), 574–94, 688, 1095–1100.

mycenaean period, from which a sizeable cemetery has been excavated.[27] The cemetery and the pottery from it can be directly compared to the contemporary cemetery at the Kerameikos. There are significant variations between the two cemeteries: the Kerameikos burials are supine, those at Salamis contracted (the graves were only 0.9–1.2 m. long); the pottery from Salamis has a 'slightly provincial' look. But there are also very close similarities: the most common vessel at both sites is the amphoriskos; very few vessel forms at Salamis are not paralleled at the Kerameikos: all but four of the decorative motifs present at Salamis are also present at the Kerameikos, and all but three of the motifs present at the Kerameikos are also present at Salamis. The finds at Salamis other than pottery are also very close to those from Athens itself. This is to be seen in contrast to the pattern of Submycenaean pottery elsewhere, where the assemblage is very different, with e.g. the amphoriskos a rare find at Argos and unknown in Elis. The only aspect of the Salamis cemetery material which sets it apart from the Athenian is its clean and abrupt finishing date: there are simply no Protogeometric traits in the Salamis material at all.

The archaeological record from Salamis between the end of the Submycenaean period and before the fifth century is thin in the extreme. On the slopes of Prophitis Elias, near the church of Ayia Kyriaki, a pit was excavated in 1978 which yielded Late Helladic and Geometric pottery. Otherwise there is no material at all before the sixth century when isolated tomb finds begin to appear (e.g. at Odhos Matrozou 2, Ambelakia).[28] What are we to make of this? How should the archaeological silence be interpreted? There is no shortage of Mycenaean or Classical evidence from Salamis, so it is difficult to put the Submycenaean presence and Geometric and Archaic absence down simply to chance. A valuable refuge site, it might well be held that Salamis was, in normal conditions and when population pressure was not problematic, not an attractive place to live. That the island had a very clear strategic importance for Athens' relations with Megara (and vice versa) did not make it a prime residential site. That the Athenians may have struggled for control of Salamis does not mean that they were also struggling for control of residents of Salamis.

There are two important conclusions that may tentatively be drawn from the archaeology. First, in as far as there is archaeological material at all from Salamis it is all culturally Athenian. This is true of Submycenaean Salamis, and it is true of late sixth-century and Classical Salamis. It appears to be true also of the small Geometric deposit. Recent finds in Megara have shown just how different the material assemblage of Geometric and Archaic Megara looked.[29] Secondly, until

---

[27] S. Wide, 'Gräberfunde aus Salamis,' *AM* 35 (1910), 17–36; C.-G. Styrenius, 'The Vases from the Submycenaean Cemetery on Salamis,' *OpAth* 4 (1962), 103–23.

[28] *AD* 33 (1978), B1 51 (Ayia Kyriaki); *AD* 37 (1982), B1 43 (Ambelakia).

[29] See *AD* 36 (1981), B1 39 and pl. 20b–d.

new archaeological finds prove the contrary we might do well to contemplate
the historical consequences of considering Salamis to have been thinly populated
in the Geometric and Archaic periods. This hypothesis would have the
additional advantage of explaining why Kleisthenes, at a time when everyone
believes Salamis to have been adjudicated into Athens' hands, did not recognize
Salamis as a deme in his new system. It may well be that, kleroukhs or no
kleroukhs, there was in 507 nothing that could reasonably be deemed a community sufficient in size to warrant representation on the Council of 500.[30]

What are the implications of this for the Salaminioi? The only period at
which the archaeology of the island suggests that a population left Salamis is
the Submycenaean period. If we are to interpret the Salaminioi as men
descended from residents of Salamis then archaeologically those residents must
have left at the end of the Submycenaean period. And if they did that then they
can hardly have moved directly to Sounion, where there is no archaeological
evidence prior to the end of the eighth century, but must have come to Athens
itself and have kept themselves sufficiently distinct there to maintain their
identity. They may indeed have been encouraged to maintain a Salaminian
identity because of the territorial claim implicit in that. (This is not a new view,
for Humphreys independently makes the same suggestion: 'I suggest that the
nucleus of the *genos* may have migrated from Salamis to Athens in the Dark
Ages, settling close to the Acropolis at first and later moving out to Alopeke';
but she takes a different view of what then happened: 'The move of one branch
to Sounion may have taken place only when the silver mines began to attract
interest, in the sixth century.')[31]

The nature of the Oskhophoria, for which the Salaminioi provided the
oskhophoroi, the young men who carried branches of vines with grapes hanging
from them, may provide some support for this interpretation. That festival
opened with a procession from Athens to the sanctuary of Athena Skiras at
Phaleron. The 'Skiras' eponym carries connotations of marginal land, and
according to Strabo (9. 393 C) Skiras was an old name for Salamis. It is attractive
to see the Salaminioi owing their responsibility for providing the marginal
adults for this festival centred on a marginal sanctuary to their own marginal
status[32] as refugees from territory that was itself marginally Athenian.[33]

[30] On the kleroukhy and its date see R. Meiggs and D. M. Lewis, *A Selection of Greek Historical
Inscriptions to the End of the Peloponnesian War*, rev. edn. (Oxford, 1988), no. 14.

[31] S. C. Humphreys, 'Phrateres in Alopeke, and the Salaminioi,' *ZPE* 83 (1990), 247. Note also
C. Sourvinou-Inwood, in R. A. Crossland and A. Birchall (edd.), *Bronze Age Migrations in the Aegean*
(London, 1972), 217–19.

[32] P. Vidal-Naquet, 'The Black Hunter and the Origins of the Athenian Ephebeia,' in R. L. Gordon
(ed.), *Myth, Religion and Society* (Cambridge,1981), 147–62 at 156–7.

[33] De Polignac (n. 20), 72 n. 89. It might equally be argued, of course, that the marginal status of
Salamis caused the name Salaminioi to be given to a group that was marginal in other ways, but in that
case either the name was bestowed when that marginal group was first established or recognized (giving

The Oskhophoria, with its procession out to a sanctuary dedicated to the goddess of the city, but to that goddess in a particular guise as protector of marginal territory, offers Athens' closest equivalent to the pattern of cult activity linking Argos and the Argive Heraion. By processing to the edge of Athenian territory, and exploiting the approach to the boundary of the territory as a way of thinking about young men approaching the boundary of manhood, the community both laid claim to *chora* as well as *asty* as comprising the city and also suggested the responsibility of the young men for maintaining the integrity of the city.

Viewed like this, it is attractive to see the Salaminioi as being further selected to establish cultic activities at Sounion when the expansion of settlement within Attica brought that within the ambit of the settled community, perhaps some time around 700 BC or shortly after. This would make the dispersion of the Salaminioi very much part of the spread of cult activity over Attica to which the archaeological evidence for the seventh century bears witness. And this would suggest that far from that cultic activity being seen as in any sense creating religious centres which acted as *rivals* of Athens these cultic developments should be seen as tied in to an overall pattern of cultic activity in which the claims of a single community to possession of the whole of the territory of Attica were increasingly clearly and strongly marked. When Solon established the first Sacrificial Calendar for the Athenians he would simply have been formalizing established practice.[34]

Conclusions

The current orthodoxy about the pattern of cult activity in Attica was built on the assumption that from time immemorial all the major Classical communities in Attica had been in existence and that Classical Attica had to be created by forcing these separate communities into a single unit. It has long been clear that there was neither archaeological nor literary support for such an assumption, but while few would now lay claim to such a view explicitly it has remained implicit in their views about the political relevance of cult activity.

I have tried to argue here that not only does the archaeology not support the orthodox view, but that it actually offers us a radically different view. The archaeological evidence points both to a great contraction of settlement in Attica on a very few sites in the Submycenaean and Protogeometric periods, and to a gradual expansion of settlement and cult activity in the eighth century

essentially the same story as presented here), or else some historical moment has to be found at which it was worth renaming the marginal group Salaminioi, and it is not clear to me that any such suitable moment prior to 507 BC is preserved in the traditions about Archaic Attica.

[34] Plutarch, *Solon* 25. 2; E. Ruschenbusch, *ΣΟΛΩΝΟΣ ΝΟΜΟΙ, Historia* Einzelschrift 16 (Wiesbaden, 1966), F83–5 (especially F83 (Steph. Byz. s.v. Hagnous) which establishes that the calendar included sacrifices outside Athens.

followed by some settlement contraction but a continued expansion of cult activity in the seventh century.

By exploiting the Classical epigraphic evidence for the responsibilities of the Salaminioi and for their places of residence in *c.*507 BC I have argued that it is not implausible that the use of cult to stake a claim to territory as well as town may well have been already a feature of Athenian community activity before 700 BC, in the Oskhophoria, and that the great seventh-century expansion of cult (including cult activity involving the Salaminioi at Sounion) should be seen in terms of the marking out of claims to an interest in the whole territory of Classical Attica by members of a community which identified itself as a single community, rather than as a mark of division. The model of classical cult activity with which I began suggests that although the members of the community may in many cases have been acting alone or in small groups that need not involve their acting in narrow sectional interests.

François de Polignac wanted to assimilate the Salaminioi to what he considered the supposedly better known cases of sixth-century processional developments at Eleusis and Brauron.[35] I, on the contrary, suggest that the case of the Salaminioi should be treated as the model. On this view Athenian cult practice and politics were linked from the beginning, and the link had nothing to do with Peisistratos. If the sixth century leaves more monumental remains to mark cult activity at Eleusis, Brauron, and elsewhere than does the seventh century then the same is true on the Athenian Acropolis itself, and indeed outside Attica. That the investment in cult activities acquires a monumental form does not require that the motivation for the investment changes. All the archaeological evidence points to cult activity outside Athens being the product of the activities of a single community. Attempts to use archaeological straws to provide Peisistratos with the sort of cult role that modern historians think he should have had, and which literary sources fail to give him, fly in the face of the overall character of the archaeological evidence. Within the past few years the one piece of evidence generally acknowledged to show Peisistratos making a cult initiative (the claim that dramatic activity at the Great Dionysia began in his time) has been challenged.[36] It is time to come to terms with how unlike the autocrats of more recent ages Peisistratos and other 'tyrants' were.

There is much speculation involved in what I have been suggesting. I am indeed less concerned to assert that the conclusions are right than to assert that the method is right. History and archaeology must talk to each other if we are to deepen our understanding of Archaic Greek history.[37]

[35] De Polignac (n. 20), 89 n. 134.

[36] M. L. West, 'The Early Chronology of Attic Tragedy', *CQ* 39 (1989), 251–4; W. R. Connor, 'City Dionysia and Athenian Democracy', in J. R. Fears (ed.), *Aspects of Athenian Democracy*, Classica et Mediaevalia Dissertationes 11 (Copenhagen, 1990) 7–32.

[37] An earlier version of this paper was read at the AIA session in Chicago, and at the University of Groningen. I am grateful to the audience on both occasions for their comments, and also to Richard Seaford, Anthony Snodgrass, and Christiane Sourvinou-Inwood who read earlier drafts.

7

Sanctuaries in the Chora of Metaponto

JOSEPH COLEMAN CARTER

University of Texas

A major criticism of current theorizing about Greek rural sanctuaries and their relation to the 'birth of the city' is that elaborate theoretical structures rest on inadequate factual bases—often on the results of early excavations and incomplete investigations. What is needed, it has been urged, are detailed studies of the phenomena, case by case.[1] The present paper, an attempt to deal with the rural sanctuaries in the territory of the Greek colony of Metaponto, is a response to this challenge.

We are fortunate that both the urban centre of the colony and the territory of the *chora* have been the object of intense research over the last quarter-century by the Soprintendenza alle Antichità della Basilicata and its collaborators, both Italian and foreign. The result is that this colonial situation is among the most fully documented archaeologically anywhere in the ancient world. At the same time our view of the nature and date of early settlement on the site of Metaponto (for example) has radically changed as a result of very recent discoveries.[2] The risk is that new discoveries resulting from ongoing work could, in a few years, make obsolete the factual bases of any attempted generalization.

The chronology of extramural sanctuaries relative to the urban centre of the polis is central to any theory of their relationship. How can we be sure when a sanctuary was founded? But even more problematic is the foundation date of Metaponto, or more precisely, of the first appearance of an urban centre.

[1] D. Asheri, 'A propos des sanctuaires extraurbains en Sicile et Grande-Grèce: Théories et témoignages', in M.-M. Mactoux and E. Geny (edd.), *Mélanges Pierre Lévêque* (Paris, 1988), 1–15.
[2] A. DeSiena, 'Contributi archeologici alla definizione della fase protocoloniale del Metapontino', *Bollettino storico della Basilicata* 6 (1990), 71–88.

Rural Sanctuaries and Urban Centre

The Dates of Metaponto

The account of the early history of Metaponto compiled by Strabo implies that there were in effect two foundings, one by the Pylians under Nestor, which he says was destroyed by the 'Samnites', and a second by Achaian settlers called by the Achaian colonists of Sybaris to resettle the site, and provide, according to Strabo's principal source Antiochos, a buffer between Taras and the rich land of Siris.[3] Strabo's text is basic, if nothing else, because it implies that the establishment of Metaponto was not a simple matter, and that it took some time. He does not, in fact, use the term *apoikia*, the proper term for founding a colony, but rather *ktisis*, a 'taking possession' of the land.

For many years now the generally accepted date for the establishment of a Greek presence on the site of the future city of Metaponto has been the middle of the seventh century BC, that is, roughly a century before the creation of the late Archaic/early Classical city, with its grid plan, impressive centre (consisting of a sanctuary with monumental temples), and agora with its massive and highly original public meeting place.[4] After more than a quarter century of systematic exploration, absolutely no evidence for a Bronze Age occupation has come to light on this site (though there is an impressive amount of it at nearby San Vito and Termitito in the environs of the later colony).[5] This fact virtually eliminates Nestor as a founder.

The long-accepted date for the historical 'founding' has begun to move gradually down from around 650 to one nearer 600 BC. The reason for this has much to do with the site known as 'Incoronata greca', and the theory which made the urban centre of Metaponto the successor of Incoronata (Ill. 7.1). Incoronata, an emporium or trading post set out by nearby Siris shortly after 700 BC on the ruins of an indigenous village (according to Orlandini's reconstruction[6]), was the victim of the Achaians who responded, if Strabo is to be believed, to the Sybarites' call. The predominance of Greek imported and inspired pottery in many contexts, the rectangular ground plan of numerous small structures, and the rare graffito in the Greek alphabet are the main support for this emporium theory. Incoronata's treatment at the hands of the Achaeans would have been the same that it had supposedly meted out to the unfortunate *indigenae*.

---

[3] D. Musti, *Strabone e La Magna Grecia: Città e popoli dell'Italia antica* (Padova, 1988), 133–9; G. Maddoli, 'I sanniti a Metaponto, un capitolo di storia Lucana', *PP* 153 (1973), 237–43; P. G. Guzzo, 'Metaponto: Dai Neleidi ai Sanniti', *PP* 38 (1983), 197–9.

[4] D. Mertens, 'Metapont: Ein neuer Plan des Stadtzentrums', *AA* (1985), 645–71.

[5] A. DeSiena, 'Termitito', and 'San Vito', in L. Vagnetti (ed.), *Magna Grecia e mondo miceneo: XXII Convegno di studi sulla Magna Grecia* (Taranto, 1982), 69–83, 97–8.

[6] Most recently: P. Orlandini, *Ricerche archeologiche all'Incoronata di Metaponto*, ii. *Dal villaggio indigeno all'emporio greco. Le strutture e i materiali del saggio T* (Milan, 1992), 28.

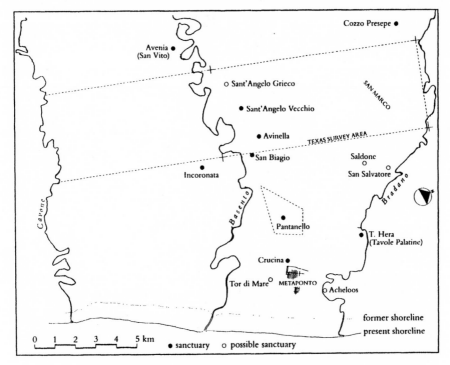

ILL. 7.1 Map showing distribution of extramural sanctuaries in the *chora* of
Metaponto

The date for the destruction of Incoronata was based on the fact that imported Protocorinthian pottery is relatively common on the site but there is no Early Corinthian[7]—whereas at Metaponto Corinthian was abundant and Protocorinthian scarce and not of good quality. The earliest known material of clearly Greek manufacture from the site of the city were terracotta figurines in the Daedalic style (Late Daedalic dated after 640 BC) and some few, locally made imitations of Protocorinthian.[8] Figurines in the Daedalic style, it should be cautioned, could have continued to be made for some time, and so are less reliable than pottery for dating.

This was the earliest material known up to 1984, when Antonio DeSiena made an unexpected discovery under the level of the grid plan of the colony (on the property of the Andrisani family) which has altered the picture very

---

[7] P. Orlandini, 'Incoronata, scavi dell'Università statale di Milano (1974–1984)', in *I Greci sul Basento: Mostra degli scavi archeologici all'Incoronata di Metaponto 1971–1984* (Como, 1986), 37.

[8] D. Adamesteanu, 'Il santuario di Apollo e urbanistica generale', in D. Adamesteanu, D. Mertens, and F. D'Andria (edd.), *Metaponto*, i. *Notizie degli scavi di Antichità*, 8, 29 Supp. (Rome, 1980), 49–58, 81–9, 171–81, 186–9.

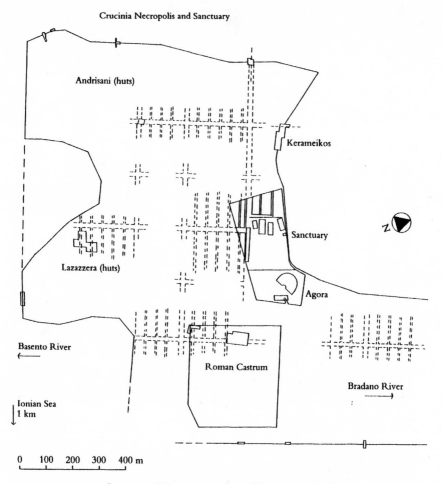

ILL. 7.2 Metaponto (adapted from DeSiena)

dramatically (Ill. 7. 2).[9] Structures, similar in form and containing a mixture of
indigenous and colonial Greek wares, of the same types as those found at
Incoronata and dated before 650/40, came to light. Subsequently more of these
structures were uncovered in soundings in the southern part of the later city.[10]
Thus, the site of the colonial urban centre was preceded by an earlier settlement,
very similar to Incoronata, or so it would appear. Few discoveries illustrate
better the danger of an argument *e silentio*.

More recent work by DeSiena, along the southern slopes of the Basento
around Incoronata, has revealed a late Iron Age indigenous village and burial

---

[9] A. DeSiena, 'Metaponto: Nuove scoperte in proprietà Andrisani', in *Siris-Poleion. Fonti letterarie e
nuova documentazione archeologica. Incontro studi—Policoro 8–10 giugno 1984* (Galatina, 1986), 135–6.
[10] DeSiena (n. 2), 87.

area of the first half of the eighth century, antedating the settlement at Incoronata greca (Ill. 7.1)[11] The similarity of the structures at this site (known as 'Incoronata indigena') to those of Orlandini's emporium (Incoronata greca) is striking, though the excavator is cautious and falls short of stating an obvious conclusion. It would appear that all the settlements along this stretch of the Basento were part of an organized development. In this light, the 'emporium' was very probably an indigenous site, with at most a Greek component, and thus a 'mixed settlement' as originally proposed by Dinu Adamesteanu.[12]

The crucial point in this development was reached about 700 BC when, according to DeSiena, a major road was built through the site of Incoronata indigena, indicating that the village may have moved into the sphere of influence of a centralized economic power. That power, it is suggested, was located on the site of Metaponto. In this scenario, the 'emporium' at Incoronata greca and the seventh-century site under the street grid of Metaponto (Andrisani) were two manifestations of an organization which had replaced the separate and apparently autonomous villages of the earlier eighth century.

What were the relations between Incoronata greca, the settlement at Andrisani, and the colony of Siris founded sometime in the first half of the seventh century? Was the earliest settlement at Metaponto, like that at Incoronata (apparently), an offshoot of the colonizing effort at Siris, or were Incoronata greca and Andrisani both indigenous sites in close commercial contact with Siris? Greek commercial contacts with Incoronata and Andrisani, in any event, antedate the foundation of Siris, as discoveries of Middle and Late Geometric pottery on both sites prove.[13] The crucial question, however, for our purpose is: from what date can we begin to speak of a colonial city on the site of Metaponto?

A series of further discoveries bears on this question. Excavation a dozen years ago under the fourth-century BC theatre in the agora revealed a truly remarkable building to which the name 'Ekklesiasterion' was quickly given (Ill. 7.3). An amphitheatre of circular form, with a rectangular orchestra, it was built up on the flat site with transported earth, held in place by a massive stone retaining wall.[14] It could have seated eight thousand![15] The most remarkable

---

[11] DeSiena (n. 2), 72.

[12] D. Adamesteanu, 'Nuovi aspetti dei rapporti tra Greci e indigeni in Magna Grecia', in D. M. Pippidi (ed.), *Assimilation et résistance à la culture greco-romaine dans le monde ancien* (Bucharest and Paris, 1976), 57. DeSiena's further discovery of predominantly flexed burials (the common indigenous rite) in a small necropolis of mid-seventh-century date is another probable indication that the population of nearby Incoronata greca was largely native.

[13] P. Orlandini, 'Un frammento di coppa mediogeometrica dagli scavi dell'Incoronata presso Metaponto', *Atti e Memorie della Società Magna Grecia* 5, 15–17 (1974–6), 177–86.

[14] D. Mertens and A. DeSiena, 'Metaponto: Il teatro-ekklesiasterion', *Bollettino d'Arte* 67. 16 (1982), 1–60.

[15] Mertens (n. 14), 20.

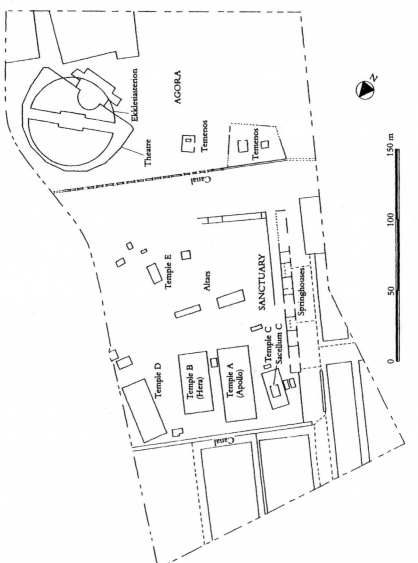

ILL. 7.3 Metaponto (from Mertens)

thing about it however—since there are other (smaller) examples of Greek buildings of this shape—is its date. The earliest stone phase of the Ekklesiasterion dates to the middle of the sixth century BC which would make it one of the earliest Greek meeting places for the assembled citizenry of which any trace remains. The earliest may have been the wooden structure which preceded it on the site. Charred remains have been interpreted as *ikria*, bleachers, and it may have had the same function as its successor. A date of about 600 has been suggested, but there is, as far as I know, no decisive proof. The wooden bleachers, if that is what they are, would point to a settlement on the site with at least one of the characteristic structures that define a polis.

The Ekklesiasterion has been associated with another structure, the sanctuary, whose earliest remains in the area of Sacellum C can be dated to the late seventh century (Ill. 7.3), and with it the ash altar and the *argoi lithoi* at the east end and along the flank of the later site of Temple B (Temple of Hera?) The *argoi lithoi*, 'unworked stones' sometimes with inscriptions (interpreted as aniconic images of Apollo), point to close cult connections with the mainland home of the Achaians.[16]

The structure known as Sacellum C was built not earlier than 600 over a charred level, indicating in all probability a wooden predecessor here as well. Between the charred level and virgin soil, DeSiena has identified Proto-corinthian geometric pottery (Thapsos cups) of about 700 BC, so there is at least a remote possibility that the cult may have been in existence as much as a century earlier. Supporting evidence for a cult at such an early date, however, is very slight.[17]

The sanctuary and the Ekklesiasterion were seen by Mertens as two components of the earliest polis.[18] At first they were considered to be associated with the clearly residential structures in Andrisani under what would be the late Archaic and Classical city—thus demonstrating continuity of function in principal areas of cult, political and commercial activity, and residence. The fact that so far no huts have been unearthed in the area of the sanctuary or agora has been cited in support of this recent reconstruction. Now, in the light of further study and the redating to the mid-seventh century BC of the Andrisani huts, it seems that a chronological gap exists, and it is too great to permit an association of the huts with the public elements, unless, of course, the charred material under Sacellum C belonged to a cult place and—an even more remote possibility—the bleachers, too, were as early as the mid-seventh century.

The destruction by fire of the assembly place and sanctuary, if they were

---

[16] D. Adamesteanu, 'Argoi lithoi a Metaponto', in *Adriatica praehistorica et antiqua: Miscellanea G. Novak dicata* (Zagreb, 1970), 307–24.

[17] DeSiena (n. 2), 87.

[18] D. Mertens, Supplement to *Enciclopedia dell'Arte Antica* (forthcoming), s.v. 'Metaponto'.

contemporaneous, may or may not have been related to the destruction by fire which consumed the dwellings at Andrisani. They may, in fact, have been three unrelated episodes. It is certain that the destruction of the huts and the wooden structure under Sacellum C could have happened at the same time, but the identity of that structure remains unclear. We can only be sure that there was a sanctuary on the site by the late seventh century when the first figurines are dated. The date of the fire that destroyed the 'bleachers' in the agora is not known for certain, nor is the function of the structure. In the case that all events took place separately, it is possible that Andrisani was, like Incoronata greca, a big village.

The archaeological evidence may be reconcilable with the historical evidence, if we assume a contemporary destruction of the presumed early cult place and 'bleachers', interpreted as having a civic function. In this view, the settlement which came to a fiery end about 600, to be replaced by that of Sacellum C and at a later date (c. 550) by the stone Ekklesiasterion was in all probability a polis— and it is just possible that its destruction is the one referred to by Strabo as the work of the 'Samnites'. The apparent refoundation of the early sixth century would then have been the work of the Achaians, and would have maintained the essential plan—sanctuary and public meeting place on the same sites—as its predecessor.

In short, the earliest securely datable evidence for cultic activity on the site of Metaponto would have corresponded closely with the establishment of at least one other structure that characterizes a polis, some time in the late seventh century BC. This, it should be cautioned, is one reconstruction of these events. Others are possible, and new facts will surely emerge which will change the picture once again. It is based on the work of others, and I have no doubt that I have reached some conclusions with which those possessing a firsthand knowledge of the full material may well disagree. Complex problems and proposed solutions have been simplified in order to take a stand on the question which is the principal aim of this paper.

Dates and Locations of the Early Extramural Sanctuaries before 600 BC

The territory of Metaponto boasts a very considerable number of sanctuaries (Ill. 7.1). A few, like that of Hera (the so-called 'Tavole Palatine'), have been known for some time. Others such as the Sanctuary of Artemis and Zeus at San Biagio alla Venella have begun to be cited frequently in the literature.[19] Sanctuary sites continue to be discovered, either by excavation or through

[19] I. Edlund, *The Gods and the Place* (Stockholm, 1987), 94–102, which provides a useful partial list and brief discussion; F. de Polignac, *La nascita della città greca: Culti, spazio e società nei secoli vii e viii a.C.* (Milan, 1991), 115.

ongoing survey work. The discussion here will be limited to those known in the territory between the Bradano and Basento Rivers and inland as far as Cozzo Presepe, which marks the furthest extension of the cultivated *chora*. The count at present is fourteen. Only those sanctuaries for which there is reliable, recent documentation will be discussed here.

The sanctuary of Artemis and Zeus,[20] located beside a good spring in a marshy hollow along Venella valley at San Biagio (Ill. 7.1), was hidden from the view of travellers along the Basento valley. It is hardly the territorial marker that the later temple of Hera (Tavole Palatine) or the altar at Cozzo Presepe were to become (see below). The cult focused on the spring which was channelled into a basin constructed of conglomerate stone. A number of structures decorated with polychrome terracotta revetments and antefixes rose on a level terrace above the spring in the sixth, fifth and fourth centuries BC.[21] If this is indeed the sanctuary of Artemis mentioned by Bacchylides, then he was more impressed by the sacred grove (*alsos*) at San Biagio than the architecture.[22]

The earliest votive figurines are contemporaneous with those of the urban sanctuaries (see Table 7.1). Images of the goddess as *potnia theron* (the mistress of the beasts) are found also in the city, and the *hieros gamos* (sacred marriage) theme seen in a plaque, where a female divinity embraces a youthful male, appears, though in different form—a marriage procession in mule-drawn cart—in the revetments associated with Sacellum C.[23] The earliest Daedalic heads from San Biagio are stylistically very like those from the area of Sacellum C and the votive deposits of the temple of Apollo. They should date to the late seventh century; that is, to the period of the first city (the one 'destroyed' by the Samnites, if the proposed reconstruction of events is accepted). The absence of terracotta figurines doesn't prove that the cult beside the spring did not exist before the late seventh century, but there is no material evidence that it did. The same argument has been applied to the sanctuary of Apollo and Sacellum C in the city (where, granted, exploration has been more thorough). The figurines demonstrate that the cult in the countryside and that in the city were roughly contemporary and further resembled each other in the emphasis on fertility (*kourotrophos* or nursing-mother type) that characterizes the great mass of these votives. This is a general characteristic of Metapontine votives. Even from sanctuaries where a male divinity was explicitly worshipped, such as Apollo in the city or Zeus at San Biagio, there are only a handful of male votive figurines.

[20] G. Olbrich, 'Ein Heiligtum der Artemis metapontina? Zur Iconographie der Terrakotta-figuren von S. Biagio bei Metapont', *PP* 31 (1976), 376–408.

[21] D. Adamesteanu, *La Basilicata Antica* (Cava dei Tirreni, 1974), 55–65.

[22] Bacchylides 11. 117–20.

[23] G. Olbrich, *Archaische Statuetten eines metapontiner Heiligtums* (Rome, 1979), 102.

TABLE 7.1 *Votive figurines in terracotta*

Sanctuaries	Late 7th cent. BC	600	600–650	550–500	500–400	400–300	Dionysos-Hades	Satyr-Nymph	After 300 BC
Urban									
Temple of Apollo	×	×	×	×	×	×	×		
Sacellum C	×	×				×	×	×	
Temple B		×	×	×	×	×	×		
Hellenistic sacellum							×	×	×
Zeus (agora)									
Apollo/Aristeas									
Castrum									×
Suburban									
Crucinia/Favole		×	×	×			×		
Tor di Mare									
Acheloos (Bradano)									
Bradano*									
Sc. of Hera (T. Palatine)				×					×
Saldone(?) isolated find	×								
San Salvatore(?)†						×		×	
Cozzo Presepe†					×				
Basento‡									
Pantanello			×	×	×	×	×	×	
San Biagio		×	×	×	×	×			
Incoronata			×	×					
Avinella			×						
Sant'Angelo Vecchio					×	×	×	×	
Sant'Angelo Griecot†					×				
Avenia (San Vito)				×					

* Beginning near the city and moving upstream.   † Dated by architecture.   ‡ Beginning near the city and moving upstream.

ILL. 7.4 Terracotta from Saldone

A single very fine Mid- to Late Daedalic male head, found in a deposit with material of later date at Saldone, is thus all the more interesting (Ill. 7.4). It suggests the possibility, at least, that San Biagio was not an isolated late seventh-century rural sanctuary, but had its counterpart along the valley of the Bradano, on the opposite side of the *chora*.

Can it be that the sanctuaries of the end of the seventh century existed in a territory otherwise devoid of settlement? While unlikely, until recently there has been no indication to the contrary. Intensive field survey, begun in 1981, of approximately a quarter of what became the *chora* of the colony in its heyday, has now made it possible to relate the distribution of rural sanctuaries to the changing settlement pattern of the *chora* (Ills. 7.5, 7.6). Several sites in the survey transect where indigenous pottery had been found suggest the possibility, at least, that a dispersed settlement of indigenous or mixed population—with its centre perhaps in the late seventh-century settlement at Metaponto (the early polis presumed to have been destroyed around 600 and later rebuilt or built over by the Achaians)—may have anticipated the dispersed farmhouses of the

ILL. 7.5 Map of Bradano to Basento survey transect showing site distribution for the period 600 to 551 BC. Farmhouses are indicated by squares, tombs by triangles

ILL. 7.6 Map of Bradano to Basento survey transect showing site distribution for the period 550 to 501 BC. Farmhouses are indicated by squares; tombs by triangles; and scatters by circles

colonial occupation by several generations or more.[24] The early sanctuaries at San Biagio and Saldone could then have served this population.[25] The sixth-century phase of the sanctuary at San Biagio and those at Tavole Palatine and elsewhere would be, in a real sense, the heirs of the earlier settlement of Metaponto and its territory.

In summary, the evidence from the *chora* demonstrates at the very least the close cultic connections of the polis and the *chora*, as they both came into being some time before 600 BC.[26]

The Sixth Century BC

The location of the site of Pantanello (Ill. 7.1), with a spring at its very heart, flanked by walls of conglomerate, with sanctuary buildings near the spring and probably also on higher ground, is quite similar to that of San Biagio, but the earliest evidence of cultic activity belongs to the first half of the sixth century BC. Post-Daedalic statuettes and a local imitation of a Mid to Late Corinthian truncated oinochoe are unambiguous testimony, found as they were in the mouth of the spring (Ill. 7.7).[27] This sanctuary has much in common, too, with Sacellum C in the city. There are close comparisons between the votive figurines, but it seems clear that Pantanello dates a generation at least after Sacellum C and San Biagio, where Early Corinthian and local imitations of it are present.

The sanctuary of Hera (Tavole Palatine) is located in a conspicuous rise on the south bank of the Bradano approximately three kilometres from the city. A large Doric temple of about 530 crowned this rise. Votive figurines appear to date the earliest use of the sanctuary to around 550, which is surprisingly late considering its prominence and its manifest role as a boundary marker. It should

---

[24] J. C. Carter, 'Taking Possession of the Land: Early Colonization in Southern Italy', in R. Scott and A. R. Scott (edd.), *Ejus Virtutis Studiosi: Classical and Post-Classical Studies in Memory of Frank Edward Brown (1908–88)* (Washington, DC, 1993), 342–67.

[25] J. C. Carter, *The Pantanello Necropolis 1982–1990* (Austin, Tex., 1990), 17. Few sites securely datable to the second half of the 7th century, besides the San Biagio sanctuary, have been identified in the countryside. One was discovered during the excavations of the necropolis at Pantanello, yielding pottery similar to that of Incoronata greca or Andrisani, though it may be somewhat later in date. A hydria with banded decoration has a parallel also at Cozzo Presepe, from a level dated about 600 BC, when a native village was replaced by the fortification wall of a Greek *phrourion*. See note below.

[26] There are some few tantalizing bits of evidence for Greek cult places that may have antedated all those of the early polis and *chora* at Metaponto: the perirrhanteria from Incoronata greca of mid-7th-century date which were, as Orlandini has shown, locally made, and for cultic use. But where? in the native or mixed villages along the Basento? P. Orlandini, 'Perirrhanterion fittile arcaico con decorazione e rilievo dagli scavi dell'Incoronata', in *Attività archeologica in Basilicata 1964–1977: Scritti in onore di Dinu Adamesteanu* (Matera, 1980), 175–238. See also D. Adamesteanu, 'Sul perirrhanterion dell'Incoronata', *PP* 41 (1986), 73–6.

[27] J. C. Carter, 'Scavi a Pizzica e Incoronata nei dintorni di Metaponto', in *Atti del 17 Convegno di studi sulla Magna Grecia 1977* (Naples, 1982), 401–7.

ILL. 7.7 Post-Daedalic figurine from
Pantanello (PZ 77.725)

have been, according to de Polignac's theory, one of the earliest cult places. This was indeed believed to be the case until quite recently.[28]

The remains of a small sanctuary building were found on one spur of the hilltop site known as Incoronata greca (see above). It belongs to the sixth

---

[28] C. Letta, *Piccola coroplastica metapontina nel Museo Archeologico Provinciale di Potenza* (Naples, 1971), 14. See also F. G. Lo Porto, 'Ricerche e scoperte nell'Heraion di Metaponto', *Xenia* 1 (1981), 36–8. Lo Porto (p. 36 fig. 21) mentions 'Proto Corinthian' pottery, but dates the 'earliest' pottery from the site 'from the late seventh to the mid-sixth century BC'. The 'Proto Corinthian', and other finds, from early investigation seem to be elusive. The earliest types of figurines published by Lo Porto (fig. 24) are of the same types as the earliest from Pantanello and Incoronata (first half of the 6th century). The sanctuaries at Tavole Palatine and Pantanello are similar in so many ways (see below) that it would not be unreasonable to suppose that they came into existence at the same time. In the larger view, the sanctuary of Hera (Tavole Palatine) on the Bradano and the sanctuary of Hera at the mouth of the Sele also make a pair. The Sele sanctuary, as recent excavations are said to prove, is no earlier than 600 and hence not older (as was long held) than the urban centre of Poseidonia: E. Greco, *Archeologia della Magna Grecia* (Bari, 1992), 152. Greco (p. 74) observes that the Sele sanctuary stood at the boundary between Etruscan-dominated Campania (later the I *Regio* of the Augustan division) and the Greek *Italía* (III *Regio*, Lucania and Bruttium). The temple of Hera at Tavole Palatine on the Bradano marked the boundary between *Italía* and Iapygia to the east, as Greco (153) notes. His stimulating suggestion (pers. comm. 1993) that the most prominent extramural sanctuaries of two Achaian colonies founded from Sybaris indicate the territorial ambitions of the only colony which might be said to have had an 'empire', would, if proved, add a new dimension to the de Polignac thesis, and to our understanding of the politics of Magna Grecia in the mid-6th century.

century, and to a different building tradition from the wattle-and-daub huts of the eighth- and seventh-century BC villages. The terracotta revetments and antefixes should date to the early sixth century,[29] while the votive figures have extremely close parallels at San Biagio (dated by Olbrich to the second half of the sixth) (Ill. 7.8).[30]

ILL. 7.8 Terracotta from sanctuary at Incoronata (IC 77.176)

A small rural sanctuary was discovered during the survey in Contrada Avinella. It was occupied already in the first half of the sixth century, to judge by the one figurine recovered together with many fragments of small votive vessels.[31]

The site of a sanctuary, with votives very similar in style to those of the middle sixth century at San Biagio and to those from the urban sanctuaries, was

[29] Carter (n. 27), 397–401.
[30] Olbrich (n. 23). Her type B, variant A, dated to c.550 closely parallels a seated female figure on a flat throne from Incoronata. This material is being studied for publication by Sarah Leach Davis.
[31] J. C. Carter, *The Territory of Metaponto 1981–1982* (Austin, Tex., 1983), 8.

reported by Adamesteanu at Masseria Avenia (San Vito).[32] This was (probably coincidentally) near the site from which a considerable amount of Mycenaean pottery has been recovered.[33]

As can be seen from the table with the earliest known dates of sanctuaries (Table 7.1), a large number of rural shrines came into existence in the sixth century, about the same time as the first massive occupation of the *chora*, and they are located along the river valleys in close proximity to contemporary farmhouses. As they appear in the context of a densely occupied territory, they cannot be, as has been urged by de Polignac, territorial markers for the polis,[34] nor do they occupy, except in a few cases (Avenia and Cozzo Presepe), a frontier between the familiar world of the *chora* and the *eschatia* or *proschoros*, the no man's land at the edge of the *chora*.

The Fifth Century BC and Later

Sanctuaries at the extreme corners of the territory were given architecturally impressive embellishment in the fifth century BC. A fine Doric capital, found at Sant'Angelo Grieco, came from a small temple and is contemporaneous with the temple of Hera II at Poseidonia.[35] That capital and a small, possibly related fragment of a fifth-century inscription on white marble are all that remain. The original site of the building has not been located, but it was probably near by. A spring flows just below the later farmhouse from which both capital and inscription were recovered.

At Cozzo Presepe, the elements of a Doric building in a style which may belong to the fifth or fourth century were found on a site with a commanding prospect up the valley of the Bradano.[36] Since no suitable foundation was discovered, the excavators have surmised that the remains belonged to an enclosure rather than a temple building—such as that of the shrine of Apollo/Aristaios that Herodotos (4. 15) describes in the agora of the city, which would have been of similar date. No sanctuary could more readily have claimed the role of territorial marker and beacon—with its position, actually on the site of the sixth-century *phrourion* (fortress), and with its walls commanding the upper Bradano valley—than the altar at Cozzo Presepe. Here, military protection was replaced by a spiritual and symbolic one. Somewhat surprisingly, no trace of cult activity remained in association. The only votive object found

[32] D. Adamesteanu, 'Problèmes de la zone archéologique de Métaponte', *RA* (1967), 25; P. C. Sestieri, 'Metaponto', *Notizie degli scavi di Antichità* 18 (1940), 120–2.

[33] DeSiena (n. 5), 97–8. University of Texas, Metaponto Survey, site 39.

[34] De Polignac (n. 19), 45–9.

[35] D. Mertens, pers. comm. No building to which the capital might have belonged is known, according to Mertens, in the city, and the monumental centre has been thoroughly explored.

[36] J. du Plat Taylor, E. McNamara, *et al.*, 'The Excavations at Cozzo Presepe (1969–72)', in *Metaponto*, ii. *Notizie degli scavi di Antichità* 8, 31 (Rome, 1977), 263–73.

(elsewhere on the site) during excavation was a Satyr and Nymph plaque, a type common around the end of the fourth century. This was the very period in which this sanctuary was demolished for a new fortification. It is probable that a spring existed somewhere on the slope of the naturally fortified—but, unfortunately, only very partially excavated—hilltop.

Remains of monumental architecture, of fourth-century BC date, were recovered in test trenches on a prominent spur at San Salvatore, along the Bradano valley in 1981. It is likely that they come from a sanctuary building (rather than a monumental tomb) somewhere in the vicinity. Columns of a temple (?) structure were also found built into a farmhouse at Saldone, excavated in 1967 by Uggeri[37] and as yet unpublished. Could this have been the successor of an earlier sanctuary at that site which had produced the Daedalic head mentioned above?

A rich variety of votive plaques and moulds are the principal evidence for a sanctuary at Sant'Angelo Vecchio.[38] Persephone by herself appears, as does the 'Dionysos-Hades' type representing a divine pair (reclining male, female with *polos* head-dress, and an infant in arms), and a standing, draped Zeus holding a sceptre: all of probably fifth-century date. To the succeeding century should be assigned the satyr in pursuit of a nymph, of the same type as that found at Cozzo Presepe. The 'Dionysos-Hades' and Satyr-Nymph plaques occur also in identical form at Pantanello, at Crucinia ('Dionysos-Hades' only), and in the urban sanctuaries.[39] At Sant'Angelo, the deposit containing this material was found near a spring, but the actual location of the cult has not been identified. While it is possible that votive objects were simply manufactured here, this is unlikely. Kilns beside the sanctuary and spring at San Biagio were producing the vases and figurines found in nearby votive deposits.[40]

A significant development of the sanctuaries coming into existence in the fifth century and later is the presence of Dionysiac elements and iconography (Sant'Angelo and Cozzo Presepe). Both these and the earlier cult places which were converted to Dionysos continue to occupy the river valleys, despite the population growth on the inland terraces in this period (Ill. 7.9).

Our uncertainty about Saldone, San Salvatore, Sant'Angelo, and the others should serve as a reminder that our knowledge of rural sanctuaries can never be complete. Some will never be found; others have been more or less completely destroyed and therefore are difficult to identify and interpret. Thus, any attempt to see a pattern in the spatial distribution of the sites will have its obvious risks.

[37] G. Uggeri, 'Kleroi arcaici e bonifica classica nella *chora* di Metaponto', *PP* 24 (1969), 52.

[38] I. Edlund, 'Scavi nella zona di Metaponto: Sant'Angelo Vecchio', *Bollettino d'Arte* 71. 39–40 (1986), 119–22.

[39] F. G. Lo Porto, 'Metaponto, scavi e ricerche archeologiche', *Notizie degli scavi di Antichità* 8, 20 (1966), 165–76. See also id. 'Nuovi scavi nella città e nella sua necropoli', *Notizie degli scavi di Antichità* 8, 35 (1981), 332.

[40] Adamesteanu (n. 21), 60–1.

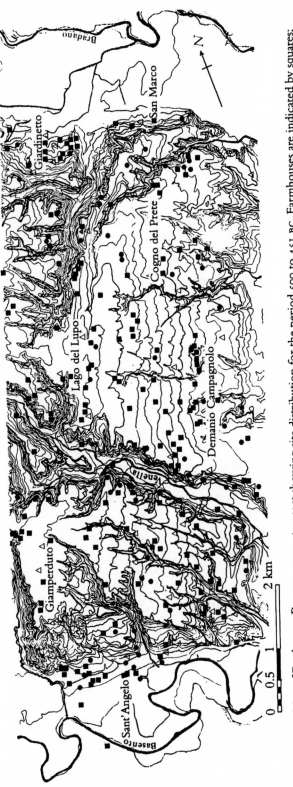

ILL. 7.9 Map of Bradano to Basento survey transect showing site distribution for the period 500 to 451 BC. Farmhouses are indicated by squares; tombs by triangles; and scatters by circles

Spatial Distribution of Rural Sanctuaries

The rural shrines described above are distributed along the river valleys in a
surprisingly regular way (Ill. 7.1). On the Bradano side, approximately three
kilometres (as the crow flies) separate the Temple of Apollo Lykeios in the city
(and the sanctuary of Acheloos), the sanctuary of Hera (Tavole Palatine), and
Saldone. There is a gap, instead, of six kilometres between Saldone and Cozzo
Presepe. San Salvatore is just one kilometre from Saldone. Along the Basento,
the same interval of three kilometres divides the Temple of Apollo in the city
(and the sanctuary at Tor di Mare) and Pantanello. From Pantanello to San
Biagio it is three kilometres. Avinella lies one kilometre, and Sant'Angelo
Vecchio two kilometres, from San Biagio, but Sant'Angelo Grieco is, again,
three kilometres from San Biagio.

The important sanctuaries along the Basento are spaced at regular three-
kilometre intervals, with other apparently smaller ones, like Avinella, at lesser
distances on tributaries reaching inland towards the higher ground of the marine
terraces. A similar arrangement is found on the Bradano. Had a sanctuary been
found at San Marco (where once existed an important Bronze Age site) midway
between Saldone and Cozzo Presepe, the symmetry would be complete.

The impression of a deliberate pattern of quasi-geometric regularity is
reinforced when one observes that the series of sanctuaries along the river
valleys each begin with a sanctuary (Tavole Palatine, Pantanello) placed sym-
metrically on the near side of the river towards the city, and on the first
substantial rise of ground above the alluvial plain. In both cases the river ran
within a few hundred feet of the site. (The river courses, especially that of the
Basento, have changed considerably since ancient times.) A direct line of sight,
from the Incoronata sanctuary site through a natural cleft in the hillside to the
sanctuary at San Biagio, does not appear to be accidental. Topographical relief
as well as linear distance must have played a role in the siting. San Biagio lies
on the north bank of the Basento two and a half kilometres from Incoronata;
Incoronata is six kilometres from Avenia on the same bank. This close spatial
relationship between Incoronata and San Biagio is complemented by the
especially close stylistic relationships among the votive figurines (as discussed
earlier).

The regular spacing of the sanctuaries along the river valleys could suggest,
at first glance, a progressive expansion of the territory in discrete waves, with
each advance inland marked by the new cult place. But the fact that there is no
progression in their apparent foundation dates rules that out immediately. The
earliest sanctuaries are not necessarily either the closest to the city or the farthest
from it. On what, then, does the regularity of the spacing depend?

Near each of the sanctuaries which lie in or close to the survey transect (San Biagio, Sant'Angelo Vecchio, Sant'Angelo Grieco, Avinella)—and in the case of Pantanello where an intensive survey was also carried out—we can be sure that by the late sixth or early fifth century there was an unusually dense cluster of dwellings belonging to individual family farms (Ills. 7.6, 7.9). The presence of a spring near each has been verified as well. More limited in number are the sanctuary sites that are also in close proximity to extensive necropoleis (Crucinia, Pantanello, and San Biagio)—a juxtaposition that does not appear to be coincidental either.

Though one or another aspect may be emphasized, in those cases where a sufficient basis exists to form a judgement, there is striking similarity between these rural cults, as well as strong iconographic links between the rural and the urban cults. The types of votive figurines are very similar. Often the same moulds seem to have been used (as at San Biagio, Incoronata, Temple of Apollo). At San Biagio and Pantanello the female image assumes a variety of characteristics (at San Biagio, for instance, she possesses elements of Aphrodite, Eileithuia, Athena, Hera, and Persephone). At Pantanello the same is true, though the variety is not so great. The cult around the spring at both sites has cathartic, fertility, nurturing (*kourotrophos*-type), healing, chthonic, and initiatory aspects. The same might have been the case at the other sanctuaries, if only we knew more about them.

In short, each sanctuary appears to serve the varied and very similar needs of its specific locale. To use a modern analogy, they are rather like parish churches. But what would have constituted a 'parish' in the Greek countryside in the mid-sixth century when these sites and the farmhouses first appear in considerable numbers?

I would like to suggest that the distribution of sanctuaries may have corresponded to a division of the *chora* made in the sixth century into a dozen or so larger units. The principal clues are: the distribution of sanctuaries, the similarity of the cults, and the fact that all are located along the river valleys, and at the mouths of tributaries which naturally divide the territory. None, as far as is known, was located in the interior, which was settled at a later date.

The division of the *chora* of Metaponto has been the object of intense investigation since 1959, when aerial photography first revealed the existence of parallel 'division lines' covering the *chora* to a distance of about fourteen kilometres into the interior and spaced some two hundred metres apart. When, in the mid-1960s, field survey began to document the hundreds of farmhouses in the *chora* dating from the sixth to the third century BC, it was argued that the 'lines' created lots for corresponding farmhouses from the very beginning of the colony. The farmhouses actually date from no earlier than the mid-sixth century. This agreed well with the historical evidence (none of it contemporary or specifically about Metaponto) that supported the theory of a primary division (*la spartizione primaria*, to use Asheri's term) of the colonial *chora* at the time of founding—a division that allotted an equal portion (*kleros*) to each individual settler.[41]

The discovery in 1986 of a 300-metre-long section of a division line—which was revealed to be a road flanked by a drainage ditch—has raised the possibility, at least, that the 'lines' may not be as old as the colony. The 'line', where it passed through the Pantanello necropolis (which came into use as early as 580), was flanked by some eighty burials, none of which was earlier in date than 480. Thus, the line was in existence by this date, but perhaps not before. Otherwise, some of the earlier tombs in the near vicinity might well have been placed beside it.[42]

Widespread changes in several areas about 500 would be consonant with a general reorganization of the *chora*—on the basis of smaller individual holdings—at this time. Limitations of space prevent a full discussion here. These developments are, briefly: 1) the number of occupied farmhouses reaches its maximum in the period 500–450 (Ill. 7.9); 2) a democratization of the necropolis occurs in the early fifth century (before 480, burial is limited to adults in relatively expensive containers); and 3) a shift from extensive pastoralism to a predominantly plough-based agriculture in the fifth century BC.

The evidence that we now have strongly suggests that a horse-breeding society—whose economy in some considerable measure was based on pastoralism and therefore favoured larger expanses of perhaps centrally controlled land over individual plots—dominated much of the sixth century, when most of the sanctuaries in the *chora* grew up.[43] That the economy of the *chora* then shifted to one based more thoroughly on the plough and adapted to small holdings is supported by the evidence of faunal remains from several sites (Incoronata, Pantanello). Horses had their heyday in the sixth century. Cattle, instead, reach an absolute majority among all the domesticated animals in the fifth century. The main use for cattle in the ancient world, as is well known, was for traction, for drawing the plough.

The huge capacity of the mid-sixth-century Ekklesiasterion—which was greater than the probable citizen population of the urban centre of Metaponto—has provided indirect evidence for a sizeable population of citizens in the *chora* in

---

[41] D. Adamesteanu, 'Le suddivisioni di terra nel metapontino', in M. I. Finley (ed.), *Problèmes de la terre en Grèce ancienne* (Paris, 1973), 49–61; D. Asheri, *Distribuzioni di terre nell'antica Grecia* (Turin, 1966), 7–13.

[42] Carter (n. 25), 25–7.

[43] Carter (n. 25), 19–24, 56–7. Cf. Bacchylides 11. 114 who describes the polis as *hippotrophos* (horse-nourishing). For representation of horses on locally produced pottery of Siris and Incoronata of the 7th century BC, see P. Orlandini, 'Altri due vasi figurati di stile orientalizzante dagli scavi dell'Incoronata', *Bollettino d'Arte* 76. 66 (1991), 6–8.

the second half of the sixth century.[44] This has been confirmed directly by the results of the survey. In large part, the farm sites of the second half of the sixth century probably belong to the end of that period, as the evidence of more precisely datable burials would indicate. It was perhaps the growing prosperity of these early settlers that stimulated changes resulting in a reorganization of the *chora*, and its division into smaller individual units defined by the division roads.

If the *chora* in the sixth century—to conclude this somewhat speculative digression—was not divided with the geometric rigidity of a grid, as it surely was in the fifth century, nevertheless it would have been divided. The placing of the sanctuaries suggests how this may have been done. The natural route for the settlement of the *chora* and penetration of the interior was along the river valleys. Along these arteries, areas of more or less uniform dimensions may have been allotted, not to individual heads of families as would be the case later on, but to larger family-based groups, who corporately as well as individually would have exploited their portions of the territory, combining more or less intensive agriculture in some areas with extensive pastoralism; these groups were probably linked by hereditary ties, by economic interests, and by a common cult.[45]

The Transformations of a Rural Sanctuary: Pantanello

Despite their number and importance, few rural sanctuaries in the territory of Metaponto have been the object of systematic investigation. Among the exceptions are San Biagio and Pantanello. Unfortunately, only partial results of the initial excavation at the complex site of San Biagio have been published.[46] The sanctuary at Pantanello has been thoroughly explored over the last twenty years and its publication is now in progress. It is possible in this latter case—and perhaps only here—to trace the development of a rural sanctuary from its inception in the early sixth century (virgin soil has been reached all over the site) to its final demise in the third century BC. This development covers the whole span of the *chora*'s

---

[44] D. Mertens, 'Metaponto e il suo territorio', in *La colonizzazione greca tra mediterraneo e Mar Nero. Simposio internazionale, Metaponto 24–28 giugno 1991* (in press).

[45] There is almost no documentary information concerning the internal organization of Metapontine society. A recent convincing correlation was made, however, of the symbols on the much discussed terracotta discs from Taras, Heraklea and Metaponto, with the symbols for local phratries in the 4th century BC on the Heraklea Tablets. T. C. Loprete and M. P. Bini, 'I dischi fittili di Eraclea', in *Studi su Siris-Eraclea* (Rome, 1989), 72–4. The discs have been cited to prove that festivals of the phratries existed at Metaponto. The cults of the Attic demes in the 5th century and later offer some suggestive analogies, especially in their relation to the cults of the urban centre. See R. Osborne, *Demos: The Discovery of Classical Attika* (Cambridge, 1985), 180, and R. Parker, 'Festivals of the Attic Demes', in T. Linders and G. Nordquist (edd.), *Gifts to the Gods* (Uppsala, 1987), 138. A recent article argues for the existence of gentilicial cults within the city of Metaponto: B. Bergquist, 'A Particular Western Greek Cult Practice? The Significance of Stele-crowned Sacrificial Deposits', *OpAth* 19. 3 (1992), 41–7.

[46] This has not prevented much discussion, e.g. M. Torelli, 'Greci e indigeni in Magna Grecia: Ideologia religiosa e rapport di Classe', *Studi Storici* 18 (1977), 48.

occupation and, as I shall attempt to show, the changing nature of the site reflects the major transformation of the *chora* and the colony in these three centuries.

The name Pantanello means 'little swamp'; a good description of what the site was and is. As a result of a sudden and dramatic shift in the water table, a shift which can be pin-pointed by excavation to about 500, the lower levels of the site including all the sixth-century levels and those fourth-century features that reutilized Archaic ones (the 'collecting basin' in particular) were below the level of the ground water. This phenomenon proved to be of fundamental importance for our understanding of the *chora* as a whole, for it caused a wide range of plant remains to be preserved. Excavation was possible only with the help of a well point pumping system (Ill. 7.10). A similar shift took place throughout the territory and in the city itself, as excavation there has also documented.

ILL. 7.10 View looking east across the excavation of the sanctuary at Pantanello and illustrating well point pumping system

The Archaic Sanctuary

In its earliest phase, dated by pottery and votive figurines to the early sixth century (as was noted above), the sanctuary was simply the spring with two channels leading from its mouth (Ill. 7.11). Votive figures were placed in small pools cut into the earth near its mouth and along the sides of the west channel. The sanctuary became more imposing sometime before the middle of the sixth

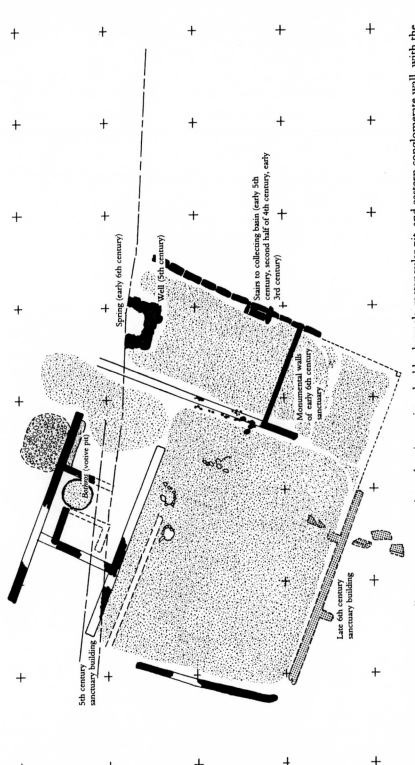

Spring (early 6th century)

Well (5th century)

Stairs to collecting basin (early 5th century, second half of 4th century, early 3rd century)

Monumental walls of early 6th century sanctuary

Bothros (votive pit)

5th century sanctuary building

Late 6th century sanctuary building

ILL. 7.11 Plan of the Pantanello sanctuary excavations, showing spring, double channels, rectangular pit, and eastern conglomerate wall, with the cobble surface of the 'collecting basin' to the east, and accumulated building phases to the west century when it was flanked by a pair of walls of local conglomerate stone (the same sort of material employed in the earliest stone shrine in the city, Sacellum C, and in the spring enclosure at San Biagio). The walls consisted of rectangular blocks a metre in length, which originally defined a rectangular temenos around the spring measuring approximately 10 by 15 metres, with the spring slightly off centre along the short north side (Ill. 7.11).

There was more, however, to this simple open-air sanctuary of the early sixth century than the spring enclosure. To the east was a cobble-paved area measuring approximately 12 by 12 metres. The 10-metre-long drystone wall at the north was intended clearly to keep the hillside in place while allowing water through (as it does to this day). Votive figurines found among the cobbles indicate that the pavement was in use at least by the middle of the sixth century. What—it may well be wondered—was the function of this very large paved surface which would have been covered with water to a certain depth?

Some idea of its original function is suggested by the better documented uses to which the area was put in the fourth century:

1. Offerings of various kinds ended up here. The pavement of cobbles was surrounded on at least three sides by walls forming a 'collecting basin'. The large quantities of plant material have been convincingly identified as 'first-fruits'—immature olives and fully preserved grapes and vines among them.[47] Large quantities of cooking ware and animal bones are evidence of sacrifice and ritual meals in the vicinity. Goat bones, for instance, are concentrated at the north end of the 'collecting basin'.[48]

2. Fragments of large vessels indicate that the basin acted as a reservoir, and fragments of perirrhanteria point to ritual bathing.[49] Parallels with other sites which have similar basins—although none of quite such ample dimensions—support this use.[50] They are to be found at mainland Greek sanctuaries: for example, at Lusoi in Arkadia, which has been compared with the sanctuary of Artemis at San Biagio alla Venella,[51] and at Perachora where the excavators originally interpreted them as basins for ritual baths,[52] but they also occur in Etruria—for example, at Veii (in comparable form).

[47] J. C. Carter, 'Agricoltura e pastorizia in Magna Grecia (tra Bradano e Basento 1987)', in G. Pugliese (ed.), Magna Grecia (Milan, 1987), 173–212.

[48] S. Bökönyi (unpublished report). For Dionysos worshipped in the guise of a goat (eriphos), at Metaponto and by Orphics, see G. Giannelli, Culti e miti della Magna Grecia (Florence, 1963), 76.

[49] J. C. Carter, 'Metapontum—Land, Wealth and Population', in J. P. Descoeudres (ed.), Greek Colonists and Native Populations (Oxford, 1990), 418.

[50] R. Ginouvès, Balaneutikè: Recherches sur le bain dans l'antiquité grecque (Paris, 1960), 375–404, passim.

[51] Olbrich (n. 20), 404–5; W. Reichel and A. Wilhelm, 'Das Heiligtum der Artemis zu Lusoi', ÖJh 4 (1901), 15–18.

[52] H. Payne et al., Perachora, i (Oxford, 1940), 120–2; but see R. Tomlinson, 'Water Supplies and Ritual at the Heraion at Perachora', in R. Hägg, N. Marinatos, and G. C. Nordquist (edd.), Early Greek Cult Practice (Stockholm, 1988), 167–71.

Water played a major role in the cult at Pantanello from the beginning. Its broad significance in Greek cults has been studied by Ginouvès and can be summarized under three general headings: (1) purification (the cathartic function); (2) initiatory purification (which kills the past to prepare for a renaissance); and (3) immediate effects (fertility, reproductivity, health and knowledge). Which of these applies to the cult at Pantanello from the sixth century—and in what degree? The same question could be asked of practically all of the cults of the *chora* as nearly all seem to incorporate water to a greater or lesser degree.[53] We do not now have, and may never possess, sufficient elements to answer this question in a definitive way, or to describe precisely the workings of the cult or the exact nature of divinities worshipped here. But on the basis of the architectural arrangements and the votive objects, especially the terracotta figurines and votive plaques together with the remains of plants and animals, I should like to offer some working hypotheses.

Mistress of the Spring

All of the Archaic votive figures are female (Ills. 7.12, 7.13). Whether they are apparently half-figures with arms outstretched, or standing figures with arms pressed across the body, or enthroned figures, they are uniformly female. They always wear the high *polos*, which in many, but clearly not all cases, indicated that the figure was meant to represent the divinity—but which divinity is she? The types are those found in the city at Sacellum C and also at San Biagio and the sanctuary of Hera at the Tavole Palatine but there too identification is elusive.

We can only be sure that the Pantanello deity was female and, given the resemblances of the figurines to those of the urban sites, more likely to be a major divinity than a nymph: one who could, like Artemis, be worshipped in an open-air shrine and like the Artemis of San Biagio, have been an all-purpose goddess of fertility. Remains of plant offerings and animal sacrifices do not help to narrow the range of choices and iconographically precise elements such as the torch (of Persephone) are too few and contradictory to be decisive—to the point that one wonders if several female divinities might not have been worshipped here.[54]

A further discovery adds a different dimension. The numerous 'Ionic cups' of sixth-century date which were deposited around the spring had their bottoms more or less carefully perforated (Ill. 7.14). There are literally hundreds of

[53] Ginouvès (n. 50), 426–8.
[54] F. Costabile, *I ninfei di Locri epizefiri* (Catanzaro, 1991). For similar iconography in an indigenous context, see D. Adamesteanu and H. Dilthy, *Macchia di Rossano: Il santuario della Mefitis* (Galatina, 1992), 64.

ILL. 7.12 Votive figurines, Pantanello (PZ 76.138; 78.73)

examples of this practice. The most obvious interpretation is that they were used for libations on the site—the liquid being funnelled by the cup directly into the spring or the ground. This practice is typical of offerings to the chthonic divinities.[55] The possibility that the female figure is, like Persephone, a power in both the upper and lower worlds is thus enhanced.

The close proximity of the sanctuary and the necropolis at Pantanello is not, I believe, a coincidence. Similarly perforated cups have been found both inside and outside burials there. An analogous juxtaposition of sanctuary and necropolis has been noted at Crucinia just outside the city walls,[56] and at San Biagio.[57] The chthonic aspect of the cult is a constant throughout its long history and is intensified in the next phase.

[55] E. F. Bruch, *Totenteil und Seelgerät im griechischen Recht* (Munich, 1926), 175–7; see also B. Rafn, 'The Ritual Use of Pottery in the Nekropolis at Halieis', in H. A. G. Brijder (ed.), *Ancient Greek and Related Pottery: Proceedings of the International Vase Symposium in Amsterdam, 12–15 April, 1984* (Amsterdam, 1984), 305–8, and G. Oikonomos, *De Profusionum receptaculis sepulcralibus* (Athens, 1921), 22–30.
[56] F. G. Lo Porto, 'Nuovi scavi nella città e nella sua necropoli', *Notizie degli scavi di Antichità* 8, 35 (1981), 292–3.
[57] C. D'Annibale, pers. comm.

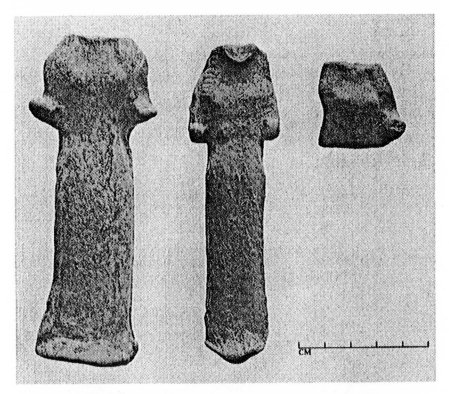

Ill. 7.13 Votive figurines, Pantanello (PZ 82.315; 78.41; 77.812)

The Fifth-century BC Sanctuary

About 500, a building with an impressive tiled roof was erected on the site (Ill. 7.11). It was oriented in an east–west direction, exactly perpendicular to the north–south walls flanking the spring, and overlapping the westernmost one. (By this time the area between the early sixth-century conglomerate walls had filled almost to the level of their upper edge.) The building—only one of whose east–west walls has been found preserved—probably measured 11 by 5.5 metres. Outside its north-west corner is a small rectangular basin which was supplied by a funnel-like channel on its long north side. The basin was empty except for fragments of coarse cooking ware. The dark coloured fill suggested fire, but there was no carbonized material in it.

This first covered structure on the site did not remain in use for long. Its replacement on high ground to the north, however, was of precisely identical dimensions and orientation (Ill. 7.15). It contained a sunken circular pit, off-centre to the north at a point (in the east–west sense) near its middle. Behind that to the west, a pedestal base, which has been interpreted as a cult statue

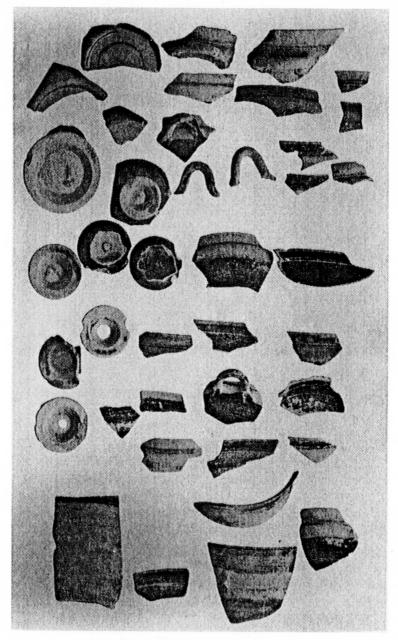

ILL. 7.14 Cups from the spring, Pantanello

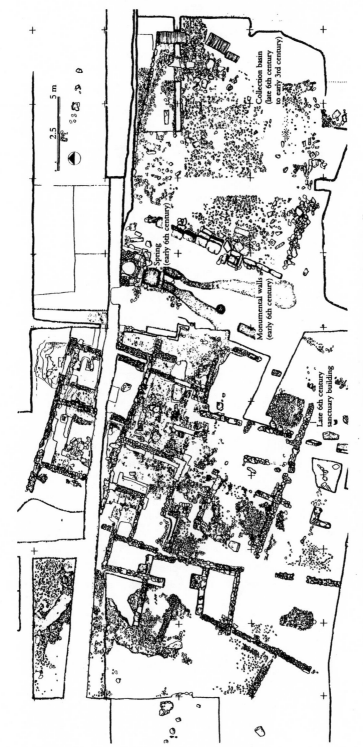

Collection basin
(late 6th century
to early 3rd century)

Spring
(early 6th century)

Monumental walls
(early 6th century)

Late 6th century
sanctuary building

5 m

2.5

ILL. 7.15 Plan of the sanctuary structures of the fifth-century BC phase, Pantanello

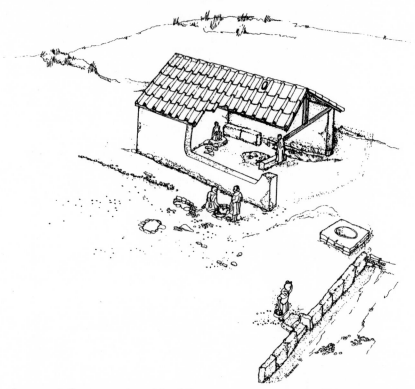

ILL. 7.16 Reconstruction of the fifth-century BC sanctuary building at Pantanello

base, was centred against a north–south wall.[58] Access to the sunken pit was limited on the east by another transverse wall of light construction and therefore probably just a low, transenna-like barrier (Ills. 7.16, 7.17).

The thick roof-fall of the structure sealed pottery of the early fifth century and contained in its upper layers other material of the second half of the fifth century. The building seems to have been in existence, then, for a brief and precisely definable period between about 475 and 425. Given its similarities to its predecessor, it is not unreasonable to suppose that the cult was simply moved up the hill to higher ground when the water table's rise made the lower site uninhabitable.[59]

The sunken pit or *bothros* within the fifth-century building (Ill. 7.16), like

[58] A large fragment of a marble acrolithic cult statue was found a few metres to the west in the context of the Roman kiln deposit which cut into this building; J. C. Carter, 'Preliminary Report on the Excavation at Pizzica Pantanello (1974–76)', in *Metaponto*, ii. *Notizie degli scavi di Antichità* 8, 31 (Rome, 1977), 478–9, fig. 54.

[59] There is some evidence that the lower site was deliberately and carefully covered over with clay. A parallel for ritual abandonment of this sort can be found in the Thesmophorion at Bitalemi outside the walls of Gela; P. Orlandini, 'Lo scavo del Thesmophorion di Bitaleme e il culto dell divinità Ctonie a Gela', *Kokalos* 12 (1966), 17.

ILL. 7.17 View of the fifth-century BC phase, looking east. The upper level of the
walls date to the fourth century BC

the rectangular basin of the lower site, contained broken coarseware amphorae
and cooking ware. A large fragment of a coarse oinochoe and numerous rims
of casseroles came to light. The pit's perimeter was defined with fragments of
amphora and pithos rims. It seemed at first to be a sunken hearth, so dark was
the soil removed from it. Analysis of this fill, however, again revealed absolutely
no charred material, no wood, no seeds or bone fragments. We were led to
conclude that it was placed where it was in order to receive exclusively liquid
offerings (or cooked vegetables or grains, which decomposed without a trace).
Sacrifices involving animals certainly took place on the site, but not here or in
the several hearth-like circular features just to the south of this building.[60]

Dionysos and his Circle

One discovery, a fragment of a votive plaque (Ill. 7.18) with the exquisitely
defined features of a satyr with his pointed ears, is, I believe, crucial for our

---

[60] R. Hägg, 'Funerary Meals in the Geometric Necropolis at Asine', in R. Hägg (ed.), *The Greek
Renaissance of the Eighth Century BC: Tradition and Innovation* (Stockholm, 1983), 189–93. See also G.
Pianu, 'Spazi e riti nell'agora di Eraclea lucana', in *Éspace sacrificiel dans les civilisations méditerranéennes de
l'Antiquité* (Lyons, 1991), 202–4.

ILL. 7.18 Head of satyr from the
bothros, fifth-century BC sanctuary
building, Pantanello

understanding of this cult. This and another earlier satyr are the first indications of the presence of Dionysos at Pantanello (though he would be very much in evidence in the last phase of the sanctuary, as we shall see). Numerous votive plaque fragments (see the discussion of Sant'Angelo Vecchio) show the bearded, reclining figure of a male identified commonly as 'Dionysos-Hades' or sometimes as the 'heroized deceased'.[61] Plaques of the same type have been found in large numbers at Taras. He is represented on a couch or *kline* holding a kantharos or other drinking cup. Beside him is the seated figure of a female divinity wearing a *polos* and holding in her left arm the figure of an infant, or sometimes a cornucopia filled with fruits. The earliest examples of this type have been placed on stylistic ground in the early fifth century, like the satyr from the *bothros* of the cult building.

Dionysos began to play an important role in the sanctuary as early as the first half of the fifth century. It should be recalled that this was the period of the democratization of the necropolis during which the division-line road had

[61] B. Neutsch, 'Der Heros auf der Kline', *Römische Mitteilungen* 68 (1961), 150–63. See also B. Kingsley, 'The Reclining Heroes of Taras and their Cult', *CSCA* 17 (1979), 201–20. At Taras, these plaques appear as early as the last quarter of the 6th century BC, and are thought to be associated with a cult of the chthonic divinities (especially as they were found close to the Tarentine necropolis). Many similar examples, in fragmentary condition, came from the votive deposit discovered at Crucinia (Favale) in a dense area of tombs just outside the north wall of Metaponto.

come into use as a burial area. Can the sudden appearance of the god here be another reflection of political change? Did he share power with the descendant of the female fertility figure of the early sixth century? Did she assume the role of his consort as the 'Dionysos-Hades' plaques might suggest? And if so, was she Persephone? These questions have been raised in regard to similar plaques found elsewhere.[62] All, I believe, can be answered in the affirmative.

ILL. 7.19 Unglazed miniature votive vessels, fifth century BC, from the spring, Pantanello

Further light is shed on the cult by the discovery around the mouth of the spring of numerous miniature unglazed vessels of a type familiar in sanctuaries throughout Magna Graecia and Sicily and in Greece itself (Ill. 7.19).[63] Krateriskoi and tiny skyphoi identical to these were found in a limited number of burials of mid-fifth-century date in the Pantanello necropolis.[64] In addition there are miniature chytrai, oinochoai, and amphorae. The shapes are those of particular importance in the rituals of the Anthesteria, a festival of Dionysos in

[62] Letta (n. 28), 14; G. Zuntz, *Persephone* (Oxford, 1971), 167.
[63] E. Gabrici, 'Il santuario della Malophoros e Selinunte', *Monumenti antichi* 32 (1927). See also H. Payne and T. J. Dunbabin, *Perachora*, ii (Oxford, 1962), 290–313.
[64] J. C. Carter, 'A Greek Rural Sanctuary—Pantanello in the Light of Recent Research 1990–1991', *AJA* 96 (1992), 371.

which special attention is paid to the souls of the departed.[65] Some of these burials can be identified (on the basis of tomb type and grave goods) as those of initiates into Orphic rites or Dionysiac mysteries.[66]

Chthonic divinities have two primary functions: 'they ensure the fertility of the land and they preside over, or have some function or other connected with, the realm of the souls of the dead.'[67] The offerings of grapes and other agricultural products in the sanctuary throughout its existence testify to the continued importance of the fertility of the field. After 500 BC the souls of the dead, to judge from the plaques and votive vessels, are of equal or greater importance.

The Final Lucanian Phase

In its final stage, the late fourth to early third century BC, a renaissance of the sanctuary took place after a period of virtual abandonment during the early fourth century. The sanctuary building of the fifth century with the central sunken pit had been buried under a layer of alluvial debris. No other building on the site rose to take its place for nearly a century. When in the late years of the fourth century a structure was built directly over the long, narrow fifth-century 'megaron', it was of a very different design (Ill. 7.11). The plan, in fact, is that familiar from thousands of examples scattered all over the *chora* of Metaponto. It would have been indistinguishable from that of contemporary farmhouses. At this time, too, the cobbled area returned to use. A clay dike blocked the flow of water to the south and created the 'collecting basin'.

From the basin's north-west end, beside the well (constructed from reused limestone blocks and placed directly over the Archaic spring), were recovered hundreds of fragments of votive plaques. There was the 'Dionysos-Hades' type (see above) in the early Hellenistic style of the late fourth century. With them was associated another type of fragmentary plaque which is also familiar both at Taras and Metaponto—the goat-legged satyr who attempts to carry off a fleeing nymph or maenad.[68] He invariably balances a large krater in his left arm and encircles the nymph with his right. She holds a cornucopia. The nymphs, the object of pursuit, are shown under a cave-like ledge surrounded by clusters of grapes. (The examples from Cozzo Presepe and Sant'Angelo in the *chora* are practically identical.) Since the Satyr-Nymph plaques were found exclusively

[65] R. Hamilton, *Choes and Anthesteria: Athenian Iconography and Ritual* (Ann Arbor, 1992), with up-to-date bibliography has recently challenged this interpretation of the festival by W. Burkert, *Homo Necans* (Berkeley, 1983), 213–26.

[66] J. C. Carter, 'Orphis in the Pantanello Necropolis', *AJA* 97 (1993), 320.

[67] W. K. C. Guthrie, *The Greeks and their Gods* (Boston, 1955), 218.

[68] A. J. N. W. Prag, 'The Terracottas', in *The Excavations at Cozzo Presepe (1969–72). Notizie degli scavi di Antichità* 8, 31 (Rome, 1983), 379–81, for Cozzo Presepe; J. C. Carter, *Excavations in the Territory, Metaponto 1980* (Austin, Tex., 1981), 14, for Sant'Angelo Vecchio; Adamesteanu (n. 8), 200–3 for the urban sanctuary; Letta (n. 28), 126–9, for the type.

ILL. 7.20 Satyr and goat,
fourth century BC, from
the collecting basin,
Pantanello

in the late fourth- or early third-century levels of the 'collecting basin', this representation must belong to the latest phase of the sanctuary (Ill. 7.20).

The foci of the cult—the spring-well, the basin, and the site of the cult building—remained constant. So, apparently, did the chthonic, Dionysiac nature of the cult. This was the period of the abundant offerings of grape and olive (mirrored by the representations of grape clusters on the plaques). All that seems to have changed significantly was the architectural form of the cult building. How significant was this?

A recent study by Fracchia and Gualtieri[69] has outlined a strong Lucanian tradition of sacred architecture in which house forms predominate. These structures are contemporary with our sanctuary and with—as I believe even more strongly now—the Lucanian presence in our territory. The late fourth century, as I have argued elsewhere,[70] saw a peaceful incursion into the *chora* of numerous Hellenized, indigenous Lucanians, the distant relatives of the pre-Greek inhabitants of the territory. Could they be responsible for this change? In the interior of Lucania, at Serra di Vaglio and Roccagloriosa, the domestic shrines seem clearly to have served as the meeting places of cults centred on the tribe or family organization. In its brief last phase, was the sanctuary at Pantanello, again, a family-based cult place?

[69] H. M. Fracchia and M. Gualtieri, 'The Social Context of Cult Practices in Pre-Roman Lucania', *AJA* 92 (1989), 217–32.

[70] Carter (n. 25), 36. See also J. C. Carter, 'The Decline of Magna Grecia in the Age of Pyrrhos? New Evidence from the Chora', in R. R. Holloway and T. Hackens (edd.), *The Age of Pyrrhos: Archaeology, History and Culture in Early Hellenistic Greece and Italy* (Providence, RI, 1992).

8

Demeter in the Ancient Greek City and its Countryside

SUSAN GUETTEL COLE

State University of New York at Buffalo

Greek conceptions of space and time were shaped by ideas that identified the world of nature with the world of the gods. The gods were thought to control the forces of nature and were believed to have their own place in the natural world. The countryside was thought to have been the home of the gods long before the birth of the first humans, and local political charter myths always placed human struggle for survival or human competition for political dominance in the context of the divine world. With the development of the walled city (*asty*) marked off as separate from its countryside (*chora*), the divine pantheon was standardized, and the functions of the gods were adapted to the new communal organization of the city-state. The gods of the countryside, however, never lost their vitality, and the history of the religious life of the Greek city is very much a history of rituals that helped the polis to maintain a balance between its nucleated centre and its rural periphery. These rituals defined the community and kept the polis embedded in the land that was believed to sustain it.

The issues of the relation between a polis and its land are stated with elegant simplicity in a late fourth-century decree from Kolophon, a small polis in western Ionia. Freed from Persian domination after the death of Alexander, the city took the opportunity to enlarge its core by extending the city wall:

to enclose the old city within the same wall as the existing city, the old city which the gods handed over to our ancestors and which our ancestors settled by building temples and altars, thereby becoming famous among all Greeks. And so, that this might be accomplished quickly, on the fourth day of the coming month, the priest of Apollo and the other priests and priestesses and the *prytanis* (eponymous magistrate) together with the *boule* and those appointed in this decree, are to go down to the old agora, and at the altars of the gods that our ancestors left behind for us, they are to pray to Zeus Soter, Poseidon who brings security, Apollo of Klaros, Mother Antaia, Athena Polias, and to all the other gods and heroes who dwell in our city (*polis*) and land (*chora*); and since benefits are bestowed, they are to hold a procession and sacrifice just as the *demos* decides.[1]

The ancient city is described as given to the people of Kolophon in former times by the gods themselves. Founding a new city is described in terms of building temples and altars, as recognition to the gods for the gift of the city. The decree requires that the priests and priestesses of Kolophon visit the altars in the old agora to acknowledge the ties between the old site and the current site of the city. The decision to build the wall is ratified by sacrifices to the major gods of the city and to all other gods and heroes who inhabit the walled city (here, polis) and its territory (*chora*). The inscription justifies the city's claim to its territory by describing that territory as a gift from the gods who dwell in the land itself. According to such beliefs, sanctuaries existed in precisely those places thought of as the natural home of the individual deity, whether in the city itself or scattered in the landscape of the city's territory.

Each polis had its own constellation of divinities. Citizens of fourth-century Kolophon knew from experience which of their gods 'dwelt' in the town and which in the countryside, and it was natural for them to consider all of these gods as belonging to the polis, just as they considered the countryside as well as the walled town to be their own. They found reassurance and derived a sense of stability from the assumption that their gods had found their city for them. The real history of city foundation, urban planning, and community development, to be sure, was much more complex, but competition between cities required foundation myths that recognized the power of the gods in order to justify claims to territory.

Common cultural consciousness, a common economic experience, and constants of social organization shaped the polis physically as well as psychically. As a result, where and how a city placed its sanctuaries is significant. The motivation for spatial order has been explained by others in terms of the power of the landscape,[2] political competition with other cities for space and territory,[3] rational planning,[4] or peculiarities of local history coupled with the function of

[1] L. Robert, 'Décrets de Kolophon', RPh 10 (1936), 158–68 (*Opera Minora Selecta* ii (Amsterdam, 1969), 1237–47). Robert dates the decree after 315, and before 306. See also I. Malkin, *Religion and Colonization in Ancient Greece* (Leiden, 1987), 151–2 (Greek text and trans.); N. H. Demand, *Urban Relocation in Archaic and Classical Greece* (Norman, Okla., 1990), 161–2.

[2] I. E. M. Edlund, *The Gods and the Place* (Stockholm, 1987), 29, distinguishing between urban, extra-urban, and rural sanctuaries, recognizes that function may have determined the location of sanctuaries just outside the city's walls, but describes rural sanctuaries in terms of 'the mysterious forces of nature'. She follows Eliade, who argues that sacred places are natural places of communion with the divine, discovered and marked by human use, but defined by an absolute holiness not dependent upon human acts.

[3] F. de Polignac, *La Naissance de la cité grecque* (Paris, 1984).

[4] I. Malkin (n. 1), 135–86, describing the process by which colonial poleis organized their sanctuaries, emphasizes the rational planning that determined not only the regular streets within the city's walls, but the location of sanctuaries outside the walls in the city's territory.

the particular deity.[5] All of these factors may have played a role, but other issues are equally important in the development of the community. I would like to propose another combination of considerations, which seems to have influenced choices of cult sites, by examining the ways in which the function of the divinity, the demands of ritual, and the social organization of the community influenced the placement of sanctuaries in relation to the city and its land. By concentrating on a single divinity and focusing on the location, arrangement, history, and uses of the relevant sanctuaries, it may be possible to isolate those features that transcended local conditions. I have chosen Demeter because she was a divinity worshipped throughout the Greek Mediterranean, she had clearly defined functions, and her main festival, the Thesmophoria, was one of the most widely observed of any Greek festival. Moreover, the general uniformity of her votives implies a certain consistency in ritual, she was often worshipped by groups clearly defined by gender, and although her sanctuaries are found both inside and outside Greek cities, there are certain striking features associated with their position, natural resources, and architectural features. A survey of her cult sites will show that the perceived character of the goddess and the demands of ritual always exerted a considerable influence.

Demeter was rarely the principal god of an ancient Greek city, but she was worshipped by the Greeks wherever agriculture was practised. Although her functions extended beyond the protection of grain, agriculture was her special province. Grain was the primary staple throughout the Mediterranean,[6] and unlike oil or wine, it was not practical to store it for protection against lean years.[7] This is perhaps the explanation for the importance of festivals linked with Demeter as a goddess of agriculture. It may explain as well the relative prominence of her sanctuaries in the landscape of the polis when compared to Athena as goddess of the olive or even Dionysos as god of wine. For the Greeks the growing, storage, and distribution of grain was a matter of life and death.[8] Many of the epithets of Demeter reflect these concerns: Chloe ('Green Shoot'), Sito ('Grain'), Himalis ('Abundance'), Ompnia ('Nourisher with Grain'), Achaia ('Reaper'), Ioulo ('Goddess of Grain Sheaves'), Haloïs ('Goddess of the Threshing Floor'), Megalartos and Megalomazos ('Goddess of Wheat (or Barley) Bread'), Hamalophoros ('Bearing Sheaves of Grain'), Polusoros ('Rich in Piles of Grain'), Soritis ('Giver of Heaps of Grain'), Karpophoros ('She who

[5] M. Jost, *Sanctuaires et cultes d'Arcadie* (Paris, 1985), 545–59.

[6] L. Foxhall and H. A. Forbes, 'Sitometreia: The Role of Grain as a Staple Food in Classical Antiquity', *Chiron* 12 (1982), 43–90.

[7] P. Garnsey and I. Morris, 'Risk and the *Polis*: The Evolution of Institutionalised Responses to Food Supply Problems in the Ancient Greek State', in P. Halstead and J. O'Shea (edd.), *Bad Year Economics: Cultural Responses to Risk and Uncertainty* (Cambridge, 1989), 102–5, for control of grain trade.

[8] Issues and strategies are discussed by T. W. Gallant, *Risk and Survival in Ancient Greece* (Stanford, Calif., 1991), 34–59, 111–16.

brings forth fruit'), and Anesidora ('She who sends up gifts').[9] Her epithet Kalligeneia ('She who brings forth beautiful offspring'), referring to the fruits of the earth, could also be used of the earth itself. As the name of the third day of the Thesmophoria, Kalligeneia could also be associated with the women who celebrated her festival and suggested a homology between the earth, the goddess, and the bodies of the women invoking her aid.

Demeter could bring food, but, as cause of deprivation, she could also take it away. In Phokis she was called Steiritis ('Barren', Paus. 10. 35. 10), and Hesychius associates her epithet Azesia with the Greek verb that means 'parch' (ἀζαίνω; Hsch. s.v. Ἀζησία). Some of Demeter's epithets are not so transparent. Even where she was clearly associated with the agricultural cycle, it is often difficult to determine what a particular epithet means. For instance, the Thesmophoria was associated with the sowing of grain, but her epithet 'Thesmophoros', 'the one who carries what has been set down', is difficult to explain. 'Thesmophoros' may refer both to the actions of the ritual (bringing up of ritual objects that had been 'set down' into pits in the earth) or to the establishment of the laws and institutions (thesmoi) of civilized life by her contribution of grain.[10] Where Demeter was not clearly associated with agriculture, the explanation is even more problematic. For instance, her Arkadian titles Melaina ('Black') and Erinys ('Avenging Fury'), not known elsewhere for Demeter, can possibly be understood as relics of very old forms of her cult.[11]

Agricultural concerns are reflected in the many sacrifices and festivals for Demeter associated with the agricultural year.[12] In Attica the Proerosia took place during the Attic month Pyanopsion in the autumn, before the ploughing for the winter crop. Ploughing is followed by sowing, and the Stenia and Thesmophoria followed in the same month, to safeguard the planting of the grain crop. In mid-winter Greeks sacrificed to Demeter Chloe, who protected the growing green shoots of grain, and they also celebrated the Haloa, in honour of the halos (threshing-floor), barren in winter, but commemorated in anticipation of the later harvest. At the time of harvest itself, in early summer, many Greek cities celebrated the Kalamaia to protect the grain stalks. The Stenia and the Thesmophoria were festivals for women from which men were excluded; the Haloa also included rituals restricted to women. In Attica many of the festivals of Demeter were celebrated at deme level, and a single modest

---

[9] M. P. Nilsson, *Griechische Feste von religiöser Bedeutung* (Berlin, 1906), 311–12; for a more complete list, see L. Farnell, *Cults of the Greek States*, iii (London, 1906), 311–25.

[10] On the much debated etymology of the epithet, see W. Burkert, *Greek Religion* (Cambridge, Mass., 1985), 243, for *thesmos* as what is set in the ground when the women imitate the sowing; cf. 246, for Thesmophoros as 'one who brings order'.

[11] Jost (n. 5), 309.

[12] A. C. Brumfield, *The Attic Festivals of Demeter and their Relation to the Agricultural Year* (New York, 1984).

deme sanctuary of Demeter could have served at different times throughout the year for all the various individual festivals. The Thesmophorion in the Piraeus was used only for women's festivals, for the Plerosia, the Kalamaia, the Skira, and, as the inscription says: 'also if the women come together on any other day according to ancestral tradition'.[13] At Eleusis Demeter's sanctuary was used for the local deme celebrations of the Thesmophoria as well as for the mysteries.[14] Demeter's rituals restricted to women could also be connected with other cults. At Thasos the same sanctuary, located just outside the wall, served for both the ancestral divinities of the local phratries (οἱ πατρῷοι) and the Thesmophoria,[15] perhaps a recognition of the need for different institutions for assimilating male and female to communal life. Strict consistency was never achieved. Demeter's calendar of festivals varied somewhat from city to city, and even the Thesmophoria, celebrated wherever grain was grown, were not fixed to the same month in every city.[16] Nevertheless Demeter's agricultural functions remained the basis of most forms of her worship.

Agricultural concerns are often reflected symbolically or indirectly in the votives dedicated to Demeter. These are so regular in type that many minor sanctuaries of Demeter may be identified by the votives alone. The most striking characteristics of Demeter's votives are their number, simplicity, and modesty. Several types of dedications to Demeter, remarkably similar from site to site, seem to reflect activities of the rites themselves. Miniature vessels for carrying water (especially small hydriai)[17] or vessels for grain (kernoi) predominate among the small ceramic objects. Figurines representing female worshippers carrying hydriai, plants, or animals (especially pigs) are also very common in sanctuaries of Demeter. These objects were dedicated by women as tokens of their participation in the rites. Small female figurines dedicated to Demeter number in the thousands, tiny hydriai in the hundreds of thousands. Small ceramic sows and piglets reflect not only the Thesmophoria, where the rotted

[13] IG ii² 1177; LSCG 36, 4th century BC. Others were also limited to a female clientele; J. Delemarre, 'Décrets religieux d'Arkésiné', REG 16 (1903), 166 (Amorgos, fourth century BC), LSAM 16 (Gambreion, 3rd century BC). From votive dedications it is obvious that some precincts of Demeter, even some specifically labelled 'Thesmophorion', could sometimes be open to men; P. Bruneau, Recherches sur les cultes de Délos à l'époque hellénistique et à l'époque impériale (Paris, 1970), 284, for the inventories of the Thesmophorion at Delos.

[14] K. Clinton, 'Sacrifice at the Eleusinian Mysteries', in R. Hägg, N. Marinatos, and G. C. Nordquist, (edd.), Early Greek Cult Practice (Stockholm, 1988), 72.

[15] C. Rolley, 'Le Sanctuaire des Dieux Patrooi et le Thesmophorion de Thasos', BCH 89 (1965), 441–83.

[16] At Athens the Thesmophoria were celebrated in the month of Pyanopsion, just before winter; at Delos the festival was celebrated in Metageitnion (late summer). The Delian schedule seems to correspond to that of Thasos, where the Thesmophoria were celebrated in the month after Hekatombaion; see F. Salviat, 'Une nouvelle loi thasienne', BCH 82 (1950), 218, 248; cf. Nilsson (n. 9), 316–18.

[17] E. Diehl, Die Hydria (Mainz, 1964), 187–92, where inventories of excavated examples make it clear that more hydriai are associated with Demeter than with any other divinity.

remains of sacrificed piglets were brought up from underground chambers, but also bear witness to the numbers of pregnant sows offered as a special sacrifice to Demeter at many sites and festivals throughout the year.[18] Ceramic pigs correspond to bones of pigs and piglets found in ash pits in sanctuaries of Demeter. Ceramic sows found at Thasos, slit open to show the foetuses inside, must reflect sacrifices similar to those performed at Mytilene, where bones of pig foetuses were found in ash pits, mixed with bones of infant and adult pigs. The fecundity of the sacrificial animal reflects a concern for female fecundity, apparent in the many kourotrophic dedications found in Demeter's sanctuaries.[19] As with any divinity, more personalized dedications show variation from these norms,[20] and Demeter's votives may not be identical at every sanctuary.[21] Nevertheless, the masses of modest dedications from individual women indicate a general consistency in the kind of ritual performed, and show that the rites of Demeter must have been open to the majority of local women, and not reserved for representative ritual specialists or small groups selected from prominent families to represent the whole. No single votive type can identify a sanctuary of Demeter if there are no inscriptions or literary accounts, but the compounding of several distinctive types together is a strong indication for Demeter at a site known only from archaeological finds and physical features.

Agricultural concerns are often reflected in the choice of sites for sanctuaries of Demeter. Rites associated with Demeter, designed to encourage agricultural success, required natural features often available only in the countryside. The ubiquitous votives associated with water indicate a concern for water, and the same concern seems to have determined the choice for sites appropriate for worship. Demeter's sanctuaries were often located near a spring or stream.[22]

---

[18] Attica: *LSCG* 20 A. 43, B. 48, 49; *LSS* 18 B. 29–30. Mykonos: *LSCG* 96. 11, 16. Lindos: *LSS* 87 A. 3, B. 2. Delos: *IG* ix 287. 68–70, 372. 103–6, 440. 36–41, 442. 198–202, 460. 66–7.

[19] T. H. Price, *Kourotrophos: Cults and Representations of the Greek Nursing Deities* (Leiden, 1978), for kourotrophic figurines in sanctuaries of Demeter.

[20] P. Gregory Warden, 'Gift, Offering, and Reciprocity', *Expedition* 34 (1992), 51–8, for heirlooms and luxury items (Egyptianizing scarabs, gems, a bronze falcon, silver satyr-mask, etc.) as dedications at Cyrene. C. Dengate, 'The Sanctuaries of Apollo in the Peloponnesos' (Ph.D., diss., University of Chicago, 1988), 116–17, on 'votive drift' and difficulty of always correlating type of votive with nature of cult or function of deity.

[21] Ceramic cakes are common for Demeter in the Peloponnese, but not so common elsewhere. Agricultural tools, surprisingly, are relatively rare; C. G. Simon, 'The Archaic Offerings and Cults of Ionia' (Ph.D., diss., University of California, Berkeley 1986), 224, 228. In some places the votives seem exclusively from female donors, but elsewhere men and women made dedications in the same sanctuary. For instance, Demeter Malophoros at Selinus, whose epithet associates her with agriculture, received weaving equipment, apparently from women, and also spears, arrowheads, and full-sized shields used in war, apparently from male worshippers; ibid. 237, 240, 249, 265.

[22] S. G. Cole, 'The Uses of Water in Greek Sanctuaries', in Hägg, Marinatos, and Nordquist (edd.), (n. 14), 164–5.

Water was necessary for agriculture,[23] and pure water was required for her rites.[24] Other features have been noticed. Béquignon has argued that the typical sanctuary of Demeter was located on the side of a hill,[25] and de Polignac has observed that, during the formative stages of the polis, the typical sanctuary of Demeter, was located just outside or near a city's walls, providing a transition between the inhabited city and its agricultural territory. Not every sanctuary, however, fits these descriptions. Many sanctuaries of Demeter were located on hillsides, a fact reflected in the *Homeric Hymn to Demeter* when Keleus instructs the Eleusinians to build a temple and altar for Demeter 'upon a projecting hill' (ἐπὶ προύχοντι κολωνῷ, 298),[26] but sanctuaries of Demeter could also be located in the plain or at the base of a hill. And while it is true that many sanctuaries of Demeter were located between the walls of the city and the city's agricultural territory, others were placed within the walls (even on the acropolis), or far outside the walls, deep in the city's rural area. Pausanias mentions sanctuaries of Demeter in 51 cities on the Greek mainland; 21 of these cities had sanctuaries of Demeter inside the city (*asty*), either on the acropolis or in the agora, 18 had a sanctuary of Demeter in a village outside the city, and 24 had sanctuaries of Demeter deep in the countryside. Pausanias rarely concerns himself with the location of a Demeter sanctuary in relation to the walls of a city.[27] When he does record distance, it is the great distance of rural sanctuaries of Demeter from towns and inhabited settlements and deep in the countryside that interests him. Recorded distances vary from the 0.7 kilometre between Akakesion (Arkadia) and the peribolos of Demeter and Despoina (Paus. 8. 37. 2) to the 11 kilometres that separated the grove and spring of Demeter Mysia from Pellene (Paus. 7. 27. 9).[28]

De Polignac's observations about peri-urban sanctuaries of Demeter are more consonant with colonial poleis than with cities of the Greek mainland. Colonial foundations, at least in their original stages, were more likely to have been built according to a deliberate plan. Cities on the Greek mainland, however, grew

[23] *POxy* ii. 221, col. 9. 18–20: '. . . and many sacrifice to Acheloos before Demeter because Acheloos is a name of all rivers and water is the source of fruit . . .'

[24] Water flowing into sanctuaries of Demeter was protected from pollution. See *IG* xii (5) 569 and xii Suppl. p. 114 (Keos); *LSCG* 65. 103–6 (Andania).

[25] Y. Béquignon, 'Déméter, déesse acropolitaine', *RA* (1958), 149–77.

[26] This line is curiously ignored by Béquignon, p. 177, in his attempt to associate Demeter with Rhea, called μήτηρ ὀρείη in the Homeric hymn. For reservations about the association, see N. Richardson, *The Homeric Hymn to Demeter* (Oxford, 1974), 295–6.

[27] He makes the relation clear only in his description of Troizen, where he describes the sanctuary of Demeter Thesmophoros as located outside the wall, on the road to Hermione, above the temple of Poseidon Phytalmios ('nourisher' or 'parent'; 2. 32.8). The sanctuary has been located above the village of Damala by G. Welter, *Troizen und Kalaureia* (Berlin, 1941), 20–2 and pls. 2, 9.

[28] The cave of Demeter Melaina on Mt. Elaios, with grove and spring, was 5.5 km. from Phigaleia (Arkadia, Paus. 8. 42. 1–2), and an unfinished temple of Demeter and Kore was 7.36 km. from Plataiai (Paus. 9. 4. 4).

more slowly, and the positioning of sanctuaries may be obscured by later adjustments dictated by political change. There are important differences between Greek cities on the mainland, Aegean cities whether on the islands or the Asian coast, and cities in other colonial areas, like Magna Graecia, Sicily, and North Africa. Historical factors like synoecism (e.g. at Kos[29]), dioecism (e.g. at Mantineia[30]), refoundation (Siris[31]), and movement of cities from one site to another (e.g. Teos[32]), as well as the ravages of decline (Tanagra[33]) could affect the placement of local sanctuaries relative to other important urban features.

Many of the mainland cities described by Pausanias had more than one sanctuary of Demeter. Leaving aside Attica, where the evidence for Demeter is far richer than Pausanias indicates, Megara, with four Demeter sanctuaries, and Hermione, with seven or more, indicate the possible diversity. At Megara there was a megaron on the main acropolis, a sanctuary of Demeter Thesmophoros on the second acropolis, another of Demeter Malophoros at the harbour, and a fourth sanctuary (with a well) in the border territory between Megara and Eleusis. Hermione, located in the southern Argolid, had at least seven sanctuaries of Demeter. Within the territory of Hermione in the southern Argolid there were four sanctuaries at some distance from the city: a sanctuary of Demeter at the village of Eileoi near the border with Troizen, a sanctuary of Demeter Thermasia on the coast north of the city, one on the mountainous headland on the sea south of the city, and a fourth at the village of Didymoi, about 3.6 kilometres from Hermione's port city of Mases. A fifth sanctuary was located in the city itself, and a sixth on Mt. Pron, not far from the city's walls.[34] Synoecism with Halieis in the Hellenistic period would have brought yet a seventh Demeter sanctuary within the province of Hermione. Clearly some Demeter sanctuaries were originally associated with local villages rather than with the central polis. Pausanias gives some indication of the vitality of the cult of Demeter in the Imperial period, but his survey does not indicate the historical complexity of sanctuary planning.

Recent excavations of Demeter sanctuaries show that in the Archaic period

[29] After synoecism at Kos in the 4th century there were at least nine sanctuaries of Demeter in the territory of a single polis; the earliest was an Archaic sanctuary at a spring just north of the town of Kos. See S. Sherwin-White, *Ancient Cos* (Göttingen, 1978), 305–12.

[30] S. and H. Hodkinson, 'Mantineia and the Mantinike: Settlement and Society in a Greek Polis', *BSA* 76 (1981), 261–5, on the dioecism of 385 BC, when the sanctuary of Demeter at Nestane might have reverted to the village. Jost (n. 5), 345–8, discusses the problems of the Koragion and Megaron at Mantineia itself.

[31] See below, p. 215.

[32] See below, p. 211.

[33] See below, p. 216.

[34] According to Michael Jameson, 'on the slope of a long hill', but not 'visible from much of the land'; 'Cultic Map of the Greek City-State', Paper presented at the American Philological Association, December 1987.

the older cities of Greece often kept their primary sanctuary of Demeter within the city's walls. Corinth and Eretria are both examples. At Corinth from the seventh to the fourth century BC the sanctuary of Demeter developed on a series of three terraces on the lower, gradual slope of the acropolis, some distance from the agora and densely inhabited areas of the city. The earliest buildings, a group of dining-rooms, date from the second half of the sixth century BC, with two later building periods of similar structures shortly after 450 and again in the late fourth century.[35] Activity diminished in the Hellenistic period, stopped after 146, and revived in the Roman period, when three small temples were built on the upper terrace in the last half of the first century. Water seems to have been important, both for purification (several of the dining-rooms were equipped with small shower stalls near the entry) and as a constituent of the ritual. Hundreds of thousands of miniature vases were among the dedications, with kalathiskoi, hydriai or hydriskai, and phialai predominating,[36] and the highest concentrations in the period from the sixth to the fourth century BC. Many of the votives were found in stone-lined pits on the terrace above the dining rooms.[37] Miniature terracotta figurines include girls and women carrying piglets and torches.[38] From the sanctuary the buildings of the agora are clearly visible in the distance, but the sanctuary itself is remote from the city centre and would have looked out over agricultural territory as well as the city.

Like the sanctuary of Demeter and Kore at Corinth, the sanctuary of Demeter at Eretria, bounded by a double temenos wall on the lower side, was located on the south-east slope leading to the acropolis, at some distance from the harbour, the agora, and the areas of domestic habitation.[39] Eretria was founded in the eighth century, but the earliest cult activity in the area of the Thesmophorion dates only from the sixth century BC. In the eighth and seventh centuries Demeter seems to have been worshipped near the major temple of Apollo Daphnephoros. A votive deposit near the temple contained more than 600 miniature hydriai, some showing women in procession.[40] The major votive deposits at the Thesmophorion on the side of the acropolis hill parallel for the most part those at Corinth (although no piglets have been found at Eretria),

---

[35] N. Bookidis and J. E. Fisher, 'The Sanctuary of Demeter and Kore on Acrocorinth, Preliminary Report IV: 1969–1970', *Hesperia* 41 (1972), 284; eid. 'Sanctuary of Demeter and Kore on Acrocorinth, Preliminary Report V: 1971–73', *Hesperia* 43 (1974), 272.

[36] E. G. Pemberton, *Corinth* xviii. 1: *The Sanctuary of Demeter and Kore: The Greek Pottery* (Princeton, NJ, 1989), 65.

[37] N. Bookidis and R. Stroud, *Demeter and Persephone in Ancient Corinth* (Princeton, NJ, 1987), 18 fig. 17.

[38] *Hesperia* 41 (1972), pl. 62d; Bookidis and Stroud (n. 37), 15 fig. 13.

[39] I. R. Metzger, *Eretria* vii: *Das Thesmophorion von Eretria* (Bern, 1985), 14 and pl. 1. The building is definitely a Thesmophorion. Roof tiles on the site are inscribed ΘΕΣΜ- (personal observation by author on site).

[40] *AR* (1982–3), 18.

with the highest concentrations in the sixth to fourth centuries. The temple and altar date from the late sixth or early fifth century; it is not known whether they survived the Persian destruction of 480.[41] A falling off of votives in the third century indicates either decline or that the worship of Demeter may have moved away from the Thesmophorion on the acropolis at that time.

In some older Greek cities Demeter's sanctuary was located between the urban centre and the agricultural territory, the pattern described by de Polignac for cities in the formative stage. This was the case at Knossos. Some of the earliest votives to Demeter have been found at Knossos, where from the eighth century to the second century Demeter was worshipped in what was originally an open-air sanctuary near a spring, on the lower slope of a hill about a kilometre from the acropolis and separated from the acropolis (and the Minoan palace) by a stream. If Knossos had a wall, this could have been an extramural sanctuary. As it is, the site is well removed from the main habitation area to the west of the palace and at least 200 metres away from the nearest traces of houses.[42] Early votives indicate nocturnal ceremonial meals in the sanctuary. Bones of sacrificial victims indicate that sheep predominated, with pigs comprising only 17 per cent. Most of the early (late eighth- and early seventh-century BC) terracotta figurines are female, including at least one kourotrophic figure.[43] By the late fifth century, when a small temple was built, the bones of sacrificial victims had become predominantly those of pigs (as many as 90 per cent).[44] Votives associated with water were common: hydriskai and hydrophoroi.[45] Until the second century, when votives seem to cease, lamps and miniature vases, especially krateriskoi, as well as hydrophoroi were popular dedications. Votive figurines (loomweights and jewellery as well as hydrophoroi)[46] indicate a primarily female clientele, but male figurines have also been found, as well as agricultural tools, weapons, and an inscribed ring dedicated 'to the Mother', by a man named Nothokrates, winner in the games.[47] Like the sanctuary of Demeter at Corinth, the sanctuary at Knossos experienced a decline in the Hellenistic period,[48] but revived again in the second half of the first century BC, when Octavian settled Campanians at Knossos, and continued into the second century AD.

Other sanctuaries of Demeter in Greece were located at some distance from town centres. A sanctuary of Demeter at Kalyvia tes Sokhas, located in a grove

[41] Metzger (n. 39), 52.

[42] S. Hood, *Archaeological Survey of the Knossos Area* (London, 1958), 20 no. 119.

[43] J. N. Coldstream, *Knossos: The Sanctuary of Demeter* (Oxford, 1973), 55 no. 60.

[44] For a marble pig's head as a dedication, see Coldstream (n. 43), 96 no. 12 and pl. 77a.

[45] Ibid. 68–70, 184.

[46] Including a ring inscribed ΔAMATP-, Coldstream (n. 43), 134 no. 25.

[47] Ibid. no. 14.

[48] Ibid. 186, compares the falling off of votives to Demeter at Axos and Gortyn in the Hellenistic period.

near a stream on a mountain side in the foothills of Mt. Taygetos, would have been about an hour and a half's walk for the women of Sparta.[49] Roof tiles inscribed ΔAMATPO[Σ] identify the sanctuary as Demeter's.[50] The earliest traces of cult activity go back to the sixth century.[51] Recognized ritual specialists, in charge of women's banquets, were exclusively female, and performed an office known from similar sanctuaries throughout Lakonia and Messenia.[52]

Literary references from the classical period, usually relating political or military crises, give some hints about the location of Demeter sanctuaries elsewhere in Greece. Two of these occur in the context of violation of the boundaries of sanctuaries normally restricted to female worshippers and illustrate the punishments expected for men who violated these boundaries. The first pertains to the sanctuary of Demeter Thesmophoros on Aigina during an early fifth-century conflict between Aigina and Athens. Herodotos tells us about a man condemned to death, who attempted to take refuge in the temple and held on to the door handles so tightly that when his pursuers cut his hands off to apprehend him, the hands remained gripped to the door (Hdt. 6. 91). Herodotos does not give the exact location of the sanctuary, but it could not have been far from the town centre because the execution was about to take place in or near the agora. The second example took place after the battle of Marathon, when Miltiades violated the sanctuary of Demeter Thesmophoros during the siege of Paros. Miltiades was trying to find a way into the city and injured his leg jumping over the wall (herkos) of the temenos of Demeter, described by Herodotos as located on a hill in front of the city (πρὸ τῆς πόλιος, 6. 134). Miltiades was not able to open the temenos door and later died of gangrene as a result of his injuries. Herodotos says the priestess who told Miltiades how to get in had revealed secrets not to be divulged to males, and implies that the injury was understood as punishment from the goddess. Two mainland sanctuaries of Demeter can be located because they were important in battle narratives. The first was just outside Plataiai, protected from pollution by Demeter herself during the battle of 479 BC. Herodotos describes a temple with temenos and grove located on a hill not far from the city (Hdt. 9. 57, 65). Although the battle of Plataiai raged all around the temenos, no Persian corpses fell in the sanctuary because, as Herodotos reports, Demeter was angry over the burning of Eleusis (9. 67).[53] The second mainland sanctuary played a pivotal

---

[49] R. M. Dawkins, 'Laconia. Sparta', BSA 16 (1909–10), 12–14.

[50] This is probably the sanctuary associated by Pausanias with the Eleusinian goddesses (3. 20. 5, 7).

[51] A Corinthian terracotta figurine and early Lakonian pottery; Dawkins (n. 49), 14, and J. M. Cook, 'Lakonia', BSA 45 (1950), 274.

[52] Cook (n. 51), 276–81; M. N. Tod, 'Notes and Inscriptions from S. W. Messenia', JHS 25 (1905), 49–53, for the office of thoinarmostria (female official in charge of banquets), a Peloponnesian title associated with the cult of Demeter and Kore. For Sparta, see LSS 64, 2nd century BC.

[53] See Paus. 9. 4. 3; Plut. Arist. 325c–f. Pritchett locates the temenos at the site of building foundations he found at Hysai on the Pantanassa ridge; see A. Schachter, Cults of Boiotia, i (London, 1981), 152–3.

role in a Spartan attack on Thebes. The Spartans were able to sneak on to the
Theban Kadmeia and capture it because the Theban men, displaced by the
women holding the Thesmophoria in Demeter's sanctuary on the Kadmeia,
had to stay down in the agora (Xen. *Hell.* 5. 2. 29).

The archaeological as well as the literary evidence shows that in the Archaic
and Classical periods sanctuaries of Demeter in Greece and the Cyclades could
be located on top of the acropolis, on the side of the acropolis, or outside the
walls of the city. Many acropolis sanctuaries of Demeter, like those at Eretria
and Corinth, were remote from other sanctuaries. Demeter at Thebes, however,
was right in the centre. Here Demeter combined agricultural and political
functions, and her location, squarely in the centre of town, reflects her central
political role. She was called Demeter Thesmophoros (Paus. 9. 16. 5), had a
temple on the Kadmeia (Ael. *VH* 12. 57), and was represented both as an
agricultural divinity rising from the earth[54] and as a political divinity, seated on
a throne, wearing a crown, and holding a sceptre.[55] Euripides recognized both
functions of Theban Demeter when he identified her with Ge and called her
possessor of Thebes, protector of the land (*Phoin.* 683–8).[56] Theban Demeter
received the sacrifice of a bull, leaders took omens at her altar when magistrates
took office[57] and before battle,[58] and soldiers dedicated booty in her sanctuary
if a battle was won.[59] Demeter nevertheless, as goddess of agriculture, continued
to be the major divinity of Theban women, and the Thesmophoria, celebrated
in midsummer, continued to be a major festival.[60]

Demeter was also an acropolis divinity at Lepreon, Mytilene, and Iasos, but
it is not likely that she played a central political role in these cities. The fourth-
century sanctuary of Demeter at Lepreon, the only excavated building in this
tiny Peloponnesian polis, was located at the very top of the acropolis and
enclosed within the city's fortification wall, overlooking the town and surrounding fields, visible in the plain below.[61] At Mytilene Demeter was located
on a rocky height overlooking the sea. Her sanctuary dates from the Archaic
period, but remained rather modest until the late Classical and Hellenistic
periods, when expansion is indicated by additional building and heavy votive
activity. The sanctuary at Mytilene seems to have been used for a variety of

---

[54] Shown rising from the earth; Paus. 9. 16. 1.

[55] Kadmos and the dragon with audience of divinities marked with non-Attic names, *ARV*² 1187,
33; Schachter (n. 53), i. 167 n. 4.

[56] For the double function and the central location, see Schachter (n. 53), i. 165–8.

[57] Plut. *De gen. Soc.* 586f, 587c.

[58] Paus. 9. 6. 5–6; Ael. *VH* 12. 57.

[59] Pind. *Isthm.* 7. 1–5; Diod. Sic. 7. 10. 2–4.

[60] An unusual time for a festival elsewhere timed to coincide with the autumn planting. As Schachter
points out (n. 53), i. 168 n. 2, other Boiotian cities must have been more conventional. The Boiotian
month Damastros coincided with Attic Pyanopsion, the month of the Athenian Thesmophoria.

[61] H. Knell, 'Lepreon: Der Tempel der Demeter', *AM* 98 (1983), 113–47.

ceremonies. Over fifteen hundred terracotta figurines represent men, women, children, birds, and animals. The building identified as the Thesmophorion dates from the late Hellenistic period, but the Thesmophoria certainly had a long history at Mytilene, as the many hydrophoroi and over five hundred lamps in the sanctuary attest.[62] Iasos had a structure for Demeter with the earliest foundations dating from the period just before the Persian wars. It was located within the wall, on the lower slope of the acropolis, not far from a series of cisterns for collection of water. Although within the wall, Demeter was not the major acropolis divinity at Iasos, and her sanctuary is situated on the lower slope of the hill, about as far away as possible from the theatre, public buildings, and main gate of the city.

Thebes, Mytilene, and Lepreon were exceptional. In most other cities sanctuaries of Demeter were either within the wall but removed from the central area or outside the wall altogether. Paros is a good example of the second pattern. Here the sanctuary was just outside the wall, or, as Herodotos says, πρὸ τῆς πόλιος, standing 'in front of the city' (6. 134). The pattern of Demeter πρὸ πόλεως was common in cities founded from Greece during the two great periods of diaspora and colonial expansion, especially in Ionian Asia Minor and Sicily. At the time of the Ionian revolt the Ephesian Thesmophoria were celebrated near the borders of the city's territory (Hdt. 6. 16). At Smyrna an inscription describes the sanctuary of Demeter Thesmophoros as πρὸ πόλεως.[63] The sanctuary of Demeter at Miletos was located 'a short way from the city' (Parth. 8. 1). The same arrangement was carried to colonial cities and refoundations from Asia Minor. For instance, at Olbia, a colony of Miletos, the temple of Demeter was located outside the walls, across a river on Cape Hippolaos (Hdt. 4. 53).[64] Teos, a city with a poor excavation record, had a temple of the Eleusinian goddesses,[65] as yet not located, but Abdera, refounded and rebuilt by Tean immigrants in 545 BC, and possibly preserving a pattern already established at Teos, had an open-air temenos of Demeter on a terrace outside the walls where terracottas and vases, including 6,000 miniature hydriai, dating from the sixth to the third century BC were found.[66]

Demeter πρὸ πόλεως was also the most common pattern in colonial cities founded during the second phase of the Greek diaspora. Thasos, founded from Paros, had a Thesmophorion on a hill above the sea, on a narrow strip of land

---

[62] C. Williams and H. Williams, 'Excavations at Mytilene, 1990', *EMC* 35, NS 10 (1991), 175–91.

[63] *ISmyrna* 655.

[64] The sanctuary is located by a graffito recording a dedication to Demeter, Persephone, and Iakchos; A.-S. Roussiaéva, 'Les Cultes agraires à Olbia pontique', *DHA* 9 (1983), 187–8. For Demeter at other colonies of Miletos along the coast of the Black Sea, see F. Graf, *Nordionische Kulte* (Zurich, 1985), 274.

[65] *SEG* 4. 598. 54, late 1st century BC.

[66] *AR* (1988–9), 84–95. For the Thesmophoria at Abdera, see Diog. Laert. 9. 43; Athen. 2. 26.

just outside the city wall.[67] A variation on this arrangement was prevalent in the western coastal colonies, but in these and other coastal cities Demeter's extramural sanctuaries usually faced not the sea, but the interior. This was the arrangement at Cyrene, where the sanctuary of Demeter was established in about 600 BC, about a generation after the city was founded. Here Demeter was located outside the wall, separated from the city by a waterway. Originally an open-air temenos near a spring, the sanctuary eventually occupied three terraces leading up from the city to the agricultural plains above the coast, linking the town centre to its agricultural territory. The sixth century BC was a time of vigorous activity at Cyrene, with what White calls a 'flood of repetitious pottery', when the sanctuary was enlarged to include two precincts with the first small buildings.[68] This development corresponded to the period of expansion into the agricultural territory of the interior. Heavy votive dedication continued until the fourth century BC, when votives began to fall off. Cyrene nevertheless continued to be an important supplier of grain to the rest of Greece, as we know from an important inscription detailing the sale of grain to forty-three cities of Greece at a time of shortage and famine in 330–326.[69] The significance of Demeter and Kore as goddesses of grain continued to be emphasized at Cyrene by a Hellenistic *defixio* that calls Demeter 'Aglaokarpos' ('She who bears splendid fruit') and an Imperial dedication to Kore 'who looks after the wheat'.[70]

Demeter was also associated with agricultural expansion in the colonial foundations in Sicily and Magna Graecia. There seem to have been several stages in the development and permanent placement of sanctuaries in the process of colonial foundation. In the first stage, where Greeks as traders and not yet permanent settlers were still only temporary residents, their sanctuaries remained on the periphery. At Etrurian Gravisca, Greek merchants and early settlers concentrated the sanctuaries of their divinities in a small area at the edge of the town's territory, where Demeter was worshipped in close proximity to Aphrodite, Hera, and Apollo.[71] In the second stage, when Greek colonists founded their own permanent settlements in new territory, the movement was from the centre to the periphery, with Demeter often one of the first divinities to appear outside the new city's walls. The best example, with clearest stratification, is Gela, where the Thesmophorion on a hill at Bitalemi was separated from the city not only by the wall, but by a river. Demeter at Gela is like Demeter at Cyrene both in the orientation of the sanctuary and in the timing

---

[67] Rolley (n. 15), 441–83.

[68] D. White, *The Extramural Sanctuary of Demeter and Persephone at Cyrene* (Philadelphia, 1984); id. 'Cyrene's Sanctuary of Demeter and Persephone', *AJA* 85 (1981), 13–30.

[69] M. N. Tod, *A Selection of Greek Historical Inscriptions*, ii (Oxford, 1948), no. 196.

[70] White (n. 21) (1981), 23.

[71] Edlund (n. 2), 76–7.

of the establishment of her extramural cult. Demeter's first votives at Gela date from 650 BC, about forty years after the founding of the city.[72] Buildings followed by the middle of the sixth century, and by the fifth the piglets and kourotrophic figurines characteristic of the worship of Demeter began to appear.[73] As the new polis established and expanded its agricultural territory in the generation after foundation, Demeter became one of the first extramural divinities, placed outside the city (at Bitalemi) to protect and nourish the new agricultural territory. As a token of this function farming tools were common dedications. There were eventually three extramural sanctuaries of Demeter at Gela.[74] The same pattern of extramural sanctuaries for Demeter was also followed at Selinus and (probably) at Akragas.[75]

The sanctuaries of Demeter at Corinth, Eretria, and Iasos illustrate a general characteristic of many sanctuaries of Demeter found within a city's walls. Although located in the 'inner' space of the city, their orientation and design exploits topographical or geographical features of the site in order to preserve the sense of isolation associated with sanctuaries outside the walls. Inside the wall, within the 'inner' space, they are nevertheless remote, either removed by distance or because they occupy an isolated level or terrace of a rising hill. Demeter could be close to the city centre, but even in these cases she often seems to turn away from inhabited areas, the agora, and other sanctuaries. The sanctuary of Demeter at Priene, for example, illustrates the remoteness of Demeter in 'inner' space. At Priene, a city that enjoyed expansion and rebuilding in the fourth century BC,[76] the sanctuary of Demeter and Kore (identified by inscribed statue bases at the entrance)[77] was located in a bounded precinct on the west end of a terrace, a steep climb above the main temple area and theatre, on the way up the cliff to the acropolis heights above. The location was perhaps chosen to take advantage of the spring that fed the lion's head fountain at the entrance to the temenos.[78] Terracotta votives from the third to the early first century BC were found deposited in the megaron beside the temple.[79] From

---

[72] de Polignac (n. 3), 114; Malkin (n. 1), 180.

[73] Price (n. 19), 183, on the historical development of the sanctuary. For the dedications, see M. Sguaitamatti, L'Offrande de porcelet dans la coroplathie géléenne: Étude topologique (Mainz, 1984). The sanctuary remained in heavy use, with new buildings constructed after a fire in 450, and lasted until the Carthaginian attack in about 405 BC.

[74] R. R. Holloway, The Archaeology of Ancient Sicily (London and New York, 1991), 56–60.

[75] Holloway (n. 74), 61–3.

[76] N. Demand, 'The Relocation of Priene Reconsidered', Phoenix 40 (1986), 35–44, argues that 4th-century Priene was an expansion of a smaller settlement on the same site, not a refoundation of a city originally located in the plain.

[77] T. Wiegand, Priene (Berlin, 1904), 148, 151; M. Schede, Die Ruinen von Priene (Berlin, 1964), 90 fig. 104, and 92 fig. 106, for a hydrophoros.

[78] Wiegand (n. 77), 148 fig. 119, with fountain at location C.

[79] E. Topfferwein-Hoffman, Ist Mitt 21 (1971), 125–60. For the Thesmophoria at Priene, see IPriene 196.

the sanctuary worshippers could look down over the temple of Athena to the agora and further, to the fields of the city in the plain below.

The situation at Pergamon to some extent parallels that at Priene. When Eumenes II created the great acropolis sanctuaries there in the early second century, his architects seem to have been conscious of the problem of maintaining elements of Demeter's rural character within the 'inner space' of the city's sacred area. Demeter Thesmophoros had occupied her own terraced sanctuary on the side of the acropolis before the third century BC,[80] and through at least three major periods of expansion and construction, the successive architects of Philetairos, Attalos I and Eumenes II respected the isolation of Demeter and kept her terrace separate from the upper level of the major acropolis cults above and the three gymnasium levels below. The separation was marked by a propylon, built by benefactions from Apollonis, wife of Attalos I, and not visible to people approaching the sanctuary until they turned the last corner and stood in the forecourt. The forecourt, bordered by a fountain enclosed in a natural rock niche, emphasized the segregation of the temenos by providing a transitional space between the communal gymnasia below and the restricted area of Demeter's sanctuary just above. Water at the entrance to sanctuaries of Demeter seems to have been more integral to the operation of the cult than water for purification contained in perirrhanteria at the entrance to other sacred precincts.[81] The fountain at Pergamon, like the fountain at the entrance to Demeter's temenos at Priene, was a permanent architectural structure, integrated into the architecture of the sanctuary, not simply a temporary or removable water vessel.

Characteristics of a countryside sanctuary could also be imitated by a later sanctuary that brought Demeter into the *asty*. At Gela, where Demeter's original sanctuary was outside the wall, separated from the city by a river, a second sanctuary was built later in the Archaic period inside the wall, on the acropolis. The votive terracottas of the later sanctuary were similar to the dedications at the earlier site, and both continued to be used through the classical period.[82] The same doubling of Demeter's sites occurred at Akragas and Heloros. At Akragas, founded from Gela, the older sanctuary, dating from the period of foundation in the early sixth century, developed outside the city around a site with two caves and springs. About a century later a more substantial temple was built on a slope along the circuit wall, closer to the other major sanctuaries of the city.[83] Providing a central sanctuary that mimicked a peripheral sanctuary

---

[80] C. H. Bohtz and W.-D. Albert, 'Die Untersuchungen am Demeter-Heiligtum in Pergamon', *AA* (1970), 391–412; C. H. Bohtz, *Altertümer von Pergamon*, xiii: *Das Demeter-Heiligtum* (Berlin, 1981).

[81] Cole (n. 22), 162. For miniature hydriai from the sanctuary at Pergamon, see Bohtz and Albert, (n. 80), 402 fig. 26. For the Thesmophoria at Pergamon, see *IPergamon* 315.

[82] de Polignac (n. 3), 115.

[83] Polyaen. *Strat.* 5. 1, for Thesmophoria at Akragas.

might have been a response to the needs of a growing urban society and may have reflected a growing complexity in the functions of the goddess, but it also provided the opportunity for a more complex ritual with processions linking the two sanctuaries and linking the city with its external territory.

There were other ways by which a country sanctuary could become a city sanctuary. If a city increased its walled territory, sanctuaries once outside the walls could become sanctuaries inside the walls. When Siris in Magna Graecia was founded by colonists from Kolophon in about 700 BC, the sanctuary of Demeter was located at a spring on a slope outside the city. Later, after refoundation from Taras in 433/2, the rural area was incorporated into the walled city and the sanctuary endured 'like an island' within the city.[84] Country-like sanctuaries could also be artificially preserved. The acropolis sanctuary of Demeter at Syracuse must have also been like a garden in the city. At Syracuse, Demeter had a very early sanctuary on Ortygia, with votives dating from the eighth century.[85] Later she assumed a special political importance when Gelon chose her in 491 as the divinity by which he united two populations brought together by his forced synoecism of Syracuse with Gela. Gelon's family had controlled the hereditary priesthood of Demeter at Gela, and when he brought a major part of the population from Gela, he built temples to Demeter and Kore on the acropolis[86] and required suspected traitors to swear allegiance to the newly reorganized polis with a great oath sworn by Demeter and Kore in that sanctuary.[87] This was the site for the Thesmophoria, a ten-day festival described later as celebrated 'in a garden' on the acropolis (Plat. *Epist.* 7. 349d).

We have observed three patterns of sanctuary location for cults of Demeter: within the city, just outside, and at the borders of the city's territory. All three patterns seem to occur in all parts of the Greek world, and common to all is the identification of Demeter with the land, whether inside or outside the city. Two points should be stressed. First, establishment of extramural sanctuaries of Demeter was not confined to the period of colonization. The practice existed before colonization, for instance at Paros, the metropolis of Thasos, and continued after the period of colonization elsewhere on the Greek mainland. Late Hellenistic sanctuaries of Demeter at Dion and Pella were extramural.[88] Secondly, Demeter's votives do not seem to vary with location of her sanctuary, whether inside or outside the city wall, and the major types of votives usually

---

[84] Edlund (n. 2), 112, for the idea of a formerly rural sacred territory preserved as an island within the city.

[85] *AR* (1976–7), 65; Malkin (n. 1), 177 n. 282. There seems to have been an early Thesmophorion at Piazza Vittoria; see G. Voza, *Kokalos* 22–3 (1976/77), 551–3, and 26–7 (1980/81), 680–5.

[86] Diod. Sic. 11. 26. 7; Cic. *Verr.* 4. 53. 119.

[87] Diod. Sic. 19. 5. 4; Plut. *Dion* 57. For the political meaning of Demeter at Syracuse, see D. White, 'Demeter's Sicilian Cult as a Political Instrument', *GRBS* 5 (1964), 261–79.

[88] Dion: *AR* (1985–6), 56; Pella: *AR* (1980–1), 29, (1982–3), 38–9.

fall into similar chronological ranges, whether found in sanctuaries in Old Greece or in colonial foundations. Demeter's ritual required water in a natural setting. The need for secrecy, whether for the mysteries or the Thesmophoria, dictated isolation. Both requirements could be most easily met outside the city, but nature and isolation could also be artificially created within the city. Finally, we should remember that although place, space, and ritual could be closely related, space could be re-created in a new place. An inscription from Tanagra demonstrates how this process worked.[89] Sometime in the late third century BC the demos of Tanagra consulted Apollo about their temple (*hieron*) of Demeter and Kore, which apparently needed to be rebuilt. They asked the god whether they should leave it where it was, move it to a site called Topos tes Euemerias ('Place of Good Weather'), or bring it into the city (polis). Apollo chose the city site, and commanded, 'Receive within the crown of the walls the goddesses who are just outside the city (προϜαστίδας) . . .' (7). Demeter and Kore, who had been formerly located 'in front of the city (*asty*)' like Demeter at Paros or Smyrna, now would have their sanctuary within the walls of the city. The procedure required a committee of three men over 30 to consult with the architect and the leaders of the city, in order to build a temple for Demeter 'as beautifully as possible in the polis, in the place where it seems best' (9–10). Ninety-eight women, probably all the married women of the community, contributed a total of 432 drachmas, most paying five drachmas each; all of their names are listed in the text. The temple was not costly, but the demos allowed three years for planning and construction. During his visit to Tanagra Pausanias failed to notice the sanctuary of Demeter and the 'Place of Good Weather', but he did remark that the people of Tanagra were exceptional among the Greeks for their consideration of the gods, because they built their sanctuaries 'far away from their houses, in an unpolluted place, kept separate from human affairs' (9. 22. 2). Demeter's new sanctuary may have been modest, but I think we can be sure that it was carefully placed.

[89] T. Reinach, 'Un temple élevé par les femmes de Tanagra', *REG* 12 (1899), 53–115; Schachter (n. 53), i. 163.

9

The Distribution of Sanctuaries in Civic Space in Arkadia

MADELEINE JOST

Université de Lille III

The distribution of sanctuaries in a region is related to the physical lie of its land, its human geography, and its political life (Ill. 9.1). Arkadia is a region where the landscape is sufficiently varied and the historical development sufficiently well known to allow an enquiry into the factors which play a part in the choice of sanctuary sites. In this paper I will examine the placing of sanctuaries, considering them both individually and as part of the network which they form in marking out the territory of a city. The factors which emerge as important in Arkadia are the factors which generally influence the placing of sanctuaries in other areas of Greece, but the particular blend apparent in Arkadia is part of what gives that region its characteristic identity.[1]

In Arkadia, as elsewhere, certain places seem destined to be considered sacred, and certain types of landscape attract cults of one divinity rather than another.

Numinous Landscapes

Among particular features of physical geography often associated with the placing of sanctuaries, are the existence of a spring, as in the spring of the Meliastai (Paus. 8. 6. 5) or of Demeter Melaina (8. 42. 2), and the existence of trees forming a sacred grove, as at Lykosoura (8. 37. 10), or near Orchomenos, where a great hollow cedar sheltered the *xoanon* of Artemis Kedreatis (8. 13. 2). Other sanctuaries were established in the naturally enclosed surroundings of the cave: the best example of this is that of Demeter Melaina, which Pausanias tells us was situated south-west of Phigaleia and consisted of an isolated mountain cave: 'a sacred grove of oak trees surrounds the cave and cold water springs from the soil'; the altar was in front of the cave (Pausanias 8. 42. 4–5).

---

[1] Further information on the sanctuaries discussed can be found in M. Jost, *Sanctuaires et cultes d'Arcadie* (Paris, 1985). See also M. Jost, 'Sanctuaires ruraux et sanctuaires urbains en Arcadie', in A. Schachter (ed.), *Le Sanctuaire grec*, Entretiens de la Fondation Hardt sur l'antiquité classique 37 (Geneva, 1992). Some of the material from that article is reused here.

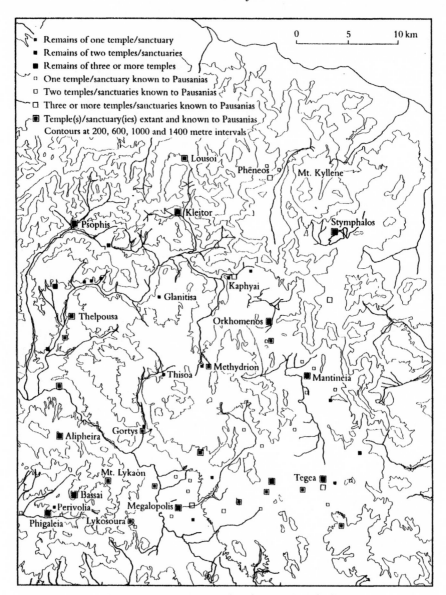

ILL. 9.1 Sanctuaries and settlements in Arkadia

Arkadian mountain peaks seem to have been exceptionally well endowed
with sanctuaries, which were generally established not at the very highest point,
which is also the most windy and most inhospitable, but a little lower down on
some more or less flat natural terrace or on a saddle. (Ill. 9.2). There is one case
of a mountain-top sanctuary which must be mentioned, however, that of

ILL. 9.2 The pass over Mount Boreion, with the sanctuary of Athena Soteira and of Poseidon at 1 and the acropolis of Pallantion at 2

Mount Lykaion, now known as Prophitis Elias and some 1,334 metres high: 'on the very top of the mountain', says Pausanias, 'there is a mound which is the altar of Zeus Lykaios' (8. 38. 7). In fact the summit of Prophitis Elias is crowned with a knoll 30 metres in diameter and 1.5 metres high, formed from earth blackened by fire and containing ash and burnt animal bones; this knoll is, as it were, grafted onto the mountain, and so the altar clearly was at the very top. This is explained by the complex character of Zeus Lykaios, who was, notably, the god associated with the atmospheric phenomena to be observed in the violent storms to which mountain tops are often host.

Finally, some parts of Arkadia (Pheneatis, Mantinike, the area of Trikolonoi in Megalopolitis) have hillocks which were treated as the tombs of heroes, some of whom were still honoured in the time of Pausanias.[2]

The choice of the sites under discussion here is dictated by the attention paid to particular features of the terrain. This is true not only for the most ancient sanctuaries, but also for sanctuaries created later, such as the sanctuary of the Great Goddesses at Megalopolis, set up in a grove in the fourth century BC.

Landscape Preferences among the Gods

If some particular landscapes are responsible for sanctuaries being established, it is also the case that some particular divinities demand one sort of terrain rather than another. This is especially clearly marked in the case of plains liable to flooding: thus, the upland plains of eastern Arkadia have a calcareous soil covered with clay and alluvium; this does not drain at all and agriculture is only possible if the katavothra, the fissures in the limestone which allow the rainwater

[2] Paus. 8. 14. 9 (Pheneatis); 8. 12. 5 (Mantinike); 8. 35. 8 (Trikolonoi).

to drain away and flooding to be avoided, are sedulously maintained. In these areas Artemis, the goddess associated with dampness, and Poseidon, the master of underground waters, are particularly often found. Artemis rules at Stymphalos, as goddess of the marsh, and she extends her influence to Alea, Orchomenos, and Kaphyai.[3] Poseidon Hippios, probably inherited from the most distant past, is the acknowledged protector of the Mantinike (Paus. 8. 10. 2–4), and is to be found also at Orchomenos (8. 13. 2) and Kaphyai (8. 23. 3).

Other parts of the plains and valleys are home to the cult of Demeter, goddess associated with the fertility of the soil and vegetation. This is particularly true of the area of ancient Azania (Thelpousa, Phigaleia, and Pheneos) where the goddess, under a variety of epithets, is linked to vegetation: at Pheneos, Demeter Thesmia taught men the rules of agriculture and brought them vegetables (Paus. 8. 15. 3–4). In the mountains, the deities to whom pastoralists address themselves are Artemis, goddess of border areas and of hunting, Hermes, honoured on Mount Kyllene as the rustic god of shepherds, and Pan, the divine goatherd and hunter who plays the syrinx. Finally in the towns, Athena, as goddess of cities, and Zeus, as protector of the social order, are particularly well represented.

The handful of examples which I have just given constitute particularly clear cases. We should not forget, however, that deities are generally polyvalent and that similar functions can be performed by different divinities, who, with a different toponymic epithet, cover different aspects of the same region.

The Network of Sanctuaries

After the examination of sanctuaries and cults individually in relation to the landscape it is time to ask what the whole picture adds up to, and to look at the network of sanctuaries in a territory in relation to the features of the landscape and the way of life pursued there. Different situations are to be discovered depending on whether, for example, one is looking at the mountainous districts of western Arkadia or the high plains of eastern Arkadia.

The city of Phigaleia and its territory offer a striking example of the placing

---

[3] Paus. 8. 22. 7–9 (Stymphalos); 8. 23. 1 (Alea); 8. 13. 2 (Orchomenos), 8. 23. 3 (Kaphyai). On the problem of drainage see J. Knauss, B. Heinrich, and H. Kalcyk, 'Der Damm bei Kaphyai und Orchomenos in Arkadien', *AA* 101 (1986), 583–611 (on Kaphyai and Orchomenos); H. Kalcyk and B. Heinrich, 'Hochwasserschutzbauten in Arkadien', *Antike Welt* 17 (2. Sondernummer) (1986), 3–14 (on Stymphalos, Pheneos, and Lake Takka); J. Knauss, 'Der Damm im Takka-See beim alten Tegea', *AM* 103 (1988), 25–36 (on the area around Tegea); J. Knauss, 'Der Graben des Herakles im Becken von Pheneos und die Vertreibung der Stymphalischen Vögel', *AM* 105 (1990), 1–52 (on Pheneos and Stymphalos).

ILL. 9.3 The site of Phigaleia in the nineteenth century (from *Expédition de Morée*)

of sanctuaries in a mountainous region. The town is situated on the edge of
the steep-sided valley of the river Neda, 'on an elevated site, sheer on almost
every side' (8. 39. 5) (Ill. 9.3). It is surrounded by compact groups of mountains
(Mount Elaion, Mount Kotilion), and some places in the countryside are very
difficult to reach. Throughout the region cultivable areas are sparse, occurring
in valley bottoms or on artificial terraces created along slopes. Pausanias mentions 'the produce of cultivated trees, particularly raisins, honey, and wool' as
an ordinary offering to Demeter (8. 42. 11), presumably because these are the
staple resources. Cultivation of cereals, mentioned by a Delphic oracle given to
the people of Phigaleia, is a precarious matter, and the Phigaleians are always
being threatened with having to live off acorns and game (8. 42. 5–7). Agriculture was the pursuit of only a small proportion of the population, which,
scattered over the territory, lived for the most part from pasturing goats and
sheep for milk and wool, and from hunting. The people of Phigaleia are to be
imagined as living like the god Pan who stayed near Bassai as a shepherd 'in a
hut made of fallen branches' and 'hunting now on one mountain and now on
another'.[4] The very structure of the town confirms the scattered residence: the
area enclosed by the fortifications has no relation to the area inhabited; it
includes enough land to be a place of refuge where the country population
from nearby areas can find protection with their flocks.

[4] *Palatine Anthology* 6. 253; Paus. 8. 42. 3.

The physical and human geography of this region is translated into religious topography by the predominance of sanctuaries in the countryside over those in the town. In the town a polis deity, doubtless Athena, was honoured along with Hermes, protector of the gymnasium, Asklepios and Hygieia, and Dionysos Akratophoros, god of the orgy who was celebrated in mysteries and theatrical performances as well as in Dionysiac festivals. In the town too the Oresthasian heroes who died for Phigaleia received annual sacrifices.[5] Finally, the sanctuary of Artemis Soteira 'formed the place of departure for the processions' (Paus. 8. 39. 5); situated in the south-east of the city, it was the place where processions gathered when setting out for the territory in which the most important sanctuaries lay.

Twelve stades above the city, to the north-east, where the Lymax meets the Neda, Pausanias records the presence of the sanctuary of Eurynome, surrounded by a very thick cypress grove and difficult of access (8. 41. 4). This sanctuary, which was a place of cult from distant antiquity, was open once a year for the festival which the city celebrated there. The old theriomorphic wooden statue of an ancient Mistress of the Waters and the creatures to be found in them (related to Artemis, it ended in a fish-tail and was held by gold chains) demonstrates the way in which remote sanctuaries could keep archaic deities alive. The same goes for Demeter Melaina, honoured, as we have seen, in a cave on Mount Elaion: the wooden cult statue of this protecting deity of vegetation had a horse's head and hair mixed with serpents (8. 42. 2–5). Along the road leading to Mount Kotilion, the citizens had to stop at the temple at Perivolia, which seems to have been part of a rather extensive sanctuary dedicated to a deity whose identity is yet to be discovered. Finally, on Mount Kotilion several cult places were grouped together: the sanctuary of Apollo Epikourios, active from the eighth century onwards, with the classical Bassai temple, and, some hundred metres below the summit, at a place known as Kotilon, two small temples of modest proportions whose exact identification is difficult because different texts claim the site for Aphrodite, Pan, Orthasia, and Artemis.[6] The number of votive offerings found on Mount Kotilion bears witness to the numerous worshippers attracted by these sanctuaries.

It is clear that for the people of Phigaleia the sanctuaries of the territory, whose gods and goddesses protected the flora and fauna, and the life and the safety of the inhabitants, were the most important religious centres: peasants, shepherds and hunters honoured them in the environment in which they lived, that is in the wild countryside. The religious topography is very largely to be

---

[5] *SEG* 23. 237 (Athena) and 240 (Hygieia); *SNG Cop.* no. 279 (Asklepios); Paus. 8. 39. 6 (Hermes and Dionysos), 8. 41. 1 (Oresthasian heroes).

[6] See Jost, *Sanctuaires* (n. 1), 90–7.

explained by the structure of the countryside and the manner in which it was occupied.

A similar religious organization, in which the country is more important than the town, is to be found in most of the mountainous districts of Azania, in western Arkadia, with some variations due to the diversity of the natural landscape. So at Thelpousa the most important cult places are dotted along the main lines of communication in a vast territory; no doubt they were easier of access that way, but the relative weight of country and town is again in favour of the country.

ILL. 9.4 The plain of Mantineia

A different situation is found in the high plains of eastern Arkadia where the organization of the territory is different and a different way of life prevailed. In these basins enclosed by mountains, the towns are mainly (with the exception of Mantineia and Tegea) sited on acropoleis, in the centre of the territory. They are surrounded by cultivable land, and if the farmer takes good care of drainage by maintaining the katavothra, the area cultivated can be extensive enough (Ill. 9.4). Agriculture therefore plays a more important part in the economy here. As the distances involved are rarely great, the owners of the fields most frequently live in the town, where they involve themselves in political activities, and leave most of the work on the land to workmen and slaves. According to Xenophon, when Epameinondas approached Mantineia 'the people of Mantineia asked the Athenian cavalry to help them ... because all their flocks were outside (sc. the walls) along with their workmen, and many children and old people of the free population' (*Hellenika* 7. 5. 15). The farms with towers found in the north-west of the Mantinike may have served this kind of arrangement. In Mantinike some villages, prior to *sunoikismos*, were also to be found in areas where agriculture required particular care, such as the Argon Pedion.[7]

In this area, therefore, the normal situation is that the majority of sanctuaries, and the most important sanctuaries, are not always found in the countryside. Tegea provides a striking example: some fifty cults are attested within the walls, and that is where the sanctuary of Athena Alea is; it is the town which is the most important hub of the city's religious life. The Athena Alea sanctuary is known from archaeology to have been in use from the eighth century. It belonged to the deme Apheidantes before synoecism,[8] and was then integrated into the new town in such a way as to strengthen its unity. From that time on the most important sanctuaries were the urban ones, even when they were concerned with providing protection for country life.

In the other basins, the situation differs from one city to another. At Orcho-menos and Stymphalos a preponderance of urban sanctuaries can be observed. At Pheneos, on the other hand, rural sanctuaries predominate: at the gates of this small town, the importance of the plain in agricultural life translates into a special importance for sanctuaries of Demeter close to the town; the major sanctuary, of Hermes, is near the border of the territory, on Mount Kyllene. The small city of Kaphyai also has one of its principal divinities, Artemis Knakalesia, on a height outside the town. But in these last two cases there are doublets within the town of the sanctuaries in question. At Pheneos Pausanias (8. 14. 10) mentions a temple close to the town, with a third-century statue by Eucheir, which is apparently simply the urban echo of the temenos and temple of Hermes on Kyllene where that god was born: ancient writers trace the cult of Hermes on Kyllene back to time immemorial, and he was honoured with an annual procession and blood sacrifices of particular solemnity.[9] When they established the temple in the plain the people of Pheneos were not trying to annex for themselves the glory with which the legendary past had surrounded the sanctuary on Kyllene, but were apparently simply trying to make the god himself present at the Hermaia games which took place in the plain, and to give an object for everyday piety. The case at Kaphyai was similar: the principal cult of Artemis Knakalesia, at which rites of initiation in honour of the goddess were celebrated every year, took place, as is normal, apart from men, on Mount Knakalos; a doublet of the sanctuary was found in the town (Paus. 8. 23. 3). I will return to the phenomenon of doublets in discussing Megalopolis. The

[7] See M. Jost, 'Villages de l'Arcadie antique', *Ktema* 11 (1986), 146–58.
[8] See M. Moggi, *I sinecismi interstatali greci*, i (Pisa, 1976), 131–9.
[9] *Homeric Hymn to Hermes*; Paus. 8. 16. 1.

important thing about Pheneos and Kaphyai is that the rural pole in these bipolar arrangements remains the most important.

Finally, at Mantineia the major cult place is the suburban sanctuary of Poseidon Hippios. From the time of the synoecism which made its unity effective, the city placed itself under the protection of this god, but without including his sanctuary within the walls: it was some seven stades from Mantineia.[10] Otherwise, however, the number of sanctuaries in the town is rather greater than that in the countryside. Overall there is a certain complementarity at Mantineia between town and country sanctuaries, and generally in these eastern plains of Arkadia there tends to be an equilibrium between the rural and the urban poles. This is also manifest in the territory of Megalopolis, but in this last case particular historical conditions have influenced the siting of sanctuaries and it is worth spending some time exploring this in detail.

The Case of Megalopolis

Few political facts or events have a significant influence on the religious topography of a region. But synoecisms are interesting in this context since, as a result of the displacement of population which they imply, they bring about a partial remodelling of the religious landscape. It is difficult to study the effect of synoecism in the case of early synoecisms (Tegea, Mantineia, Heraia), but for the fourth century BC we have explicit testimonies. Synoecism agreements between Orchomenos and Euaimon and between Mantineia and Helisson show that it was normal to respect local cults: 'the cult ceremonies of Euaimon will be celebrated each month at Euaimon in the accustomed manner', and the sacrifices of Helisson are, similarly, to be accomplished on the traditional site.[11] The study of the religious measures accompanying the synoecism of Megalopolis casts a bright light on the politics of religion.

The exact date of the synoecism of Megalopolis, between 371/0 and 368/7, and the precise list of participants, remain subjects for controversy between historians,[12] but there is no doubt that it involved a very large region with some particularly ancient religious traditions, above all in Parrhasia. The object of synoecism was to ensure the political unity of the new city of Megalopolis and of its territory, in which some villages were left. To soften the obligation for most of the Arkadians in the region to leave their 'little homeland' for the Great City, the powers establishing the city exploited the political potential of religious

---

[10] Paus. 8. 10. 2–4. See most recently M. Moggi, 'Processi di urbanizzazione nel libro di Pausania sull' Arcadia', *RFIC* (1991), 46–62.

[11] See S. Dušanić, 'Notes épigraphiques sur l'histoire arcadienne du IVᵉ siècle', *BCH* 102 (1978), 333–46 (for Orchomenos and Euaimon); G. J. and M. J. Te Riele, 'Hélisson entre en sympolitie avec Mantinée: Une nouvelle inscription d'Arcadie', *BCH* 111 (1987), 167–88 (for Mantineia and Helisson).

[12] See most recently S. Hornblower, 'When was Megalopolis Founded?', *BSA* 85 (1990), 71–7.

unity, avoiding totally uprooting people by maintaining the old sanctuaries of the territory and creating urban cult centres adapted to the transplanted population.

Apart from Lykosoura, which retained the status of a city 'because of its sanctuary of Despoina' (Pausanias 8. 28. 6), only a few settlements remained with the status of *komai* (villages) of Megalopolis; these kept their sanctuaries, both urban and extra-urban. The most interesting case is that of Gortys, a small town which served as a distant defence for the city, where a new prosperity can be detected in its sanctuaries in the fourth century BC; but one might also cite Theisoa and its sanctuary of the Great God, or Methydrion and the suburban temple of Petrovouni, whose religious vitality after synoecism is archaeologically attested.[13]

In the old towns that were systematically depopulated through synoecism, the sanctuaries often remained, maintained by Megalopolis even when the rest of the settlement was falling into ruins: Pausanias attests this for Basilis in Parrhasia, where the cult of Demeter Eleusinia was still active in the second century AD (8. 29. 4), and for Akakesion, where the statue of Hermes Akakesios remained in place (8. 36. 10). Looked after by the city, these sanctuaries simply changed status, becoming sanctuaries of the territory of Megalopolis, on the same level as the old rural sanctuaries. The case of Trapezous whose *xoana* were transferred to the capital must be regarded as an exception, provoked by the rebellion of this city against synoecism (8. 28. 6, 8. 31. 5).

The old rural sanctuaries generally continued to be honoured. Archaeology has even allowed the detection of renewal in the fourth century at remote little sanctuaries such as that of Glanitsa, as well as at the great Parrhasian sanctuary of Zeus Lykaios, which became the major cult place of the Arkadian Federation. Cult places which were deserted are rare; one instance is provided by the sanctuary of Pan at Berekla, for which archaeological evidence does not extend beyond the fifth century, no doubt because it was so far from any settlement.

Overall the religious restructuring of the territory of Megalopolis consisted more of changing the status of old cult places than in any new topographical distribution. The most important change brought about in the religious landscape of the region was in fact the creation of urban sanctuaries in the town of Megalopolis. Some of these answered urban preoccupations—the defence of the city and its territory, political and social life, arts and crafts. Others took up the cults of the territory, so as to establish in the town a traditional ensemble of gods designed to arouse in the new citizens a consciousness of belonging to a community. The most interesting phenomenon in this regard, of which

---

[13] See Jost (n. 7), 146–58.

Megalopolis offers several examples, is the founding of 'doublets' of the most sacred cult places of the territory.

The 'peribolos of stones with a sanctuary of Zeus Lykaios', which Pausanias (8. 30. 2–3) speaks of, is particularly characteristic. 'This is not to be entered, but one can take in the interior at a glance: there are altars of the god, two tables, as many eagles as tables, and a marble statue of Pan. This last is known by the epithet Sinoeis, a name which derives from the name of the nymph Sinoe.' The structure of the sanctuary, the prohibitions with which it is surrounded, and the cult objects which it encloses, show clearly that the complex cult of Zeus Lykaios on Mount Lykaion, which Pausanias describes elsewhere (8. 38. 6–7) has been transposed. The *abaton*, here enclosed by a low wall, is a replica of that on Lykaion; altars replace the mound of cinders on Prophitis Elias (and two tables are reserved for offerings); the eagles, no doubt less monumental than those on Mount Lykaion, recall the two columns crowned with eagles which flanked the sacred way on the mountain. All in all, the most important elements of the sanctuary of Zeus are present, adapted to an urban environment and grouped in the smaller space of a temenos wall. The presence of Pan in this enclosure also recalls Mount Lykaion, where the two divinities had neighbouring sanctuaries, although the epithet Sinoeis indicates some contamination with another cult which originated, apparently, in the region of Bassai-Phigaleia.

The establishment of this cult doublet at the moment of synoecism does not imply transfer of cult; on the contrary it responds to a desire to respect the cradle of the cult of Zeus Lykaios. The sanctuary on Mount Lykaion in fact saw a period of great prosperity in the fourth century, and an increase in the number of pilgrims: far from plundering the site, as Kourouniotis believed in the case of the gold eagles,[14] the city established new votive offerings there and had several buildings erected in the Kato Kambos valley; inscriptions from the area of the hippodrome (*IG* v. 2 549–50) show, moreover, the wide attraction of the Lykaia in this period, when the sanctuary of Zeus on the mountain became the religious centre of the new Arkadian Federation. At Megalopolis itself there is no question of games, still less of the curious phenomena to be observed on Lykaion of which Pausanias speaks (loss of shadow for anyone penetrating the *abaton*, ritual of the Hagno spring), or of human sacrifices like those celebrated on the peak of Lykaion, the practice of which seems connected with the making wild of a place where violence and primitive cruelty flourish in a way which would not be acceptable in the town.

In short, one should not see in the sanctuary doublets at Megalopolis any intention of rivalling the sanctuaries of the countryside. On the contrary, the

---

[14] K. Kourouniotis, 'Anaskaphai Lukaiou', *AE* (1904), 177.

new city was trying to place itself under the protection of the god who, from archaic times, had effectively constituted a centre of political and religious unity for the Parrhasians and had in the fifth century come to symbolize Panarkadian aspirations.

Zeus Lykaios was thus the linchpin in efforts to cement the union between the new citizens. But regional legends too had to be evoked by the city sanctuaries. A temple of Hermes Akakesios was constructed in the agora of Megalopolis, in imitation of that in the village of Akakesion; the original statue was left in place in the deserted village and a copy was executed for Megalopolis, of which only the marble tortoise, a memorial of the invention of the lyre, remained in Pausanias' time (8. 30. 6). The importance accorded to Hermes at Megalopolis is very characteristic of the desire of the founders of the Federation to strengthen the new unity of south-west Arkadia by founding it upon religious traditions. Making light of the legend popular throughout the Greek world according to which Hermes was born on Kyllene, they wanted to strengthen the Parrhasian version, and perhaps by their exploitation of the resemblance between the toponymic epithet of the god and the Homeric epithet *akaketa*, the obscure village of Akakesion became the home of the official Arkadian tradition concerning the early childhood of Hermes: the god became the son of one Akakos, son of Lykaon. Once more, this was not a matter of robbing Akakesion; on the contrary, the temple at Megalopolis glorified the religious importance of this site.

Two contradictory sentiments can be seen to lie behind the politics of cult doublets in Arkadia, as they can also be seen behind cult doublets in Attica:[15] the idea that the principal sanctuary in the countryside has a character of its own that is bound to the place where it is situated and cannot be transposed elsewhere; and the desire to create some reminder in the town of the rural sanctuary, not to rival its prestige or assume control of it but rather to recognize its importance and the loss which its total absence from the town would create.

The Network in Action

As a result of the physical and the human geography, remodelled in the end as a result of historical events, the religious landscape of Arkadia sometimes had its principal pole as the countryside, and sometimes, less often, as the town. In both cases the cult attachment of all the sanctuaries to the city, with its political centre in the town, and the complementarity between rural and urban sanctuaries, was made concrete by religious processions which went out from the town to the countryside.

---

[15] Cf. R. G. Osborne, *Demos: The Discovery of Classical Attika* (Cambridge, 1985), 154–77.

The mobilization of the rural and the urban populations for periodic festivals in great sanctuaries in the countryside was in Greece, as is well known, a way of increasing the cohesion of the social groups by the common activities that those festivals involved. In Arkadia, long processions climbed each year from Pheneos to Mount Kyllene and from Phigaleia to the cave of Demeter Melaina and Mount Kotilion; on arrival, sacrifices were made on the altar. On Kyllene blood sacrifices were offered to Hermes, and, according to Geminos (*Elementa astronomiae* 17. 3), 'when at the end of a year one returns to the sanctuary . . ., the bones of the victims and the ash of the hearth are to be found in the same state in which they were left, totally unaffected by wind or rain, because the clouds and windy conditions only come about lower than the summit of the mountains'. At the sanctuary of Demeter Melaina 'the products placed on the altar in front of the cave are the fruits of cultivated trees, particularly raisins, honeycombs, and wool that has not been worked at all and is still full of yolk; when they have been put on the altar they are sprinkled with oil. This is the customary practice both for individual sacrifices and for the annual sacrifice offered by the community of Phigaleians' (Paus. 8. 42. 11).

One sacrifice offered in the Megalopolitis shows vividly the desire of the new city to enjoy a symbiotic relation with the sanctuaries of its territory. 'On the occasion of the annual festival of Apollo Parrhasios, sacrifices are made in the agora at Megalopolis of a wild boar to Apollo Epikourios. Immediately afterwards the victim is carried in procession to the sanctuary of Apollo Parrhasios, accompanied by the music of the *aulos*. There the thighs are jointed and the flesh of the victim is consumed on the spot' (Paus. 8. 38. 8). Apollo Parrhasios had a sanctuary 'in the east part of the mountain range of Lykaion'; his epithet derived from the ancient name of the territory in which Megalopolis stood, Parrhasia, and the existence of an annual cult shows how concerned the Megalopolitans were to maintain religious traditions in existence before synoecism in order not to cut the region off from its past. The ceremony is exceptional, since the different phases of the sacrifice take place in two different sanctuaries of Apollo several kilometres apart: the throat of the victim is slit at Megalopolis, but the distribution of the portions between gods and men and the feast take place in the countryside. In this way an urban sacred place, one which itself owes its sacredness to the rural sanctuary of Apollo Epikourios at Bassai from which its cult statue came, and a rural sanctuary, whose god evokes the antiquity of the region, are closely linked.

The religious topography of Arkadia is marked by the complementarity between urban and rural sanctuaries. In this land whose economy is overwhelmingly rural, the countryside, rather than the town, is impregnated with the sacred: rural sanctuaries outnumber those of the town. But the town, to which the sanctuaries of the territory are administratively attached, is the element that gives unity, the place from which the processions emanate. Over the centuries the influence of physical and human geography on the founding of sanctuaries has sometimes been corrected by the political element. The result is a network of subtle correspondences, varying from one city to another, between the sanctuaries of the countryside and those of the town.

Translated by Robin Osborne

10

Trees in the Landscape of Pausanias' Periegesis

DARICE BIRGE

Loyola University, Chicago

Without the information that we derive from Pausanias, our knowledge of ancient Greece would be immeasurably poorer. His *Periegesis*, however, is not objectively comprehensive; it reflects the interests and preferences of its author. Indeed, Pausanias' predilections and his particular concerns as traveller and student of ancient Greece are well known.[1] One might note, for instance, that on occasions, he found cult statues worth mentioning, but not the temples in which they were housed, and that he ignored constructions from the period of Roman rule in favour of much older monuments. We may view the limits of Pausanias' field of vision more positively if we do not regard his omissions as expressions of idiosyncratic connoisseurship and distaste for all that is new. We might rather consider his monuments and the territory through which he travelled as making up a sacred landscape that was the main vehicle for the display and expression of social and religious monuments, customs, and ideologies that belonged to an otherwise irretrievable past.[2] Pausanias wrote as a native inhabitant of a notional land, so to speak, which none the less could be made real by attaching explanations and stories to particular sites, monuments, and natural features. By means of the cult activities that he observes and performs (as an initiate into mysteries, for example) and the stories that he tells, Pausanias constructs a cultural matrix, extending through space and time, on which a Greek resident of the Roman province of Achaia might depend.

This paper is concerned with a particular group of landmarks in the territory through which Pausanias travelled: single trees and stands of trees. Trees differ from boundary stones, commemorative dedications, and the like in that they are not artificially produced but rather are natural elements of the landscape.

---

[1] I would like to thank Susan Alcock and Robin Osborne for their patience and their helpful advice. For recent discussion of Pausanias' special interests, see C. Habicht, *Pausanias' Guide to Ancient Greece* (Berkeley, 1985), 4–5, 23–4 (with bibliographical note at p. 23, n. 91), 130–7.

[2] The relationship between Pausanias and Greece summarized here has been effectively demonstrated by J. Elsner, 'Pausanias: A Greek Pilgrim in the Roman World', *Past and Present* 135 (1992), 3–29 and S. E. Alcock, *Graecia Capta: The Landscapes of Roman Greece* (Cambridge, 1993), esp. pp. 201–14.

Stationary and visible, they may serve as spatial markers within a physical, tangible territory; stationary and long-lived, they may also be temporal markers, in that they relate a particular moment in the past, as one point in the whole passage of time, to the present. Do Pausanias' trees act as such markers: to what extent do they exist within two landscapes, one visible and present, and the other past and intangible?[3]

Pausanias obviously could not catalogue each landmark tree in Greece. When we find that he mentions trees in only a few particular contexts, we should not therefore assume that trees were rare in second-century AD Greece. In fact, in the course of describing Mt. Parnes in Attica, Pausanias mentions that the area is good for boar-hunting; though he does not mention trees, the presence of boar implies the existence of forest.[4] Although we may extrapolate a few wooded tracts from clues such as this, any generalizations that we make for the whole collection of trees mentioned in Pausanias' *Periegesis* are valid only within that collection. We may consider reasons for which Pausanias found some trees notable, but we can say nothing about why other trees were invisible from his point of view and hence unmentioned in his text.

Taken together, Pausanias' trees are widely distributed across terrain that had long been exploited and altered by various human activities.[5] In most instances his trees grow in sanctuaries of gods and heroes, although they are not completely restricted to cultic contexts. Pausanias does not usually identify closely the physical environment in which trees grow: by a stream, on a hillside, or the like. He often indicates, however, their situation relative to their respective cities: most are in the countryside but some thrive in urban areas.

Most of the trees to which Pausanias refers fall into four main categories depending on the number of trees he reports and their contexts. The first category I will discuss includes stands of trees, identified by species or with words such as *drumos* or *dendra*, that are simply noteworthy features of the physical landscape and unassociated with any cult practices. A second group includes single trees, likewise identified by species. Stands of trees identified by species or as *dendra* and associated with hero shrines make up a third group.

[3] I consider here only trees that Pausanias reports in the topography of the cities he describes in Roman Achaia, not those to which he alludes that are located in places outside the geographical scope of his work (e. g. the grove at Gryneion, 1. 21. 7, and the *fegos* at Dodona, 8. 23. 5).

[4] As has been recognized by R. Meiggs, *Trees and Timber in the Ancient Mediterranean World* (Oxford, 1982), 381.

[5] For alterations in the landscape of Greece, see Tj. van Andel, E. Zangger, and A. Demitrack, 'Land Use and Soil Erosion in Prehistoric and Historical Greece', *JFA* 17 (1990), 379–96; Tj. van Andel and C. Runnels, *Beyond the Acropolis: A Rural Greek Past* (Stanford, Calif., 1987), esp. 110–13, 135–53 for the period of Pausanias; O. Rackham, 'Ancient Landscapes', in O. Murray and S. Price (edd.), *The Greek City from Homer to Alexander* (Oxford, 1990), 85–111; and T. Wertime, 'The Furnace versus the Goat: the Pyrotechnologic Industries and Mediterranean Deforestation in Antiquity', *JFA* 10 (1983), 445–52. S. E. Alcock, 'Roman Imperialism in the Greek Landscape', *JRA* 2 (1989), 5–34, discusses land use in the Roman period.

The last category contains stands of trees, identified with the word *alsos* (sacred grove), that grow in sanctuaries of deities as opposed to heroes.[6] Such distinctions indicate that Pausanias categorized trees in relation to combinations of location, cultic associations, references to legendary events, and accompanying monuments so as to reveal and define the various places of trees in his cultic topography. By examining the array of contexts into which he placed his trees—flourishing festival sites, cult places in disrepair, hero shrines, locations of historical events and so on—it is possible to judge the essential characteristics of Pausanias' trees and to discover to what extent they are venerated remnants of a distant past, markers of special territory, symbols of wilderness, or other such social adaptations of a natural feature. We begin by examining briefly the category of non-sacred stands of trees that Pausanias identifies by species.

Stands of Trees as Features of the Physical Landscape

Pausanias is careful to provide histories and legends for the cities of Greece and their monuments. His descriptions of natural, physical features and qualities are, however, few and relatively brief. Those that he includes mainly involve locations of sources of water, areas with good hunting, sitings of towns and shrines, and the like. Such descriptions concern aspects of the countryside that are as significant and consequential to local inhabitants as they are to the travelling author of a descriptive geography.[7] Among these Pausanias includes a few reports of wooded land, but generally he de-emphasizes greenery, although, as a provider of shade and an indicator of the presence of water, it presumably would have been of everyday practical importance.

The few stands of trees that are unequipped with either legends or monuments grow in border territories.[8] Certainly in reality such stands of trees need not have been limited to borders, although trees in general may have had better chances of survival in places that were relatively difficult for woodcutters to reach. In an analysis of Pausanias' work *per se*, however, it is not necessary to

---

[6] *Alsos* is used in Homeric epic for stands of trees in shrines of gods. In the following several centuries the word takes on wider metaphorical and scientific applications, but it continues to be used for sacred, wooded territory until the end of antiquity.

[7] For example, courses, qualities, and sources of rivers: 8. 6. 6 (Inachos), 2. 38. 7 (Tanaos); underground rivers: 1. 38. 1 (Rheiti), 5. 7. 1 and 8. 54. 1–3 (Alpheios); qualities of water: 2. 34. 1 (hot springs at Methana), 8. 18. 4–5 (Styx at Pheneos), 3. 22. 7 (drinking water for Geronthrai). Situations of cities: for example, Sparta, on hills without a real acropolis (3. 17. 1); Heraia, on a slight incline (8. 26. 1); Methydrion, on a high hill (8. 36. 1); Pheneos, with a sheer acropolis (8. 14. 4).

[8] For instance, stands of trees without legends or monuments grow near Genesion on the Argolid-Lakonian border, 2. 38. 4–5; at Skotitas, on the Argolid-Lakonian border, 3. 10. 6; and near the Elis-Messenian border and the remains of Skillous, 5. 6. 4. The *drumos* called Aphrodision between Psophis and Thelpousa (8. 25. 1), and the *drumos* at Alalkomenai from which the Plataians took wood to make their *xoana* that were burned at the Boiotian Daidala festival (9. 3. 4), have cultic connections.

decide whether stands of trees with no cultic or legendary connections actually grew more commonly in border territory or close to cities. The relative absence of 'secular' stands of trees without stories, and their marginal location in his *periegesis*, corresponds to the emphasis that Pausanias places on city-oriented historical and cultic monuments, the importance of which is sustained by local tradition and informants. Pausanias' virtual omission of stands of trees that were to him simply natural features confirms the choices he has made that characterize his work in general.

Single Trees

Single trees appear more likely to have grown in or very close to urban centres than in distant, outlying areas, although Pausanias does not cite enough examples to provide a meaningful pattern of distribution. They stood out among the sights of comparatively wealthy cities as well as in relatively small settlements. For example, the famous original olive tree, which Athena produced in her contest with Poseidon, was one of the attractions on the Athenian acropolis; the tree grew miraculously after the Persians destroyed it.[9] Between the agora and the acropolis at Troizen were a laurel that grew from material used in the purification of Orestes, a wild olive that sprouted from Herakles' club, and a myrtle tree that the lovesick Phaidra mutilated, all having flourished since the legendary past.[10] Close to Kaphyai in Arkadia (ὀλίγον δὲ ὑπὲρ τὴν πόλιν) was a plane tree called Menelais, planted by Menelaos when he came there to raise an army against Troy. A pomegranate tree with bloody fruit, very near (ἐγγύτατα) the Neistan gate at Thebes, marked the tomb of Menoikeus, who killed himself in defence of Thebes.[11] Two other single trees grew perhaps at a slightly greater distance from their city centres: an olive tree at the Academy outside Athens, six stadia from the Dipylon Gate, is said to be the second that ever appeared; the wild olive tree in which the reins of Hippolytos' chariot became entangled could be seen near the shore outside the centre of Troizen.[12]

A few single trees by Pausanias' account are not close to any concentration of settlement. In the southern Argolid one might still see an olive bent by Herakles beside the Epidauros–Asine road, in land that had been left waste (ἑτέρωθι ἀναστάτου γενομένης χώρας: 2. 28. 2). A shrine and an oak dedicated

[9] 1. 27. 2 and 8. 23. 5.
[10] Laurel, 2. 31. 8; wild olive, 2. 31. 10; myrtle, 1. 22. 2 and 2. 32. 3.
[11] Kaphyai: 8. 23. 4; Thebes: 9. 25. 1. For other instances of notable single trees, see 3. 22. 12 (Boiai, at the site of the foundation of the city); 8. 13. 2 (Arkadian Orchomenos, the location of a *xoanon* of Artemis); 8. 19. 2–3 (Kynaithai); 2. 37. 4 (home of the Hydra at the source of the Amymone river at Lerna).
[12] Athens: 1. 30. 2; Troizen: 2. 32. 10. Note also the unique situation of the wild olive (*kotinos*) in the Panhellenic sanctuary of Zeus at Olympia (5. 15. 3); it was distinguished from stands of trees in both the Pelopion and the larger Altis.

to Pan are the last monuments that Pausanias describes in Tegean territory on the road towards Thyrea (8. 54. 4). Although he records no legend, epithet, or specific cult practice for this apparently functioning shrine, he may have found it significant because, as the last notable sight in Tegean territory, it marked a political boundary of sorts.

Pausanias rarely points out single trees that are noteworthy for what they produce.[13] Furthermore, although he may have passed many trees that served as informal boundary markers, Pausanias did not make it a practice to note landmark single trees that associated a parcel of land with a contemporary controlling polity.[14] Some single trees grow at active cult places: the sanctuary of Zeus at Olympia, the Athenian Acropolis, Pan's shrine near Tegea, and Arkadian Orchomenos.[15] Nevertheless, Pausanias does not generally point out single trees in the sanctuaries he visits, although such trees would be comparable to two other kinds of sights he finds notable: natural features with legendary associations and artefacts that, as 'heirlooms', are displayed in sanctuaries.[16]

The single trees that are significant to Pausanias commemorate events of the Greek past. They recall incidents of local importance involving gods or figures of legend, such as the introduction of the olive and the Athenian recovery after the Persian invasion, the labours and travels of Herakles, and the defence of Thebes against the Seven.[17] The presence alone of a living memorial of the past seems to be sufficient for such a purpose; if the events that single trees memorialize were ever re-created or recalled in contemporary cultic observances, Pausanias did not consider it necessary to describe such practices. Because they commemorate auspicious occurrences (the post-Persian renewal of Athens, the successful defence of Thebes, the beneficial deeds of Herakles), one might claim that single trees signify a kind of ideal political soundness. In this capacity the locations of single trees are associated with events that helped to establish Classical city-states. Nevertheless, as is the case with 'secular' stands of trees, Pausanias did not deliberately or obviously identify them as topographical markers functioning within a second-century AD political structure.

[13] See, however, 4. 34. 4 for a spring flowing from beneath a plane tree, twenty stadia off the road between Messene and Korone, that provides water for Korone, and 8. 19. 2–3 for a plane tree, two stadia from Kynaithai in Arkadia, whose waters cure people bitten by mad dogs.

[14] Pausanias does not explicitly connect the olive on Mt. Koryphos (2. 28. 2; see above), which overlooks the sanctuary of Asklepios, to any current Epidaurian boundary, but he offers the possibility that Herakles planted it to mark the border between the territory of Epidauros and Asine to the west.

[15] While Pausanias does not offer direct evidence that the shrines near Tegea and Orchomenos were active, we might presume that they were not abandoned.

[16] Natural features: springs made by Atalanta's spear (3. 24. 2), and the hoof of Bellerophon's horse (9. 31. 3), stones left over from the clay from which Prometheus made people (10. 4. 4), et al.; heirlooms: a folding chair made by Daidalos in the temple of Athena Polias on the Athenian Acropolis (1. 27. 1), a pillar from Oinomaos' house at Olympia (5. 20. 6), et al.

[17] Note that longlived trees at Samos, Dodona, and elsewhere may also simply testify to the great age of their shrines: 8. 23. 5.

Stands of Trees at Hero Shrines

Stands of trees, usually not labelled with *alsos*, that grow at shrines and tombs of heroes are functionally related to historically significant single trees.[18] Their presence often prompts Pausanias to recount pertinent events from the legendary past, sometimes including the death of the hero whose tomb they mark.[19] Also like single trees, the small number of wooded hero shrines shows no apparent pattern with regard to location within the territory of cities. Four were in or close to their cities, as, for example, the Aiakeion at Aigina, ἐν ἐπιφανεστάτῳ τῆς πόλεως (2. 29. 6).[20] Others are apparently more distant from flourishing urban centres: the Hyrnethion (2. 28. 3; 6–7) lay between Epidauros town and the Asklepieion,[21] and the shrine of the hero Argos (2. 20. 8 and 3. 4. 1), destroyed by the Spartan Kleomenes, lay south-east of Argos in the area of Tiryns, about eight kilometres in a straight line from the urban centre of Argos. The grave mound of Kallisto, covered with trees, some unproductive and some presumably cultivated for their produce, is crowned with a shrine of Artemis Kalliste (8. 35. 8); it lies approximately half-way between Methydrion and Trikolonoi in Arkadia (137 stadia, or roughly 28 km., apart) near the *chorion* of Anemosa and the ruined city of Phalanthos.[22] Finally, the trees in the Pelopion at Olympia are distinguished from those of the larger Altis (5. 13. 1–2) within which the Pelopion lies.

---

[18] The shrine of Ino at Megara: 1. 42. 7; of Hyrnetho near Epidauros: 2. 28. 3, 6–7; of Aiakos in Aigina: 2. 29. 6, 8; of Pelops at Olympia: 5. 13. 1–2; of Alkmaion at Psophis (a μνῆμα): 8. 24. 7; of Kallisto in Arkadia: 8. 35. 8; the burial place of the Argive commanders in the campaign of the Seven against Thebes, at Glisas: 9. 19. 2. The wooded shrine of Argos outside Argos (2. 20. 8, 3. 4. 1), appears in Pausanias' account of Kleomenes' defeat of the Argives, rather than in a topographical description. For two instances of a hero shrine described with *alsos*, see p. 238.

[19] Accompanying the description of the *heroon* of Ino is the story of how her body was washed ashore and buried (1. 42. 7); mention of Hyrnetho's tomb prompts the story of her brothers' plot against her husband and her death (2. 28. 3–7); Aiakos alone was able to propitiate Zeus on behalf of all the Greeks and thereby end a drought (2. 29. 7–8); Alkmaion's tomb recalls his flight from Argos, two marriages, and death at the hands of the brothers of Alphesiboia, the wife he took in Psophis (8. 24. 8–10). Since he referred earlier (5. 1. 6–7), to Pelops' vanquishing of Oinomaos, Pausanias mentions instead in his description of the Pelopion (5. 13. 2, 4–7), Pelops' posthumous career as hero: the foundation of his shrine and the vicissitudes of his shoulder-blade at the end of the Trojan War as well as an association of Pelops with Lydia that ties him to Pausanias' probable home. Although there may have been landscaping at tombs of the ordinary deceased, Pausanias makes no mention of it and apparently did not find such memorial plantings noteworthy.

[20] See in addition the shrine of Ino at Megara (1. 42. 7); Alkmaion's tomb ἐν Ψωφίδι (8. 24. 7), according to some scholars in the south-western quadrant of the city (G. Papandreou, 'Ereunai en Kalabrutois', *Praktika* (1920), 145, pace C. Bursian, *Geographie von Griechenland* (Leipzig, 1868–72), ii. 261–2); and the burial mound of the Argives near the ruins of Glisas (9. 19. 2; N. Papachatzis, *Pausaniou Ellados Periegesis: Boiotika kai Fokika* (Athens, 1981), 123, nn. 2 and 3).

[21] See N. Papachatzis, *Pausaniou Ellados Periegesis: Korinthiaka kai Lakonika* (Athens, 1976), 216 n. 2.

[22] The locality of the grave of Kallisto has been identified with the village of Chrysovitsi, approximately 15 km. north of Megalopolis (E. Curtius, *Pelop.* 1. 305); see J. G. Frazer, *Pausanias's Description of Greece* (London, 1898), commentary on 8. 35. 8, and most recently M. Jost, *Sanctuaires et cultes d'Arcadie* (Paris, 1985), 190.

Scholars have associated hero shrines in general, at least in earlier periods of Greek history, with the marking of territory.[23] Like non-wooded hero shrines throughout Pausanias' work, however, and *heroa* of the post-classical era in general, Pausanias' wooded hero shrines were not obviously markers of outlying, agricultural territory at which social groups could symbolically validate their existence and unity.[24] As Pausanias would have it, at the end of the sixth century BC the wooded shrine of Argos marked a point at which Argives defended their city. Perhaps one may extrapolate from its role as a defensive military position that at that time the shrine of Argos acted as one element of a city-*chora* network. Nevertheless in the second century AD Pausanias does not acknowledge the existence of a successor to the Archaic grove. Hyrnetho may likewise have preserved Epidauros through loyalty to her Epidaurian husband in the face of familial (Argive) treachery, but her deed, as Pausanias records it, was not directly connected with a particular parcel of land, nor did it necessarily require a memorial in extra-urban territory. Pausanias may imply that these two *heroa* marked outlying territory, but in neither case does he claim that the function of territory-marking was obviously vital to the existence of the shrine. Just as Pausanias did not note cult practices in general at wooded hero shrines, so he acknowledged no currently active belief or ritual that recognized these shrines as explicit markers of Argive or Epidaurian political identity or power.[25]

Both wooded and non-wooded hero shrines had little construction that Pausanias thought worth mentioning. He notes only that Pelops' temenos featured a stone wall and statues, and he implies the existence of a *bothros* for sacrifice; Hyrnetho's shrine was notable only for its regulation prohibiting the removal of fallen branches.[26]

There seems to be no correlation between the location of a wooded hero shrine or the wealth of its city and the quality or number of the monuments the shrine contained; all *heroa* are comparably simple, in Pausanias' eyes, as far as architecture and dedications are concerned.

[23] See, for instance, F. de Polignac, *La Naissance de la cité grecque* (Paris, 1984), 127–50; A. Snodgrass, 'Les Origines du culte des héros dans la Grèce antique', in G. Gnoli and J.-P. Vernant (edd.), *La Mort, les morts dans les sociétés anciennes* (Cambridge, 1982), 107–19; A. J. M. Whitley, 'Early States and Greek Hero-Cult: A Re-appraisal', *JHS* 108 (1988), 175–82.

[24] As regards public cult activities, Pausanias notes only that the Megarians offered an annual sacrifice to Ino; Pelops received honours at Olympia with a sacrificial ritual in which it seems that both Eleans and *xenoi* could participate (5. 13. 3). For post-classical hero cult, see S. E. Alcock, 'Tomb Cult and the Post-Classical Polis', *AJA* 95 (1991), 455.

[25] An exception to Pausanias' silence on hero cults is the shrine of Trophonios at Lebadeia, which significantly is described with the term *alsos*; see p. 238.

[26] See also the monuments of Aiakos (2. 29. 6, 8), Alkmaion (8. 24. 7), Ino (1. 42. 7), and Kallisto (8. 35. 8).

Stands of Trees (*Alse*) at Shrines of Gods

Stands of trees identified with the term *alsos* make up the largest category of trees that Pausanias mentions; the word *alsos* designates some forty-five groves.[27] They grow throughout the entire region Pausanias describes, in city centres as well as in suburban and rural territory; they are dedicated to numerous different deities; they are associated with a variety of dedications, constructions, cult practices, and historical events; and they belong to both complex and simple sanctuaries. In short, Pausanias records roughly twice as many examples of sacred groves as he does of trees in his other three categories together.

Generally Pausanias uses *alsos* to identify plantings in shrines of deities as opposed to those in hero shrines and in non-sacred settings. There are exceptions, however, and a glance at these will help to define the limits of Pausanias' general use of the term. *Alsos* occurs only once in a context that is likely to have been secular: near the river Pieros, not far from Pharai in Achaia, an *alsos* contains plane trees so large that people can dine and sleep in their hollow trunks (7. 22. 1). Pausanias uses *alsos* twice for stands of trees at *heroa*: at the oracle of Trophonios at Lebadeia (9. 39. 2, 4) and the shrine of the hero Argos outside Argos (2. 20. 8 and 3. 4. 1; see p. 237). Both shrines operate as more than simply the grave markers of heroes. Pausanias presents himself as a full participant in the oracular ritual at the shrine at Lebadeia. The Argives sought asylum (unsuccessfully) at the shrine of Argos; their treatment at the hands of Kleomenes and his eventual punishment underscore the supernatural, supposedly inviolable quality of the grove as refuge. These two shrines (with qualities that belong also to non-wooded shrines of deities) provide refuge and counsel for worshippers in the present or the recent past as well as memorials of a distant age.

In a few cases Pausanias uses species names instead of *alsos* for stands of trees that are associated with shrines of deities. At Aulis (9. 19. 8), palm trees grow in front of the sanctuary (πρὸ τοῦ ἱεροῦ) of Artemis. Pausanias may mean to place special emphasis on the species of tree (living palm trees appear nowhere else in his work) or he may be avoiding the ambiguous phrase *alsos pro tou hierou*, which might have suggested the presence of two shrines. Two shrines of Asklepios, at Titane (2. 11. 6) and Epidauros Limera (3. 23. 7), contain *kuparissoi* and *elaiai* respectively. Here, Pausanias mentions species names in connection with stories of the foundations of the shrines; perhaps these two stands of trees

---

[27] At 7. 23. 9, Schubart's emendation of *allos* for *alsos* in Αἰγιεῦσι δὲ Ἀθηνᾶς τε ναὸς καὶ ʽʽΗρας ἐστὶν ἄλσος supports Pausanias' statement that follows on the concealing of the statue of Hera, which would have been easier in a structure than in a stand of trees; N. Papachatzis, *Pausaniou Ellados Periegesis: Achaika kai Arkadika* (Athens, 1980), 144 n. 1. Note also the substitution of *alsos* for *allos* at 2. 29. 1, proposed by Siebelis and followed by Rocha-Pereira: (in Epidauros) ναοὶ δὲ ἐν τῇ πόλει καὶ Διονύσου καὶ Ἀρτέμιδός ἐστιν ἄλσος.

recall particular moments in the past, in the manner of single trees.[28]

Pausanias' specific use of *alsos* appears more striking when it is compared to occurrences of peribolos and temenos, both of which designate various types of clearly defined space. Pausanias uses peribolos to describe some thirty-three cult places; it sometimes refers to city walls, either under construction (e.g. Messene, 4. 27. 7) or enclosing a decayed and depopulated city (e.g. Mycenae, 2. 16. 5 and Arkadian Orchomenos, 8. 13. 2); occasionally peribolos is attached to a smaller enclosed space in which public activity occurs.[29] The term appears much more commonly in Pausanias' descriptions of cultic space, where it refers equally to both *heroa* and shrines of deities.[30] Temenos describes approximately forty shrines in Pausanias' work. Although it does not appear in a non-sacred context, as peribolos and *alsos* do, temenos may be applied to the shrine of a hero or a divinity.[31] Occasionally by temenos Pausanias implies an open-air shrine (of Asklepios at Epidauros town, 2. 29. 1) and sometimes a roofed structure (of Roman emperors at Sikyon, 2. 8. 1, located in what was formerly the *oikia* of a tyrant; of Zeus, with a *naos*, at Megara, 1. 40. 4). Often, however, Pausanias does not describe the amount and type of constructions and dedications at temene, for instance at the shrines of Isis at Corinth, 2. 4. 6 (with two temene) and of Boreas at Megalopolis, 8. 36. 6. Of the three terms, all of which Pausanias uses with roughly the same frequency, *alsos* is the most strictly limited to a single kind of sacred space, that is, a wooded tract of land making up or contained in a sanctuary of a god. Pausanias, it seems, separated trees in public space into categories that were more well-defined than those within the ranges of meaning he applied to peribolos and temenos. The characteristics shared by Pausanias' groves do not, however, imply any differences between sanctuaries with trees and those without trees. There is no way of knowing how many of the shrines at which Pausanias does not mention trees actually were treeless. Nevertheless the common characteristics of *alse*, which differentiate them from Pausanias' three other categories of trees, reveal the degree of precision with which Pausanias considered trees and cult places, a

---

[28] Pausanias' use of the species name in the phrase πιτύων δένδρα at Isthmia (2. 1. 7), may emphasize the physical qualities of the pines in the sanctuary, that is, their straight growth, as compared to the ordinary untended pines in its vicinity. At Heraia myrtles and other cultivated trees formed borders between *dromoi* beside the Alpheios, near baths and two temples of Dionysos (8. 26. 1). Here, rather than being simply landscaping, the myrtles may have marked a gymnasium-type area. Elsewhere *dromos* as a topographical feature generally signifies a race-track rather than a place for promenades. Outside Phigaleia *kuparissoi* grow at the shrine of Eurynome (8. 41. 4–5), whom Pausanias identifies as an Okeanid, and therefore, possibly, dissociates from the Olympian gods' *alsos*.

[29] Peribolos for athletic facilities: Elis, 6. 23. 1–5; for agora: Pharai, 7. 22. 2.

[30] Peribolos occurs, for instance, in descriptions of the shrines of Aiakos in Aigina, 2. 29. 6, 8 and of Neoptolemos in Delphi, 10. 24. 6. The peribolos at the Olympieion in Athens (1. 18. 6, 9), includes several roofed structures; that of Zeus in Megalopolis (8. 30. 2), is apparently relatively simple.

[31] E.g. for heroes, Phylakos at Delphi, 10. 8. 7, and Bellerophon at Corinth, 2. 2. 4; for gods, Zeus on Mt. Ithome, 4. 3. 9, and Aphrodite at Patrai, 7. 21. 10.

precision not so readily apparent in his use of peribolos and temenos. We will now examine these shared characteristics.

Somewhat over half of the *alse* that Pausanias mentions grew in shrines dedicated to Olympians: Demeter (six), Artemis (four or five), Apollo (four), Poseidon (four), Zeus (two or three), Athena, Aphrodite, Ares, Hermes, all the gods (one each), Hera (perhaps one); Pausanias also names temples of Apollo and Aphrodite in a grove at Patrai.[32] Groves at shrines of Demeter and Kore together, Despoina, and the Megalai Theai add an additional five or six,[33] and the lesser figures, Pan, Eros, Hebe, Asklepios, the Kabeiroi, nymphs, Trophonios, the Meilichioi, the Dioskouroi, and the Sikyonian Eumenides, each have one grove. Cultic monuments and titles do not indicate that these deities, with shrines to which Pausanias attributes groves, were concerned specifically with trees as products of agriculture or indicators of wilderness.

Pausanias reports various sources of water in or near almost half his shrines with *alse*, but water is not limited to his wooded shrines. *Krene* and *pege* identify approximately eighty other sources of water at shrines in which trees are unreported, although the physical environment suggests they might have been present. It seems, then, that for Pausanias, mention of one of these elements, grove or water source, does not require mention of the other. Quite often these ostensibly treeless but well-watered sites are connected with nymphs, heroes, and deities (Hera, Hermes, Dionysos) that in general in Pausanias' work do not possess *alse*. The relatively common occurrence of *alsos* at shrines of Demeter, Artemis, Apollo, and Poseidon may conform to some particular cultic associations of Pausanias, but we should note that it also corresponds to the large number of shrines in general, wooded and non-wooded, that Greek literature reports for these deities.

Financial resources, building materials, and architectural competence were not required to maintain a stand of trees. Nevertheless, the sacred groves that Pausanias noted were not restricted to simple shrines containing nothing more than an altar and a few humble dedications. The term *alsos* could signify a part of a larger *hieron*, along with altars, statues, stoas, and one or more temples, such as at the shrine of the Megalai Theai (Demeter and Kore) at Megalopolis (8. 31. 1–7). In other cases *alsos* includes sacred territory and the structures it contained, such as the Altis at Olympia (5.10.1 and 5. 13. 1).[34] Some *alse* were

---

[32] For discrepancies as regards groves of Hera and Artemis, see n. 27; for groves of Zeus see n. 33 below.

[33] Jost associates the grove within the precinct of the Megalai Theai at Megalopolis with a temple of Zeus also within the precinct; see M. Jost, 'Les Grandes Déesses d'Arcadie', *REA* 72 (1970), 144.

[34] Other examples are the *alse* at Andania, Epidauros, and Helikon. For the sanctuary at Andania and its problematic group of deities see J. Heer, *La personnalité de Pausanias* (Paris, 1979), 180–5. For the shrines of the Muses on Helikon see G. Roux, 'Le Val des Muses et les musées chez les auteurs anciens', *BCH* 78 (1954), 22–48, and P. W. Wallace, 'Hesiod and the Valley of the Muses', *GRBS* 15 (1974), 5–24.

connected with no temple, altar, or cult statue belonging to a single shrine, but rather with several distinct but contiguous cult places: at Patrai temples of Apollo and Artemis stood in a park-like grove, adjoining which were a shrine of Demeter with an oracle and two shrines of Serapis.[35] Such complexes of structures and wooded open space may have originated as simple shrines, but there is no evidence that they necessarily remained so at the time of Pausanias.

Pausanias specifically locates a few groves within urban centres: at Anthedon, Geronthrai, Megalopolis, Phlious, and Tithorea,[36] and by implication at Kyrtones, Leuktra, Marios, Patrai, Aigion, and Epidauros Limera (the last named by species, not called *alsos*).[37] Myrtles at Heraia grew in an area of public buildings; the grove of the Meilichioi at Myonia seems to have been in the city, in contrast to a notable shrine of Poseidon, which is *huper ten polin*.[38] Archaeological evidence suggests that the wooded shrine of Asklepios at Titane is near the town's acropolis.[39] In some fifteen other cases, such as at Kolonos Hippios outside Athens and at Potniai outside Thebes, extramural groves grew a short distance away (roughly 10 stadia) from their cities.[40] An equally sizeable group of wooded shrines grew at greater distances from the population centres with which Pausanias associates them.[41]

In several cases it is possible that Pausanias' wooded sanctuaries provided a locus for cult that connected a city centre with its *chora*. Approximately a third of Pausanias' outlying groves are dedicated to deities who also have shrines in the cities with which the groves are associated.[42] Chance must not be discounted, however, since about half of Pausanias' groves belong to four deities—Demeter,

---

[35] Note also the Kraneion grove on the outskirts of Corinth, with a temenos of Bellerophon, a temple of Aphrodite, and the grave of Lais (2. 2. 4), and the grove on Mt. Pontinos near Lerna, within which Pausanias saw statues of Demeter, Dionysos, and Aphrodite and a temple of Dionysos (2. 37. 1–2).

[36] Anthedon, 9. 22. 5; Geronthrai, 3. 22. 6; Megalopolis, 8. 30. 10–31. 1, 8. 31. 5; Phlious, 2. 13. 3–4; Tithorea, 10. 32. 10.

[37] Kyrtones (two groves), 9. 24. 4; Leuktra, 3. 26. 5; Marios, 3. 22. 8; Patrai, 7. 21. 11; Aigion, 7. 23. 9; Epidauros Limera, 3. 23. 7.

[38] Heraia, 8. 26. 1; Myonia 10. 38. 8.

[39] See *IG* iv. 436, a dedicatory inscription to Asklepios built into the wall of a church on the acropolis of Titane, Papachatzis (n. 21), 112, fig. 106; and K. Krystalli-Botsi, *AD* 30 B. 1 (1975 (1983)), 59.

[40] For instance, the shrine of Despoina near Lykosoura (8. 37. 10); of Poseidon near Athens (at Kolonos Hippios: 1. 30. 4); of Artemis near Kaphyai (8. 23. 6–7); of Hermes near Korseia (9. 24. 5); of Demeter near Megalopolis (8. 36. 6); of Apollo near Pharai in Messenia (4. 31. 1).

[41] For example, the shrine of Demeter Kabeiraia and Kore, 25 stadia or more outside Thebes (9. 25. 5); of Demeter Melainis, approximately 30 stadia outside Phigaleia (8. 42. 12); of Poseidon, at the deserted site of Trikolonoi and 33 stadia outside Megalopolis (8. 35. 6); of the Muses on Mt. Helikon, approximately 40 stadia from Thespiai (9. 31. 3); of Demeter Mysia, 60 stadia from Pellene (7. 27. 9); of Zeus at Nemea, approximately 100 stadia from Argos (which, with some relatively brief exceptions, generally controlled the games from the fifth century BC; 2. 15. 2–3); and that of Zeus at Olympia, some 300 stadia from its sponsoring city of Elis (5. 10. 1; 6. 22. 8 for distance).

[42] Shrines at the city centres of Thespiai, Epidauros, Argos, Elis, Mantineia, Pellene, and Tegea correspond respectively to sanctuaries of the same deities on the flanks of Mt. Helikon (Muses), west of Epidauros (Asklepios), at Nemea (Zeus), at Olympia (Zeus), outside Mantineia (Demeter), 60 stades from Pellene (Demeter), and at the foot of Mt. Parthenios (Demeter).

Apollo, Artemis, and Poseidon—whose cults and monuments were generally prominent in Pausanias' second-century Greece. A number of outlying wooded shrines around Megalopolis, however, are more likely to have complements in the city itself. They have chronological primacy over their urban equivalents in Megalopolis, which was founded at the synoecism of the Arkadians in 371 BC.[43] Such non-urban wooded shrines as these would not have been 'colonized' from their city centres, but rather would have been subsumed by a city as cult places of some importance in their own right. In any case, city centre-*chora* pairs of shrines suggest that some groves were not isolated from cities' cultic networks.

Some cities with a number of notable sights possessed sacred groves in shrines with much construction, contrary to wooded (and non-wooded) hero shrines, which Pausanias regularly represents as architecturally and artistically simple. Groves without 'tourist attractions' appear likely to belong to equally unimpressive towns, if Pausanias connects them to towns at all. For instance, outside the otherwise unremarkable *polisma* of Korseia in Boiotia is a grove containing nothing noteworthy except a statue of Hermes (9. 24. 5); on the other hand, in Lebadeia, a typical prosperous city, the grove of Trophonios contains at least two temples and several statues.[44]

Although the majority of the *alse* that Pausanias mentions did not grow in simple shrines, there is no reason to assume that unpretentious cultic installations, wooded or not, were necessarily rare in Greece in the second century AD. Hermes' grove with its statue outside Korseia is only one noteworthy example out of a great number of similar, relatively simple sanctuaries.[45] Perhaps Pausanias neglects to mention groves at such shrines because, owing to his particular concern with shrines representing the Hellenic past, he is unlikely to describe many shrines in which he saw no features that were ideologically meaningful to him. Consequently a wooded shrine worth mentioning often includes notable monuments and, in addition, is supervised by a city that maintains noteworthy monuments and buildings elsewhere in its territory. Such an association between stands of trees and man-made features contrasts with Pausanias' wooded hero shrines (as well as with his non-wooded *heroa*), which communicate their connection with the heroic, Hellenic past by stories alone.

Contrary to his treatment of single trees and stands of trees at hero shrines,

---

[43] Outlying wooded Megalopolitan shrines belong to Parrhasian Apollo, at Kretea on Mt. Lykaion (8. 38. 2, 8); to Pan, on the peak of the same mountain (8. 35. 8); to Despoina, associated with Demeter at Lykosoura (8. 37. 10); to Demeter, five stadia from Megalopolis (8. 36. 6); the sanctuary of Poseidon at Trikolonoi (8. 35. 6) is possibly associated with a shrine in Megalopolis itself. For Megalopolitan cults, see M. Jost, 'Pausanias en Mégalopolitide' *REA* 75 (1973), 245–67, Jost (n. 22), index s.v. Mégalopolis, and Jost's chapter in this volume.

[44] In addition to the monuments at Lebadeia, see for instance descriptions of groves at Aulis (9. 19. 6–8), at Epidauros (2. 27. 1–6), and in the territory of Sikyon (2. 11. 3: Demeter and Kore; 2. 11. 4: Eumenides).

[45] Alcock (n. 2), 175, 201–9.

Pausanias does not generally associate groves at shrines of gods with historical or legendary events. Of the few such connections that Pausanias makes, most have nothing to do with the foundation of the sanctuary and none specifically concern the planting of trees. The breach of asylum at the shrine of Argos (2. 20. 8 and 3. 4. 1), the burning of the grove of Poseidon at Kolonos Hippios (1. 30. 4), and the flooding of Helike, where only the tree-tops in Poseidon's shrine remained visible (7. 24. 12), concern instead the destruction of groves. Pausanias tells of the foundation of cults and shrines on Mt. Pontinos (2. 36. 8–37. 2), at the shrine of Kabeiraian Demeter and Kore outside Thebes (9. 25. 5), and at the river Herkyna by the grove of Trophonios at Lebadeia (9. 39. 2–3), but in all three cases he does not directly connect sanctuary foundation and the planting of groves.[46]

Pausanias does not refer to abandoned groves that were no longer a vital part of contemporary beliefs and cult practices; indeed, derelict groves might have been unrecognizable.[47] Although he mentions abandoned temples, Pausanias does not indicate that where buildings had once been erected, dedications set up, and rituals performed, worshippers could consciously maintain the sanctity of a site by virtue of a sacred grove. None the less several groves—for example, at Aulis, Potniai, and Tithorea—flourished in decrepit or partially abandoned cities and sanctuaries.[48]

Neither legend nor history associates groves with a different, bygone era—a vanished period of prosperity or a time when the grove was new. Instead, rules and regulations, processions, and festivals and cult practices open to all or only to initiates at many of the wooded shrines that Pausanias mentions show that his noteworthy wooded shrines had the same value for their communities as did Pausanias' flourishing sanctuaries in general. A number of them were the sites of festivals that may well have required shelter from wind, rain, and sun for a sizeable number of celebrants. Visitors from a wide territory, which in some cases included the whole Greek world, must have gathered for the cultic and athletic events at the Panhellenic sanctuaries at Olympia and Isthmia,[49] for

[46] In two cases, a grove simply provides the setting for a legendary or historical event: the death and burial of Saron in connection with the sanctuary of Saronian Artemis at Troizen (2. 30. 7 and 10), and an incident in which children were wrongly accused of impiety at the sanctuary of Artemis Kondyleatis near Kaphyai (8. 23. 6).

[47] Presumably, without enforced rules against woodcutting, an accessible but neglected sacred grove would soon become a wood-lot or a treeless patch of ground where wood was valuable and an undistinguished *drumos* where it was not.

[48] Shrines in disrepair need not have been completely abandoned; in some, votive 'heirlooms' were displayed and cult activities were carried out. For ruins (*ereipia*), see Alcock (n. 2), 207–8.

[49] As for other Panhellenic games sites, trees at the sanctuary of Apollo at Delphi are problematic; we have only poetic references to laurels and a grove, e.g. Pindar, *Paean* 6. 14; Euripides, *Ion* 76. Evidence for Roman activity at the sanctuary of Zeus at Nemea indicates that it was not entirely abandoned in the second century AD, when Pausanias reported a grove of cypresses (2. 15. 2). See D. Birge, L. Kraynak, and S. G. Miller, *Nemea* i: *Topographical and Architectural Studies* (Berkeley, 1992), pp. xxx, 26. For fifth- and fourth-century BC evidence for trees at Nemea, see ibid. 85–96.

the Mouseia on Mt. Helikon, and for the medical treatment obtainable at the sanctuary of Asklepios at Epidauros. Less widely famous, but also doubtless attended by many participants, were the rituals for initiates that Pausanias calls *teletai* or *orgia*, celebrated at sanctuaries with groves at Andania, Heraia, Megalopolis, Mt. Pontinos, and perhaps Potniai. Sizeable portions of nearby populations must have congregated for sacrifices and festivals that Pausanias mentions at the wooded shrines at Geronthrai, Myonia, and Phlious; near Kaphyai, Pellene, Phigaleia, Sikyon (at two separate shrines), and Troizen; and on Mt. Lykaion at the sanctuary of Apollo Parrhasios and, before Pausanias' time, at the sanctuary of Pan.[50] Besides distinguishing *alse* from other categories of trees, Pausanias apparently imagines groves as sharing characteristics that have little to do with non-Olympian cults, primordial states of existence, or makeshift shrines in the shadow of a glorious past. Well-to-do cities with notable monuments tended to manage wooded shrines that were similarly well equipped. While groves prospered at shrines of deities like Demeter and Apollo, who had cultic associations with the territory outside cities where groves often grew, Pausanias does not directly or explicitly associate such groves with sanctified nature or with agricultural cults.[51] Instead, he emphasizes their existence in actively functioning shrines, closely associated with the flourishing cultic network that in various ways connected city centres to their surrounding territories. Nor does Pausanias regard specific groves as the sites of supernatural communication with an intangible, divine realm. Rather, the specific details he does add involve processions, *teletai* and *orgia*, entrance rules, regulations against removal of material, and the like at approximately half his shrines with sacred groves. Such wooded sanctuaries are settings for contemporary practices that belong to flourishing, city-oriented cults.

Pausanias associates trees so closely with sanctuaries that his *Periegesis* rarely includes trees that do not live within some explicitly cultic or political environment. Moreover, the existence of trees is subordinate to the essential character of the site in which they are found: Pausanias' approximately four dozen wooded shrines, with their statues and festivals, seem no different from the hundreds of shrines he describes without mentioning trees. Likewise, the single trees that he mentions are similar to historical markers that are not trees, and his wooded *heroa* are similar to hero shrines without trees. It is not even necessarily true that sites at which Pausanias mentions no trees were indeed

[50] For *teletai* and *orgia* at wooded shrines see 4. 33. 5 (Andania), 8. 26. 1 (Heraia), 8. 31. 5 (Megalopolis), 2. 36. 7 and 2. 37. 2 (Mt. Pontinos), 9. 8. 1 (Potniai). For other festivals see 3. 22. 7 (Geronthrai), 10. 38. 8 (Myonia), 2. 13. 4 (Phlious), 8. 23. 7 (Kaphyai), 7. 27. 9–10 (near Pellene), 8. 41. 5–6 (Phigaleia), 2. 11. 3 (Demeter and Kore near Sikyon), 2. 11. 4 (Eumenides near Sikyon), 2. 32. 10 (Troizen), 8. 38. 8 (Parrhasian Apollo on Mt. Lykaion), and 8. 38. 5 (Pan on Mt. Lykaion).

[51] See Susan Cole's contribution to this volume (Ch. 8), and D. E. Birge, 'Sacred Groves and the Nature of Apollo', in J. Solomon (ed.), *The Source of Apollo* (Tucson, Ariz., 1993), 9–19.

treeless, and the actual extent of 'secular' woods and stands of trees in the territory that Pausanias describes is unknowable. We can reach no definitive conclusions, then, concerning the actual presence of trees in various settings in second-century AD Greece.

Pausanias neither gives trees a single meaning nor treats them similarly wherever he finds them. They are not simply shade-producers or displaced signifiers of sacred nature; they share neither a single, utilitarian function, a distinctive supernatural quality, nor a use as objects of worship.[52] The categories by which Pausanias distinguishes non-sacred stands of trees, single landmark trees, and groups of trees in both hero shrines and shrines of deities depend on the social environment in which the trees grow more than on physical attributes such as species or number. As a consequence of his interests in artefacts, architecture, and customs that persist from an earlier era, Pausanias gives the trees in his *Periegesis* various associations with venerable, Hellenic features of Roman Achaia. Single landmark trees and groups of trees at hero shrines maintain a stronger connection with the distant, intangible past than with the contemporary cities' visible territory, in which they grow. Pausanias makes their existence at a particular spot notable by using ordinary language—species names or *dendra*—and narratives that attest to their existence as links, by means of their extraordinarily long lives, between the otherwise unattainable past and the ordinary, visible, present world. On the other hand, the trees that Pausanias identifies with the specialized term *alsos* grow in flourishing shrines of deities that fully belong to the visible, contemporary world. By their collectively perpetual existence, however, Pausanias' groves provide an unvarying setting for cult activities that, by their continued performance, help to maintain and make visible the Hellenic past in Roman Greece.

[52] Trees seem not to have received the same reverence as some other natural objects, such as the thirty stones at Pharai which the locals venerated (σέβουσι), and called by the names of gods (7. 22. 4).

Minding the Gap in Hellenistic and Roman Greece

SUSAN E. ALCOCK

University of Michigan

One of the oft-repeated, if less than popular, maxims of archaeological research is that negative evidence—the absence of material traces of human activity—is just as valuable as the richest and most copious of finds. While other papers in this volume are by and large concerned with where sanctuaries *were* placed, here I am equally interested in the problem of where they *were not*: or rather by cases where known sanctuaries disappear or cease functioning. My general argument is two-fold: first, that the Hellenistic and Early Roman era saw a relative decline in activity at rural sanctuaries, with this gap being followed (in some instances) by a Late Roman resurgence; and second, that this pattern betrays not only a considerable transformation of the religious landscape of Greece, but major transitions within the society that shaped and inhabited it.

Two underlying points should be established before proceeding. First is the 'cultic depth' of the ancient Greek countryside, the sheer range of places and things venerated. Pausanias, the second-century AD pilgrim and author, can be plumbed for a catalogue of these various shrines, describing worship at springs, rocks, stones, trees, caves, tombs—not to mention the more familiar built environment of temples and altars. The range is extensive, from overwhelmingly impressive to barely noticeable. Indeed it is impossible to avoid the conclusion that some ancient holy places will forever remain invisible to the latter-day investigator, as de Polignac and Wright also note (this volume). The second point involves the 'temporal depth' of rural cult activity. Sacred landscapes (as this volume demonstrates in a variety of contexts) are shifting and fluid by nature, much as diachronic patterns of human settlement have proved to be, a development especially documented in recent years through the practice of archaeological surface survey. This fluidity has too frequently been masked through an assumption of static Greek religious practices, an over-emphasis on a few major and long-lived sanctuaries, and an over-dependence upon Pausanias—a second-century AD source who is none the less frequently taken as gospel for ritual behaviour in earlier times.

As far as 'cultic depth' is concerned, not surprisingly most attention has been paid to sites which develop into major rural sanctuaries (e.g. Argive Heraion; Apollo Epikourios at Bassai; Panhellenic shrines), cults boldly and deliberately visible in the countryside. By contrast, the focus here will be upon smaller, 'minor' rural cults—a very difficult category to define (especially upon the basis of often limited material remains) and of necessity a somewhat arbitrary one. What is meant in this context is a cult which, at least in large part, appealed to and depended upon the local rural population; such shrines would not be particularly large, nor particularly monumentalized, nor particularly blessed with rich votives. Above all, these are rural cults that rarely appear in our literary or epigraphic sources, with the possible exception of Pausanias, as will be seen later.

In order to locate such sanctuaries, and to trace their long-term history, we are thus reliant chiefly upon archaeological evidence. Yet while it is true that some minor rural shrines have been located and excavated, these remain relatively limited in number, especially when compared to the attention paid to urban sanctuaries. Moreover, many of those that have been explored tend to be in certain kinds of spectacular (or at least very obvious) settings, such as mountain tops or caves. In other words, the case could be made that we possess only a limited, and biased, sample of rural cults.

Surface Survey and the Sacred Landscape

When classical archaeologists first began to acknowledge the overwhelming urban bias of their investigations and sought to rectify their understanding of rural settlement and land use, one response was the adoption of intensive surface survey. Intensive survey has dramatically altered modern perceptions of habitation and land use in the ancient countryside, not least in terms of their variability through time.[1] Most surveys have concentrated their attention on human settlement (e.g. farmsteads, hamlets, villages) in the landscape, but a range of other types of sites and rural activities has also been recovered (e.g. cemeteries, sheepfolds, kilns, quarries, mines).[2] Given that background, how have survey projects dealt with evidence for cult in the countryside?

---

[1] For general treatments of survey in Greece: J. F. Cherry, 'Frogs Round the Pond: Perspectives on Current Archeological Projects in the Mediterranean Region', in D. Keller and D. Rupp (edd.), *Archaeological Survey in the Mediterranean Region*, BAR Int. Ser. 155 (Oxford, 1983), 375–416; R. Osborne, *Classical Landscape with Figures* (London, 1987), 53–74; A. M. Snodgrass, *An Archaeology of Greece: The Present State and Future Scope of a Discipline* (Berkeley, 1987), 93–121; 'Survey Archaeology and the Rural Landscape of the Greek City', in O. Murray and S. Price (edd.), *The Greek City: From Homer to Alexander* (Oxford, 1990), 113–36.

[2] For modern analogies: P. Murray and P. N. Kardulias, 'A Modern Site-survey in the Southern Argolid, Greece', *JFA* 13 (1986), 21–41.

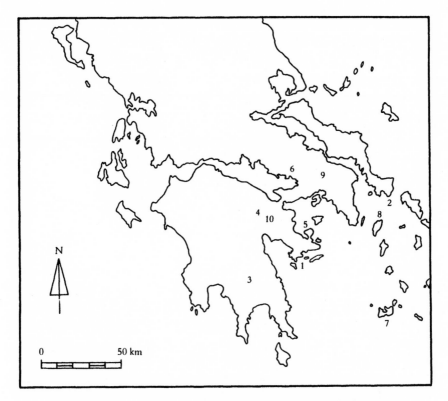

ILL. 11.1 Location of survey projects (see Table 11.1 for key)

That question had not previously been asked in any systematic fashion, and it is clear that no systematic answer can yet be given—not least because almost all of the survey projects involved remain at a preliminary stage of publication.[3] At this point, however, a wide range of results seems apparent: from surveys blessed with several shrines, to projects which posit one or two, and those which lay claim to none. A brief review of some relevant investigations might clarify this variability and help to identify which features were considered the hallmarks of rural cult (see Ill. 11.1 and Table 11.1).

The Argolid Exploration Project in the *Southern Argolid* (1), one of the first intensive surveys undertaken in Greece, identified a variety of 'special purpose' sites, sites 'defined negatively, by the lack of those characteristics thought to belong to settlements, the absence of any objects indicating that someone lived on them. The identification may be made easier by a few column drums, or a

---

[3] I refer here to the situation in mainland Greece and the islands; for a quite different South Italian perspective, see Carter, this volume (Ch. 7).

TABLE 11.1   *Survey projects* (see Ill. 11.1)

Survey region reported	Approximate area studied	Number of rural sanctuaries
1. Southern Argolid	44 km²	c.7
2. Southern Euboia	41 km²	6
3. Lakonia	70 km²	'several'
4. Nemea Valley	50 km²	2
5. Methana	10.5 km²	2
6. Boiotia	55 km²	1
7. Melos	30 km²	0
8. Keos	20 km²	0
9. Skourta Plain	44 km²	0
10. Berbati	4.5 km²	0

find of bones uprooted from a grave, but more often a degree of uncertainty remains here also.[4] The following rural sanctuaries were identified: for the Geometric–Classical period (approximately the tenth to third century BC) some seven definite and two possible shrines, for the Hellenistic to Middle Roman era (approximately the third century BC to third century AD), one possible shrine, for the Late Roman era (fourth to seventh century AD), one definite and one possible shrine.[5] While details about individual proposed cases are lacking at this point, what does emerge clearly is an overall impression of a Geometric through Classical floruit for a handful of rural cults.

Donald Keller, in his individual survey of the area around ancient Karystos in *Southern Euboia* (2), also identified some half-dozen sanctuaries, often in prominent settings, and almost all of Archaic or Classical (or Archaic to Classical) date. Common finds included fine black glaze pottery (often open-shaped vessels) together with occasional votive plaques or figurines, and in one case even a religious inscription. Proposed sanctuaries also usually boasted some form of architectural elaboration, such as temenos walls, cut blocks, bedrock niches, basins or channels. The schist bedrock of Southern Euboia allows such features, as well as the foundations of secular buildings such as farmsteads, to be more readily preserved than in many other survey zones.[6]

[4] T. H. van Andel and C. N. Runnels, *Beyond the Acropolis: A Rural Greek Past* (Stanford, Calif., 1987), 159–60.

[5] Van Andel and Runnels (n. 4), 160, table 1. See also C. N. Runnels and T. H. van Andel, 'The Evolution of Settlement in the Southern Argolid, Greece: An Economic Explanation', *Hesperia* 56 (1987), 309, table 1.

[6] D. R. Keller, 'Archaeological survey in Southern Euboea, Greece: A Reconstruction of Human Activity from Neolithic Times through the Byzantine Period' (Ph.D., diss., Indiana University, 1985). One of the sites involved, at Plakari, appears to begin activity in the Protogeometric period. For farmhouses in this area: D. R. Keller and M. B. Wallace, 'The Canadian Karystia Project: Two Classical Farmsteads', *EMC/Classical Views* 32, NS 7 (1988), 151–7.

The *Lakonia* survey (3) has recorded an as yet unspecified number of Archaic, Classical, and Hellenistic shrines in the countryside; at least one Archaic sanctuary yielded figures of ithyphallic males. Votive figurines and fine pottery appear to have characterized these assemblages.[7]

The *Nemea Valley* Archaeological Project (4) lays claim to fewer cult places than the surveys reviewed above. Apart from the Panhellenic sanctuary of Zeus at Nemea itself, only two out of some hundred-odd sites have been identified as possible rural sanctuaries. A previously known mountain-top ash altar to Zeus Apesantius on Mount Apesas (Pausanias 2. 15. 3) was intensively studied through surface collection. Ceramic finds ranged from late Geometric down to Hellenistic times (being primarily of Archaic and Classical date), with a possible trace of Late Roman material as well. A more surprising, because completely unheralded, discovery was made on a bulldozed and deep-ploughed bluff top overlooking the present day National Highway as it runs through the Tretos Pass. Finds there included miniature votive cups, Attic black and red figure pottery, black glazed wares, and a late Classical moulded figure representing a bearded male. Tiles and cut blocks were also found, making a very strong case for the presence of a rural shrine of late Geometric to late Classical date (perhaps primarily dating from the fourth century BC), resting atop a much earlier, Early Helladic settlement site.[8]

Two Archaic sanctuaries were discovered in the course of surveying the *Methana* peninsula (5), both characterized by the presence of votive skyphoi. One of these shrines (above the settlement at Oga) is known to have been abandoned in the early fifth century, when a temple (near Kounoupitsa) appeared, which continued in use into the Hellenistic period.[9]

The *Boiotia* survey (6), working in the south-western part of that region, is one of the longest-running survey projects in Greece (with intensive fieldwalking beginning in 1979). Yet apart from the previously known sanctuary of Poseidon at Onchestos (Pausanias 9. 26. 5), only one other site has tentatively been proposed as a rural sanctuary. At nearly four hectares, this site (Plains B2) is very large compared to the known sizes of other rural shrines, and produced 'not only an unusual number of worked masonry blocks, but also two sherds carrying carefully incised (if fragmentary) inscriptions'. Schachter has suggested that this may possibly be the sanctuary of Herakles Hippodetes (Pausanias 9.

---

[7] W. G. Cavanagh and J. H. Crouwel, 'Laconia Survey, 1983–86', *Lakonikai Spoudai* (1988), 77–88; *AR* (1983/84), 27–9; *AR* (1984/85), 25; *AR* (1987/88), 26; cf. W. G. Cavanagh, 'Surveys, Cities and Synoecism', in J. Rich and A. Wallace-Hadrill (edd.), *City and Country in the Ancient World* (London, 1991), 97–118, at 110–13.

[8] J. C. Wright, J. F. Cherry, J. L. Davis, E. Mantzourani, S. B. Sutton, and R. F. Sutton, Jr., 'The Nemea Valley Archaeological Project: A Preliminary Report', *Hesperia* 59 (1990), 607, 611–12, figs. 7–8. I thank the directors of this project for unpublished information on these locations. For previous work at Mount Apesas, J. Wiseman, *The Land of the Ancient Corinthians* (Göteborg, 1978), 106–8.

[9] *AR* (1984/85), 21–2; *AR* (1985/86), 28; *AR* (1987/88), 23.

26. 1).[10] On present evidence, the site's history spanned the Archaic to Roman periods.

It is worth observing that several other intensive surveys, albeit usually of smaller territorial coverage than those named above—e.g. *Melos* (7), *Keos* (8), *Skourta Plain* (9), *Berbati* (10)—to date report the discovery of no rural cult places at all.[11]

From this review, what has generally been taken to identify a rural sanctuary? Epigraphic material or architectural remains (blocks, column fragments) present the most unambiguous evidence. In terms of ceramic finds, votives or figurines, together with fine ware pottery (often of open shapes), consistently turn up. Certain locations (mountain tops, bluffs) also help clinch the identification. In cases where these factors are combined, matters appear more or less straightforward. A devil's advocate might ask, however (especially after reading Pausanias), whether all rural shrines would be quite so well defined, and whether survey projects might be missing less obvious, more amorphous instances of cult. Survey archaeologists have, it is true, been relatively restrained about 'finding religion' in the landscape, perhaps in reaction to some of the previous predilections of the discipline, and on the whole continued caution seems the wisest course. Identifying ritual activity in the past without ambiguity is a general archaeological problem, and separating votive from domestic assemblages becomes even more problematic when working with surface finds alone.[12] This is especially true given the long history of occupation and mutability of function of many survey sites; the same location can serve a number of purposes over the centuries, of which a shrine may represent only one phase. Defining precisely what constitutes a site (of *any* sort) is a complex process in con-

---

[10] J. Bintliff and A. M. Snodgrass, 'The Cambridge/Bradford Boeotian Expedition: The First Four Years', *JFA* 12 (1985), 139–40, 149, table 7.

[11] Melos: J. F. Cherry, 'Appendix A: Register of Archaeological Sites on Melos', in C. Renfrew and M. Wagstaff (edd.), *An Island Polity: The Archaeology of Exploitation in Melos* (Cambridge, 1982), 291–309. Keos: J. F. Cherry, J. L. Davis, and E. Mantzourani, 'Greek and Roman Settlement and Land Use', in eid., *Landscape Archaeology and Long-Term History: Northern Keos in the Cycladic Islands*, Monumenta Archaeologica 16 (Los Angeles, 1991), 327–47. On Keos, only the excavated sanctuary at Ayia Irini proved to have a historic period shrine, lasting as late as the 3rd century BC: 'the existence of other shrines or temples outside the polis centre remains to be demonstrated (p. 335)'; M. E. Caskey, 'Ayia Irini, Kea: The Terracotta Statues and the Cult in the Temple', in R. Hägg and N. Marinatos (edd.), *Sanctuaries and Cults in the Aegean Bronze Age* (Stockholm, 1981), 127–35. Skourta Plain: M. H. Munn and M. L. Z. Munn, 'Studies on the Attic–Boiotian Frontier: The Stanford Skourta Project, 1985', in J. Fossey (ed.), *Boiotia Antiqua*, i: *Papers on Recent Work in Boiotian Archaeology and History* (Amsterdam, 1989), 73–127. Berbati: B. Wells, C. N. Runnels, and E. Zangger, 'The Berbati-Limnes Archaeological Survey: The 1988 Season', *OpAth* 18 (1990), 207–38.

[12] C. Renfrew, *The Archaeology of Cult: The Sanctuary at Phylakopi* (London, 1985). From a survey context: 'While one might expect to identify graves or sanctuaries from a concentration of painted and other fine wares, rural sanctuaries, in particular, may be difficult to recognize ...': R. F. Sutton, Jr., 'Ceramic Evidence for Settlement and Land Use in the Geometric to Hellenistic Periods', in Cherry *et al.* (n. 11), 248. The determination of the precise deity involved presents an even greater difficulty, and this is rarely attempted for minor shrines without some form of textual attribution.

temporary survey methodologies, and for cult sites especially it is best that a somewhat loose range of potential diagnostic features be allowed. None the less, the processes that lie behind their identification in each individual case must be made more firmly explicit – not least in order to determine whether *genuine* regional differences in cult behaviour are emerging in these survey data, or whether the resulting patterns rather reflect an archaeological agnosticism on the part of the investigators involved. If, for the sake of argument, survey results are accepted at face value, then they suggest the presence of *significant* variation in the density of minor rural cults in the regions studied—an unexpected and intriguing observation, given the generally accepted ubiquity of sanctuaries in the Greek landscape.

Sizing Up the Gap

If conclusions about the regional patterning of cult remain tentative, what about the chronological range of such activities? In the sample of survey evidence, a heavy emphasis lies on the Archaic and Classical periods, with some cults beginning earlier in Geometric times, and others extending into the Hellenistic epoch. In other words, the rural sanctuaries observed through archaeological survey can broadly be assigned to the Archaic–Hellenistic era, a period—in central and southern Greece—of intensive land use, a dispersed settlement pattern, a 'full' countryside. Conversely, the subsequent centuries (termed the Late Hellenistic and Early Roman periods in most survey chronologies) saw a relatively 'empty' landscape, largely devoid of human settlement: a pattern which now appears paralleled by the abandonment of these small country cults.[13] On present evidence therefore, at least for certain areas of Greece, a direct correlation exists between levels of rural settlement and minor rural shrines.

If sanctuaries can thus drop out of use, they can also be reactivated. From an examination of one sub-sample of rural sanctuary sites (in some instances examined through excavation rather than surface collection), a further pattern emerges. One well-investigated example is the sanctuary of Zeus (possibly Zeus Ombrios) on Mount Hymettos in Attica. Together with simple enclosure walls and open-air altars, Protogeometric, Geometric, and Archaic finds were discovered, as well as Late Roman material (particularly lamps of the late fourth/early fifth centuries AD); each period was represented by significant quantities of material. The site's investigator, Langdon, explained the chronological gap observed as reflecting the agricultural history of Attica and its relative

---

[13] It is also worth noting that other types of 'special purpose' sites (kilns, quarries, cemeteries) also disappear from this early imperial countryside; S. E. Alcock, *Graecia Capta: The Landscapes of Roman Greece* (Cambridge, 1993), esp. 33–92.

dependence on internal resources. Local populations felt the need to pray to Zeus as a weather deity in periods of greater *autarkeia*, less so when foreign imports were assumed to be largely supplying the region's needs (e.g. Classical to early imperial times). Such an interpretation today may seem flawed (it is unlikely that Attica was *ever* uninterested in a local food supply), but that leaves the Hymettian cult pattern, with its break in activity between Archaic and Late Roman times, to be explained.[14]

Nor does Hymettian Zeus stand alone; other mountain-top shrines point in the same direction (if generally less clearly). A shrine, again possibly to Zeus Ombrios, on Mount Parnes yielded up Geometric and Archaic material, then 'Roman' lamps.[15] Surface reconnaissance at the Zeus sanctuary on Mount Kokkygion in the Southern Argolid (Pausanias 2. 36. 2) discovered an enclosure, as well as many open vessels of Archaic to Classical date; the lower body of a Roman lamp of the third or fourth century AD was also present. On Mount Arachneion in the Argeia, relatively limited investigation appears to have located the altars of Zeus and Hera: 'when rain is needed they sacrifice to them here' (Pausanias 2. 25. 10). Masonry foundations were discovered, together with sherd concentrations (mainly from open shapes), suggesting use of the summit from the later eighth until at least the sixth century BC 'with sporadic use probably into the Roman era'.[16] Finally, a hilltop shrine of Zeus Messapeus, originally discovered by the Lakonia survey, revealed when subsequently excavated traces of Geometric to Classical activity, with no apparent signs of subsequent use 'until very much later, in the third–fourth centuries AD, when regular activity at the site is demonstrated by hundreds of mould-made terracotta lamps . . .'; 'it seems possible that activity in the Roman period began amid the remains of a ruined shrine.'[17]

---

[14] Fragments of some 120 lamps were found, as well as two late imperial coins (Constantius, Arcadius). M. K. Langdon, *A Sanctuary of Zeus on Mount Hymettos* (Princeton, NJ, 1976), 87–95; P. Garnsey, *Famine and Food Supply in the Graeco-Roman World* (Cambridge, 1988), 89–164; G. Fowden, 'City and Mountain in Late Roman Attica', *JHS* 108 (1988), 55.

[15] No more precise dating of this Roman material is available. Langdon (n. 14), 84, 100–1; *AR* (1959/60), 8; *AR* (1960/61), 5; E. Vanderpool, 'Newsletter from Greece', *AJA* 64 (1960), 269. Langdon also mentions the altar of Zeus Panhellenios on Aigina, an excavation which was never fully published, but from which the pottery was said to range from Geometric down to Late Roman times: Langdon (n. 14), 81 n. 12.

[16] Mount Kokkygion: M. L. Zimmerman Munn, 'The Zeus Sanctuary on Mt. Kokkygion above Hermion, Argolis' (Paper delivered, 87th General Meeting of the Archaeological Institute of America, Washington, DC, Dec. 1985); Langdon (n. 14), 108. Mount Arachneion: D. W. Rupp, 'The Altars of Zeus and Hera on Mt. Arachneion in the Argeia, Greece', *JFA* 3 (1976), 261–8; Langdon (n. 14) 107–8. The mountain-top shrine of Mount Apesas, already mentioned as a cult site studied by the Nemea Valley Archaeological Project, produced a hint of Late Roman, in addition to primarily Archaic and Classical material, see n. 8 above, and Langdon (n. 14), 107.

[17] H. W. Catling, 'Zeus Messapeus near Sparta: An Interim Report', *Lakonikai Spoudai* (1990), 276–95, esp. 281. For the period of reuse, the excavator, Hector Catling, even suggests that 'there was such a large number of abandoned offerings left about from the sanctuary's previous use that . . . they

A further number of reactivated shrines, usually in high or inaccessible places and often dedicated to Zeus, have been documented in Attica, where Garth Fowden collected information about various religious sites exhibiting use in broadly the Archaic to Hellenistic era, with a subsequent Late Roman florescence. At one small Attic mountain-top shrine with three periods of activity (Geometric, Late Classical, and Late Roman), the investigator, Lauter, at first had doubts about the cultic significance of the later finds (lamp fragments); the further discovery, however, of another 'summit cult' (at Varkiza) with a similar material range supported the notion of a late imperial renaissance.[18] Near Varkiza was found yet another shrine which fell out of use in the Hellenistic period, yet possessed a number of lamps from 'middle and late imperial times'. A small church was later constructed on this site, possibly in the fifth or sixth century AD. Caves too were involved in this development; the Cave of Pan, the Nymphs, and Apollo (the Vari cave) contained nearly one thousand fifth- and sixth-century AD Roman lamps which, together with late imperial coins (Constantine to Arcadius), represented reuse of the site after a break since the second century BC. Originally, this reuse was interpreted as Christian in nature (with the pagan sculptures present first being smashed), but the return of pagan worship to this locale is not at all unlikely. The Cave of Pan on Mount Parnes reveals a similar history, with Late Roman lamps (over two thousand in total) suggesting a pagan presence at least into the fifth century AD. Fowden argues cogently that caves, 'an obvious place to look for cultic continuity in difficult times', may have been deliberately sought out for pagan worship in response to a growing Christian influence. Moreover, an elite, often philosophical, interest in such cult places (for example, because of Platonic associations with the Vari cave) may have stimulated their late imperial use, though as Fowden remarks we 'must of course assume that most of their visitors were simple local people'.[19]

This Late Roman revival is by no means universal; as far as can be determined, the great majority of 'dead' sanctuaries remain dead. But enough signs of a resurgence appear (in most cases without having been explicitly sought by archaeologists) to merit some brief comparison of the two periods of cult florescence. The Archaic–Hellenistic period and the Late Roman era have something very much in common. From the results of intensive surface survey, it is clear that these are the two 'peak' periods of ancient rural activity, of

may have been deliberately picked up and offered by those who came to the shrine with their mould-made lamps and other contemporary offerings' (p. 286). See also *AR* (1989/90), 22–4.

[18] The first of these shrines may be to Zeus Anchesmios; the Late Roman material found there dated to the later 2nd or 3rd century AD. Fowden (n. 14), 56; Langdon (n. 14), 101–2; H. Lauter, *Der Kultplatz auf dem Turkovuni* (Berlin, 1985), 148–9, 157; H. Lauter and H. Lauter-Bufe, 'Ein attisches Höhenheiligtum bei Varkiza', in *Festschrift zum 60. Geburtstag von Werner Böser* (Karlsruhe, 1986), 304–5.

[19] Fowden (n. 14), 56–7. On the cave of Pan at Vari: C. H. Weller, M. E. Dunham, I. C. Thallon, L. S. King, A. Baldwin, and S. E. Bassett, 'The Cave at Vari', *AJA* 7 (1903), esp. 284–5, 335–49. On Parnes, A. Skias, 'To para ten Phylen antron tou Panos', *AE* (1918), 1–28.

intensive cultivation, of dense settlement. Survey archaeologists have known for some time that the sites of former 'Classical' farmsteads were resettled in late imperial times; it now seems that at least some neglected rural shrines were likewise revivified.

Exploring in detail this apparent correlation between numbers of rural cults and levels of rural activity in these 'peak' periods is not the direct subject for this paper, but a few general comments can be made. Obviously, sheer propinquity could serve as one fundamental explanation: more time and labour expended in the countryside (as indicated by more substantial archaeological traces) would facilitate cult maintenance. Intensified cultivation might provoke a perceived greater need for agricultural propitiation, or for the use of cult by families or small-scale rural communities to establish claims to the possession of land. Such relatively pragmatic factors, factors involved in the structuring of everyday life in the countryside, no doubt played a great part in the diachronic development of minor rural cults. Yet other motivations too must be considered, including changes in religious fashions or even in the choice of religious adherence itself; Fowden's suggestion concerning the preferred location of the often inaccessible Late Roman shrines—'well away from interfering Christians'—is interesting in this context. Christianity's progress through Roman Greece (especially outside the major urban centres) is difficult to trace, and doubtless was a prolonged process, but certainly the 'closing down' of major pagan shrines seems apparent by the late fourth century AD, well before the terminal use of the minor cults examined here.[20] Finally, changing attitudes towards the countryside, the evolution of the bonds linking town and country, and the likely constituency of rural cult patrons are additional factors which could mould a sacred landscape.

What this range of factors makes clearest, perhaps, is the danger inherent in equating the earlier and later 'peak' periods of rural cult activity. While the rural landscapes that survey has recovered for the Archaic–Hellenistic and the Late Roman epochs may 'look' rather similar, the two periods were in fact markedly different in their systems of land ownership and social organization; settlement patterns must be interpreted accordingly. Just so for interpreting rural shrines: cult location may remain unchanged, but the prayers and aspirations of its worshippers need not. For religious practices no less than for any other aspect of human behaviour, an historically sensitive contextual approach is necessary.

---

[20] Fowden (n. 14), 57; F. R. Trombley, 'Boeotia in Late Antiquity: Epigraphic Evidence on Society, Economy and Christianization', in H. Beister and J. Buckler (edd.), *Boiotika. Vorträge vom 5. Internationalen Böotien-Kolloquium* (Munich, 1989), 221–3 ; Cl. Vatin, 'Les Empereurs du IVᵉ siècle à Delphes', *BCH* 86 (1962), 229–41. The frequency with which the dedicatee in these Late Roman cases can be identified as Zeus would also ultimately demand attention.

Bridging the Gap

The complexity of pressures involved in rural cult maintenance, or neglect, can in part be demonstrated by an examination, not of a 'peak' period, but of the intervening 'gap', established as spanning approximately the Hellenistic to the Late Roman era (approximately third century BC–third/fourth century AD). As already noted, most rural cults observed through surface survey vanish at this time. Writing in the late second century AD, Pausanias appears at points to corroborate such a trend; on his travels he observes ruined sanctuaries, temples without roofs, missing cult images.[21] Combined with the drastic reduction in rural habitation and other signs of human activity (almost unanimously reported by survey projects in Greece), it would seem simple enough to reconstruct for this period an abandoned landscape, forsaken both by mortals and by gods.

Matters are not so straightforward, however. Human utilization of the countryside perforce continued, if at a less intensive, less archaeologically visible level; the continued urban life of Greece would otherwise have quickly proved impossible. And the gods maintained a significant presence in that landscape as well. Running concurrently with Pausanias' account of defunct sanctuaries (and easily outnumbering them) are his descriptions of the many apparently flourishing rural cults (at a variety of scales) which form such a dominant feature of his *Guide to Greece*. But what then to make of the apparent discrepancy between our textual and our archaeological sources? Is the proposed 'gap' in rural cult activity simply illusory?

Unless textual authority is automatically given precedence (a dubious decision given what has been said about the 'cultic' and 'temporal' depth of rural cult practices), some means must be found of correlating Pausanias with current archaeological evidence. Three proposals can be made: the first challenges the reliability of our archaeological understanding, the second questions the accuracy of Pausanias' *Guide*, the third accepts both and attempts to reconcile them. For the first, Madeleine Jost, perturbed at the number of Arcadian sanctuaries where archaeological documentation ceases in the fourth to third centuries BC, yet which appear to be extant in Pausanias' time, concluded that at least in some cases the site's 'condition of preservation' must be held accountable. Thus, ritual activity at such sites endured, but with the later phases of use lost to latter-day investigators.[22] Change in dedicatory practices is another potential

---

[21] For a sample of defunct or dilapidated sanctuaries: Pausanias 2. 12. 2, 2. 36. 2, 2. 36. 8, 3. 22. 10, 7. 22. 11, 8. 35. 5, 8. 41. 10, 8. 54. 5, 10. 38. 8. J. G. Frazer, *Pausanias' Description of Greece*, i (London, 1898), p. xiv; Alcock (n. 13), 200.

[22] M. Jost, *Sanctuaires et cultes d'Arcadie* (Paris, 1985), 549. The additional question arises of just how assiduously early explorations in particular were looking for a full chronological range of material. An even more fundamental challenge, of course, is the problem of the archaeological sample: just how much remained to be discovered after various geomorphological and cultural processes had worked their will upon ancient landscapes? Survey investigators are cognizant of this problem; for example, the

hypothesis; in this scenario, worship would have continued, while leaving only minimal (or no) material traces. There is, to the best of my knowledge, no independent reason to posit a radical change in votive practices at this time, but it must be offered as a possibility, and one that only further work (particularly detailed and well-published excavation of this type of small-scale sanctuary site) can resolve. At this point, while the quality of much of the archaeological data admittedly remains problematic, to dismiss without further exploration the general trends suggested would be an unhelpfully negative response.

As for the accuracy of Pausanias' *Guide*, to what extent might the account have been distorted by the intangible forces of nostalgia and local memory? The Hellenistic and Early Roman epoch, an era marked for the Greek cities (poleis) by the gradual loss of independence and the encroachment of external powers, witnessed the development of a conscious archaism in their self-representation. Myth, legend, and heroic genealogies were increasingly invoked to provide a sense of identity and of purpose, as well as to spin a web of interrelationships among the political units of the Mediterranean world.[23] Might not antique cults in the countryside, preserved in memory but no longer actively patronized, have been described to the traveller by the local informants Pausanias often consulted, thus presenting the image of a 'busier' sacred landscape than actually existed? In this scenario, present abandonment of shrines would, on the whole, be less meaningful than the memory of their former existence. Yet while it is difficult to overestimate the influence of the Hellenic past upon Pausanias and his perceptions, the power of nostalgia in shaping his account should not be exaggerated. Such misrepresentation might be the case when Pausanias, working from hearsay evidence alone, undertook no personal autopsy of a site, as has been suggested, for example, for some of the mountain-top shrines already mentioned.[24] But when (as was more common) the pilgrim did personally visit a sanctuary, if he saw it in neglect, he so reported it. Pausanias was no tourist of the Romantic era, indifferent to contemporary human activity, revelling in ruins; he was instead an observant participant in contemporary religious practice. His testimony—that in the middle of our apparent 'gap', numerous rural locales were still the focus for active cult—must be accepted.

Southern Argolid survey noted that Pausanias claimed a sanctuary of Demeter was still standing on the Iliokastro plateau, yet the survey found absolutely no trace of any activity at the relevant date: van Andel and Runnels (n. 4), 113. No doubt, in specific instances, material traces have been irretrievably lost. Yet, as always with survey-derived analyses, it is the enduring general pattern which requires attention.

[23] P. A. Cartledge and A. J. S. Spawforth, *Hellenistic and Roman Sparta: A Tale of Two Cities* (London, 1989), 190–211; A. J. S. Spawforth and S. Walker, 'The World of the Panhellenion: I. Athens and Eleusis', *JRS* 75 (1985), 78–104; 'The World of the Panhellenion: II. Three Dorian Cities', *JRS* 76 (1986), 88–105; P. Veyne, *Did the Greeks Believe in their Myths?: An Essay on the Constitutive Imagination* (Chicago, 1988), 71–8. On Pausanias, J. Elsner, 'Pausanias: A Greek Pilgrim in the Roman World', *Past and Present* 135 (1992), 3–29; C. Habicht, *Pausanias' Guide to Ancient Greece* (Berkeley, 1985).

[24] Langdon (n. 14), 102 n. 11; Munn (n. 16); Rupp (n. 16), 267 n. 16.

How then to reconcile our archaeological and textual sources? Perhaps by returning to where we began—to the 'cultic depth' of the countryside. Within the great range of rural religious practices, some shrines indeed endured (for Pausanias to witness), while others did not (as archaeological research has observed). But what then distinguished the survivors? And what did the defunct cults lack?

Possible answers to these questions can be organized around the twin concepts of scale and significance. The shrines which disappear, by and large, are fairly categorized as 'minor' operations—relatively small, relatively simple.[25] Pausanias, on the other hand, seems often preoccupied with a larger, more impressive body of sanctuaries, as his frequent descriptions of temples and dedications reveal. One line of distinction then could be drawn between major and minor, big and little shrines, with the former category as the more normal survivors.

A closer reading of Pausanias, however, makes it clear that judging by scale alone would be an inadequate measure of success. For Pausanias also reports a not inconsiderable number of small and undistinguished shrines, places apparently lacking any significant degree of architectural elaboration. At this juncture, the issue of significance must come into play. All cult locations, obviously, are meaningful in some sense to some audience, so what levels of significance, what meanings must a shrine have borne to guarantee continued patronage? Without claiming it as the only explanation, one general theme can be identified: the thread connecting the enduring rural cults (including and perhaps most markedly the smaller shrines) to the past history of the host city. Many of these shrines possessed a link to the foundation or early development of their communities and thus (for the inhabitants of Roman Greece) to their identity; association with mythic or legendary events established credentials in the eyes of others, Greek and non-Greek alike.[26] The preservation of such venerable places, with their investment in civic memory, thus worked to ensure the preservation of the community itself: a matter of grave concern in this era, especially to those individuals who controlled civic destinies.

That observation raises the issue of the nature of cult patronage. During this period, authority within the cities was increasingly transferred to urban-based elite families, and their intervention in the organization and maintenance of

---

[25] The only clear exception to this rule so far is the Boiotia survey's Plains B2 (Sanctuary of Herakles Hippodetes?), which is also, of course, anomalous in its chronological range (Archaic to Roman times).

[26] Examples include places venerated for their particular antiquity (Pausanias 4. 34. 7, 7. 25. 13, 8. 10. 2–3) or associated with local legendary occurrences (Pausanias 2. 18. 1, 2. 32. 7–9, 8. 23. 6–7, 8. 34. 1–2). Tombs of heroes or other mythic or historical figures are also frequently noted (e.g. Pausanias 2. 12. 4, 7. 17. 8, 8. 11. 1, 8. 12. 8, 8. 54. 4, 9. 2. 2). Border sanctuaries continued to play a role in territorial demarcation at this time, Alcock (n. 13), 118–20. For an in-depth study of one civic ritual, G. M. Rogers, *The Sacred Identity of Ephesos: Foundation Myths of a Roman City* (London, 1991).

various cults (urban and rural) is eminently clear.[27] As far as the countryside
was concerned, attention to larger, more renowned, or otherwise 'higher status'
sanctuaries was particularly manifest. This emphasis derived in part from an
escalating competition between such wealthy families, and between their
respective cities. Ritual became an active weapon in such rivalries, with, not
surprisingly, some sanctuaries proving more potent allies than others in terms
of their age, size, or splendour. Strategic deployment of resources would target
certain cults in the countryside for support, while others were left out of such
elite calculations.

If size, status, entrenchment in civic memory, and the backing of powerful,
urban-based patrons can be identified as chief characteristics of surviving cults,
then those that disappear are, to an extent, thus negatively defined: small-scale,
lacking in significance at the wider community level, primarily the concern of
unimportant local audiences. Yet does this necessarily account for why such
shrines ceased functioning, rather than continuing quietly along some parallel
course? At this point, the radical transformation of the Hellenistic and Early
Roman countryside must be brought to bear on the problem. This transformation involved, as has been said, a dramatic decline in signs of human
settlement and activity in the countryside, a development owing in part to
overall demographic loss, in part to an increasingly urban orientation at this
time—an orientation which would work, ultimately, to marginalize (eco-
nomically and politically) many within Greek society. The ritual sphere was
deeply implicated in these developments. With the fracturing of previously close
relations between rural activities and rural shrines, worship in the countryside
became instead a matter for conscious and deliberate investment of effort.
Such investment was not universally forthcoming, however, and cult in the
countryside passed into the domain of powerful, centrally-based agencies.
Other, more modest expressions of rural worship, even when based on generations of votive practices, were abandoned.

Like the proverbial glass, the sacred landscape of the Hellenistic and Early
Roman period could be seen as either half-full or half-empty. In earlier thinking
on this subject, I saw it as half-full, applauding the continued presence of rural
sanctuaries: 'As far as town–country relationships were concerned, sanctuaries
worked to preserve the union of the polis. . . . thanks in part to these ritual ties,
the final disruption of that relationship, and the end of the polis as a coherent
territorial unit, do not belong to the period studied here . . .'[28] I now wonder

[27] Jost (n. 22), 126–7, 550–1; L. Migeotte, 'Réparation de monuments publics à Messène au temps
d'Auguste', BCH 109 (1985), 597–607; J. H. Oliver, 'Epaminondas of Acraephia', Greek, Roman and
Byzantine Studies 12 (1971), 221–37; A. J. S. Spawforth, 'Agonistic Festivals in Roman Greece', in S.
Walker and A. Cameron (edd.), The Greek Renaissance in the Roman Empire (London, 1989), 196–7;
Alcock (n. 13), 210–12.
[28] Alcock (n. 13), 207.

if a 'half-empty' reading is not equally appropriate, and perhaps even more revealing. The relinquishment of small-scale cults, together with the role they played in articulating the rural existence of a substantial portion of the population, testifies (however distantly) to a major upheaval in the religious landscape, and thus to a radical restructuring of local allegiances and indeed emotions—the depths of which we are just beginning to comprehend.[29] In this case, paradoxically, it is negative evidence which most deeply illuminates the complexities, and painful transitions, of the era.

[29] For indications of somewhat similar developments in roughly contemporary Italy, M. H. Crawford, 'Italy and Rome', *JRS* 71 (1981), esp. 60; M. W. Frederiksen, 'Changes in the Patterns of Settlement', in P. Zanker (ed.), *Hellenismus in Mittelitalien* (Göttingen, 1976), 34–55. A version of this paper was presented at the Laurence Seminar, 'Agriculture and Settlement in Classical and Later Greece', held at the Faculty of Classics, University of Cambridge, June 1992, and organized by John F. Cherry, Jack L. Davis, and Anthony M. Snodgrass. I would like to thank all the participants in that seminar for their comments. My title will sound familiar to anyone who has travelled extensively on the London Underground.

INDEX